Business Law

Business Law

Jon Rush and Michael Ottley

THOMSON

Australia • Canada • Mexico • Singapore • Spain • United Kingdom • United States

THOMSON

Business Law
Jon Rush and Michael Ottley

Publishing Director	Publisher	Development Editor
John Yates	Patrick Bond	Laura Priest
Production Editor	**Manufacturing Manager**	**Marketing Manager**
Sonia Pati	Helen Mason	Katie Thorn
Typesetter	**Production Controller**	**Printer**
Meridian, Berkshire	Maeve Healy	Canale, Italy
Cover Design	**Text Design**	
Nick Welch	Design Deluxe, Bath, UK	

Copyright© 2006 Jon Rush and Michael Ottley

The Thomson logo is a registered trademark used herein under licence.

For more information, contact Thomson Learning, High Holborn House; 50–51 Bedford Row, London WC1R 4LR or visit us on the World Wide Web at: http://www.thomsonlearning.co.uk

ISBN-13: 978-1-84480-173-2
ISBN-10: 1-84480-173-X

This edition published 2006 by Thomson Learning.

British Library Cataloguing-in-Publication Data
A catalogue record for this book is available from the British Library

Brief contents

Part 5 Consumer employment and agency law 283

Part 6 Test your knowledge 337

Contents

Part 1 English legal system

1 What is law?

2 How the law is enforced

Part 2 Contract

3 Contract law: an introduction

4 Contract formation: getting agreement

5 Contract formation: certainty of terms and consideration

8 Discharge of contracts, performance and remedies for breach

9 Validity of contracts (1)

12 Other business-related torts and vicarious liability

Part 4 Company law

13 Business associations

14 Incorporation

15 Capital

16 Company management

Consumer, employment and agency law

22 Agency

Part 6 Test your knowledge

English legal system

Contract

Consumer, employment and agency law

How to use the tables of cases and legislation

Looking up case law

The table of cases contains references such as *Holwell Securities v Hughes [1974]* 1 All ER 161. This reference will allow you to look up that case in a law library. 'All ER' refers to 'All England Law Reports'. Once you have found the part of the library that contains this series, you need to find the volumes relating to 1974 (they should be in date order). There may be several volumes for 1974, but the '1' before the words 'All ER' indicates that you need to look at Volume 1. Finally, 161 gives you the page number for the start of that case report. You may also be able to look up cases using electronic databases. Unless the case is fairly recent, you will generally need to access a subscription database, which normally means that either you or your law library will have to pay an access charge. Access to a range of more recent cases is available free of charge over the internet from the following websites:

- House of Lords rulings (from 1996): www.parliament.uk/judicial_work/judicial_work.cfm

- Court of Appeal and High Court rulings (from 1996): www.bailii.org/

Looking up legislation

The table of statutes contains references such as the Unfair Contract Terms Act 1977 (discussed in Part 2). This reference will allow you to look up that Act in a law library. For example, Acts of Parliament are published in a series of volumes called *Statutes*, which are in date order. You would also be able to find this Act in a publication such as *Halsbury's Statutes*, although that book is organised by subject; you would need to consult the index to find out which volume contained the text of the Unfair Contract Terms Act 1977. You may also be able to look up legislation using electronic databases. Unless the legislation is fairly recent, however, you will generally need to access a subscription database, which normally means that either you or your law library will have to pay an access charge. Access to more recent legislation (1988 onwards) is available free of charge over the internet from the Office of Public Sector Information website: www.opsi.gov.uk.

Table of cases

Table of legislation

Preface

Business law is an extremely broad subject. Those new to law often find it somewhat dry and perhaps overwhelming, both in terms of the sheer volume of material and its complexity. In writing this book, our aim was to explain business law in straightforward terms and show how it affects today's businesses (and therefore why it is worth knowing about). We have tried to resist the temptation to put down everything we know about the subject (after all, this is precisely what many a lecturer has told his or her students *not* to do when writing exam answers or essays). Instead, we have concentrated on the 'core' subject areas covered by the majority of degree courses featuring a business law element. By adopting this approach, we have been able to devote more space to clear explanations of the topics that students often find difficult. In particular, we have sought to tackle head on some of the key questions that students often ask themselves about the subject using the 'FAQ' (frequently asked questions) textboxes. Another novel feature is the inclusion of textboxes headed 'Reality check', which provide up-to-date examples to demonstrate how principles of business law – many of which were developed in an age when business was done very differently from today – continue to be relevant to modern business practices.

For the benefit of students facing exams in the subject, the revision section includes chapter summaries in bullet-point format, definitions of key terms from the relevant chapter and self-test questions. And for those readers who want more detail, the companion website features a range of additional material, including more in-depth analysis of certain topics, tutorial exercises and hyperlinks to other relevant websites. We hope that the end result is a book that not only makes business law readily comprehensible, but actually brings the subject alive for the reader.

We have attempted to ensure that the law was correctly stated as at January 2006.

Jon Rush and Michael Ottley
January 2006

Acknowledgements

Both authors would like to thank Pat Bond and Laura Priest at Thomson Learning and the following reviewers who provided helpful feedback on earlier drafts:

Michael Connolly, University of Westminster
Edgar Forbes, Bournemouth University
Jennifer Lee, University of Liverpool
Omar Masood, University of East London
Richard Morris, University of Central England
Ronke Shoderu, London Metropolitan University
Ruth Soetendorp, Bournemouth University
Janet Wilson-Ward, Bath University

Walk-through tour

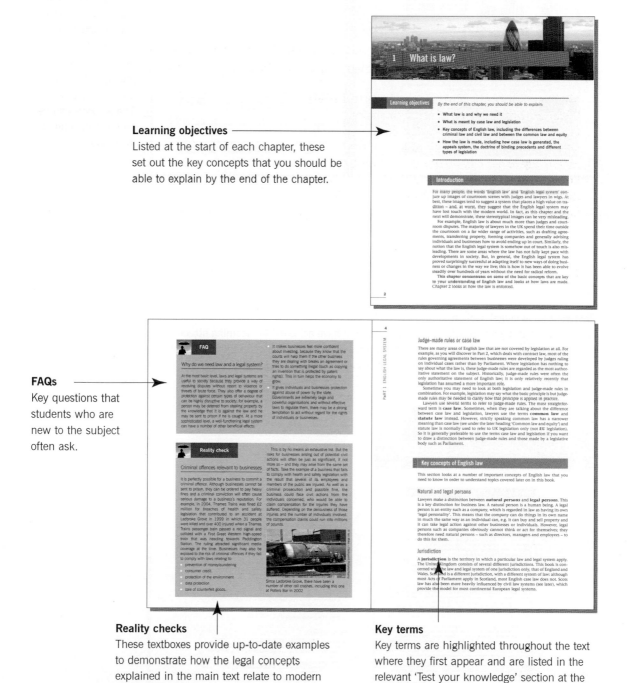

Learning objectives
Listed at the start of each chapter, these set out the key concepts that you should be able to explain by the end of the chapter.

FAQs
Key questions that students who are new to the subject often ask.

Reality checks
These textboxes provide up-to-date examples to demonstrate how the legal concepts explained in the main text relate to modern business practices.

Key terms
Key terms are highlighted throughout the text where they first appear and are listed in the relevant 'Test your knowledge' section at the back of the book.

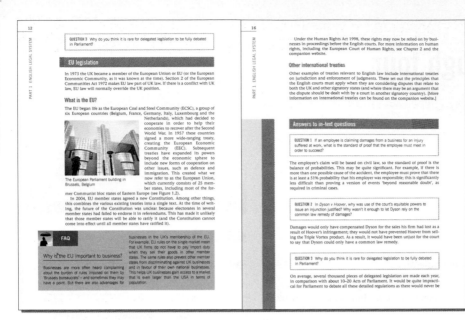

In-text questions and answers

Short questions about how the law you have been reading about applies to certain situations not covered in the main text. You might try jotting down your answers as you go. The answers can be found at the end of each chapter.

'Test your knowledge' section

This section is designed to help you test whether you have achieved the learning objectives for each chapter. It should also assist with exam revision. For each chapter there is a bullet point summary, a list of key terms with definitions and a series of quick quiz questions (with answers).

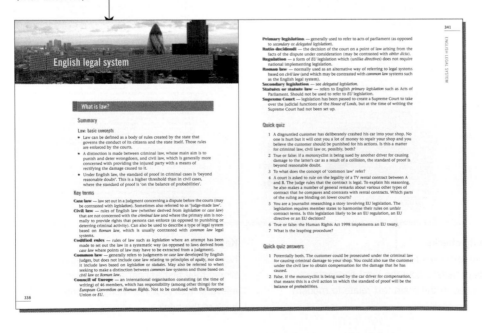

A companion website accompanies

Business Law
Jon Rush and Michael Ottley

Visit the *Business Law* accompanying website at *www.thomsonlearning.co.uk/rush_ottley* to find further teaching and learning material including:

For students

- Additional questions with answers for each chapter
- Quiz containing multiple-choice questions for each part
- Biannual update bulletins to the book that will consist of brief details of any major common law, statutory and constitutional developments affecting the currency of the book
- Additional material including more in-depth analysis of certain topics and links to other relevant websites

For lecturers

- PowerPoint slides containing relevant information from each chapter to help with revision

PART ONE

English legal system

This part, which consists of two chapters, deals with the English legal system, including:

- **What law is and why we need it (Chapter 1)**
- **How the law is made (Chapter 1)**
- **How the English court system works (Chapter 2)**
- **How the law is enforced (Chapter 2)**

It is essential for businesses to have a good understanding of the law and the legal system in which they operate. You will need to have a good grasp of these issues in order to understand the other topics covered in this book. Knowledge of the subjects covered in this part is also useful in everyday life. For example, it will help you understand what your options are if you ever find yourself having to think about taking legal action – or if someone is taking legal action against you. It is worth remembering that, at the time of writing, over 1 million court proceedings are begun every year in England and Wales; so the odds are that, at some stage, you or someone you know will come into contact with the English legal system.

1 What is law?

Learning objectives

By the end of this chapter, you should be able to explain:

- **What law is and why we need it**
- **What is meant by case law and legislation**
- **Key concepts of English law, including the differences between criminal law and civil law and between the common law and equity**
- **How the law is made, including how case law is generated, the appeals system, the doctrine of binding precedents and different types of legislation**

Introduction

For many people, the words 'English law' and 'English legal system' conjure up images of courtroom scenes with judges and lawyers in wigs. At best, these images tend to suggest a system that places a high value on tradition – and, at worst, they suggest that the English legal system may have lost touch with the modern world. In fact, as this chapter and the next will demonstrate, these stereotypical images can be very misleading.

For example, English law is about much more than judges and courtroom disputes. The majority of lawyers in the UK spend their time outside the courtroom on a far wider range of activities, such as drafting agreements, transferring property, forming companies and generally advising individuals and businesses how to avoid ending up in court. Similarly, the notion that the English legal system is somehow out of touch is also misleading. There are some areas where the law has not fully kept pace with developments in society. But, in general, the English legal system has proved surprisingly successful at adapting itself to new ways of doing business or changes in the way we live; this is how it has been able to evolve steadily over hundreds of years without the need for radical reform.

This chapter concentrates on some of the basic concepts that are key to your understanding of English law and looks at how laws are made. Chapter 2 looks at how the law is enforced.

What is law?

Law can be defined as a body of rules created by the state that governs the conduct of its citizens and the state itself. The rules are enforced by the courts – that is to say, if a person thinks that another person or the state has broken the law, he can ask a court for a ruling on this question. The court normally has power to make an order against the person who broke the rules. For example, the order might require that person to stop breaking the law or to pay compensation (known as *damages*) to the injured party. The process of enforcement by the courts is examined in more detail in Chapter 2. This chapter concentrates on the nature of the rules themselves and how they are made.

Where does English law come from?

Talking about English law as a set of rules might suggest that they must be written down somewhere in some vast encyclopaedia of law. However, the reality is rather less convenient. There are two major sources of English law – legislation and case law – and you may need to look at both in order to find out what the law is.

Legislation

The nearest thing that the English legal system has to a written rulebook are laws such as Acts of Parliament, which are known as **legislation**. An encyclopaedia of all the legislation currently in force would run to hundreds of volumes – but even that would not be sufficient to contain all the rules of the English legal system. Legislation is dealt with in more detail later in the chapter.

FAQ

Why do we need law and a legal system?

At the most basic level, laws and legal systems are useful to society because they provide a way of resolving disputes without resort to violence or threats of brute force. They also offer a degree of protection against certain types of behaviour that can be highly disruptive to society; for example, a person may be deterred from stealing property by the knowledge that it is against the law and he may be sent to prison if he is caught. At a more sophisticated level, a well-functioning legal system can have a number of other beneficial effects:

- It makes businesses feel more confident about investing, because they know that the courts will help them if the other business they are dealing with breaks an agreement or tries to do something illegal (such as copying an invention that is protected by patent rights). This in turn helps the economy to grow.

- It gives individuals and businesses protection against abuse of power by the state. Governments are extremely large and powerful organisations and without effective laws to regulate them, there may be a strong temptation to act without regard for the rights of individuals or businesses.

Judge-made rules or case law

There are many areas of English law that are not covered by legislation at all. For example, as you will discover in Part 2, which deals with contract law, most of the rules governing agreements between businesses were developed by judges ruling on individual cases rather than by Parliament. Where legislation has nothing to say about what the law is, these judge-made rules are regarded as the most authoritative statement on the subject. Historically, judge-made rules were often the only authoritative statement of English law; it is only relatively recently that legislation has assumed a more important role.

Sometimes you may need to look at both legislation and judge-made rules in combination. For example, legislation may say what the basic principle is but judge-made rules may be needed to clarify how that principle is applied in practice.

Lawyers use several terms to refer to judge-made rules. The most straightforward term is **case law**. Sometimes, when they are talking about the difference between case law and legislation, lawyers use the terms **common law** and **statute law** instead. However, strictly speaking common law has a narrower meaning than case law (see under the later heading 'Common law and equity') and statute law is normally used to refer to UK legislation only (not **EU** legislation). So it is generally preferable to use the terms case law and legislation if you want to draw a distinction between judge-made rules and those made by a legislative body such as Parliament.

Key concepts of English law

This section looks at a number of important concepts of English law that you need to know in order to understand topics covered later on in this book.

Natural and legal persons

Lawyers make a distinction between **natural persons** and **legal persons**. This is a key distinction for business law. A natural person is a human being. A legal person is an entity such as a company, which is regarded in law as having its own 'legal personality'. This means that the company can do things in its own name in much the same way as an individual can, e.g. it can buy and sell property and it can take legal action against other businesses or individuals. However, legal persons such as companies obviously cannot think or act for themselves; they therefore need natural persons – such as directors, managers and employees – to do this for them.

Jurisdiction

A **jurisdiction** is the territory in which a particular law and legal system apply. The United Kingdom consists of several different jurisdictions. This book is concerned with the law and legal system of one jurisdiction only, that of England and Wales. Scotland is a different jurisdiction, with a different system of law: although most Acts of Parliament apply in Scotland, most English case law does not. Scots law has also been more heavily influenced by civil law systems (see later), which provide the model for most continental European legal systems.

You may also see the term jurisdiction used in a slightly different context. For example, before a court can rule on a dispute, it will need to consider whether it has the power to make such a ruling. If the people involved in the dispute are asking the court to do something it does not have power to do, the court may say that it has 'no jurisdiction' to make a ruling.

Common law and civil law jurisdictions

England and Wales is known as a **common law** jurisdiction. This refers to the fact that English law is based largely on case law, i.e. judge-made rules – although as we have seen, common law systems also make use of **codified rules** set out in legislation. Other common law jurisdictions are Australia, Canada, India, South Africa and the United States of America. Common law jurisdictions may be contrasted with **civil law** jurisdictions (such as France or Germany), where judge-made rules play a less important role and somewhat greater reliance is placed on a set of codified rules. Civil law jurisdictions are sometimes referred to as legal systems based on **Roman law**. [You can find out more about the differences between the two systems on the companion website.]

Civil and criminal law

Another concept that is key to your understanding of English law (and most other legal systems) is the distinction between civil law and criminal law. Note that we are now using the word civil in a different sense from the civil law jurisdictions just described.

Criminal law prohibits behaviour that is considered so undesirable that the state itself will normally take action to enforce it and may impose relatively severe penalties. For example, if a person has stolen something, he may be prosecuted by the Crown Prosecution Service in conjunction with the police; if found guilty, then at the very least he will have a criminal record (indicating the state's disapproval of his behaviour) and may well be given a prison sentence.

Civil law is generally concerned with conduct that is not regarded as serious enough to warrant criminal penalties (although this is not to say that breaches of civil law cannot have serious consequences and there are some examples of the civil law being used to pursue aims more commonly associated with criminal law – see, for example, the discussion of regulators in Chapter 2). Instead of the state taking action on their behalf, individuals or businesses are normally expected to take legal action themselves and the sanctions involved are generally less severe (e.g. they do not include imprisonment). Whereas criminal law penalties are more concerned with deterrence, punishment and indicating the state's disapproval, civil law remedies are usually more concerned with providing the injured party with a means of rectifying the damage caused to them. For example, if a business has broken a legally binding agreement with another business, the civil law will allow the injured party to claim compensation from the party who is at fault. Generally speaking, it is not possible to obtain this type of remedy by bringing criminal proceedings. There are certain limited circumstances in which victims of criminal conduct are able to obtain compensation but these are beyond the scope of this book.

Different courts and procedures are used to deal with criminal and civil law cases; these are explained in Chapter 2.

Standard of proof in civil and criminal cases

The other key difference between the civil and criminal law is the standard of proof. In a criminal case, it is necessary to prove beyond reasonable doubt that the person accused of the crime is guilty. This is a very high standard of proof. In civil cases, the standard of proof is lower; a breach of the law only needs to be proved on the balance of probabilities. This means that if there are two versions of what happened, the court will rule in favour of the version it considers to be the more probable – even if the version in question is only 1% more probable than the other version.

> **QUESTION 1** If an employee is claiming damages from a business for an injury suffered at work, what is the standard of proof that the employee must meet in order to succeed?

Reality check

Criminal offences relevant to businesses

It is perfectly possible for a business to commit a criminal offence. Although businesses cannot be sent to prison, they can be ordered to pay heavy fines and a criminal conviction will often cause serious damage to a business's reputation. For example, in 2004, Thames Trains was fined £2 million for breaches of health and safety legislation that contributed to an accident at Ladbroke Grove in 1999 in which 31 people were killed and over 400 injured when a Thames Trains passenger train passed a red signal and collided with a First Great Western high-speed train that was heading towards Paddington Station. The ruling attracted significant media coverage at the time. Businesses may also be exposed to the risk of criminal offences if they fail to comply with laws relating to:

- prevention of moneylaundering
- consumer credit
- protection of the environment
- data protection
- sale of counterfeit goods.

This is by no means an exhaustive list. But the risks for businesses arising out of potential civil actions will often be just as significant, if not more so – and they may arise from the same set of facts. Take the example of a business that fails to comply with health and safety legislation with the result that several of its employees and members of the public are injured. As well as a criminal prosecution and possible fine, the business could face civil actions from the individuals concerned, who would be able to claim compensation for the injuries they have suffered. Depending on the seriousness of those injuries and the number of individuals involved, the compensation claims could run into millions of pounds.

© Ian Miles – Flashpoint Pictures/Alamy

Since Ladbroke Grove, there have been a number of other rail crashes, including this one at Potters Bar in 2002

Common law and equity

Another concept that is key to your understanding of the English legal system is the distinction between **common law** and **equity**. So far we have used the term 'common law' to describe the difference in approach between the English legal system and those of countries with civil law systems – in particular, the fact that the English legal system is based primarily on judge-made rules. However, the term common law is also used to distinguish between judge-made rules that are based on a concept known as equity (called **equitable rules**) and those that are not (known as common law rules).

A brief history of equitable rules

Equitable rules originated in the fourteenth century. At first, they could only be applied by a special court – the court of the Lord Chancellor, also known as the Court of Chancery. Principles developed by the ordinary courts were known as common law rules. The Court of Chancery evolved in order to deal with petitions from citizens to the king. These citizens often had complaints that could not be dealt with in the ordinary courts because, at the time, judges were often very reluctant to extend or modify the common law in response to new situations – even where this resulted in obvious injustice. The principles applied by the Court of Chancery, by way of contrast, focused more on the moral position of the parties to the dispute, mainly because Lord Chancellors were usually clergymen.

Equity: the current position

The position now is that all courts can apply equitable principles. These principles are capable of overriding inflexible common law rules. However, equitable principles may only be applied at the court's discretion, i.e. where certain relatively strict conditions are met. In particular, the court must normally be satisfied that:

- the application of the common law rule would cause injustice
- the person seeking to modify the application of the common law rule has behaved fairly (lawyers sometimes say that the person in question must have 'clean hands').

Equitable powers will be explored in more detail in the chapters of Part 2 dealing with equitable remedies for breach of contract, such as injunctions. However, an example of the use of equitable powers is given in the 'Reality check' textbox.

 Reality check

Dyson v Hoover (2001)

Vacuum cleaner wars

Dyson had invented a new type of bag-less vacuum cleaner based on a revolving cylinder. His invention was protected by a patent, giving him the exclusive right to make use of the invention for 20 years. His company successfully sued rival vacuum cleaner manufacturer Hoover for copying his invention (and infringing his patent) with its bag-less Triple Vortex model. Under the common law, Dyson could only have claimed damages for the infringement. However, the court agreed to use its equitable powers to issue an injunction, preventing Hoover from selling any more Triple Vortex cleaners until Dyson's patent had expired (by the time of the injunction, it only had about a year to run).

> **QUESTION 2** Why was use of the court's equitable powers to issue an injunction justified in this case? Why wasn't it enough to let Dyson rely on the common law remedy of damages?

Case law

English law relies heavily on judge-made rules or case law. However, this does not mean that judges are free to make new rules of law whenever they please. In reality, their freedom to do so is often quite limited. In the vast majority of cases, for example, the role of judges is simply to apply established principles. Provided those principles are sufficiently clear, there is no need for judges to make new law. The principles may be set out either in legislation or in an earlier case dealing with similar issues, known as a **precedent**. Judges and lawyers can find out what was decided in these cases because the rulings are normally published (see the section entitled 'How to use the tables of cases and legislation' accompanying the tables at the beginning of this book).

The doctrine of binding precedents

There are two types of precedent:

- *Binding precedent* – a decision on a point of law that the court is obliged to follow, even if the court itself disagrees with it.
- *Persuasive precedent* – a decision on a point of law that the court is not obliged to follow, but it may choose to use the case as a guide.

The difference between these two types of precedent is explained in more detail under the later heading 'Precedents and judicial creativity'. As far as binding precedents are concerned, the general rule is that decisions made by higher courts must be followed by lower courts (see Figure 1.1). Where a court believes that there may be some doubt over the correctness of a binding precedent, its only option is to allow an appeal to a higher court (which may be in a position to over-rule the precedent). Figure 1.1 shows the appeals structure for civil law cases.

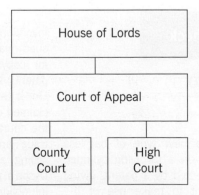

Figure 1.1 Civil court hierarchy

The House of Lords

The highest court in the English legal system is the **House of Lords**. This is another legal term that can have two meanings, depending on the context. Sometimes it is used to refer to one of the Houses of Parliament (the other House of Parliament is the **House of Commons**); when the House of Lords acts in this capacity, its role is to scrutinise legislation (this is explained under the later heading 'UK legislation'). The House of Lords also acts as the highest court of the English legal system. When the House of Lords acts in this capacity, a panel of senior judges, known as Law Lords, hears appeals against rulings of the lower courts. The panel normally consists of five Law Lords (other members of the House of Lords who are not judges take no part in this aspect of the House of Lords' work – their main role is to scrutinise legislation).

Decisions of the House of Lords are binding on all other English courts. The House of Lords itself will normally follow its own previous decisions. It is free to depart from what it said in an earlier precedent if, for example, it concludes that the law needs to be changed to reflect changes in society or the principles set out in an earlier precedent may have undesirable consequences that were not appreciated at the time. However, it is normally reluctant to do this as it creates uncertainty; as a result, such decisions are rare in practice.

The proposed Supreme Court

In 2005 Parliament passed legislation to take away the judicial functions of the House of Lords and create a **Supreme Court** to carry out this role. Instead of appealing a case to the House of Lords, lawyers will appeal to the Supreme Court. You can find out more information about these changes on the companion website. However, these proposals will take time to implement and, at the time of writing, the Supreme Court was not expected to be set up until 2008. We have therefore continued to use the term 'the House of Lords' to refer to the highest court in the English legal system.

The Court of Appeal

Below the House of Lords, the court hierarchy is different for civil and criminal cases. So far as civil cases are concerned (which are more relevant to the topics covered in this book), the next highest court is the **Court of Appeal**. Its decisions are binding on all lower courts, but not the House of Lords. The Court of Appeal generally follows its own earlier decisions, unless they are inconsistent with a later House of Lords decision. In addition, the Court of Appeal may overrule its own earlier decisions where:

- there are two earlier Court of Appeal decisions that appear to conflict – in such a case, the Court of Appeal must decide which one to follow; or
- the earlier decision failed to take account of an important point of law.

The lower courts

For civil cases, the courts below the Court of Appeal have to follow earlier decisions of more senior courts, such as the House of Lords and the Court of Appeal, but they are not bound by their own previous decisions.

Appeals (for both civil and criminal cases) must normally make their way up through the court hierarchy. For example, where a case started in the High Court, an appeal must normally be made first to the Court of Appeal; it can only be appealed to the House of Lords once the Court of Appeal has taken its decision on the case. However, if the point of law in question is already the subject of a binding Court of Appeal precedent, it may be appealed directly to the House of Lords (on the grounds that there is no point in referring it to the Court of Appeal, since the latter is bound by its own previous decisions). This is known as the 'leapfrog' procedure. In practice, however, it is rarely used.

Precedents and judicial creativity

The effect of the system of precedents – particularly binding precedents – is that English judges often have very limited scope to make new law. Whenever a higher court has given a ruling on a particular point of law, judges in any lower courts must normally follow that ruling. However, there is an important exception to this.

A distinction is made between what a court says when applying the law to the facts of a case and other comments made by the court about what the law is. For example, if the House of Lords is asked to rule on a dispute about payment of loans, it may make some general observations about this subject, such as how the law would be expected to work in various hypothetical situations, in order to explain the reasons for its ruling. Such observations are known by the Latin term

FAQ

The old v the new

If the lower courts are faced with a House of Lords' precedent that is 200 years old, are they still obliged to follow it?

Legally, the lower courts are obliged to follow *all* binding precedents, no matter how old they are. This highlights one of the potential problems of the precedent system, which is that it can make it difficult for the law to move with the times; if a binding precedent arose 200 years ago and has never been overruled, it remains the law, even though society may well have changed so much in the meantime that the precedent causes considerable difficulties. However, in practice, such problems are rarer than you might expect. There are several reasons for this. First of all, a judge may be able to avoid having to follow a precedent by choosing to **distinguish** it; this is where he decides that the facts of the case before him are different from those of the precedent,

which means he is not obliged to follow it. Second, as we shall see when we look at contract law in Part 2, many precedents have stood the test of time surprisingly well; while the facts may sometimes seem somewhat quaint to our modern eyes, the basic principles remain helpful in resolving today's legal disputes. Third, in areas where the approach used in case law was felt to be particularly outdated, Parliament has often intervened with legislation to change the law and introduce a more modern approach.

The Houses of Parliament, London

obiter dicta. They are not binding on lower courts (although they are likely to be highly persuasive). It is only the **ratio decidendi** of the House of Lords' decision that the lower courts are obliged to follow; this is a Latin term referring to the part of the decision involving the application of the law to the actual facts of the case at hand.

UK legislation

With the notable exception of European legislation and international treaties (see later), all legislation relevant to the English legal system is made by Parliament or with Parliament's authority. Parliament consists of the House of Commons (made up of 659 elected Members of Parliament) and the House of Lords (whose members are not elected). Scotland has its own parliament, but this is beyond the scope of this book, which is only concerned with the law of England and Wales. Wales also has its own assembly, but at the time of writing its powers in relation to legislation were fairly limited.

Types of UK legislation

There are two main types of UK legislation:

- Acts of Parliament, sometimes also referred to as **primary legislation** or statutes
- **delegated legislation**, sometimes also referred to as **secondary legislation**.

Delegated legislation is made by bodies outside Parliament, such as government departments, usually under powers delegated to them by Acts of Parliament. While the relevant Act will normally set out the basic principles to be followed, delegated legislation tends to be more concerned with detailed, technical regulations setting out how those basic principles should be implemented in practice. Delegated legislation is also sometimes used where there is a need to adapt regulations fairly frequently in response to changing circumstances. This is because delegated legislation can be enacted in far less time than an Act of Parliament as it is not usually fully debated. [You can find out more about UK legislative procedure and legislation generally on the companion website.] To find out how to look up UK legislation, see the section entitled 'How to use the tables of cases and legislation' at the beginning of this book.

Reality check

Communications Act 2003

How delegated legislation is used in practice

The Communications Act 2003 establishes a framework for the regulation of communications providers such as internet service providers and telecoms firms. Although the Act itself runs to more than 400 clauses and 19 schedules, this was not sufficient to deal with all the technical regulations relating to this area; these are set out in numerous pieces of delegated legislation issued by the telecoms regulator OFCOM and the Department of Trade and Industry under powers delegated to them by the Communications Act.

QUESTION 3 Why do you think it is rare for delegated legislation to be fully debated in Parliament?

EU legislation

In 1973 the UK became a member of the European Union or EU (or the European Economic Community, as it was known at the time). Section 2 of the European Communities Act 1972 makes EU law part of UK law. If there is a conflict with UK law, EU law will normally override the UK position.

What is the EU?

The EU began life as the European Coal and Steel Community (ECSC), a group of six European countries (Belgium, France, Germany, Italy, Luxembourg and the

Netherlands), which had decided to cooperate in order to help their economies to recover after the Second World War. In 1957 these countries signed a more wide-ranging treaty, creating the European Economic Community (EEC). Subsequent treaties have expanded its powers beyond the economic sphere to include new forms of cooperation on other issues, such as defence and immigration. This created what we now refer to as the European Union, which currently consists of 25 member states, including most of the for-

The European Parliament building in Brussels, Belgium

mer Communist bloc states of Eastern Europe (see Figure 1.2).

In 2004, EU member states agreed a new Constitution. Among other things, this combines the various existing treaties into a single text. At the time of writing, the future of the Constitution was unclear because electorates in several member states had failed to endorse it in referendums. This has made it unlikely that those member states will be able to ratify it (and the Constitution cannot come into effect until all member states have ratified it).

FAQ

Why is the EU important to business?

Businesses are more often heard complaining about the burden of rules imposed on them by 'Brussels bureaucrats' – and sometimes they may have a point. But there are also advantages for businesses in the UK's membership of the EU. For example, EU rules on the single market mean that UK firms do not have to pay import duty when they sell their goods in other member states. The same rules also prevent other member states from discriminating against UK businesses and in favour of their own national businesses. This helps UK businesses gain access to a market that is even larger than the USA in terms of population.

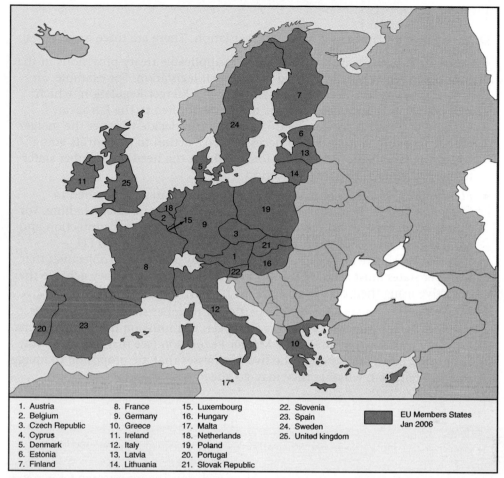

1. Austria	8. France	15. Luxembourg	22. Slovenia
2. Belgium	9. Germany	16. Hungary	23. Spain
3. Czech Republic	10. Greece	17. Malta	24. Sweden
4. Cyprus	11. Ireland	18. Netherlands	25. United kingdom
5. Denmark	12. Italy	19. Poland	
6. Estonia	13. Latvia	20. Portugal	
7. Finland	14. Lithuania	21. Slovak Republic	

EU Members States
Jan 2006

Figure 1.2   Map of the European Union

By signing up to the EU, member states agree to abide by the relevant EU treaties and EU legislation. If there is a conflict between EU law and national law, EU law always wins. However, all member states have a say in the making of EU legislation and although membership places certain limits on national sovereignty, it also has a number of advantages, some of which are highlighted in the FAQ textbox headed 'Why is the EU important to business?'

Treaty provisions

Some rules of EU law are set out in the various treaties themselves. For example, there are provisions prohibiting anticompetitive behaviour, such as an agreement between businesses to fix their prices rather than compete with one another. Some (but not all) of these provisions may be relied on directly in national courts. For example, a UK company that has been forced to pay a higher price for goods as a result of an illegal price-fixing agreement could claim compensation in the national courts of an EU member state on the basis of provisions of the EU treaty; there would be no need for the UK firm to show that any national laws had been broken. Where a treaty provision can be relied on in this way without the need for national legislation, it is said to be 'directly applicable'.

EU legislation

Other rules of EU law are set out in EU legislation. There are three main types:

- *EU regulations*: these are similar to directly applicable treaty provisions in that they take effect without the need for national legislation. For example, an important **regulation** for businesses is the EU Merger Regulation, which requires all mergers above a certain size to be notified to the European Commission (this is so that the Commission can decide whether the merger may reduce competition and, if necessary, take action to prevent its going ahead). This regulation came into force without the need for member states to enact their own national legislation.

- *EU directives*: these set out measures that member states are required to implement using their own national legislation by a particular deadline. For example, in Part 5 we will look at a number of UK consumer protection and employment law measures that were introduced in response to EU **directives**. Unlike a regulation, a directive only sets out the objectives that member states must achieve; it is up to member states how they achieve that objective using their own laws.

- *EU decisions*: these are addressed to particular member states, businesses or individuals. For example, when the European Commission has completed its assessment of a merger under the Merger Regulation (see first point), it will issue a **decision** addressed to the two businesses that are proposing to merge; this will tell them whether they may go ahead with their merger.

FAQ

How does the EU legislate in practice?

You might think that the most common form of EU legislation would be regulations, However, in practice, directives tend to be used more often than regulations – despite the fact that directives involve 'extra work' (in the sense that member states have to enact their own legislation in order to implement them). The main reason for this is that member states have different legal systems; using a directive allows them to choose how best to 'translate' the measures they have agreed with other member states into national legislation that fits in with their own legal system. You can find out more about the EU, its institutions and its legislative procedures on the companion website.

QUESTION 4 What happens if a member state fails to implement a directive properly?

International treaties

International treaties are an increasingly important source of English law. We have already seen one example of this in the influence of the EU, which is based on international treaties. However, there are numerous other treaties that the UK has agreed to and that therefore affect English law. Treaties are effectively agreements between states; they often result from negotiations within international organisations such as the United Nations or the World Trade Organisation. They do not usually have to be ratified by the UK Parliament, although Parliament will often be called on to pass legislation to implement treaty provisions (most international treaties are not directly applicable in the same way as the EU treaties, i.e. they need to be 'translated' into national laws before they can be relied on by businesses or individuals).

The European Convention on Human Rights

For example, the UK is a signatory to the **European Convention on Human Rights (ECHR)**. This treaty was drawn up by the **Council of Europe** in 1950. The Council is a separate organisation from the EU; at the time of writing, it had 46 members in total, including most EU members but also non-EU countries such as Russia and Turkey. For many years, individuals and businesses in the UK could not rely on convention rights when they brought disputes before the English courts because the government had not enacted any legislation to permit this. Anyone with a complaint involving human rights had to appeal to the **European Court of Human Rights (ECtHR)** in Strasbourg, which is considered in more detail in Chapter 2. This was a very lengthy procedure because the person had first of all to exhaust their rights of appeal in the English legal system, taking their case all the way to the House of Lords if necessary. However, the position has now changed as a result of the Human Rights Act 1998, which incorporated the convention into English law.

Human rights and businesses

Under the European Convention on Human Rights, businesses as well as individuals can have rights. The following are of particular importance:

- *The right to a fair trial (Article 6)*: businesses have used this to challenge the procedures adopted by bodies such as planning authorities, by arguing that they were not given a fair hearing.
- *The right to private and family life (Article 8)*: businesses have used this right to challenge what they consider to be overly intrusive reporting by the media.
- *The right to freedom of expression (Article 10)*: businesses have used this right to challenge legislation restricting advertising.
- *The right to property (Article 1 of Protocol 1)*: businesses have used this right to challenge legislation on taxation and compulsory purchase of property (see the case of **Stretch v UK (2003)**, which is discussed in Chapter 2, and **Wilson v First County Trust (2003)**, which is discussed in Chapter 20).

Under the Human Rights Act 1998, these rights may now be relied on by businesses in proceedings before the English courts. For more information on human rights, including the European Court of Human Rights, see Chapter 2 and the companion website.

Other international treaties

Other examples of treaties relevant to English law include international treaties on jurisdiction and enforcement of judgments. These set out the principles that the English courts must apply when they are considering disputes that relate to both the UK and other signatory states (and where there may be an argument that the dispute should be dealt with by a court in another signatory country). [More information on international treaties can be found on the companion website.]

Answers to in-text questions

QUESTION 1 If an employee is claiming damages from a business for an injury suffered at work, what is the standard of proof that the employee must meet in order to succeed?

The employee's claim will be based on civil law, so the standard of proof is the balance of probabilities. This may be quite significant. For example, if there is more than one possible cause of the accident, the employee must prove that there is at least a 51% probability that his employer was responsible; this is significantly less difficult than proving a version of events 'beyond reasonable doubt', as required in criminal cases.

QUESTION 2 In *Dyson v Hoover*, why was use of the court's equitable powers to issue an injunction justified? Why wasn't it enough to let Dyson rely on the common law remedy of damages?

Damages would only have compensated Dyson for the sales his firm had lost as a result of Hoover's infringement; they would not have prevented Hoover from selling the Triple Vortex product. As a result, it would have been unjust for the court to say that Dyson could only have a common law remedy.

QUESTION 3 Why do you think it is rare for delegated legislation to be fully debated in Parliament?

On average, several thousand pieces of delegated legislation are made each year, in comparison with about 10–20 Acts of Parliament. It would be quite impractical for Parliament to debate all these detailed regulations as there would never be enough time to do this. While this may sound undemocratic, the government may consult on delegated legislation before it is made – so there is often an opportunity for businesses and the wider public to have their say. Having said that, because of the lack of democratic scrutiny, the use of delegated legislation for some purposes remains controversial. [For more information on this, see the companion website.]

QUESTION 4 What happens if a member state fails to implement a directive properly?

If a member state fails to implement an EU directive properly, the European Commission can bring an action against it in the European Court of Justice (this is explained in Chapter 2).

2 How the law is enforced

By the end of this chapter, you should be able to explain:

- **The role of the High Court, the County Court and tribunals in the English civil court system**

- **The roles of the European Court of Justice and the European Court of Human Rights**

- **The procedure for bringing a civil action**

- **What is meant by arbitration and alternative dispute resolution**

- **The role of regulators in enforcing the law**

- **How the law may be enforced against the state**

Introduction

In Chapter 1, we looked at how laws are made. But laws are not much use without an effective system of enforcement to ensure that they are actually followed in practice. This system is mainly provided by the courts, which provide a forum for the resolution of disputes involving possible breaches of the law. Their role is primarily reactive, in that they take decisions on matters brought before them by the state, businesses, individuals or other organisations. Here are some examples of how this process works in practice:

- Where businesses or individuals are in dispute with one another, they may decide to start court proceedings in order to enforce their legal rights. For example, a business that is owed money by a customer may seek a court order requiring the customer to pay. If necessary, the court may authorise measures such as the use of bailiffs to seize property belonging to the customer in order to pay the sums owed to the business. But resolving legal disputes of this type does not have to involve going to court. For example, two businesses that are in dispute may use arbitration or alternative dispute resolution instead (as explained later in the chapter).

- Some laws are enforced by the state or by institutions operating with its authority. As we have seen, the criminal law involves the state bringing a prosecution against an individual or an organisation in the criminal courts. The state is responsible for starting the procedure, but the final decision on whether the law has been broken and what should be done about it is made by the court.

- Some laws are capable of being enforced without having to go to court. For example, regulatory bodies such as the Financial Services Authority can decide that a business has breached certain legislation (e.g. the Financial Services and Markets Act 2000) and impose penalties, such as fines, without having to go to court at all. However, if the business in question disputes the decision, a court may well become involved at that stage, when it will have to consider whether the regulator's decision was correct.

Different procedures and courts are used depending on the nature of the dispute or the alleged breach of the law.

Types of court

In Chapter 1, we looked at the court hierarchy in connection with the topic of binding precedents. This involved looking at the court structure 'from the top down', because we were looking at how the decisions of more senior courts are normally binding on lower courts. We are now going to look at the court structure 'from the bottom up'; this will illustrate how the type of court used depends on the type of case, in particular whether the case involves civil or criminal law.

Civil law cases: the County Court and the High Court

The two most important courts dealing with civil cases are the **County Court** and the **High Court**. The High Court is based in London, although there are district registries in larger regional cities. It tends to be reserved for more complex or specialist cases or cases where larger sums of money are at stake. The County Court has more venues (over 200 at the time of writing) and tends to deal with matters that are less complex or where less money is at stake. Hearings in both courts are normally in front of a single judge (the vast majority of civil cases are conducted without juries, which tend to be reserved for more serious criminal law cases).

A case must start in the County Court unless the claim is worth more than £15,000 (£50,000 if the claim relates to personal injuries). If the claim is worth less than this, it is possible to ask the County Court to transfer the case to the High Court. However, the court must be persuaded that:

- the case is complex
- the case involves an important point of law
- the County Court's procedures or remedies are not appropriate to deal with the case.

At the time of writing, the government had announced that its long-term aim is to merge the County Court with the High Court in order to create a single civil court for England and Wales. You can find out more about these proposals on the companion website.

As we saw in Chapter 1, appeals from decisions of either the County Court or the High Court in civil cases are made to the Court of Appeal, with a further right of appeal from the Court of Appeal to the House of Lords. The only exception to this is where the leapfrog procedure applies, allowing a direct appeal from the County Court or the High Court to the House of Lords (see Chapter 1). There is not usually any right of appeal from the House of Lords, although in certain cases it may be possible to appeal to the European Court of Human Rights or the **European Court of Justice** (see under 'European courts' later).

Tribunals

The County Court and the High Court are not the only courts that deal with civil law cases. Some civil cases, such as those concerned with employment matters, may also be dealt with in specialist courts known as **tribunals**. For example, a person wishing to bring an action against their employer for unfair dismissal will normally start their case in the employment tribunal.

Tribunals generally have a more informal procedure, intended to make it easier for individuals to represent themselves instead of using a lawyer. They normally consist of a panel of three members, one of whom is normally legally qualified, while the others will normally have specialist knowledge in the relevant field (e.g. in employment tribunals, the other panel members will normally include one person with experience of working in the personnel department of a business and one person who has worked as a union official). Decisions of tribunals can be appealed to higher courts. Appeals from the majority of tribunals are generally made to the High Court or in some cases direct to the Court of Appeal (and then to the House of Lords). In areas such as employment law, where there is a large volume of cases, appeals are heard by another specialist tribunal, known as the Employment Appeal Tribunal (appeals from that tribunal's decisions are to the Court of Appeal and then to the House of Lords).

The criminal court system

The system of courts for dealing with criminal cases is different from the system for civil cases. Instead of starting in the County Court or the High Court, criminal cases normally start in either the **Magistrates Court** or the **Crown Court**.

The vast majority are dealt with in the Magistrates Court. These tend to be cases that are either relatively straightforward or involve less serious offences. There is no jury; hearings take place before three magistrates (sometimes also known as 'justices of the peace'), most of whom do this job voluntarily (only a small number are paid a salary to do it). Unlike judges, most magistrates are not legally qualified but are given some formal training before taking up their duties. They are also advised by a clerk of the court, who *is* legally qualified. Jury trials are reserved for cases dealt with in the Crown Court, which tends to deal with more complex criminal cases or those involving more serious offences. Trials in the Crown Court are presided over by a judge. [You can find out more about criminal court procedures on the companion website.] This chapter concentrates on the civil court system because it is more relevant to most of the topics you will cover in the remainder of this book.

European courts: the ECJ and the ECtHR

Certain cases that begin life in the courts of the English legal system may be referred to the European Court of Justice (ECJ) or the European Court of Human Rights (ECtHR). Although they are often confused with one another, these two courts are entirely separate and carry out entirely different functions. The key differences are as shown in Table 2.1.

The European Court of Human Rights, Strasbourg, France

This means that if your case is concerned with a point of EU law, you cannot involve the ECtHR in Strasbourg; if national courts cannot deal with the point, the relevant court will be the ECJ in Luxembourg. Equally, if your case is concerned with a point of human rights law, the relevant court will be the ECtHR in Strasbourg.

Referrals to the ECJ and ECtHR

A further key difference concerns the way in which cases are referred to these courts. For a case to be heard by the ECtHR, it must first go all the way through the appeals system of the English courts (up to the House of Lords if necessary). The ECtHR is therefore effectively a final court of appeal in relation to points of law concerning human rights (but it cannot consider any other issues). By contrast, cases may be referred to the ECJ at a much earlier stage. For example, if the High Court, the County Court or a tribunal decides that a case before it raises a question of EU law, it can refer that question to the ECJ. There is no requirement for the case to be appealed before such a reference is made. However, the ECJ will

Table 2.1 Functions of the ECJ and the ECtHR

	European Court of Justice	*European Court of Human Rights*
Relevant law	Treaties, regulations, directives and decisions of the European Union	The European Convention on Human Rights 1950
Jurisdiction	The 25 member states of the European Union	The 46 member states of the Council of Europe (entirely separate from the European Union – see Chapter 1)
Role	(i) Assists national courts by answering their questions on the interpretation of EU law (ii) Rules on whether EU institutions and member states have complied with EU law	Rules on whether member states of the Council of Europe have complied with the European Convention on Human Rights. Effectively acts as a final court of appeal once a case has reached the most senior national court of appeal
Location	Luxembourg	Strasbourg (France)

not decide the outcome of the case itself; it will merely give an answer on the point of EU law put to it by the referring court. The case will then come back to the referring court for a decision (which must take account of the ECJ's ruling on the point of EU law).

Reality check

Arsenal FC v Reed (2003)

In 2002, the High Court referred a number of questions to the ECJ concerning trademarks owned by Arsenal FC. These questions arose because Arsenal FC had taken legal action against a trader, Matthew Reed, who had been selling unofficial Arsenal merchandise outside the club's ground. For example, he sold scarves featuring the word 'Arsenal' and the 'Gunners' logo, which are registered trademarks. Arsenal FC argued that Mr Reed was acting illegally, because he did not have the club's permission to use these trademarks. Mr Reed argued that he would only be breaking the law if he had misled consumers into thinking that he was selling official club merchandise; he maintained that consumers would not be confused because there was a notice on his stall saying that all the merchandise was unofficial. The ECJ ruled that Mr Reed was wrong; it pointed out that when goods left the stall, consumers could still be confused into thinking that the merchandise was official (which would be an infringement of Arsenal FC's trademark rights). The High Court

referred this question to the ECJ because the law on trademarks is subject to an EU directive designed to ensure that trademarks are given the same protection throughout the EU. Unusually, when the case came back before the High Court, after the ECJ's ruling, the English judge decided that the ECJ had not answered his question properly and that he did not have to follow its decision; however, Arsenal FC appealed to the Court of Appeal, which ruled that the ECJ had answered the question properly and its ruling had to be followed.

QUESTION 1 In *Arsenal v Reed*, if the High Court judge had concluded that the ECJ's ruling had answered his question properly, would he have been obliged to follow it?

The dual role of the ECJ

Besides helping national courts interpret EU law, the ECJ also has power to rule on whether the actions of EU institutions such as the European Commission are lawful and whether EU member states have infringed EU law (e.g. by failing to implement a directive on time). This is discussed further under the later heading 'Enforcing the law against the state'. When the ECJ acts in this capacity, there is no need to start proceedings in a national court; applications can be made direct to the ECJ.

Bringing a claim in the civil courts

The procedure followed by courts of the English system varies depending on the type of case. As civil cases are most relevant to the topic of business law, this section outlines the procedure that might be followed in a typical civil case. It is based on the fictional scenario in the following case study.

Case study

Alpha Business Machines Limited sells computer equipment. It has supplied some hardware to a business customer at a cost of £30,000. The customer paid a deposit of £5000, with the remaining sum due on delivery. Alpha has delivered the equipment and sent an invoice for the remaining £25,000. The customer has refused to pay; it argues that some of the equipment does not work. Alpha's engineers have looked into the complaint and they believe that the problems are the fault of the customer. The customer does not accept this and still refuses to pay. Eventually, Alpha decides to start legal action to recover the £25,000.

Claimants and defendants

In this scenario, Alpha would be referred to as the claimant. The **claimant** is the person who starts the legal action. You may sometimes see the word **plaintiff** used instead of claimant. This term was abandoned following the 'Woolf reforms' of the civil courts system, which were implemented in 1999, but you are very likely to come across it in older cases and textbooks. The Woolf reforms (named after a senior judge, Lord Woolf) were intended to simplify procedures; as part of this process, an attempt was made to introduce more straightforward English terminology in place of words such as plaintiff. The customer in this scenario would be the **defendant**, which refers to the person on the 'receiving end' of the legal action. The defendant and the claimant are known collectively as the **parties** to the legal action.

Getting legal assistance

Alpha would not be required to appoint lawyers to represent it in its claim; there would be nothing to stop it from representing itself – e.g. its managing director could conduct the whole case on behalf of the company. However, legal action is often a complex and time consuming process and Alpha's managers probably have their hands full running their business. So it is likely that they would instruct lawyers to assist them.

Solicitors

Alpha's first port of call would probably be a firm of **solicitors**. They would advise Alpha initially on whether it had a claim that was worth pursuing. They would also normally advise on what the risks might be. For example, they would normally point out that if Alpha loses, it will probably have to pay some or all of its customer's legal costs for defending itself against the claim. Solicitors will often write a 'letter before action' warning the potential defendant that legal action is being considered. Sometimes the threat of legal action is sufficient to achieve the desired result (e.g. in this case it might be enough to persuade the customer to pay up).

Barristers

If Alpha decides to proceed with the claim, its solicitors would normally instruct a **barrister** to represent the firm in court. Historically, barristers were the only lawyers who could present a case in court; solicitors did not have the necessary 'rights of audience'. This position was altered by the Courts and Legal Services Act 1990, which permitted solicitors who have obtained an additional qualification to represent their clients in court. However, relatively few solicitors have taken up this opportunity and it remains common for barristers to be instructed once a case comes to court. Because barristers specialise in advocacy (i.e. representing their clients before a court), they are generally more skilled than solicitors at presenting a client's case to a judge. Firms of solicitors tend to carry out a wider range of activities on behalf of their clients, such as drafting agreements, transferring property or forming companies.

Starting the claim

Alpha or its lawyers will need to fill out a claim form and send it to the court, together with the relevant administrative fee. The court will then arrange for a copy of the form to be sent to the defendant (Alpha's customer). The defendant has to respond to this within the time limits specified by the court. If it fails to do

FAQ

Isn't it expensive to use two sets of lawyers?

There would be nothing to stop a firm like Alpha from only instructing a barrister (or a solicitor qualified to appear in court). But barristers tend to work as individuals with relatively few support staff and may not have the time or the resources to deal with all the necessary paperwork. Firms of solicitors tend to be better equipped to carry out these tasks. Provided work is divided up sensibly between solicitors and barristers, the client should not be paying twice for the same work. In addition, two heads can often be better than one when it comes to making decisions about how to get the best result.

so, Alpha may be able to apply for a ruling in its favour (and the defendant will be deprived of the opportunity to put its side of the case).

In the scenario we are looking at, it is likely that the defendant would respond by filing a **defence**. That defence would probably include the argument that it was not obliged to pay the £25,000 because the equipment did not work properly. It might also include a **counterclaim**, which is a claim by the defendant for compensation (or some other remedy) from the claimant. For example, in this case, the defendant might argue that as a result of the problems with the equipment, it has incurred costs of £10,000. It will argue that these costs should be deducted from any amounts awarded to Alpha.

Case allocation

The next stage is for the case to be allocated to one of the 'tracks' summarised as follows:

- *The small claims track*: this is for claims of up to £5000 (although larger claims can be dealt with in this track if both parties agree). The procedures are designed to make it easier for parties to represent themselves, rather than instruct lawyers. As a result, the small claims track is often used for disputes between businesses and consumers.

- *The fast track*: this is for claims that are more than £5000 but not exceeding £15,000. As the name implies, the aim of the procedures is to resolve the dispute fairly quickly, so this track tends to be reserved for cases that appear to be relatively straightforward. For example, it would not be suitable for cases where a significant amount of evidence will need to be considered.

- *The multi-track*: this is for claims of over £15,000 (or less than this where the court concludes that the fast track or small claims track procedures would not be appropriate, e.g. because the case is complex). The multi-track gives judges a wide discretion to manage the case as they see fit. For example, if there is a great deal of evidence to be considered, the judge can give instructions as to how and when this should be dealt with.

Sometimes the process of case allocation may lead to the case being assigned to a different court. Cases on the small claims track or the fast track would normally be dealt with in the County Court. Cases on the multi-track could be dealt with in either the High Court or the County Court, depending on which one the judge considered to be more appropriate.

> **QUESTION 2** Which track do you think Alpha's case would be assigned to?

Case management and disclosure

Judges have quite extensive powers to impose deadlines on the parties to carry out tasks in preparation for the trial such as exchanging written evidence (a process known as **disclosure**). In Alpha's case, there would need to be disclosure of evidence about the customer's claims that the equipment did not work properly (and Alpha would need to provide evidence to support its argument that the problems were the fault of the customer).

Settlement

It is possible for the parties to settle their dispute at any time, even where legal action has already begun. Sometimes the process of disclosure will lead one party to conclude that their case is not as strong as they thought it was, which may encourage them to reach an agreement rather than pursue the matter to a full trial. Indeed court procedures are designed to encourage this. For example, in Alpha's case, the defendant customer could decide to make a payment into court of, say, £10,000. This would put Alpha in a difficult position because if it were to be awarded compensation of less than this amount, it will have to pay the customer's legal costs (which could be considerable). Equally, if Alpha made the customer an offer to settle and is then awarded the same amount or more at trial, Alpha can ask the court to order the customer to pay a higher level of interest on that amount.

The trial

If the case goes to trial, there will be a hearing before the judge. The parties will normally be represented by a barrister or a solicitor with an advocacy qualification, who will take the judge through the arguments and explain the supporting evidence. For example, in Alpha's case, the judge would probably be asked to look at the contract for supply of the equipment. He might also be asked to look at experts' reports on whether the equipment was working properly or not.

Evidence can also take the form of testimony from witnesses. For example, Alpha might submit witness statements from its engineers stating that they had carried out tests on the equipment to prove that it was working properly. Alternatively, Alpha might call the engineers to present their evidence to the court in person. If the defendant disputed that evidence, it could ask for the engineers to be questioned by its lawyers (this is known as **cross-examination**). The role of the judge at this stage is primarily to listen to the evidence and arguments presented to him or her and reach a view on which party should win the case.

The judgment

After the hearing, a written judgement will be produced explaining the reasons for the decision. The most common remedy is an award of financial compensation, known as **damages**, although the court may order other types of remedy. These are considered in more detail in Chapter 8.

> **QUESTION 3** If Alpha won its case, how much would the court order the defendant to pay? Would it be £25,000 or could it be more than this? Assume that the defendant's counterclaim failed.

Executing judgment

Even if Alpha had won its case, its customer could still refuse to pay. In order to enforce payment, Alpha might have to return to court in order to apply for one of the following:

- a **charging order**: this means that the defendant cannot sell any of its property until it has paid the amount owed to the claimant.
- a **garnishee order**: this is an order against the defendant's bank or some other person holding money belonging to the defendant, which prevents payment of that money to anyone other than the claimant.
- a **writ of fieri facias**: this allows the claimant (or bailiffs acting on its behalf) to seize the defendant's property and sell it (but only up to the value of the amount claimed).
- **attachment of earnings**: if the defendant is an individual, his or her employer can be required to pay some of the defendant's salary direct to the claimant in order to pay off the amount owed.

An alternative to this is to start insolvency proceedings against the defendant, which are explained in more detail in Part 4. Such proceedings can result in the defendant's property being sold in order to pay its debts. However, if the defendant owes money to many other businesses or individuals, there is no guarantee that the claimant will get its money back.

Resolving disputes outside court

Court proceedings can be time consuming, expensive and may attract adverse publicity (because the proceedings are held in public and may be reported in the media). As a result, some businesses favour resolving disputes through arbitration or alternative dispute resolution.

Arbitration

Arbitration refers to a procedure where the parties to a dispute agree to appoint someone to resolve it (an **arbitrator**) and to be legally bound by the arbitrator's decision. It is quite common for agreements between businesses to contain clauses requiring any dispute to be referred to arbitration rather than resolved in the courts. The key advantages over court proceedings are as follows:

- *Confidentiality*: hearings are usually in private so it is easier to avoid bad publicity.
- *Flexibility*: the parties can organise the proceedings to fit the nature of the dispute (although their freedom to do so is constrained somewhat by the requirements of the Arbitration Act 1996).
- *Specialist knowledge of arbitrator*: an arbitrator can be appointed who has specialist knowledge of the technical issues involved in the case (which may be preferable to a judge who knows about the law, but does not know much about the technical background to the dispute).

Arbitration can sometimes be cheaper than court proceedings but this is not always the case. It is usually necessary to instruct lawyers and similar procedures are often involved, e.g. disclosure. It is also normally necessary to pay the arbitrator. As a result, arbitration can sometimes be more expensive than going to court. It is possible to appeal against a decision of an arbitrator (usually to the High Court). However, appeals are generally only possible where there has been a serious irregularity or the arbitrator was wrong on a point of law.

Alternative dispute resolution

Alternative dispute resolution (ADR) is a broad term that may be used to refer to any method of resolving disputes not involving arbitration or court proceedings. The key point to note is that the outcome of the procedure is not binding on the parties. If the parties are happy with the outcome, there is nothing to prevent their entering into a legally binding agreement to abide by it – but they cannot be forced to do this. ADR offers greater flexibility than arbitration or court proceedings and there is a wide variety of different schemes. It can also be cheaper, although this depends on the procedure adopted and how much the mediator has to be paid.

The role of regulators

Historically, the civil law was enforced primarily by individuals and businesses asserting their rights through the court system. The role of the state was primarily confined to enforcing criminal law by bringing prosecutions in the criminal courts. As society and the economy have become more complex, it has become more common for the activities of businesses to be regulated by the civil law as well as the criminal law. The task of enforcing such regulation is increasingly carried out by independent regulators acting with the authority of the state.

Many of these regulators can issue decisions against businesses, including fines, without having to go to court (although their decisions can normally be appealed to courts). The advantage of such an approach is that it is not dependent on businesses or individuals taking legal action to enforce their rights (which they will often be prepared to do only as a last resort); powerful, state-funded regulators are better placed to take enforcement action where they believe that it is in the public interest. This is also an example of the civil law being used to pursue aims more commonly associated with criminal law, namely deterrence of undesirable conduct and punishment by the state for engaging in such conduct. Some examples illustrating the impact of regulators' decisions on businesses can be found in the 'Regulators in action' textbox. (Regulators will be discussed in more detail in Chapter 20.)

Reality check

Regulators in action

- *Football shirts*: in 2003 the Office of Fair Trading (OFT) fined Manchester Utd, JJB Sports and a number of other retailers a total of £18.5 million for fixing the price of replica football shirts in breach of the Competition Act 1998.

- *Exaggerated oil reserves*: in 2004 the Financial Services Authority (FSA) fined the oil company Shell £17 million for exaggerating the amount of its oil reserves (misleading shareholders into thinking that their shares were more valuable than was actually the case). This was in breach of the Financial Services and Markets Act 2000.

- *TV shopping*: in 2004 communications regulator OFCOM fined TV channel Auctionworld £450,000 for serious failures to comply with its code of practice on broadcast advertising. When Auctionworld failed to pay, OFCOM revoked its licence to broadcast under the Communications Act 2003.

Enforcing the law against the state

So far we have concentrated on how the law is enforced against businesses or individuals. But what if the state (or bodies acting on its behalf such as regulators) breaks the law? There are several ways in which the state can be called to account.

Judicial review

In the English legal system, the main remedy against the state is provided by a procedure known as **judicial review**. This allows individuals or businesses to ask a court (usually the Administrative Division of the High Court) to rule on whether a decision taken by the state (or a public body acting with the authority of the state) was lawful. (See the 'Judicial review' textbox.)

Breaches of EU law

If the breach concerns EU law, such as the failure to implement a directive, the European Commission may bring proceedings against the relevant member state in the ECJ. For example, in 2001 France was found by the ECJ to have infringed EU law by maintaining a ban on British beef. The European Commission then threatened to ask the ECJ to impose fines on France but withdrew the threat when the French government backed down and lifted the ban.

Reality check

Judicial review: Interbrew SA v Competition Commission (2001)

In 2001 the Belgian brewing firm Interbrew applied for judicial review of a decision taken under UK merger control legislation by a regulator called the Competition Commission. Merger control legislation is designed to prevent firms acquiring a dominant market position by simply buying up their competitors. The decision would have forced Interbrew to sell the brewing company Bass, which it had just bought. Interbrew argued that the Competition Commission's procedures had been unfair. The High Court agreed and ruled that the Competition Commission's decision should be 'quashed'

(declared invalid). The government asked another competition regulator, the Office of Fair Trading, to reconsider the merger; although Interbrew was still forced to sell some of its brewing interests in the UK, it achieved its main objective, which was to keep Bass.

Breaches of human rights

As explained in Chapter 1, the Human Rights Act 1998 means that individuals can sue the government for breaching their human rights. The case outlined in the following textbox was begun before the act came into force, but it shows how human rights can be used to prevent the state acting unfairly towards individuals and businesses.

Reality check

Human rights: Stretch v UK (2003)

Dorchester Borough Council granted a 22-year lease of a light industrial estate to a businessman called Michael Stretch, with an option to renew for a further 21 years. Mr Stretch had taken the lease on the understanding that he would be able to renew it in order to secure an adequate return on his investment. However, when he requested a renewal, he was told that the option was unenforceable. This was because the council had acted beyond its powers and should never have granted the option in the first place. Having exhausted his UK rights of appeal, Mr Stretch appealed to the ECtHR, arguing that the council's refusal to renew the lease breached his right to property under Article 1, Protocol 1 of the European Convention on Human Rights. The ECtHR agreed and awarded him damages. It accepted that the council would be acting illegally if it permitted the renewal, but said that it was wrong that Mr Stretch was left without any remedy under English law; at the very least, he should have been able to claim compensation for the fact that he had been misled by the council.

QUESTION 4 If the human rights issues in *Stretch v UK (2003)* had come before the English courts after the Human Rights Act 1998 came into force, rather than before, what difference would it have made?

Answers to in-text questions

QUESTION 1 In *Arsenal v Reed*, if the High Court judge had concluded that the ECJ's ruling had answered his question properly, would he have been obliged to follow it?

Yes, but only in the sense of following the principles set out in the ECJ's ruling. As we saw in Chapter 1, EU law (including judgments of the ECJ) takes precedence over national law. However, where a question is referred from a national court, the ECJ does not tell the national court what to decide; it merely sets out the principles that the national court should apply when reaching its decision. So in this case, the ECJ did not say that the national court should find in favour of Arsenal – it simply set out the correct interpretation of EU trademark law and left it up to the national court to apply that interpretation to the facts of the case.

> **QUESTION 2** Which track do you think Alpha's case would be assigned to?

Because the value of its claim is over £15,000, Alpha's case would probably be assigned to the multi-track. If it were considered to be a relatively straightforward case, it would probably be dealt with in the County Court (even if Alpha had issued its claim in the High Court).

> **QUESTION 3** If Alpha won its case, how much would the court order the defendant to pay? Would it be £25,000 or could it be more than this? Assume that the defendant's counterclaim failed.

The court would order the defendant to pay £25,000 together with interest on that sum from the date on which it should originally have been paid until the date of actual payment. It would normally order the defendant to pay Alpha's reasonable legal costs as well.

> **QUESTION 4** If the human rights issues in *Stretch v UK (2003)* had come before the English courts after the Human Rights Act 1998 came into force, rather than before, what difference would it have made?

Until the Human Rights Act 1998 came into force, parties could not rely on provisions of the European Convention on Human Rights in proceedings before the English courts. Had the Act been in force, it would have enabled Mr Stretch to make a claim for compensation based on Article 1, Protocol 1 in the English courts. Had he been able to do this, it is possible that his case would not have needed to be appealed all the way to the ECtHR.

Website summary

The book's website contains the following material in respect of Part 1:

- PowerPoint slides containing relevant information from each chapter to help with revision
- Four additional questions with answers per chapter
- Quiz containing 10 multiple-choice questions for each part
- Biannual update bulletins to the book, which will consist of brief details of any major common law, statutory and constitutional developments affecting the currency of the book

PART TWO

Contract

This part deals with contract law, which is a key element of most courses on business law. Businesses make contracts all the time – with their suppliers, customers, employees and advisers. As the following chapters will demonstrate, businesses that do not pay sufficient attention to contracts do so at their peril. Knowledge of contract law is also useful in everyday life; for example, it will ensure that you know what your rights are if you buy from a shop goods that later turn out to be defective. Contract law is not an easy subject and some of the cases you will learn about may strike you as rather quaint and old fashioned. But the basic principles contained in those cases are often as important today as they were over 100 years ago.

The chapters in Part 2 deal with the following aspects of contract law:

- **How contracts are made**
- **What contracts say and how the courts interpret them**
- **Factors that can lead to contracts being invalid**
- **How contracts are enforced by the courts**

3 Contract law: an introduction

Learning objectives

By the end of this chapter, you should be able to explain:

- **Why contract law is important**
- **What the 'basic ingredients' of a legally binding agreement are**
- **What types of contract have to be in writing in order to be valid**
- **What is meant by express terms, implied terms and the notion of 'freedom of contract'**
- **What the courts can do to enforce contracts**

Introduction

This chapter introduces a number of key concepts relating to contract law and explains how it is relevant to businesses today. These key concepts are examined in more detail in the chapters that follow, but it is helpful to have a sound grasp of the basics and how they fit together before moving on to tackle the trickier aspects. In the interests of keeping things simple to start with, this chapter does not contain many cases – these are dealt with in the chapters that follow.

What is a contract?

A contract is an agreement between two or more individuals or businesses that is legally binding. The individuals or businesses who have made the agreement are known as the parties. Although many contracts are in writing, the vast majority of contracts are not required to be written down; provided the necessary ingredients of a legally binding agreement are present, a contract can come into existence based on nothing more than a conversation between the parties.

If one of the parties fails to keep a promise made in the contract, the other parties can take them to court. This is what differentiates a contract from other types of agreement that do not give rise to legal rights and obligations. For instance, if you agree to meet a friend for lunch and you have offered to pay, you will have made an agreement. But that agreement is unlikely to be viewed as giving rise to legal rights and obligations; at most, you will simply have a moral obligation to keep the promise you made to your friend. If, on the other hand, you and your friend start up a business together and you each sign a written agreement setting out how the profits will be shared, then you have probably entered into a contract. Should your friend try to stop you from obtaining your share of the profits, you would normally be able to take him or her to court in order to obtain your agreed share.

Why are contracts important?

Trust is not enough

Without contracts, businesses would have to rely entirely on trust in their dealings with other businesses or with individuals. Trust is all very well if relatively little is at stake. But few people would feel comfortable about relying entirely on trust

 Reality check

Baird Textiles

Why trust is not enough

Baird Textiles Holdings v Marks & Spencer (2001) concerned a dispute between the high street retailer Marks & Spencer and one of its main clothing suppliers, a UK-based firm called Baird Textiles. The two companies had worked closely together for 30 years. Over that time, Baird had invested heavily to meet its customers' needs and sales to Marks & Spencer had grown to over £100 million a year (representing 30–40% of Baird's total turnover). In 1999, however, Marks & Spencer decided to source more of its clothing from overseas firms. It informed Baird that it would not be ordering any more clothes from it after the end of the current production season.

Baird did not have a formal, written contract with Marks & Spencer. Although Marks & Spencer had always ordered significant volumes of clothing from Baird in the past, it had never committed itself to ordering large amounts over the longer term (e.g. 2–5 years ahead). On the contrary, both parties had chosen to operate outside a long-term contractual framework; their relationship was

based mainly on trust, rather than on legal rights and obligations. This led the Court of Appeal to conclude that the only legally binding commitment by Marks & Spencer to Baird consisted of its promise to pay for the clothing that it had ordered for the next production season – nothing more. In particular, there was no legal obligation on Marks & Spencer to compensate Baird for the loss of such a major customer or the sizeable investments that Baird had made over the course of their 30-year relationship.

when they were making a significant purchase, like buying a house – particularly when buying from someone they have never met before. Equally, banks or building societies would be unlikely to lend people the money to buy houses unless they had some means of recovering that money if the borrower failed to pay it back. This is where contracts play a key role, because they give people the confidence to proceed with a transaction, reassured by the knowledge that if the other party fails to meet its promises, it will normally be possible to seek some form of legal remedy. If there were no system for making and enforcing legally binding agreements, large parts of the economy would probably grind to a halt. The perils of relying on trust alone are illustrated in the 'Reality check' textbox headed 'Baird Textiles'.

> **QUESTION 1** In *Baird v Marks & Spencer*, if Baird had agreed a formal, long-term contract with Marks & Spencer, how could this have protected its position?

The dangers of promising too much

Awareness of contract law is important because businesses make contracts all the time. Most businesses will have hundreds, sometimes even thousands of contracts – with suppliers, customers, employees, auditors, the landlord of any rented premises, advertising agencies, marketing and PR consultancies, recruitment agencies, lawyers and so on. Because these agreements are legally binding, businesses need to be confident that they can deliver on any promises they make. If they are unable to meet those promises, the other party may (among other things) be able to take them to court to claim compensation (known as damages). The perils of making promises that you may not be able to meet are illustrated in the 'Reality check' textbox headed 'The Hoover free flights fiasco'.

Reality check

The Hoover free flights fiasco

The dangers of promising too much

In the early 1990s, the vacuum cleaner manufacturer Hoover offered free airline tickets to customers who bought a new Hoover product. At first, the promotion appeared to be working well and sales of Hoover products increased significantly. However, Hoover had underestimated demand for the free flights offer. Hoover could, of course, have refused to make good on its promise once it felt that the cost of providing the flights had become too high – but this would have had two major disadvantages. First, it would have been extremely bad publicity.

Second, it would have exposed Hoover to a large number of legal claims from customers, who would have argued that Hoover was in breach of contract. These factors appear to have persuaded Hoover that the best policy was to honour its promise in the majority of cases. Despite this, a number of customers were refused tickets and took Hoover to court. Not all of them were successful; for example, some had been offered tickets but chose not to accept them because they were at inconvenient times. However, those who were unjustifiably refused tickets did succeed in court. They were awarded damages equivalent to the value of the free flights they should have been offered. Although Hoover did not go out of business as a result of the promotion, it lost a great deal of money; while the promotion generated about £30 million in additional sales, it cost Hoover about £50 million to provide the free flights.

Common misconceptions about contract law

Before we move on to looking at the key ingredients of a contract, it is worth taking a moment to address some common misunderstandings about contract law.

Not about fairness

Sometimes people think that contract law generally is primarily concerned with achieving fairness. While that may be broadly true of some branches of the law, contract law is not really concerned with fairness – at least not in the sense that most people would understand the word 'fair'. For example, most people would not regard the outcome of the Baird Textiles case referred to above as 'fair'. But the courts expect businesses to be able to look out for themselves. When they are asked to look at contracts between businesses, the courts generally see themselves as merely giving effect to what the parties have agreed. If there were no agreement or the agreement is very unfair to one party, then in most cases, the courts will not intervene to readjust the balance on grounds of fairness alone.

Not entirely logical

Some people expect the law generally – and contract law in particular – to be an entirely logical, coherent set of rules. However, contract law has evolved over several hundred years based on a mixture of case law and legislation. Some of it is based on cases that were decided when society and the economy was very different from the way they are now, so they may produce odd results when applied to today's businesses. No one has ever attempted to codify it all into a single, coherent system. And even where Parliament has intervened with legislation, it has not always succeeded in making the legal position easy for businesses (or students of business law) to understand.

So you should not be surprised if you find yourself thinking that some aspects of contract law are rather unsatisfactory. But this is a problem with all legal systems. It is also worth remembering that English law remains popular as a choice of governing law for many international contracts (which could equally well choose the law of some other country, such as the United States). This shows that, despite its imperfections, English contract law remains well respected by many businesses.

Key ingredients of a contract

As we have seen, not all agreements are legally binding. The courts will only enforce agreements that have certain key 'ingredients'. The main ones are now outlined briefly and will be explored in more detail in the following chapters.

Intention

The parties must intend their agreement to be legally binding. This is known as **intention to create legal relations**. For example, in the Baird Textiles case mentioned earlier, lack of intention was one of the main reasons why the Court of Appeal ruled that there was no long-term contract with Marks & Spencer; the parties had decided not to have a contract governing their long-term relationship and had chosen instead to rely primarily on trust.

Agreement (offer and acceptance)

The parties must also have reached agreement. This may sound obvious, but the reality is more complex than many people imagine. In order to prove that there is agreement, you need to show that there has been a valid **offer** followed by a valid **acceptance**. For example, imagine that you are negotiating with another business to supply a computer system. You draw up two quite different proposals, which you send to your customer. These would be regarded as two separate offers. The customer then sends you a fax saying 'Yes, I agree to your proposal. Please start work on Monday.' The customer might well think that he or she has a contract with you – and could sue you if you fail to start work on Monday as requested. But legally, a court would probably say that you have not reached agreement. This is because the customer has not indicated which of the two options he or she has agreed to, so there is no acceptance.

Certainty of terms

Even where they are satisfied that the parties have reached agreement and intended that agreement to be legally binding, the courts will not enforce an agreement if its terms are unclear or do not contain enough detail. Lawyers refer to this as **certainty of terms**. Unless the courts can work out what the parties intended, they will not normally fill in any gaps that the parties have left in their agreement. This was another reason why the Court of Appeal said that there was no long-term contract in the Baird Textiles case mentioned earlier; the parties had never discussed how long their relationship should last or how much Marks & Spencer should buy in future, so it was impossible for the court to work out what any long-term agreement should actually say.

Consideration

The courts will not normally enforce agreements where one party promises to do something but the other party has not promised anything in return. This is known as **consideration**. For example, in a contract for the supply of clothing, there will be a promise by the supplier to deliver the clothing and a promise by the customer to pay for it. The customer's promise to pay is consideration for the supplier's promise to deliver – and vice versa. However, you should not assume that whenever a business claims to offer something 'free of charge', there is no binding contract because of a lack of consideration. For example, in the Hoover free flights promotion referred to earlier, customers did not have to pay the full cost of the flights being offered – but they had provided consideration in the form of payment for a Hoover product (which included an offer of airline tickets).

Formalities

Sometimes, a contract will only be valid if it is made in a certain way. Lawyers refer to such requirements as **formalities**. For example, the following agreements cannot be enforced unless they are in writing:

- agreements for the sale or transfer of an interest in land such as a contract to buy a house or a lease (Law of Property (Miscellaneous Provisions) Act 1989)
- agreements governed by the Consumer Credit Act 1974
- agreements for the transfer of shares in a limited company (Companies Act 1985)
- cheques (Bills of Exchange Act 1882).

The importance of formalities in practice is illustrated by the 'Reality check' headed 'The ITV Digital case'. For the vast majority of contracts, there are no special requirements – so in many cases, it is perfectly possible to have a legally binding agreement that is *not* written down. However, it is generally preferable to have a written document because otherwise it may well be difficult to prove what has been agreed.

 Reality check

The ITV Digital case

The importance of formalities

In 2000 the Football League sold the rights to broadcast football matches from Divisions 1–3 (but not the Premier League) to ITV Digital for £240 million. ITV Digital was not a success and went out of business. It still owed significant sums of money to the Football League – but there was no point in the Football League suing ITV Digital because the company did not have enough money to pay its debts. Instead, the League sued ITV Digital's majority shareholders, Granada plc and Carlton Communications plc (these two companies have since merged to form ITV plc). Granada and Carlton had been able to continue in business because ITV Digital was a limited liability company (see Chapter 13 for an explanation of limited liability).

The Football League argued that Granada and Carlton had given a guarantee that they would pay any money owed if ITV Digital went out of business. Guarantees of this type are only valid if certain formalities are complied with. These were originally set out in the Statute of Frauds 1677 (which is still in force). While the guarantee itself does not need to be in writing and could take the form of an oral promise, there must be some written evidence of it, such as a statement from the person giving the guarantee acknowledging the fact that they made such a promise. The written evidence also needs to be signed by the person giving the guarantee. The law imposes these requirements because guarantees are viewed as onerous obligations that should not be entered into lightly. The act of writing it down and signing it is intended to give the person offering the guarantee an opportunity to think seriously about it before going ahead.

In this case there was no written document that met these requirements; the only written agreement was between the Football League and ITV Digital (after that contract had been signed, the Football League had tried to get Granada and Carlton to sign a written guarantee, but they had refused). The court also ruled that there was insufficient evidence that Granada and Carlton had ever intended to give a guarantee in the first place. The League was therefore unable to recover the money it was owed by ITV Digital. Although it managed to sell the TV rights to the football matches to another broadcaster, it was forced to accept much less than the £240 million it had agreed with ITV Digital. See *Carlton Communications plc and Granada plc v The Football League (2002)*.

© Nick Kennedy/Alamy

Making contracts by electronic means

Some legislation relating to formalities has had to be amended to enable the relevant contracts to be made electronically. For example, while agreements for the transfer of land only have to be in writing, the law also requires a formal document (known as a conveyance) transferring the land into the name of the new owner. The government had to amend the relevant legislation in order to allow these documents to be executed electronically, because the original legislation was based on the assumption that paper documents would be used. These changes were made under the Electronic Communications Act 2000 (ECA).

The ECA also deals with electronic signatures. When electronic signatures first came out, there was some doubt over how they would be viewed by the courts. However, the ECA makes it clear that the courts should recognise electronic signatures, provided they are satisfied on the evidence presented to them that the signature is genuine. [More information on the law concerning formalities and making contracts electronically can be found on the companion website.]

> **QUESTION 2** In view of what has been said about formalities, do you think it is possible as a general rule to make a contract by an exchange of emails? Do you think any special formalities should be required if email is used?

Capacity

A contract will not normally be enforceable if one of the parties did not have the legal power to make it. Lawyers refer to a person's ability to make contracts as their **capacity**. The general rule is that if it should have been obvious to one party that the other party did not have capacity, then the contract will not be enforceable. For example, if a person is obviously so drunk that they do not know what they are doing, then they will not be regarded as having the necessary capacity to make a contract. These rules are discussed in more detail in Chapter 10.

The contents of the contract

Terms

The contents of a contract are known as the **terms**. These are discussed in more detail in the chapters that follow. **Express terms** are those that have actually been agreed between the parties. Sometimes contracts contain very little by way of express terms – in which case the courts may 'read in' terms in order to fill in any gaps in what the parties have agreed. These are known as **implied terms**. But as we have seen, if the parties have failed to agree key terms, the courts may refuse to enforce their agreement because it is too uncertain.

> **QUESTION 3** Think about the terms of the contract you would make when you buy a pair of shoes from a shop. Would most of the terms be express or implied?

What do contracts say in practice?

Exactly what a contract says will vary considerably depending on what it is designed to do. But to give you some idea of what contracts may deal with, a typical contract for the sale of goods will normally cover the following issues:

- what goods need to be supplied
- when the goods have to be delivered by
- how much the customer has to pay for the goods
- what standards the goods must meet (in terms of quality etc.)

- what the supplier may be responsible for if something goes wrong and how much it will have to pay the customer in compensation (usually known as exclusions and limitations of liability)
- the circumstances in which the parties can terminate the contract
- whether the contract is governed by English law (or the law of another jurisdiction)
- whether disputes will be dealt with by the courts or by some other method, such as alternative dispute resolution or arbitration.

More material about what contracts say in practice, including example contracts, can be found on the companion website.

Freedom of contract – and its limits

Generally, the parties are free to include whatever terms they like in their contract. This is an important principle of English contract law and is known as **freedom of contract**. However, there are certain types of agreement and certain terms that the courts will not enforce. For example, the courts will not enforce agreements that are against the law, such as an agreement between suppliers to fix the prices of the goods they sell instead of competing with one another (such an agreement would be illegal under the Competition Act 1998 and possibly also under European law).

Similarly, there are situations where the courts will not enforce certain individual terms in contracts (even though they may be prepared to uphold most of the other terms of the agreement). For example, the law controls the extent to which businesses can use an **exemption clause** to exclude or limit their liability if something goes wrong. Unless the exemption clause meets certain conditions, the courts will not allow a party to rely on it in order to prevent the other party from claiming damages (or to limit the amount of damages that party can claim). All these issues are discussed in more detail in the chapters that follow.

How contracts are enforced

If a business has made a legally binding agreement but fails to do what it promised to do, it will be in breach of contract. The other party can normally take that business to court to enforce the agreement. How the court will respond depends on the nature and seriousness of the breach. In theory, courts can do any of the following (which are explored in more detail in Chapter 8):

- Order a party to pay compensation to the other party for the loss that it has suffered – this is known as damages.
- Order a party to carry out its promises – this is known as **specific performance**.
- Order a party not to do something – this is known as an **injunction**.
- Issue a statement clarifying the status of a contract or what the parties' obligations are – this is known as a **declaration** and both parties are obliged to comply with it.

In practice, an order to pay damages is by far the most common remedy; declarations, injunctions and orders for specific performance are comparatively rare.

Answers to in-text questions

> **QUESTION 1** In *Baird Textiles v Marks & Spencer*, if Baird had agreed a formal, long-term contract with Marks & Spencer, how could this have protected its position?

If the parties had drawn up a formal, long-term contract, Baird could have protected its position by insisting that Marks & Spencer committed to a minimum level of purchases in each year. It could also have required Marks & Spencer to give Baird several years' advance warning before terminating the agreement. This would have given Baird more time to adapt to the prospect of life without Marks & Spencer as a major customer; for example, it might have allowed it to find new customers to replace Marks & Spencer and so avoid having to make cutbacks in its staff or production facilities. If Marks & Spencer had failed to give the required advance warning and had terminated the contract immediately, Baird would have been able to claim compensation for breach of contract. For example, if Marks & Spencer had been required to give 2 years' advance warning, Baird could have claimed the value of 2 years' worth of business.

> **QUESTION 2** In view of what has been said about formalities, do you think it is possible as a general rule to make a contract by an exchange of emails? Do you think any special formalities should be required if email is used?

For most types of contract, no special formalities are required – so it is perfectly possible for a legally binding agreement to be made by an exchange of emails. Lack of an electronic signature would not prevent a contract coming into existence, provided the court were satisfied that the parties intended to make a legally binding agreement. Indeed, there have been a number of cases where the courts have ruled that a contract was formed following exchange of emails where no electronic signatures were used and no special formalities were observed. [See companion website for details.]

> **QUESTION 3** Think about the terms of the contract you would make when you buy a pair of shoes from a shop. Would most of the terms be express or implied?

When you buy a pair of shoes from a shop, you agree to buy the shoes for a particular price, usually marked on the shoes. Sometimes, the shop assistant might also tell you about their returns policy. But those will often be the only *express* terms of the contract – all the other terms will be *implied*. For example, the shop will normally be subject to a number of obligations implied by consumer protection law, e.g. it will be regarded as having made you a promise that the shoes will be of satisfactory quality (so if they fall apart after a week, you would normally be able to take them back and demand a refund or a replacement). For more detail, see Chapter 20 on consumer protection.

4 Contract formation: getting agreement

Learning objectives

By the end of this chapter, you should be able to explain:

- **How the courts decide whether a person intended to enter into a legally binding agreement**

- **How the courts differ in their treatment of business transactions as compared with social and domestic agreements**

- **What is meant by offer and acceptance**

- **How the law views advertisements and other commercial communications that may lead a person to enter into a contract**

- **What happens if a person wishes to withdraw an offer they have made**

- **How the law deals with contracts made by various different means of communication, e.g. post, fax or email**

Introduction

This chapter deals in detail with two of the key ingredients of a legally binding agreement that were discussed briefly in Chapter 3, namely:

- intention to create legal relations
- agreement – or the process of offer and acceptance.

The other key requirements for a legally binding agreement – certainty of terms, consideration and capacity – are dealt with in Chapter 3.

Intention to create legal relations

The courts will only enforce agreements if they are satisfied that the parties intended them to be legally binding. As explained in Chapter 3, if you agree to buy lunch for a friend, you have made an agreement – but that agreement will not normally be regarded as giving rise to a contract because neither of you intended your obligations to be legally enforceable.

How the courts approach intention

The courts cannot be expected to see inside the minds of the parties in order to work out whether they really did intend to make a legally binding agreement. They have to look at the outward appearances, i.e. how the parties behaved and the overall context in which they made their agreement. This is known as the **objective approach** to intention (as opposed to the **subjective approach**, which would involve trying to work out the state of mind of the parties):

> In contracts you do not look into the actual intent in a man's mind. You look at what he said and did. A contract is formed when there is, to all outward appearances, a contract. A man cannot get out of a contract by saying 'I did not intend to contract' if by his words he has done so. His intention is to be found only in the outward expression which his letters convey. If they show a concluded contract, that is enough.
>
> Lord Denning in *Storer v Manchester City Council (1974)*

The importance of context

When considering intention, the courts will normally look at the context in which the agreement was made. A distinction is made between the following situations:

- *business agreements*: businesses are normally regarded as having intention to create legal relations
- *social or domestic agreements*: friends or family members are not normally regarded as having intention to create legal relations.

These are known as **presumptions**. The courts use them as their starting point for consideration of intention but they are not necessarily decisive. For instance, it is possible for a party to an agreement made in a business context to show that it was not intended to be legally binding. This is known as rebutting a presumption. Some examples of this are discussed now.

FAQ

Do businesses ever make agreements that are *not* intended to be legally binding?

Generally, businesses want their agreements to be legally binding because, otherwise, they cannot be enforced through the courts and will be entirely dependent on trust. However, when two businesses are negotiating an important deal, they will often mark the documents 'Subject to contract'. This is to indicate that any exchange of documents is not intended to give rise to a legally binding agreement at that stage – because the two businesses only want to be legally bound when they are both happy with the terms of the deal. Sometimes they will also agree 'heads of terms'. These usually summarise the key points of the deal and will sometimes be detailed enough to be used as a legally binding agreement. However, they are not normally intended to be legally binding and will usually include special wording to make this clear; their main purpose is normally to set out the key principles to be included in an even more detailed agreement, which *will* be legally binding.

Business agreements

Businesses can **rebut** the presumption that their agreements are intended to be legally binding by pointing to strong evidence that the opposite was intended. For example, in **Rose & Frank Co v J R Crompton & Bros (1925)**, Crompton, an English manufacturer of paper tissues, appointed Rose & Frank as its exclusive agent to sell its tissues in Canada and the USA. Crompton decided to terminate the agreement early. It refused to supply Rose & Frank with any tissues at all, even though it had accepted a number of orders from the firm. Rose & Frank sued it for breach of contract. The agreement included the following wording: 'This arrangement is not entered into nor is this memorandum written as a formal or legal agreement and shall not be subject to legal jurisdiction in the courts of the United States of America or England.' The House of Lords ruled that this wording was sufficient to rebut the normal presumption that when a business makes an agreement, it intends to be legally bound.

However, if no such wording is included, a business will normally have difficulty convincing a court that it did not intend to be legally bound. For example, in the Rose & Frank case, the House of Lords also considered various orders that Rose & Frank had submitted to Crompton (and that Crompton had agreed to supply). As there was no evidence to rebut the normal presumption that the two businesses intended to be legally bound, the House of Lords ruled that the orders did give rise to legally binding contracts for sale of specific quantities of tissues. The non-binding agreement only related to the appointment of Rose & Frank as exclusive agents of J R Crompton in North America (and not to individual orders for tissues).

More examples of situations where business agreements may not be legally binding can be found on the companion website.

> **QUESTION 1** In *Jones v Vernons Pools (1938)*, Jones claimed that he had sent in a winning football pools coupon but Vernons refused to pay out, stating that the coupon had never been received. The court ruled that the agreement could not be enforced because the coupon stated that the agreement was 'binding in honour only'. Do you think this result was fair and would the case still be decided in the same way today?

Social and domestic agreements

The main reason why the courts treat social and domestic agreements differently from business agreements is that friends and family members do not normally expect their agreements to have legal consequences; when they make agreements, they are usually relying on trust rather than the threat of enforcement by the courts. The source of this presumption is the case of **Balfour v Balfour (1919)**, where the Court of Appeal ruled that a promise by a husband to pay his wife an allowance while he was working abroad was not legally binding.

It is possible to rebut the presumption where there is evidence that the parties did intend their agreement to be legally binding. For example, in **Merritt v Merritt (1970)**, the court upheld an agreement by a husband to pay maintenance and transfer the house into his wife's name (once she had paid off the mortgage). Unlike the agreement in Balfour, the agreement in Merritt had been made after the relationship had broken down; this indicated that the parties were no longer relying on their trust in one another and expected the agreement to have legal consequences. Today, however, someone in Mrs Balfour's position would probably be able to seek an order for maintenance payments through the family courts, based on family law.

It is also possible to rebut the presumption by showing that the agreement in question had a *commercial* character. For example, in **Albert v Motor Insurers Bureau (1971)**, the House of Lords ruled that an agreement to give someone a lift on a regular basis was legally binding. In that case, the agreement was regarded as having a commercial character because the driver was prepared to take anyone, provided that they paid him; he did not insist that his passengers were friends. However, it is far more common for such agreements to be regarded as lacking intention to create legal relations. For example, in **Coward v Motor Insurers Bureau (1963)**, the court ruled that an agreement to give a friend a lift to work on a motorbike (in return for a small payment) was not binding. Unlike the agreement in *Albert*, it was based primarily on friendship and the payment was not sufficient to give it a commercial character.

Offer and acceptance

It is not enough for two parties to show that they merely *intended* to make an agreement. They must actually have reached agreement. The courts will find that there has been agreement where there is a valid offer followed by a valid acceptance. Offer and acceptance may be defined as follows:

- *Offer*: a statement of the terms on which a person (known as the **offeror**) is prepared to enter into a contract, which will become legally binding if accepted by the person to whom it is addressed (known as the **offeree**).

- *Acceptance*: an unconditional expression of willingness to be legally bound by all the terms of an offer, which has been properly communicated to the offeror (and gives rise to a legally binding agreement).

Offers and invitations to treat

There are many situations in which businesses make statements that look very much like offers because they appear to set out key terms of an agreement, such as the price of goods. However, many statements of this type are not in fact offers but merely an **invitation to treat** – that is to say, a statement or action designed to draw the customer into negotiations, as a prelude to the process of offer and acceptance. Consider the following examples:

- *Advertisements*: in **Partridge v Crittenden (1968)**, the court ruled that an advertisement in a magazine for 'Bramblefinch cocks and hens' at the price of 25 shillings was not an offer but merely an invitation to treat.

- *Goods on display in a shop*: in **Pharmaceutical Society of Great Britain v Boots Cash Chemists (1953)**, the court ruled that goods displayed on the shelves of a supermarket, with prices attached, were also invitations to treat.

- *Answers to requests for information*: in **Harvey v Facey (1893)**, the defendant was asked what price he would accept for a piece of land called 'Bumper Hall Pen'. His response was: 'Lowest price for Bumper Hall Pen, £900.' The claimants replied that they were prepared to pay that amount. The court said that there was no contract because the defendant had not made an offer; his reply was simply a response to a request for information.

An offer must be made with the intention that it will become binding as soon as it is accepted by the offeree. In the cases just examined, the courts ruled that this intention was missing; the sellers did not intend to be legally bound as soon as a customer said 'Yes, I will buy these goods at the price you have indicated.' What the sellers intended to happen was for the customer to approach them and make an offer to buy the goods (e.g. by taking the goods to the supermarket checkout). The sellers would only be legally bound if they then accepted the customer's offer.

When an advertisement may be an offer

Although most advertisements and similar statements made in advance of an agreement will be regarded as invitations to treat, this is not always so; each case needs to be examined individually. A famous example of an advertisement that was *not* an invitation to treat is discussed in the Carlill case study textbox.

More examples of the distinction between an offer and an invitation to treat can be found on the companion website.

Carlill v Carbolic Smoke Ball Company

In **Carlill v Carbolic Smoke Ball Co Ltd (1893)**, a company claimed in an advertisement that regular use of its 'smoke ball' product would prevent influenza. It offered £100 to anyone who caught the disease after using the product and stated that £1000 had been placed in a special bank account in case there were any claims. Mrs Carlill bought the product, used it regularly but still got influenza. The company argued that the claim in the advertisement was a 'mere puff', which was not intended to be taken seriously. The Court of Appeal disagreed. It said that the reference to the deposit of £1000 showed that the possibility of claiming £100 was serious; it therefore amounted to an offer, rather than an invitation to treat. That offer was made to the whole world rather than to a specific person. It would become a binding contract if the product were used as instructed by any person who had seen the advertisement and that person went on to catch influenza.

> **QUESTION 2** You want to buy some books from a website. The website contains descriptions of the various books available, their price and the terms on which the website operator will supply them to you (e.g. delivery times etc.). Is this an offer?

Communication of offers

For there to be a valid contract, all the terms of an offer must be properly communicated to the offeree before acceptance. At first sight, this principle may sound obvious; after all, it would clearly be absurd if a person could be regarded as having accepted an offer before they have been given the chance to find out what the offer consisted of. But consider the Alpha Business Machines scenario in the case study below – which, although fictional, is actually quite common in practice.

Withdrawal of offers

Once an offer has been made, it can normally be withdrawn (or **revoked**) at any time before the offeree has accepted it – even if the offeror has stated that the offer will remain open for longer. In *__Routledge v Grant (1828)__*, the defendant offered to purchase the claimant's house. He said that his offer would remain open for 6 weeks, but withdrew it before that period had expired. The claimant chose to ignore the withdrawal and argued that he was able to accept the offer at any time within the 6-week period. The court said that the defendant was entitled to withdraw his offer at any time before it was accepted, even if the 6-week period had not expired. The promise to keep the offer open for 6 weeks was not legally binding

Case study

Alpha Business Machines sells computer equipment. It has been in discussions with a potential customer (which it has never supplied before) over a possible contract. Alpha sends its potential customer a fax setting out the key terms on which it is prepared to enter into a contract, such as price, delivery date and specifications of the equipment. The fax also says (in very small print) 'Subject to our standard terms and conditions of sale'. **Standard terms** are usually pre-printed agreement forms designed to save businesses the trouble of negotiating a detailed formal agreement. The potential customer has never been sent a copy of Alpha's standard terms.

A court would probably say that the fax amounts to an offer because Alpha has indicated an intention to be legally bound. However, Alpha's standard terms do not form part of this offer, because Alpha has failed to communicate them to its customer. This may be quite disadvantageous for Alpha, because standard terms often contain clauses that are very important if the parties get into a dispute. For example, the standard terms may contain clauses (known as *exemption clauses*) that try to limit how much Alpha would have to pay if something went wrong (e.g. the equipment did not work properly). The key cases relating to this area are covered in Chapter 6, dealing with incorporation of terms and exemption clauses; but it is worth remembering that those cases are all based on the basic principle that all the terms of an offer must be communicated to the offeree.

because the claimant had not offered anything in return for that promise (so there was no consideration – this will be explained in more detail in the next chapter).

Any decision to withdraw an offer must be communicated to the offeree before acceptance takes place. In **Byrne v Van Tienhoven (1880)**, the defendant, which was based in Cardiff, sent the claimant a letter on 8 October withdrawing its offer to sell 1000 boxes of tin plates. However, the claimant, which was based in New York, only received the letter of withdrawal on 20 October – which was after it had sent its acceptance of the offer by telegram on 11 October. The court ruled that the defendant had failed to communicate the withdrawal of its offer in time and a legally binding agreement had come into existence on 11 October.

Expiry of offers

Once made, an offer does not normally last forever. Sometimes, as in *Routledge v Grant* (see earlier), the offeror will specify an expiry date. However, even in cases where no expiry date has been given, the courts are generally reluctant to regard an offer as having an indefinite lifespan. In **Ramsgate Victoria Hotel v Montefiore (1866)**, Montefiore made an offer to buy some shares in a company. He heard nothing from the company for 5 months, when he was told that the shares had been allotted to him and he was required to pay for them. By this time, Montefiore no longer wanted the shares. The court ruled that his offer was not open ended; shares were products that could change in price quite significantly over a fairly short time and it was only appropriate to regard the offer as being open for a 'reasonable' period. Given that 5 months had passed since the offer was made, the court said that a reasonable period for accepting the offer had expired (which meant that the offer had lapsed and the company was unable to accept it). Having said that, much depends on the surrounding circumstances. For example, if Montefiore's offer had concerned products with a more stable value than shares, the court might well have concluded that the offer should have remained open for as long as 5 months – or possibly even longer.

 FAQ

Why are most of the cases concerning offers over 100 years old?

How can they still be relevant to today's businesses?

Many of the cases dealing with the principles of offer and acceptance date from the 1800s, when Britain was in the throes of industrialisation. This development triggered a major expansion in trade, which was accompanied by a corresponding increase in the number of legal disputes involving businesses. In order to resolve these disputes in a fair and consistent manner, the courts developed detailed rules on the process of making agreements. They broke down this process into three main elements – (i) invitation to treat (sometimes triggering a period of negotiation), followed by (ii) offer, followed by (iii) acceptance. While much has changed since the 1800s, the fundamental process of making agreements has not. Today's businesses may advertise on the internet or on television, but they are essentially doing the same thing as the Carbolic Smoke Ball Co Ltd in the late 1800s. Similarly, although today's businesses may conduct their dealings by email or fax rather than letter or telegram, they are essentially doing the same thing as the two businesses in *Byrne v Van Tienhoven* in 1880. The textbox headed 'Reality check: Pickfords v Celestica' on page 52 contains a modern example of how the principles of offer and acceptance continue to be relevant to today's businesses.

Acceptance and counteroffers

When the offeree accepts an offer, he must do so *unconditionally*; he cannot choose to accept some but not all of the terms, neither can he add new terms. If he tries to do this, the courts will say that no agreement has been reached and that the offeree is in fact making his own offer – which the other party can either accept or reject. This new offer is referred to as a **counteroffer**, which is said to 'destroy' the original offer.

In *Hyde v Wrench (1840)*, the defendant offered to sell his farm to the claimant for £1000. The claimant's agent submitted an offer of £950, which the defendant agreed to consider. Several days later, the claimant wrote a letter stating that he would pay the full £1000. By this time the defendant had decided not to sell, but the claimant argued that a legally binding agreement had come into existence, based on his acceptance of the original offer of £1000. The court disagreed with the claimant's argument. It said that the claimant had made a counteroffer to purchase the property for £950. This counteroffer had 'destroyed' the original offer to sell the property for £1000. As the original offer was no longer in existence, it could not be accepted – and the defendant could not be forced to sell his farm to the claimant.

The battle of the forms

The approach taken in *Hyde v Wrench* gives rise to a situation known as the **battle of the forms**. This is where two businesses are conducting negotiations based on their own standard terms. Standard terms have two main advantages:

* they help to save time that would otherwise have to be spent negotiating the detail of the contract
* they are usually drafted in favour of the business offering to use its standard terms as the basis of the contract (so the resulting agreement will normally be more favourable to that business than if it had been fully negotiated).

Most suppliers of goods or services have standard terms of supply of one sort or another. Many larger businesses, such as supermarkets, also have standard terms of purchase. A common problem when two such businesses negotiate is that each wants to use its own standard terms – but it is usually impossible for both of them to apply. Several documents may be exchanged in negotiations, each referring to a different set of standard terms. Each new document usually amounts to a counteroffer, which destroys the previous offer contained in the previous document. Lawyers call this the battle of the forms.

In *Butler Machine Tool Co Ltd v Ex Cell-O Corporation (England) Ltd (1979)*, Butler offered to sell machine tools on its standard terms and provided a quotation for the price. Those terms contained a clause that allowed the price of the goods to be increased above the level of the quoted price, should the cost of manufacture increase. The buyer, Ex Cell-O, responded with a document referring to its own standard terms, which did not include a clause allowing price increases (and which required Butler to supply at no more than the quoted price). Ex Cell-O's document included a tear-off slip, which Butler signed and returned. The slip stated: 'We accept your Order on the Terms and Conditions stated thereon.' When Butler claimed a price that exceeded its original quotation, Ex Cell-O refused to pay the extra sum, arguing that the contract was based on its own standard terms (which did not include a clause allowing price increases). The Court of Appeal agreed that Ex Cell-O was not obliged to pay the extra sum. It said that Ex Cell-O's document amounted to a counteroffer, which destroyed Butler's original offer (including the price variation clause). Butler had accepted Ex Cell-O's standard terms by returning the tear-off slip.

Given that the basic principles governing acceptance and counteroffers have been in existence for over 100 years, you might think that they would have become so familiar to today's businesses that they rarely cause any problems in practice. However, the 'Reality check' textbox shows how they continue to give rise to disputes.

Reality check

Pickfords Ltd v Celestica Ltd (2003)

Acceptance and counteroffers: still causing problems after all these years

Pickfords, a removals firm, was asked to provide a quotation to Celestica, an IT firm, for the cost of moving its office furniture and other equipment to new premises. Two quotations were provided. The first was based on a rate per lorry load and Pickfords suggested that Celestica should budget for a total cost of around £100,000 (but did not offer a guarantee that the price would be no higher than this). The second quotation, which was sent about 2 weeks later, was much more detailed and followed a survey of Celestica's premises. It offered to carry out the move for a fixed price of £98,760. Celestica then sent Pickfords a fax entitled 'Confirmation', which appeared to refer to the first quotation but included the words 'Not to exceed 100K'. Pickfords argued that a contract came into existence based on the second quotation and demanded payment of £98,760. Celestica argued that it had accepted the first quotation and was only obliged to pay an amount based on the number of journeys made (which it claimed would amount to about one-third of what Pickfords were claiming). The Court of Appeal said that both quotations were offers, but the first quotation was clearly designed to be replaced by the second, more detailed quotation. Celestica's fax appeared to be an attempt to accept the first quotation, but this was not possible because that offer had been withdrawn. Neither could the fax be regarded as a clear and unconditional acceptance of the second offer (because it made no reference to the second quotation). The correct analysis was that the fax amounted to a counteroffer by Celestica, based on the terms of the first offer (i.e. on a per-journey basis), but with a price cap of £100,000; the result was that Celestica was only obliged to pay £30–40,000. Pickfords had accepted this counteroffer by its conduct in going ahead with the work (this concept is explained later under the heading 'Acceptance by conduct').

QUESTION 3 Is it always the case that, where two offers are made, the second will revoke the first? In *Pickfords v Celestica*, what should Pickfords have done if it wanted to ensure that the work was carried out based on the second quotation?

Communication of acceptance

As we have seen, an acceptance will only be valid if it is unconditional, i.e. the offeree is clearly signifying his agreement to *all* the terms of the offer. A further requirement is that acceptance must normally be communicated to the offeror (subject to certain exceptions – see later under the heading 'Offeror may dispense with communication'). This is so that the offeror knows that his offer has been accepted. It is a key event in the formation of a contract because once acceptance has been communicated, both parties become legally bound (assuming, of course, that the other key ingredients of a legally binding agreement are present (see Chapter 3 for a brief summary of these)).

For example, in **Felthouse v Bindley (1862)**, Felthouse had been negotiating with his uncle over the sale of a horse. His uncle wrote him a letter saying: 'If I hear no more about him, I consider the horse mine at £30 15s.' Felthouse never responded to this letter, although in his own mind he had already decided to accept his uncle's offer. He had instructed an auctioneer, Bindley, to sell his farming stock, but told him that the horse was no longer for sale. However, Bindley forgot to withdraw the horse from auction. The uncle brought a claim against Bindley in tort (see Part 3). This claim was based on the existence of a contract with his nephew for the sale of the horse. The court ruled that the claim against the auctioneer could not succeed because there was never any contract with the nephew. Although the uncle had made an offer and the nephew had accepted that offer in his own mind, the nephew's acceptance had never been communicated to the uncle.

Acceptance by conduct

Communication of acceptance does not have to take place by means of a clear written or spoken acknowledgement. However, it must take the form of some positive act that indicates to the offeror that his offer has been accepted. For example, in **Brogden v Metropolitan Railway Co (1877)**, an agreement for the supply of coal was drafted but never signed by the parties. Brogden made some amendments to it and sent it to the railway company's agent, who put it in a drawer. Later on, Brogden tried to argue that the agreement was not binding because the railway company had never communicated its acceptance of the version that he had amended. The House of Lords disagreed. It said that the railway company communicated its acceptance by its conduct in going ahead with the agreement, either by placing an order with Brogden or by accepting the first delivery of coal. A more recent example of acceptance by conduct is provided by the case of *Pickfords v Celestica*, referred to earlier.

> **QUESTION 4** In *Felthouse v Bindley*, the nephew told the auctioneer to withdraw the horse from sale. This was a positive act in response to the uncle's offer. Why wasn't it sufficient to amount to communication of acceptance by conduct? Would it have made any difference if the auctioneer *had* told the uncle about the nephew's action?

Offeror may dispense with communication

Sometimes, an offeror may make it clear that he does not need to be notified of the offeree's acceptance. For example, in *Felthouse v Bindley*, the uncle's letter saying, 'If I hear no more about him, I consider the horse mine' meant that the nephew could probably have accepted by silence had he chosen to do so. However, the nephew could not be required to do so because he had never agreed to an arrangement involving acceptance by silence.

Sometimes the offeror's willingness to dispense with communication of acceptance can be inferred from the nature of the transaction itself. In *Carlill v Carbolic Smoke Ball Co* (see earlier), the company argued that there was no contract because Mrs Carlill had not communicated her acceptance. The court said that it was clear from the advertisement that the company did not expect people like Mrs Carlill to notify it of their acceptance of its offer. The whole point of the advertisement was to encourage people to buy smoke balls and a requirement to notify the company of purchases would have made the offer less attractive.

The postal rule

The other major exception to the requirement that acceptance must be communicated is the **postal rule**. In cases where this rule applies, a letter of acceptance that has been properly addressed and posted will be communicated as soon as the letter is posted (rather than when it is received). This is so even if the offeror never receives the letter. The rule was established in the case of **Adams v Lindsell (1818)**. It is essentially a rule of convenience, developed in response to disputes over what should happen if an acceptance were lost in the post. The courts effectively decided that the risk of a postal acceptance not getting through should be borne by the offeror, not the offeree. This may seem unfair to the offeror. However, the offeror is in a position to protect himself against the postal rule. In particular, the rule does not apply where the offeror indicates that post is not to be used for communicating acceptance or that he will only be bound when he actually receives the acceptance – see **Holwell Securities v Hughes (1974)**.

The rule has been applied to acceptances by telegram (where, like the post, there was normally a delay between sending and receipt because the message had to be delivered to the recipient). However, the courts have refused to extend the postal rule to more modern forms of communication such as telex or fax. In

FAQ

Does the postal rule apply to email?

At the time of writing, English courts have not ruled on whether the postal rule applies to email. Communication by email can be virtually instantaneous – but sometimes there can also be a significant delay in receipt. For this reason, some commentators have suggested that the postal rule should apply to email. However, as we have seen, the courts have been reluctant to extend the scope of the postal rule to new forms of communication. Today's businesses can also choose between many different means of communication besides email – and they can always protect themselves against the risks of delayed receipt by agreeing their own rules about

when acceptance takes place. The companion website includes information on the Electronic Commerce (EC Directive) Regulations 2002, which contain some provisions dealing with ordering over the internet and making contracts by exchange of emails. However, these do not resolve the question of when acceptance is communicated in English law.

Entores v Miles Far East Corporation (1955), the defendants (based in Amsterdam) accepted an offer from the claimants (based in London) by telex. Later on, a dispute arose and the Court of Appeal had to decide where acceptance took place in order to determine whether English or Dutch law applied. The defendants argued that if the postal rule applied, then acceptance took place when the telex was sent (which meant that Dutch law would apply). The Court of Appeal said that the postal rule did not apply here because communication by telex was virtually instantaneous, like a telephone conversation, so the parties were in almost the same position as they would have been if they were negotiating face to face. Acceptance took place when it was actually communicated to the claimants (in London), not when it was sent (in Amsterdam).

> **QUESTION 5** If a faxed acceptance arrives at a business's office in the middle of the night, when no one is there to read it, does acceptance take place as soon as the fax arrives?

Answers to in-text questions

> **QUESTION 1** In *Jones v Vernons Pools (1938)*, Jones claimed that he had sent in a winning football pools coupon but Vernons refused to pay out, stating that the coupon had never been received. The court ruled that the agreement was not binding because the coupon stated that the agreement was 'binding in honour only'. Do you think this result was fair and would the case still be decided in the same way today?

This outcome may strike you as unfair, given that Jones had paid for his coupon and (assuming he had posted it in time), he was probably not to blame for it not having been received by Vernons. However, the court was concerned that if such arrangements were legally binding, pools companies would be faced with many thousands of legal actions from people claiming that they had posted a winning coupon. A number of cases in the late 1990s confirmed that the ruling in *Jones v Vernons Pools* is still good law. However, it is doubtful whether most businesses could successfully use the same tactic where they were dealing with individual consumers. As explained in Chapter 20, on consumer protection, the law gives special protection to consumers against attempts by businesses to exclude their legal liability. It is only likely to tolerate clauses stating that agreements between businesses and consumers are not binding in exceptional circumstances, such as football pools agreements. With business-to-business contracts, however, wording stating that the agreement is not binding will normally be sufficient to rebut the presumption that businesses intend to be legally bound when they make agreements (as was the case in *Rose & Frank v J R Crompton*). This is because, unlike consumers, businesses are expected to look out for themselves when they make agreements.

> **QUESTION 2** You want to buy some books from a website. The website contains descriptions of the various books available, their price and the terms on which the website operator will supply them to you (e.g. delivery times etc.). Is this an offer?

You might think that this would amount to an offer – after all, it seems to be a statement of terms on which the website operator is prepared to contract. But in order to be an offer, it needs to be capable of giving rise to a binding contract as soon as you communicate your acceptance to the website operator – and it is not in the website operator's interest for this to happen. For example, he would not want to be legally bound to supply you if he did not have enough books in stock or if you had ordered goods in the past but failed to pay for them. If the website has been set up with the principles of offer and acceptance in mind, it should make it clear that when you fill in the online order form, you are in fact making an offer to buy the books (based on the terms and prices stated on the website). The website operator can then decide whether to accept or reject your offer (having checked that the goods are in stock or that your credit record is acceptable). The acceptance will normally take place when the website operator sends you a confirmation email. This, at any rate, is what should normally happen if the website operator has considered the implications of the law on offer and acceptance. But in practice, these points are sometimes overlooked – so you should not be surprised to discover that some website operators may well have allowed themselves to become legally bound from the time they receive your order form.

> **QUESTION 3** Is it always the case that where two offers are made, the second will revoke the first? In *Pickfords v Celestica*, what should Pickfords have done if it wanted to ensure that the work was carried out based on the second quotation?

Where two offers are made, the second will only revoke the first if it is clear that this was what the offeror intended. Clarity is required because revocation of an offer must be communicated to the offeree (see *Byrne v Van Tienhoven*). Although Pickfords did not say 'we are now revoking our first offer', the Court of Appeal said that this should have been obvious to Celestica because the second quotation was much more detailed than the first (and was clearly intended to replace it). However, if Celestica had asked for two different quotations, one on a per-load basis and one based on a fixed price, so that it could choose between them, then both offers would have remained in existence (even had they been made at different times). So it is not the case that a second offer will always revoke a previous offer; it all depends on the circumstances. In order to ensure that the work went ahead on the basis of the second quotation, Pickfords should have replied to Celestica's fax with a counteroffer of its own, referring to the second quotation. This would have destroyed Celestica's counteroffer. If Celestica had failed to respond and the work had gone ahead, the court would probably have ruled that Celestica had accepted Pickfords' counteroffer by conduct – and Pickfords would have been able to claim their fixed fee of £98,760.

QUESTION 4 In *Felthouse v Bindley*, the nephew told the auctioneer to withdraw the horse from the sale. This was a positive act in response to the uncle's offer. Why wasn't it sufficient to amount to communication of acceptance by conduct? Would it have made any difference if the auctioneer *had* told the uncle about the nephew's action?

The nephew's action was a positive act but since the uncle was unaware of it, the court ruled that the nephew's acceptance had not been validly communicated. If the auctioneer had told the uncle, this could have amounted to valid communication of acceptance – but only if he had been authorised to do so by the nephew. For example, in **Powell v Lee (1908)**, a schoolteacher was told by a member of the appointment board that the board would accept his offer to take up employment at a school. However, the board later changed its mind. The court ruled that acceptance had not been validly communicated because the board member had not been authorised by the board to do so.

QUESTION 5 If a faxed acceptance arrives at a business's office in the middle of the night, when no one is there to read it, does acceptance take place as soon as the fax arrives?

In **Brinkibon v Stahag Stahl (1983)**, the House of Lords indicated that an acceptance sent by telex, which arrived out of office hours, might not be communicated immediately, as would normally be the case with electronic communications of this type. The thinking behind this appears to be the recognition that, if the offeror's office is shut, then the parties cannot be said to be in 'instantaneous communication'. However, the acceptance would probably be validly communicated as soon as the office had reopened, rather than when the fax was actually read (because the offeror would be expected to have an efficient system for getting the fax to the person to whom it was addressed).

Contract formation: certainty of terms and consideration

By the end of this chapter, you should be able to explain:

- **What is meant by certainty of terms and why it is important**
- **Ways in which the courts can 'read in' missing details that might otherwise make a contract too uncertain to enforce**
- **What is meant by consideration and privity of contract and why they are important**
- **Typical situations in which a contract cannot be enforced because there is no consideration**

Introduction

In Chapter 4, we looked at two of the key ingredients of a legally binding agreement, namely:

- intention to create legal relations
- agreement (offer and acceptance).

But even where both intention and agreement are present, there may be no contract because certain other key ingredients are missing, such as certainty of terms or consideration. These were outlined briefly in Chapter 3 and are examined in more detail in this chapter. In some cases, failure to comply with formalities may also result in the courts deciding that there is no contract, as has already been explained in Chapter 3. Capacity is discussed in more detail in Chapter 10.

Certainty of terms

The courts will not enforce an agreement if its terms are unclear or do not contain enough detail. Lawyers say that such a contract is **void** for uncertainty. As we saw in ***Baird Textiles v Marks & Spencer (2001)***, discussed in Chapter 3, lack of certainty was one of the reasons why Baird had no remedy in contract law when Marks & Spencer terminated its supply arrangement (which was worth over £100 million each year to Baird). Similarly, in **Scammell v Ouston (1941)**, the House of Lords ruled that a hire purchase agreement for a van was too uncertain to be enforced because it did not contain any clear indication of the payments to be made, neither did it set out the other hire purchase terms (e.g. it did not say at what stage the hirer should have been able to purchase the vehicle). However, there are some situations in which the courts may be prepared to 'read in' or 'imply' the missing terms (see Chapter 3 for an explanation of implied terms). This may allow the agreement to be enforced, even where it appears at first to be unclear or lacking in detail. Implied terms are discussed further in Chapter 6 on the terms of the contract.

Terms implied by performance

Where the parties have actually been carrying out their agreement, the courts may be able to look at how the parties have behaved in the past in order to work out what the agreement would have said (had the parties bothered to write it down in sufficient detail). In **Foley v Classique Coaches (1934)**, the court rejected arguments that a written agreement for supply of petrol was void for uncertainty because it did not state the exact price of the petrol. A key factor in the court's reasoning was that the parties had been dealing with one another for 3 years and, during that time, the lack of detail in their agreement had not prevented them from agreeing a price. The court said that the original agreement had to be read as if it contained a term requiring the price of the petrol to be reasonable. Whether it was reasonable could be decided by looking at the prices charged during the previous 3 years and comparing them with the prices of other petrol suppliers. Another reason for deciding to uphold the agreement was the presence of a dispute resolution clause (see later).

 FAQ

How much detail needs to be missing from an agreement before it is too uncertain to enforce?

It is impossible to answer this question in terms of a percentage. For example, you might have an agreement where 99% of the clauses are very detailed indeed, but the remaining 1% is not detailed enough and deals with an issue of great importance. At the other extreme, you may have a situation where very little was agreed before work began, but the courts take the view that since the parties have actually been carrying out the work, they must be regarded as having a workable agreement. This can make the topic of certainty of terms seem quite confusing. The key to making sense of it is to remember that the courts tend to apply the principle of certainty with a fair degree of flexibility. If they think that a business is simply using the requirement for certainty as a way of avoiding obligations that were clearly intended to be legally binding at the time the contract was made, they will usually look for ways of avoiding having to conclude that the agreement is void. This often involves looking at some of the ways of 'reading in' the missing details, which are outlined later. However, as we shall see, the facts of the case must provide the courts with enough evidence to be able to fill in the missing details.

Previous courses of dealing and custom and practice

Where the parties have done business in the past, the courts may be able to look at earlier agreements in order to work out what a more recent agreement, relating to similar matters, would have said (had the parties bothered to write it down). Lawyers call these past transactions a **previous course of dealing**. Similarly, the courts may be able to 'fill in the gaps' in an agreement that would otherwise be void for uncertainty by reference to well-known terms in the industry that the parties would have included had they thought about it. Lawyers say that these terms are based on **custom and practice**.

For example, in **Hillas v Arcos (1932)**, Hillas had agreed to buy wood from Arcos for 1 year, with an option to buy more timber the following year. Arcos, which did not have enough wood to supply Hillas for a second year, argued that the option was void for uncertainty as it did not contain key details (such as how much Hillas would have to pay for timber during the following year). The House of Lords ruled that these missing details could be read into the agreement by looking at what the parties had done in the past (e.g. in the first year of the agreement) and by reference to custom and practice in the timber industry (e.g. terms which timber merchants usually included in their agreements).

Agreements to agree and dispute resolution clauses

An 'agreement to agree' is where a contract includes a term such as 'the parties will negotiate a detailed contract for the sale of the business on fair and reasonable terms'. The courts will usually refuse to enforce terms of this type because they are too uncertain. They are also reluctant to interfere because they see it as being the task of the parties, not the courts, to write their own agreements. For instance, in **iSoft Group plc v Misys Holdings Ltd (2003)**, two software firms made an agreement that included a term very similar to the example given earlier. The Court of Appeal ruled that the term was void for uncertainty, as it would be impractical for a court to decide what would be a fair and reasonable price for the business or what the other terms of the agreement should be. However, the Court of Appeal also said that the agreement might have been enforceable had the parties agreed on a mechanism for resolving disputes over what the terms of the business sale should be. These mechanisms are known as *dispute resolution clauses*. They can sometimes help to 'save' an agreement that might otherwise have been void for uncertainty. For example, in *Foley v Classique Coaches* (see earlier), although there was no provision for setting the price, the court said that the

Reality check

Cable & Wireless v IBM (2002)

ADR clauses – too uncertain to enforce?

As explained in Part 1, it is becoming increasingly common for businesses to seek to resolve disputes by ADR or alternative dispute resolution, instead of using the courts. For many years, it was thought that a clause in a contract that said that the parties had to use ADR was unenforceable on the basis that it was an agreement to agree (and therefore void for uncertainty). This meant that if only one party wanted to use ADR, the other party could not be forced to do so – so ADR only worked where both

sides were prepared to go down that route of their own free will. However, in *Cable & Wireless plc v IBM UK Ltd (2002)*, the High Court ruled that such clauses *may* be enforced provided they refer to a sufficiently detailed ADR procedure. In that particular case, the contract referred to comprehensive ADR procedures laid down by the Centre for Dispute Resolution (CEDR). The High Court's decision was also motivated by the desire to encourage out of court settlement of disputes wherever possible, so as to prevent the courts having to deal with too many cases. This is another example of the courts taking a fairly flexible, practical approach to the requirement that contracts need to be certain in order to be enforced. [More information on CEDR can be found on the companion website.]

contract should be upheld because the parties had agreed on a mechanism for dealing with such omissions. A more recent example, concerned with a slightly different issue, is explained in the 'Reality check' textbox highlighting **Cable & Wireless plc v IBM UK Ltd (2002)**.

Consideration

The courts will not normally enforce agreements where one party promises to do something but the other party has not promised anything in return. Lawyers say that such agreements lack consideration. The person making the promise is known as the **promisor**. The person to whom the promise is made is known as the **promisee**. Consideration is closely related to the principle of **privity of contract**. This is the rule that a person can only enforce a contract if he is a party to that contract. In most cases, a person will only be regarded as a party to the contract if he has provided some consideration (although there are exceptions to this, some of which are examined later).

Basic principles governing consideration

Lawyers divide consideration into two types:

- **executory consideration**: a promise that will be carried out in the future
- **executed consideration**: an act that has already been done.

For example, where payment for services has been made in advance, lawyers would say that the customer has provided executed consideration; the supplier, by the same token, has still to carry out his obligations, so his consideration is executory.

FAQ

Why is consideration important?

In many business situations, there is no need to think very hard about consideration; for example, in a contract for the sale of goods, one party's promise to supply is consideration for the other's promise to pay – and vice versa. However, there are other scenarios where failure to think about consideration can cause more problems. For example, imagine that you are buying a business. The seller says that you can have 2 weeks to think about it and he promises that, during that time, he will not sell the business to anyone else. You contact him a week later to say that you want to buy the business but find that he has already sold it to one of your competitors. You would not be able to sue the seller because you have provided no consideration in exchange for his promise to keep the offer open for 2 weeks. If, however, you had paid him to keep the offer open, then that would almost certainly have been sufficient to make his promise enforceable.

When deciding whether an agreement is supported by consideration, the courts apply three main rules, each of which is explored in more detail in the remainder of this section:

- *Consideration must move from the promisee* – this rule concerns the *person providing consideration*.
- *Consideration must not be in the past* – this rule concerns the *timing of consideration*.
- *Consideration must be sufficient* – this rule concerns *the types of promise that may qualify as consideration*.

Consideration must move from the promisee

This rule states that a person cannot normally enforce contractual rights unless he has provided consideration. It is also referred to as the principle of privity of contract. The rule originated in **Tweddle v Atkinson (1861)**, where two fathers, Tweddle and Guy, agreed that they would each pay a sum of money to Tweddle's son. Guy died before he had paid his share of the money. Tweddle's son sued the executor of Guy's estate, but the court said that he was unable to enforce the agreement. This was because he had provided no consideration. Only Tweddle senior could enforce the agreement, since only he had provided consideration for Guy's promise.

The privity rule can cause problems where the parties to an agreement clearly intended a **third party** – such as the son in *Tweddle v Atkinson* – to benefit from their agreement. This has led Parliament to intervene with legislation – the Contracts (Rights of Third Parties) Act 1999 – that overrides the common law position and allows parties to enforce contractual rights where they have provided no consideration.

Contracts (Rights of Third Parties) Act 1999

Enforcing contractual rights without consideration

The Contracts (Rights of Third Parties) Act 1999 allows the parties to a contract to agree that a person who has not provided consideration (known as a 'third party') can enforce certain rights under that contract. The Act applies to agreements where the court is satisfied that:

- the parties intended to confer a benefit on the third party
- the third party can be clearly identified by name, class or description.

For example, in the property sector, buildings such as office blocks are usually owned initially by developers, who sell them to commercial landlords (and then move on to develop other sites). In order to build the office block, the developer will usually contract with a construction firm. The construction firm will make various promises to the developer about the quality of its work. However, a legal problem arises when the developer sells the office block to a landlord. Since the landlord has provided no consideration to the construction firm, it cannot sue the construction firm in contract law if something goes wrong (it might be able to do so in tort, but its remedies are likely to be more limited – see Part 3). Traditionally, developers got around this problem by requiring construction firms to make the same promises to landlords in the form of a **deed**. A deed is a special form of contract requiring particular formalities. Promises made in a deed do not need to be supported by consideration – so it would not matter that the landlord had not provided any consideration to the developer. However, the Contracts (Rights of Third Parties) Act 1999 provides a new way of overcoming the problem, which avoids the need for deeds. It allows the construction firm to say in its contract with the developer that any promises about the quality of the building are made not only for the benefit of the developer, but for the benefit of a third party – the landlord. The landlord can then sue the construction firm direct for breach of those promises – even though it has provided no consideration in exchange for those promises. But remember that the Act only applies where that is what the parties to the contract intended – if they have excluded the Act, as is often the case, then the normal rules of privity of contract will apply. [More information on the Act can be found on the companion website.]

Consideration must not be in the past

If a person makes a promise after the contract has been made, that promise cannot be consideration for the earlier promise. Lawyers refer to it as 'past consideration'. For example, in **Roscorla v Thomas (1842)**, the seller of a horse promised the buyer that it was 'sound and free from vice'. This turned out to be untrue, but the buyer was unable to sue the seller for breach of this promise because it was made *after* the horse had been sold (and did not therefore form part of the seller's offer). In order to enforce the promise, the buyer would have needed to provide 'fresh' consideration to the seller, such as an additional payment. Alternatively, he could have obtained an assurance from the seller *before* he purchased the horse (in which case the price he had agreed to pay would have been sufficient consideration for the seller's promise about the horse being 'sound and free from vice' and he would not have had to pay any extra).

This rule is not always rigidly applied by the courts. For example, in **Re Casey's Patents (1892)**, Stewart asked Casey to exploit an invention in which he was joint owner of the patent rights. Casey helped to turn the invention into a profit-making venture. Stewart later wrote to him stating that: 'In consideration of your services … [we] hereby hereby agree to give you one-third share of the patents above mentioned […]. This is in addition to and in combination with our agreement of the 29th November last.' After Stewart's death, his executors argued that Casey had not provided any consideration for the promise of a one-third share of the patents, because Casey's work had been done before that promise was made, i.e. his consideration was in the past. The Court of Appeal disagreed, saying that when Casey had been asked to do the work, there was an implied promise of future payment in some form. The letter from Stewart merely confirmed that promise and made it clear that payment would be in the form of a one-third ownership of the patents.

Consideration must be sufficient

Consideration can take many forms. For example, it can be something positive, such as a promise to pay for goods or to supply them. It can also be something negative, such as a promise not to sue someone. It must normally have some value in the eyes of the law, which is what lawyers mean when they say that 'consideration must be sufficient'. For example, in **White v Bluett (1853)**, the court ruled that a promise by a son not to bore his father had no value. However, in **Chappell & Co v Nestlé Co Ltd (1959)**, a court was prepared to regard chocolate wrappers as valuable consideration, even though their value in monetary

Reality check

Consideration need not be adequate

Bank for sale – going cheap!

In 1995, Barings, the UK's oldest merchant bank, faced collapse, having accumulated debts of over £800 million. The crisis had arisen because of the activities of one of its traders in the Far East, Nick Leeson, whose story has since been turned into a film called *Rogue Trader*. Initially, Leeson made significant gains for the bank but his success did not last. He gambled increasing amounts of money in an attempt to recover his losses, while concealing the amounts at stake. By the time managers discovered the true extent of the losses, it was too late. Barings was eventually sold to Dutch bank ING for only £1. This token consideration could not be said to bear any relation to the economic value of the assets and the staff of Barings, which (ignoring the bank's debts) would have been worth a considerable sum. However, legally, it would have enabled ING to argue – if necessary – that it had provided sufficient consideration to enforce the promises made to it in the sale agreement.

CAPITOL/THE KOBAL COLLECTION/CHEDLOW, PAUL

Ewan McGregor as Nick Leeson in *Rogue Trader*

terms was miniscule (customers who sent in the wrappers as proof of purchase were entitled to a copy of a record at a reduced price). In addition, the value of consideration provided by one party does not have to correspond to the value of consideration provided by the other party. This is what lawyers mean when they say 'consideration need not be adequate' (see the 'Reality check' textbox).

Although the basic principle that consideration must be sufficient is fairly straightforward, there are a number of more complex aspects of the rule, which are examined in more detail later. These are:

- performance of an existing obligation
- part-payment of debts
- **promissory estoppel**.

Performance of an existing obligation

A promise to do something that you are already obliged to do cannot normally be sufficient consideration. For example, in **Collins v Godefroy (1831)**, Collins was obliged by a court order to appear as a witness in a case involving Godefroy. Godefroy was keen to ensure that Collins turned up and promised to pay him 6 guineas if he attended. Godefroy later failed to pay and Collins tried to enforce the promise. The court ruled that, since Collins was already obliged to attend as a result of the court order, his promise to do so was not good consideration for Godefroy's promise to pay.

The same logic applies where a person is already obliged to do something by a contract. In **Stilk v Myrick (1809)**, the captain of a ship promised to pay the crew extra to complete the voyage because two sailors had deserted. When the captain failed to pay, one of the sailors sued him for the extra money. The court said that the captain's promise was not enforceable because the sailor had provided no additional consideration in exchange for it; the sailor was merely agreeing to do something that he was already obliged to do, namely sail the ship home (and the desertion of only two sailors had not made this task significantly more difficult). This case contrasts

Williams v Roffey Brothers (1990)

Roffey had a contract to refurbish flats for a housing association. It subcontracted the carpentry work to Williams, who underestimated the amount of work involved, fell behind schedule and got into financial difficulties. This created a problem for Roffey, as its contract with the housing association contained clauses requiring Roffey to pay compensation for late completion of the work. Roffey promised to pay Williams an extra £575 per flat if he managed to get the job done on time. Roffey later argued that this promise was unenforceable, because Williams was merely doing something that he was already obliged to do (as in *Stilk v Myrick*). The Court of Appeal ruled that Roffey was obliged to pay. There were two main reasons why it decided not to follow *Stilk v Myrick*:

- The payment was offered by Roffey on its own initiative, without any pressure (or 'duress') being applied by Williams (duress is considered in more detail in Chapter 10).
- Roffey obtained a benefit from the promise, as it resulted in Williams finishing enough of the flats on time for Roffey to avoid making compensation payments to the housing association.

with **Hartley v Ponsonby (1857)**, where 17 sailors out of a total crew of 36 deserted and the captain made a similar promise of extra money to the remaining crew. The court said that the promise was enforceable because each sailor had effectively had to do the work of almost two men. This was considerably more than they had originally agreed to do. It therefore amounted to 'fresh' consideration for the captain's promise. *Hartley v Ponsonby* shows that the courts do not apply the rule in *Stilk v Myrick* rigidly, regardless of the facts. Another more recent example of this flexible approach is **Williams v Roffey Brothers (1990)**, which is explained in the case study textbox.

> **QUESTION 3** In *Williams v Roffey*, why was Williams unable to rely on *Hartley v Ponsonby*? Can you think of any criticisms of the decision in *Williams v Roffey*?

Part-payment of debts

As we have seen, where one party promises additional money but the other party does not promise to do anything additional in return, the extra payment cannot normally be enforced (because promising to perform an existing obligation is not good consideration). What happens where one party owes £100 but claims that the other party agreed to accept £80? As you might expect, the promise to accept less money is not usually enforceable – because the party owing the money (the **debtor**) has not provided any consideration in return for that promise. However, if the debtor promises to do something different from his original obligations, this will normally be sufficient to amount to consideration for the promise to accept part-payment of the debt.

For example, in **Pinnel's Case (1602)**, Pinnel promised Cole that he would accept £5 instead of the £8 that Cole actually owed him. The court said that Cole could only enforce Pinnel's promise if he had provided fresh consideration. In fact, Cole had provided fresh consideration by agreeing to pay Pinnel the £5 at an earlier date, so the promise was enforceable (although Pinnel won the case on a technicality). Pinnel's Case may be ancient but it was confirmed by the House of Lords in **Foakes v Beer (1884)** and remains the law.

> **QUESTION 4** In *Pinnel's Case*, all Cole had promised in return for Pinnel's promise to accept £5 was to pay the money at an earlier date. Cole's promise was unlikely to be worth £3 to Pinnel – so why did the court decide that it amounted to good consideration?

Promissory estoppel

As we have seen, a promise to accept part-payment of a debt is generally only enforceable if the debtor has promised to do something over and above what he was obliged to do in the original agreement. Debtors cannot rely on *Williams v Roffey*, where one party was allowed to enforce a promise even though he had done nothing more than he was obliged to do – see **Re Selectmove (1995)**. However, where a promise to accept part-payment has been made, the courts may use their equitable powers to stop a creditor from recovering the whole of the debt

Central London Property Trust Ltd v High Trees House Ltd (1947)

High Trees leased a block of flats in London from Central London Property Trust (CLT) during and after the Second World War. During the war, High Trees had difficulty paying the rent because it did not have enough tenants for the flats. As a result, CLT agreed to accept a reduced rent. After the war had ended, High Trees continued to pay at the reduced rate. CLT claimed that it was now entitled to the full rent, as the flats had begun to fill up again. The court said that CLT was entitled to claim the full rent for the last 6 months of 1945 (i.e. after the war had ended). It also considered whether CLT could have claimed the full rent for the period *during* the war. Based on *Pinnel's Case*, the answer to this question would appear to be 'yes', because High Trees had not provided any new consideration in return for CLT's promise to accept part-payment. However, High Trees had assumed that it would never be required to pay the full rent during the war. As High Trees had (quite reasonably) relied on CLT's promise, the court said it would be unfair to allow CLT to go back on that promise – and it would use its equitable powers to prevent any such claim.

(see Part 1 for an explanation of equity). A debtor can ask a court to use these powers where he is faced with a claim for payment of the full amount and has provided no new consideration in return for the promise of part-payment. Lawyers refer to such use of equitable powers as promissory estoppel. It is also commonly said that: 'Promissory estoppel can only be used as a shield, not a sword.' This refers to the fact that it can only be used as a defence to a claim for payment of the full amount. The case in which the principles of promissory estoppel were developed – ***Central London Property Trust Ltd v High Trees House Ltd (1947)*** – is outlined in the case study textbox.

After the *High Trees* case, promissory estoppel was raised again in ***D&C Builders v Rees (1965)***, where a firm of builders had promised to accept £300 instead of the £483 to which they were entitled under their original contract.

FAQ

Why are there so many exceptions to the three general rules on consideration?

It is certainly true that there are a significant number of exceptions to the three general rules on consideration (namely (i) consideration must move from the promisee; (ii) consideration must not be in the past; and (iii) consideration must be

sufficient). Sometimes the exceptions can start to seem more important than the principles themselves; for example, there has been a vast amount of academic discussion of *Williams v Roffey* and the *High Trees* cases. They have attracted such attention precisely because they seem to run against the grain of some of the basic principles on consideration. However, in practice, cases such as *Williams v Roffey* and *High Trees* have been applied rarely, if at all. The general rules, meanwhile, continue to be used by the courts to resolve the vast majority of disputes concerning consideration.

However, the builders had been in financial difficulties at the time and had been told by their customers that unless they accepted £300, they would get nothing. As we have seen, the courts will only help a person using their equitable powers if that person has acted fairly himself. In this case, the court said that the customers had effectively taken advantage of the builders' financial difficulties. As a result, it would not be fair to allow the customers to use promissory estoppel as a defence to the builders' claim for payment.

Answers to in-text questions

> **QUESTION 1** In *Baird Textiles v Marks & Spencer* (discussed in Chapter 3), the parties had been dealing with one another for 30 years, yet the agreement was too uncertain to be enforced. Why was the outcome different from *Foley v Classique Coaches*?

It is not always possible for the courts to look at the past behaviour of two businesses in order to work out what their agreement should have said, had the parties bothered to draft one. In the *Baird* case, the Court of Appeal ruled that it was impossible to say how long any such agreement should have lasted because in practice, despite the 30-year relationship, the parties had never planned much further ahead than the next clothing season. There was nothing in the parties' behaviour that the court could use to work out whether the alleged long-term agreement should have lasted 5, 10 or even 20 years.

> **QUESTION 2** Can you think of a way in which a previous course of dealing might help a business that had entered into a written agreement with a customer but forgotten to include its standard terms as part of its offer?

As we saw in Chapter 4, an offer must be communicated to the offeree; by forgetting to include its standard terms as part of its offer, the business in this question has failed to communicate them to the customer, which means they cannot form part of the offer (and the customer cannot therefore be bound by them). However, if the business has dealt with this customer before on similar matters, a court might decide that the standard terms should be 'read into' the agreement based on a previous course of dealing.

> **QUESTION 3** In *Williams v Roffey*, why was Williams unable to rely on *Hartley v Ponsonby*? Can you think of any criticisms of the decision in *Williams v Roffey*?

Williams could not rely on *Hartley v Ponsonby* because he had not performed obligations over and above what was originally expected of him – he had only done what he was originally obliged to do. One criticism of the Court of Appeal ruling in *Williams v Roffey* is that it effectively amounted to a reward for Williams' mismanagement; after all, the delay in completing the flats arose not because of anything that Roffey did, but because Williams had underquoted and got into financial difficulties. However, the Court of Appeal was in a difficult position. If it had ruled in favour of Roffey, this might have encouraged businesses to make promises of extra payments that they had no intention whatsoever of keeping (and that could not have been enforced in the courts); this could have given rise to even greater unfairness.

> **QUESTION 4** In *Pinnel's Case*, all Cole had promised in return for Pinnel's promise to accept £5 was to pay the money at an earlier date. Cole's promise was unlikely to be worth £3 to Pinnel – so why did the court decide that it amounted to good consideration?

The court's decision can be seen as an early illustration of the rule that consideration must be sufficient – but need not be adequate. This means that the value of the debtor's promise need not correspond to the value of the creditor's promise. In *Pinnel's Case*, for example, the court said that Pinnel's promise would also have been enforceable if, in return, Cole had promised to give Pinnel some goods (even if those goods were worth far less than the £3 that Cole would otherwise have owed).

By the end of this chapter, you should be able to explain:

- How the courts decide whether a particular term of a contract is a condition or a warranty and why this is important

- When terms may be implied into a contract, including the terms implied by legislation into contracts for the supply of goods and services

- How the courts deal with disputes over which documents or statements form part of the contract (incorporation of terms)

Introduction

As we saw in Chapter 3, contracts are important to businesses because they contain legally binding promises; these are set out in the terms of the contract. If one party fails to keep its promises (or, to put it another way, *breaks* the terms of the contract), the other will normally be able to take legal action, such as suing the first party for damages. This chapter is concerned with situations where there is a dispute over the terms of the contract. It deals with the following issues:

- How the courts decide whether a particular term is a **warranty** or a **condition** (this determines the remedies available to the party complaining about the other party's failure to comply with a term). This topic is essential to your understanding of Chapter 8, which examines remedies for breach of contract.

- How the courts decide what the terms of the contract are (for example, whether all the terms are contained in a formal written agreement or whether there may be other terms that have not been written down or are contained in other documents); this is dealt with under the headings of implied terms and **incorporation of terms**.

The section on implied terms also deals with the terms implied by legislation into contracts for the supply of goods and services. All these topics are essential to your understanding of the way in which the courts approach **exemption clauses**, which are explained in Chapter 7. Exemption clauses are terms that attempt to exclude or limit the liability of one party.

Conditions and warranties

As we saw in Chapter 3, a typical contract for the supply of goods will contain many different terms, such as price and payment, deadlines for delivery and standards of quality. Some terms will be more important than others. Terms that are of crucial importance to the contract are normally classified as conditions, whereas less important terms are referred to as warranties.

A term requiring a customer to pay for the supply of goods will normally be a condition, because payment is clearly a key element of the bargain that the parties have made. Breach of a condition allows the innocent party to regard the contract as being at end (or **repudiate** the contract) and claim damages for any loss that it has suffered. Breach of a warranty means that the innocent party can only claim damages.

A term requiring delivery by a particular date will often be regarded as a warranty unless it is clear from the contract itself or the surrounding circumstances that the deadline for delivery was a key part of the parties' bargain. So if the supplier fails to deliver by the deadline, the customer will only be able to repudiate the contract at that stage if it can show that the requirement to deliver by that particular date was a condition; if the delivery date is merely a warranty, then the customer will normally only be able to repudiate once a reasonable time has elapsed and the supplier has still failed to deliver. More examples of conditions and warranties can be found later, under the heading 'Terms implied by legislation'.

Innominate terms

The example of delivery clauses shows how it can sometimes be difficult to determine whether a particular term is a warranty or a condition. The courts refer to such terms as **innominate terms** (because whether they are classified as a warranty or a condition depends on the nature of the breach). This terminology originates from the case of ***Hong Kong Fir Shipping Co Ltd v Kawasaki Kisen Kaisha Ltd (1962)*** (usually refered to as the '*Hong Kong Fir* case'), which concerned a term stating that a ship would be 'in every way fitted for cargo service'. Clearly, there could be both minor and very serious breaches of this term. The court ruled that a breach of this term would only be treated as a breach of condition if it deprived the innocent party of 'substantially the whole benefit of the contract' (e.g. the ship was so far below the standard required that it was unseaworthy and could not sail).

> **QUESTION 1** Is there a difference between the legal concept of warranty and warranties offered by suppliers of products such as cars or computers?

Implied terms

In Chapter 5, we looked at a number of situations where the courts may be prepared to uphold an agreement based on implied terms, where the agreement would otherwise have been too uncertain to enforce. Exactly the same approach may be used where the dispute is not concerned with whether there is actually an agreement, but whether the agreement contains a particular term. For example, if the parties have dealt with one another in the past, the courts may be able to imply a particular term based on a previous course of dealing (see Chapter 5 for relevant case law). There are also a number of other circumstances in which the courts may find that an agreement contains implied terms.

Terms implied for business efficacy

Generally, the English courts are quite reluctant to conclude that a contract contains implied terms. However, they may be prepared to do so where the term in question meets the following conditions:

- It must be obvious to a reasonable person, i.e. if the parties were asked about it at the time the contract was made, then assuming they were both reasonable people, they would have said, 'Oh, of course, that goes without saying' – see **Shirlaw v Southern Foundries Ltd (1939)**.
- It must be necessary for 'business efficacy', i.e. in effect, the contract will not work without it. See the example discussed in the FAQ textbox.

The courts may also imply a term where neither of these tests is met, but the term is required as a matter of law. For example, in **Liverpool City Council v Irwin (1976)**, the House of Lords ruled that, because the council was landlord of a block of flats, it was obliged to maintain the lifts and rubbish chutes; even though the council's contract with its tenants was silent on this point, a term was implied requiring it to carry out such maintenance.

 FAQ

What does 'business efficacy' mean in practice?

In *The Moorcock (1889)*, a ship was damaged when it ran aground at low tide, while unloading at a jetty. When the ship's owners claimed damages, the owners of the jetty argued that they had made no express promise in their contract that the jetty would be a reasonably safe place to unload for a ship of that size. The Court of Appeal, however, ruled that such a promise had to be implied. This was because, without such a term, the contract would have amounted to nothing more than an opportunity to damage the ship – which was clearly not what either of the parties had intended. Indeed, without such a term, the efficacy of the jetty owners' business would be completely undermined, as no rational ship owner would be interested in paying for unloading space that was not reasonably safe.

> **QUESTION 2** *The Moorcock* dates from before the 'obviousness' test in *Shirlaw v Southern Foundries*. Do you think it meets that test?

Terms implied by legislation

Terms may also be implied into contracts by legislation. In some cases, such terms may be implied even in situations where the parties did not intend them to be part of the contract or have tried to exclude them. There are many examples of this, but in this chapter we will concentrate on terms implied into contracts for the supply of goods and services.

Sale of Goods Act 1979

Under the Sale of Goods Act 1979 (SGA), the following terms may be implied into contracts for the sale of goods, even if the express terms of the contract contain no promises at all about the goods (Table 6.1).

Table 6.1 Terms implied into contracts for sale of goods

Section	Implied term	Explanation	Always implied?
12	The seller must have the right to sell the goods	The seller must have the right to sell the goods to the buyer, either because he owns them or has been appointed as agent on behalf of the owner. For example, this term would be breached if the seller had rented the goods (and had not been given the right to sell them by the actual owner)	Implied into all contracts for sale of goods
13	Goods sold by description must correspond to their description	For example, this term will be breached if a sofa is described as 'blue' but it turns out to be red (even if there is nothing else 'wrong' with the sofa)	Implied into all contracts for sale of goods where the goods were sold by reference to their description
14(2)	The goods must be of satisfactory quality	See below for explanation	Only where the seller is acting as a business (does not apply to private sales)
14(3)	The goods must be fit for their purpose	See below for explanation	Only where the seller is acting as a business (does not apply to private sales)
15	If goods are sold by sample, the quality of the sample provided must correspond to the quality of the bulk	For example, if a buyer is sent a sample of fabric, the full consignment of fabric (known as the 'bulk') must be of the same quality as the sample. The bulk must also be of satisfactory quality, unless a reasonable inspection of the sample by the buyer would have revealed the defect	Only where the seller is acting as a business (does not apply to private sales)

Dealing as a business

Sections 14(2), 14(3) and 15 SGA only apply where the seller is dealing 'in the course of a business'. For example, they would not apply if you sold your car (which was for non-business use only) by advertising it in the paper as a private seller. So if the car broke down two days after the sale, the buyer would probably be unable to sue you for breach of contract (unless he got you to promise that the car was in good working order).

However, the concept of dealing 'in the course of a business' is fairly wide – see **Stevenson v Rogers (1999)**. For example, if you were selling a van that you used mainly for business purposes, then you would probably be acting in the course of a business. As a result, the terms implied by sections 14(2), 14(3) and 15 would form part of your contract with any buyer (unless you were able to exclude them – this is discussed in Chapter 7, which deals with exemption clauses). So if the van breaks down two days later, the buyer may well be able to sue you for breach of those terms.

Satisfactory quality

When assessing satisfactory quality, the courts are required to consider the 'description of the goods … and all other relevant circumstances', including any public statements made about the goods by the supplier or the manufacturer. To meet the requirement of satisfactory quality under section 14(2) SGA, goods must generally:

- be fit for the purpose for which they are normally supplied
- be safe
- be free from defects, including minor ones
- function properly for a reasonable period of time
- have a reasonably satisfactory finish and appearance.

Safety and fitness for normal purposes are usually requirements whatever price the products are sold at. For example, in **SW Tubes Ltd v Owen Stuart Ltd (2002)**, the Court of Appeal ruled that a second-hand mechanical saw was not of satisfactory quality because its drive belt kept breaking (which meant it could not be used) and it had no guards to protect users against injury (which meant it was unsafe).

Brand-new goods are generally expected to meet higher standards of quality and even minor defects (such as blemishes on the paintwork of a new car) will be likely to constitute a breach of section 14(2). An example of a product that did not meet this standard is discussed later under the heading 'Effect of breaching SGA and SOGASA implied terms'. However, if the goods are second hand or are being sold at a relatively low price, the courts will not necessarily expect their quality to meet such high standards, particularly where the seller has drawn the buyer's attention to any defects before the sale. For example, in **Bartlett v Sidney Marcus Ltd (1965)**, the seller of a second-hand car had pointed out that its clutch was worn and the price took account of the fact that the car was not in perfect condition. This meant that when the clutch failed shortly after the sale, the seller was not in breach of the implied term as to satisfactory quality.

Reality check

Jewson v Kelly (2003)

When is a boiler fit for its purpose?

Jewson, a firm of builders' merchants, had supplied boilers to Mr Kelly for installation in some flats, which Kelly intended to sell. When he came to sell them, he found that they produced poor energy efficiency ratings (which meant that he was not able to sell the flats for as much money as he had hoped). He argued that the boilers were not of satisfactory quality under section 14(2) SGA because they should have been able to achieve the energy efficiency ratings used by surveyors when valuing the flats. He also argued that Jewson was in breach of section 14(3) SGA because it had been aware of the specific purpose for which the boilers were required (i.e. for installation in flats, which he intended to sell). The Court of Appeal disagreed on both points. It said that boilers were commonly used for the purposes of providing hot water and heating, not for achieving particular levels of energy efficiency. Since there was no complaint about the former, the boilers were of satisfactory quality under section 14(2). As for fitness for purpose under section 14(3), Mr Kelly had only indicated that the boilers were for installation in some new flats and had said nothing specific about energy efficiency ratings. In the circumstances, it was not reasonable to expect Jewson to realise that he needed the boilers to achieve particular levels of energy efficiency.

Fitness for purpose

Section 14(3) SGA implies a term into all contracts for the sale of goods that the goods must be fit for their purpose. There is some overlap here with section 14(2), which requires goods to be fit for the purpose for which they are *commonly used*. Section 14(3) gives the buyer additional protection in situations where he has indicated to the seller that the product is needed for a specific purpose (which may not be a purpose for which the product is commonly used). However, as illustrated by the case of ***Jewson v Kelly (2003)***, highlighted in the 'Reality check' textbox, a seller will not be in breach of section 14(3) if the buyer has failed to make clear exactly what his requirements are (and the goods turn out to be unsuitable for his purposes).

> **QUESTION 3** If a person bought a child's soft toy for use by their pet dog as a plaything and the dog was injured when it chewed up the toy, could that be a breach of section 14(2) or 14(3) SGA?

Supply of Goods and Services Act 1982

The Supply of Goods and Services Act 1982 (SOGASA) applies to contracts for:

- the supply of services only, e.g. a taxi service
- the supply of a mixture of goods and services, e.g. where a builder/decorator provides materials (goods) *and* carries out building work (services)

- rental (as opposed to sale) of goods (note that if the contract is for hire purchase, rather than rental, i.e. the customer may be able to buy the goods at the end of the contract, another statute applies – the Supply of Goods (Implied Terms) Act 1973 – which is not covered in this book, although its provisions are very similar to those of SOGASA regarding rental contracts).

Where the contract includes supply of goods (i.e. mixed goods and services contracts and rental contracts), SOGASA implies terms that are essentially the same as those in sections 12–15 SGA. The key difference is that where the goods are only being rented, there is no implied term that the supplier can transfer ownership of the goods to the customer (because the customer will be expected to return them at the end of the period of rental). The sections of SOGASA relevant to goods are summarised in Table 6.2.

The terms implied by SOGASA into contracts for supply of services include the following:

- *Section 13*: the supplier will carry out those services with reasonable care and skill.
- *Section 14*: the supplier must carry out the services within a reasonable time (unless the time for performance has been fixed in the contract itself).

'Reasonable care and skill' is measured by reference to the standards that a reasonably competent provider of the relevant services could have been expected to meet. It does not entitle the customer to expect above-average levels of skill or attention to detail. However, the customer will normally be able to demonstrate a breach if it can show that the service fell short of standard industry practices. For example, in **The Simkins Partnership v Reeves Lund & Co Ltd (2003)**, Simkins engaged Reeves to install a new telephone system. Reeves left voicemail ports unbarred, which allowed fraudsters to access Simkins' telephone system and run up charges of £17,200. The court found that a reasonably competent installer of telephone systems would have been expected to bar the voicemail ports, as this was generally recognised to be good practice in the industry. Reeves had therefore breached the implied term of reasonable care and skill.

Table 6.2 SOGASA sections relevant to goods

Implied term (and equivalent SGA reference)	Contracts for mixed supply of goods and services	Rental contracts
Title (s12 SGA)	Section 2 SOGASA	Section 7 SOGASA **NB** Supplier only promises that it can rent the goods to customer (not that it can sell them)
Description (s13 SGA)	Section 3 SOGASA	Section 8 SOGASA
Satisfactory quality (s14(2) SGA)	Section 4(2) SOGASA	Section 9(2) SOGASA
Fitness for purpose (s14(3) SGA)	Section 4(3) SOGASA	Section 9(5) SOGASA
Sale by sample (s15 SGA)	Section 5 SOGASA	Section 10 SOGASA

Effect of breaching SGA and SOGASA implied terms

The terms implied by SGA and SOGASA are generally regarded as conditions of the contract. As we have seen, this means that the customer may not only claim damages but may also repudiate the contract. In the case of a sale of goods contract, repudiation means that the customer can reject the goods and demand his money back. However, there are two important limits on the buyer's right to reject goods:

- *Acceptance*: the buyer must reject the goods within a reasonable time; if he fails to do so or acts in a way that suggests he has accepted the goods (e.g. by waiting an unreasonable amount of time before rejecting them or, in some cases, by using the goods), the right to reject is lost and the buyer can only claim damages. Two contrasting cases concerning the right to reject are considered in the 'Reality check' textbox that follows.

- *Minor breaches and business purchasers*: where the breach is of section 13, 14 or 15 (or their equivalents in SOGASA) and the breach is so slight that it would be unreasonable to reject them, then the customer can only claim damages. In these cases, the breach is regarded as a breach of warranty, not a breach of condition. This only applies to business purchasers, not consumers.

Reality check

Clegg v Andersson (2003) and Jones v Gallagher (2004)

To reject or not to reject?

In *Clegg v Andersson (2003)*, Mr Clegg bought a yacht costing about £250,000 from Andersson. He took delivery in August 2000 and used it for sailing. However, he found that the yacht had various handling problems and took it back to Andersson for repair. In February 2001 Andersson informed him that the problems were due to an overweight keel, which was quite a serious defect as it affected the safety of the vessel. Three weeks later, Clegg wrote to Anderson rejecting the yacht on the grounds that it was not of satisfactory quality. Andersson argued that Clegg had lost the right to reject because he had been in possession of the yacht for over 6 months and had sailed in it. The Court of Appeal accepted that delay in rejection or use of the goods could often be regarded as evidence that a buyer had accepted the goods (and

(continued overleaf)

therefore lost the right to reject). However, in this case, the buyer had not been aware of the extent of the defect until February 2001. Three weeks was a reasonable time in which to exercise the right to reject. There was no doubt that Clegg had the right to reject given the seriousness of the defect and the fact that the yacht was both new and fairly expensive. A contrasting case is *Jones v Gallagher (2004)*, where the buyers argued that they were entitled to reject a fitted kitchen because it was not of satisfactory quality. However, they did not indicate that they wished to reject until seven months after the kitchen had been completed. Unlike in *Clegg*, there was no evidence that Mr & Mrs Jones had been unaware of the extent of the problem. Their delay in pursuing their complaints about the kitchen, combined with the fact that they had used it in the meantime, suggested that they did not consider the defects to be so serious that the kitchen had to be rejected in its entirety. The Court of Appeal therefore ruled that they had lost their right to reject (although they were awarded £2500 in damages).

Additional rights for consumers

Customers who are consumers have certain additional rights where they have purchased goods and the supplier is in breach of the relevant provisions of SGA or SOGASA. A person 'deals as a consumer' if he did not make the contract in the course of a business or did not hold himself out as doing so (this definition is discussed in more detail in Chapter 20, on consumer protection). As a result of amendments to the SGA and SOGASA made by the Sale and Supply of Goods to Consumers Regulations 2002, consumers who do not wish to reject the goods or claim damages may choose between the following additional remedies:

* requiring the supplier to replace the goods within a reasonable time
* requiring the supplier to repair the goods within a reasonable time
* or accepting a reduction in the price.

The rights to repair or replacement are not available where it would be disproportionately expensive to carry them out. The 2002 regulations made a number of other changes to SGA and SOGASA, which were intended to make it easier for consumers to obtain redress for substandard goods. These are explained in Chapter 20, on consumer protection. They are not covered here as they are not strictly relevant to the topic of implied terms.

Incorporation of terms

Contracts are not always set out in a single written agreement that has been signed by both parties. It is perfectly possible to have a contract based on an oral agreement (so there is no written documentation at all). Alternatively, the terms of the contract may be contained in a potentially confusing mixture of oral statements and a variety of written documents. Indeed, it is quite common for parties to get into disputes over what the terms of the contract actually say, particularly where a number of documents have been sent back and forth during negotiations but no formal agreement has been signed.

The courts have therefore developed a number of rules to help them decide whether a term has been included as part of the final agreement. Lawyers refer to these rules as dealing with incorporation of terms. The rules are particularly important in relation to exemption clauses, but they are also relevant to other types of term.

The general rule

The courts will not regard a term as having been incorporated into a contract unless the term was brought to the attention of the other party *before* acceptance. For example, in **Olley v Marlborough Court (1949)**, a hotel tried to argue that it was not responsible for the theft of some valuables from one of its bedrooms. It pointed out that there was a notice in the bedroom itself stating that the hotel would not be liable for such loss. The court ruled that the contract with the hotel guests was made when they booked the room in the lobby of the hotel; since the notice was not brought to their attention until after acceptance had taken place, it was not incorporated as a term of the contract (and so was not binding on the guests).

Signed documents

Where a party has signed a document, the courts will assume that he has read and understood its contents; as a result, any terms contained in that document will normally be regarded as having been brought to the attention of that party and will therefore be incorporated into the contract. For example, in **L'Estrange v Graucob (1934)**, the claimant signed the supplier's standard terms for the purchase of a vending machine, which did not work properly. This document stated that no warranties were given about the quality of the machine (which effectively meant that the seller had no liability if the machine did not work). The claimant argued that, since she had not read the document before signing it, she was unaware of its terms; as a result, she claimed, none of the written terms formed part of the contract with the seller and a term had to be implied stating that the machine would be reasonably fit for its purpose. The court said that her signature on the document indicated that she agreed to its terms – even if she had not read them.

 FAQ

The rule on signed documents

If you sign an agreement for the purchase of a second-hand car from a dealer, are you bound by all its terms – including any exclusions of liability?

Not necessarily. For example, as we have seen, someone who was in Ms L'Estrange's position today would be able to argue that the contract contained implied terms about the quality of goods on the basis of the Sale of Goods Act 1979. The clause used by the seller to exclude any terms relating to the quality of the machine could be challenged under the Unfair Contract Terms Act 1977, which is explained in Chapter 7. In addition, if you were buying the car from a business for your own private purposes (rather than for use in your own business), you would benefit from quite extensive protection against clauses of this type – regardless of whether you had signed the agreement. This is explained in Chapter 20 on consumer protection. However, while consumers often benefit from more lenient treatment, the courts are rarely sympathetic towards business people who have failed to read documents they have signed.

Unsigned documents or notices

Where the agreement consists of several unsigned documents or notices, the courts will need to be satisfied that enough was done to draw attention to the relevant term before the contract was made. The general rule is that the more likely it is that the term will have harsh or unexpected effects on one party's normal rights, the more effort needs to be made to draw attention to it before acceptance. For example, in *Thornton v Shoe Lane Parking (1971)*, a motorist was injured in an accident as he was collecting his car from a car park. The accident was partly the fault of the car park owners. They tried to argue that they were not liable for any injury to customers based on various notices at the car park and on the ticket. Lord Denning remarked that terms that were particularly harsh, such as exemption clauses, would only be incorporated if a special effort had been made to draw attention to them. In this case, he thought that the term in question was 'so wide and so destructive of rights' that: 'It would need to be printed in red ink with a red hand pointing to it – or something equally startling.'

Similarly, in **Interfoto Picture Library Ltd v Stiletto Visual Programmes Ltd (1988)**, the Court of Appeal ruled that not enough had been done to draw attention to a clause contained in some standard terms (which had not been signed). The clause required the customer to pay a daily penalty for late return of photographic transparencies from a picture library. The customer argued that it was not aware of the clause. The Court of Appeal concluded that this term was so harsh that the picture library should have done more to bring it to their customers' attention (for example, by putting it in bold type or referring to it specifically in a covering letter). However, as demonstrated by the example in the 'Reality check' textbox, not all terms need to have special attention drawn to them in this way.

Reality check

O'Brien v Mirror Group Newspapers Ltd (2001)

Should competition rules have been printed in red ink with a red hand pointing to them?

In *O'Brien v Mirror Group Newspapers Ltd (2001)*, the *Mirror* newspaper ran a scratchcard competition offering prizes of £50,000. Due to an administrative error, Mr O'Brien was one of about 1400 people who thought they had won. The *Mirror* had published the rules of the competition in full when it was first announced, but not in subsequent issues (although reference was made to the rules on each scratchcard and

in each edition of the newspaper where the competition was run). Rule 5 stated that there were only a limited number of prizes each day and if the number of claimants exceeded the number of prizes, then the winners would be selected by a simple draw. Mirror Group referred to rule 5 to justify not awarding Mr O'Brien a prize. The majority of the Court of Appeal stressed that – unlike the exclusions of liability challenged in cases such as *Thornton v Shoe Lane Parking* and *Interfoto v Stiletto* – the rule in question was not a particularly harsh term, such as an exemption clause. Consequently, less effort was required to bring it to the attention of the other party. [Details of further cases dealing with incorporation of terms and unsigned documents or notices can be found on the companion website.]

> **QUESTION 4** Could the outcome in *Interfoto v Stiletto* have been different if there had been a previous course of dealing?

Terms and pre-contractual representations

As a general rule, statements made by the parties in negotiations (either in writing or orally) will not normally be regarded as terms of the contract; where this is the case, lawyers call them **pre-contractual representations**. It is possible to sue a party for making a pre-contractual representation that is false; this is explained in the section of Chapter 9 dealing with misrepresentation. However, in this chapter, we are only concerned with statements made in negotiations that may be regarded as terms of the contract. The courts generally look at four factors when considering whether such statements may amount to terms:

- the importance of the statement
- whether the maker of the statement had special knowledge or skill
- whether the parties had put their agreement in writing (and whether the written document contained any reference to the statement)
- the timing of the statement.

For example, in **Bannerman v White (1861)**, the buyers of a consignment of hops told the sellers that they did not want any hops that had been treated with sulphur. The sellers said that none of the hops had been treated with sulphur, but this proved to be untrue. When the buyers sued for compensation, the sellers argued that their statement about the hops was not a term of the contract because it had been made in negotiations. The court noted that the buyers had made it clear on several occasions how important it was to them that the hops had not been treated. It also noted that the sellers were in a better position than the buyers to know whether sulphur had been used; as such, they could be said to have 'special knowledge or expertise'. In the circumstances, the statement was to be regarded as a term of the contract.

In **Routledge v McKay (1954)**, by contrast, the purchaser of a motorbike was unsuccessful in arguing that a statement about the age of the vehicle amounted to a term of the contract. The seller had told him that he thought the motorbike had been registered in 1941 or 1942, based on what had been written in its logbook. This statement proved to be wrong, but the court said that it could not be regarded as a term of the contract. First of all, there had been a delay of a week between the making of the statement and the conclusion of the contract, during which the purchaser could have asked the seller to check whether the logbook was correct. Second, the agreement was made in writing and contained no promises about the age of the motorbike. The court took the view that if this issue had been so important to the buyer, he should have asked for such a promise to be included.

FAQ

Putting it in writing

When a business enters into a written agreement, can it ever be 100% sure that the agreement sets out all the terms of the contract?

Where two businesses have gone to the trouble of drafting a written agreement, the courts will normally be quite reluctant to accept arguments that statements made during negotiations (and not included in the written agreement) are terms of the contract. Many agreements also contain 'entire agreement clauses', which usually say something like: 'This agreement constitutes the entire agreement between the parties and supersedes all previous statements or negotiations relating to the subject matter of this agreement.' These clauses are intended to make it more difficult for one of the parties to argue that terms should be implied (except where they are implied by statute) or that a pre-contractual statement should be incorporated as a term – and, in practice, they are often effective. So while it is generally impossible to be 100% sure that a written agreement contains all the terms of the contract, there are many situations where businesses can be fairly confident that this is the case. [You can find out more about entire agreement clauses on the companion website.]

Answers to in-text questions

> **QUESTION 1** Is there a difference between the legal concept of warranty and warranties offered by suppliers of products such as cars or computers?

Suppliers of products such as cars or computers tend to use the word 'warranty' in a fairly specialised sense to refer to a promise that if the product goes wrong during a particular period, they will repair or replace it free of charge. Lawyers use the concept of warranty to refer to a much wider range of promises, i.e. any promise contained in a contract that is not a condition. Legally, there is nothing wrong with a computer supplier calling a promise to repair the product a warranty; it is intended to indicate that if the product goes wrong, the customer is not entitled to reject it and demand a refund, but may claim damages if the supplier fails to repair or replace it. However, as we have seen, it is up to the courts to decide whether such a term is a warranty or a condition; what the parties have called it is not necessarily decisive.

> **QUESTION 2** *The Moorcock* dates from before the 'obviousness' test in *Shirlaw v Southern Foundries*. Do you think it meets that test?

Another way of looking at *The Moorcock* is to consider what the parties would have said had they been asked whether the contract contained a term stating that the jetty was safe; it seems likely that they would have replied: 'Oh, of course, that goes without saying' (because, so far as the jetty owners were concerned, any other reply would have tended to deter customers from using the jetty to unload ships). So in that respect, the implied term in *The Moorcock* would seem to meet the test in *Shirlaw v Southern Foundries*.

> **QUESTION 3** If a person bought a child's soft toy for use by their pet dog as a plaything and the dog was injured when it chewed up the toy, could that be a breach of section 14(2) or 14(3) SGA?

In *Jewson v Kelly*, Sedley LJ suggested that the answer to this question was that section 14(2) SGA would normally only be breached if the toy would have been unsafe when handled by a child, not a dog; this was because use as a pet toy was not a purpose for which such a toy would commonly be used. However, it was also necessary to consider the circumstances in which the toy was sold. For example, had the toy been bought in a pet shop, the buyer would be justified in assuming that it was safe to give it to his dog (and there *would* be a breach of section 14(2)). Equally, if the buyer had specifically asked the seller if the toy was suitable for pets as well as children and been told that it was, then there would be a breach of section 14(3) SGA.

> **QUESTION 4** Could the outcome in *Interfoto v Stiletto* have been different had there been a previous course of dealing?

If the customers in the Interfoto case had dealt with the picture library before and had been sent the company's standard terms on previous occasions without objecting to them, it is possible that they would have been regarded as having had sufficient notice of the clause. For example, in **Spurling v Bradshaw (1956)**, a term excluding liability for damage to barrels of orange juice stored at a warehouse was found to be validly incorporated, even though no special attempt had been made to draw attention to it. The court ruled that, since the terms had been sent to the owner of the barrels several times in the past, he must have been aware of what they said. At first sight, the outcome of *Spurling v Bradshaw* may seem somewhat harsh. However, in practice, it is quite common for owners of goods placed in storage to arrange insurance for them and, had the owner of the barrels done this, he would probably not have needed to sue the owner of the warehouse. Against that background, the term excluding liability on the part of the warehouse operator was not as surprising or as onerous as it may initially appear; this may explain why a previous course of dealing amounted to sufficient notice of the term.

7 | Exemption clauses

By the end of this chapter, you should be able to explain:

- **How businesses use exemption clauses to limit their liability if they are in breach of contract**

- **The methods courts have developed to control the use of exemption clauses (i.e. the rules on incorporation and construction of exemption clauses)**

- **How the use of exemption clauses is limited by legislation, in particular the effect of the Unfair Contract Terms Act 1977 and how the courts have applied it in practice**

Introduction

Even where businesses have entered into a fairly comprehensive written agreement, some of the terms may not be legally binding. For instance, there are special rules governing exemption clauses. These are terms of the contract that attempt to limit or exclude the **liability** of one party to the other. If you buy a car from a dealer, the dealer may include a term in the contract of sale stating that he does not have to pay you any compensation if you are injured in an accident because the car was faulty. For reasons explained later, it is very unlikely indeed that the courts would uphold such a term.

There are three areas of law the courts can use to prevent the abuse of such clauses:

- the common law rules on **incorporation of terms**
- the common law rules on **construction**
- legislation, namely the Unfair Contract Terms Act 1977 and (in the case of consumers only) the Unfair Terms in Consumer Contracts Regulations 1999.

This chapter also looks at the extent to which the terms implied by the Sale of Goods Act 1979 and the Supply of Goods and Services Act 1982 can be excluded. You may want to remind yourself of those terms before reading this chapter (see Chapter 6).

Incorporation

When considering exemption clauses, the courts normally look particularly care-fully at whether such terms have been properly incorporated – because if they have not, then they are not legally binding. The law on incorporation of terms has already been discussed in Chapter 6, as it is relevant to all terms (not just exemption clauses). However, it is essential to consider it when answering exam questions about exemption clauses because, in practice, it acts as an important control on the use of such terms.

> **QUESTION 1** In order to be properly incorporated, is it always essential for exemption clauses in written contracts to have special attention drawn to them, e.g. by being printed in bold letters?

Construction

If an exemption clause has been properly incorporated, the courts will go on to examine the wording in some detail. This process, which is known as 'construing' the clause (hence the term 'construction'), can also lead to a ruling that the term in question cannot be relied on. There are two main rules of construction that are relevant here:

- *The need for clear wording*: because the effect of an exemption clause is often quite harsh, the courts require them to be drafted in a way that makes their scope quite clear. An example of this is given in the 'Reality check' textbox (on the following page) highlighting ***Casson v Ostley PJ Ltd (2001)***.

- *The contra-proferentem rule*: the courts interpret exemption clauses narrowly, against the interest of the party seeking to rely on them ('contra' is Latin for 'against' and 'proferentem' is Latin for 'the one who put it [i.e. the term] forward'). For example, if a notice on a car park states that 'All cars are left at owner's risk', it might be sufficient to exclude liability for damage to a car – but it will not be sufficient to exclude liability for injury to the owner of the car, because the wording only refers to cars. The **contra-proferentem rule** is relevant here because even if the car park owner tries to argue that the wording was intended to exclude liability for injuries to car owners as well, the courts will not give the notice a wider interpretation – if the car park owner had wanted to exclude liability to owners, he should have made this clear.

Reality check

Casson v Ostley PJ Ltd (2001)

Construction of exemption clauses in practice

Casson's farm was damaged by a fire, which appeared to have been caused by Ostley, a firm of builders who had been engaged to carry out some work on some of the farm buildings. Under the heading 'Insurance', Ostley's standard terms contained a clause stating that all existing structures and unfixed materials shall be 'at the sole risk of the client as regards loss or damage by fire and the client shall maintain a proper policy of insurance against that risk in an adequate sum'. Ostley argued that this clause prevented it from being liable, even where the fire was caused by its own negligence. The Court of Appeal criticised several aspects of the drafting of this term. First of all, the fact that the clause appeared under the heading 'Insurance' was confusing; it made it look as if the clause was concerned only with insurance issues, when in fact it was an attempt to exclude liability (and should therefore have been put under a heading such as 'Liability' or 'Limitations and exclusions'). Second, the Court of Appeal thought that most customers would be quite surprised to learn that Ostley had no liability for fires caused by its own negligence and that the effect of such a term could be quite harsh. In view of this, it ruled that the wording needed to state quite explicitly that Ostley was excluding liability for fires caused by its own negligence; since the clause failed to do this, it could not be relied on by Ostley to exclude its liability to Casson.

> **QUESTION 2** In *Casson v Ostley*, would it have made any difference had Casson signed the contract?

Legislation

The Unfair Contract Terms Act 1977 (UCTA) allows parties to challenge certain types of exemption clause on the grounds that they are too harsh. This legislation was introduced in response to concerns that businesses were often including exemption clauses in agreements that were so wide they relieved the supplier of almost any liability. However, as explained earlier, the courts will only look at UCTA if they are satisfied that the exemption clause passes the tests of incorporation and construction already outlined.

UCTA is not a straightforward piece of legislation and many of its clauses are peculiarly drafted. In recognition of this, the Law Commission has published proposals to simplify the legislation; details of these are available on the companion website.

Unfair Terms in Consumer Contracts Regulations 1999

A consumer who wishes to challenge an exemption clause can also do so under the Unfair Terms in Consumer Contracts Regulations 1999 (UTCCR), which implement an EU directive. As a result, when considering whether an exemption clause may be valid against a consumer (as opposed to a business), it is necessary to consider both UCTA and the UTCCR. The UTCCR are explained in detail in Chapter 20, which deals with consumer protection (the same chapter also includes a detailed discussion of the differences between UCTA and UTCCR in relation to contracts with consumers).

Business liability

UCTA only applies to contracts where a business is seeking to limit or exclude its liability. For example, if you buy a second-hand car from a dealer, then UCTA could potentially apply because the dealer is acting as a business. However, if you were to buy the same car from an individual selling in a private capacity, UCTA would not apply at all; so if you sign a document saying 'sold as seen' and 'I accept that the seller has no further liability to me', you would not be able to use UCTA to challenge that exemption clause.

Negligence: section 2 UCTA

Section 2(1) of UCTA says that exemption clauses that seek to limit or exclude liability for death or personal injury caused by negligence are *always* void and unenforceable. For example, had the contract in *Casson v Ostley* contained a clause that said 'The supplier shall not be liable for any injury caused to any person', this would have been automatically void under section 2(1) UCTA.

Note that 'negligence' in section 2 can refer to both (i) carelessness in carrying out contractual obligations; and/or (ii) liability in the tort of negligence, which is explained in Part 3. Liability in the tort of negligence may arise wherever someone owes another person a 'duty of care'. It can exist alongside contractual liability. For example, a supplier normally owes a customer a duty of care in negligence, as well as various contractual obligations. If the supplier breaches its duty of care (e.g. by failing to exercise sufficient care when the goods are delivered, resulting in an injury to the customer), it could be sued in the tort of negligence as well as contract.

Section 2(2) of UCTA says that exemption clauses that try to limit or exclude liability for damage *other than personal injury or death* caused by negligence *may* be void and unenforceable – but only if they fail the **reasonableness test**. For example, a clause in a contract with a firm of builders that said, 'The suppliers [i.e. the firm of builders] shall not be liable for damage to any of the client's property, howsoever caused (including damage caused by negligence on the part of the suppliers)' could be challenged under section 2(2). This is because the wording is sufficiently wide to exclude the builders' liability if they are careless in carrying out their contractual obligations or if they breach their duty of care to the client in the tort of negligence. The reasonableness test is explained later.

Breach of contract: section 3 UCTA

Section 3 of UCTA deals with clauses seeking to limit liability for breach of contract. It says that such clauses may be void and unenforceable if they fail to meet the reasonableness test, but, unlike section 2, it only applies in two situations:

- Where the person whose rights are affected by the exemption clause is a consumer (as noted earlier, the party relying on the exemption clause must be a business for UCTA to apply at all).
- Where the exemption clause is contained in the standard written terms of the business seeking to rely on it.

For example, it is quite common for contracts to contain clauses that state that the liability of the supplier for any breach will be limited to the total value of the price payable by the customer under the contract. If that price were £10,000, but

FAQ

In practice, what are the main differences between section 2 UCTA and section 3 UCTA?

Section 2 only applies where there is an attempt to exclude liability for negligence; section 3, by way of contrast, can be used to challenge an exemption clause limiting or excluding liability for a breach of contract that does not involve negligence. For example, if a builder failed to complete work by a date specified in the contract due to factors beyond its control, such as the failure of one of its suppliers to deliver on time, there would be a breach of contract – but that breach would not be caused by the negligence of the builder. Nevertheless, the failure to finish on time would still be seen as the builder's responsibility under the contract – and any

attempt by the builder to limit or exclude such liability could be challenged as unreasonable under section 3 UCTA (provided the customer is a consumer or the contract is on the builder's written standard terms). This is not to say that excluding or limiting liability for such breaches will always be unreasonable – that will vary according to the circumstances of the case (see later).

The new Scottish Parliament building: 3 years late and 10 times over budget

the customer had suffered a loss of £50,000, it could use section 3 to challenge the £10,000 limit of liability – but only if the customer were a consumer or the contract were on the standard written terms of the supplier (which was a business). The following definitions are crucial when considering section 3:

- *Consumer*: for the purposes of UCTA a consumer is any party who is not acting in the course of a business (this concept is examined in more detail in Chapter 20, on consumer protection; see Chapter 6 for detail on what the courts regard as acting 'in the course of a business').

- *Standard written terms*: this concept has generally been interpreted quite widely by the courts as covering not only pre-printed forms but also any exemption clause regularly put forward by a business as its starting point for negotiations.

SGA and SOGASA implied terms: sections 6 and 7

In Chapter 6, we looked at the terms implied into contracts for the supply of goods by the Sale of Goods Act 1979 (SGA) and the Supply of Goods and Services Act 1982 (SOGASA). Sections 6 and 7 of UCTA deal with attempts to exclude the implied terms relating to goods (section 6 deals with SGA and section 7 with SOGASA). However, they do *not* deal with the terms implied by SOGASA relating to services. As with section 3 UCTA, consumers and businesses are treated differently:

- *Consumers*: where the buyer is a consumer, businesses cannot limit or exclude liability under any of the terms implied by SGA or SOGASA relating to goods.

Note that, unlike section 3 UCTA, there is no need to consider whether the exemption clause meets the reasonableness test – any term attempting to limit or exclude liability under the SGA or SOGASA implied terms against consumers is automatically void.

- *Businesses*: where the buyer is a business, the terms implied by SGA and SOGASA relating to title of goods cannot be excluded at all. However, the other implied terms relating to goods (e.g. satisfactory quality, fitness for purpose etc.) may be excluded if the exemption clause meets the reasonableness test (see later). Note that, unlike section 3 UCTA, there is no need to consider whether the contract is on standard written terms.

There is some overlap between sections 2–3 UCTA and sections 6–7; for example, an exemption clause in a consumer contract that attempted to exclude liability for goods that were unsafe (and that caused injury to both people and property) would fall foul of most of the provisions of UCTA that have already been discussed. But the worked example in the 'Reality check' textbox shows how there are some situations where an exemption clause can only be challenged using a more limited 'armoury' of UCTA provisions.

Reality check

The importance of sections 6–7 UCTA in practice

A brewery has entered into a contract (which is not on standard terms) for supply of beer to a large chain of pubs. The pub chain is unhappy with two aspects of the brewery's performance, which it claims have resulted in a loss of £100,000. First, some of the beer supplied was not fit for consumption and had to be thrown away (but no one was injured). Second, the brewery has failed to make various deliveries on time (so the pub chain has lost profit on anticipated sales of the beer). When the customer threatens to sue for £100,000, the brewery responds that it has made no promises (express or implied) about the quality of the beer and, in any event, its contract with the customer states that its liability is limited to £50,000.

Since the contract is not on standard terms and, furthermore, the buyer is not a consumer, section 3 UCTA has no application to this situation. Section 2(1) UCTA has no application here because no one has been injured or killed. Sections 6–7 UCTA will be relevant because the brewery has attempted to exclude the SGA implied terms concerning satisfactory quality and fitness for purpose. This exclusion will only be valid if it meets the reasonableness test. Sections 6–7 can also be used to challenge the limitation of the brewery's liability to £50,000 insofar as it limits liability for breach of the SGA implied terms. However, the pub chain's position is weaker when it comes to its claim for loss of profits due to failure to deliver the beer on time. Here, the pub chain's claim will be limited to £50,000 unless it can show that the failure was due to negligence – in which case it will be able to challenge the limit of liability under section 2(2) UCTA. So in this particular scenario, it is sections 6–7 UCTA that are likely to prove most helpful to the pub chain – sections 2(1) and 3 are irrelevant and it is debatable whether section 2(2) will assist.

QUESTION 3 Can a business or a consumer use section 7 UCTA to challenge an exclusion of liability for breach of section 13 SOGASA (implied term of reasonable skill and care)?

The reasonableness test

When considering whether a term meets the reasonableness test under UCTA, the courts look at 'the circumstances which were, or ought reasonably to have been known to or in the contemplation of the parties *when the contract was made*' (section 11). Schedule 2 and section 11(4) UCTA give some further guidance on what circumstances the courts should take into account:

- *Bargaining strength of the parties*: if one of the parties is in a weak position to negotiate changes to an exemption clause, the courts will generally be more likely to regard the clause as unreasonable (but this depends on what the clause actually says). If the parties have equal bargaining power, however, the courts will normally be more inclined to uphold the clause (because this means that the party seeking to challenge the clause could probably have negotiated changes to it at the time the contract was made).

- *Inducement to accept the term*: if the party challenging the exemption clause received an inducement in return for its agreement to the clause, the courts will generally be more likely to regard the clause as reasonable. For example, if a customer has secured a reduction in the price in return for agreeing to an exemption clause, the courts will normally be more likely to uphold the clause.

- *Knowledge of the existence and extent of the term*: if the party challenging the exemption clause can show that he could not reasonably have been expected to know of the term or to appreciate its true effect (perhaps because it was not very clearly worded or hidden away in a document that did not look like a contract), this may well make the courts more inclined to regard the clause as unreasonable.

- *Whether liability is accepted only if certain conditions are complied with*: in contracts for the sale of goods, terms are often included that require the buyer to notify any claims to the seller within a particular time period e.g. 1 week from delivery. If a fault emerges after that period, the seller may try to argue that it has no liability at all. If it was not reasonable (at the time the contract was made) to expect the buyer to comply with this condition (because the time period is too short for the buyer to determine whether the goods are in working order), the courts will normally be less inclined to uphold the exemption clause.

- *Goods made to special order*: where goods supplied under the contract were manufactured to the special order of the customer, the courts will generally be more inclined to regard certain types of exemption clause as reasonable. For example, where the customer is responsible for the design of the goods, it may be perfectly reasonable for the supplier to limit or exclude its liability to the customer if the design proves unsatisfactory in practice.

- *Resources of the parties and availability of insurance*: where one party has access to large financial reserves or would easily be able to obtain insurance against potential claims, it may be unreasonable for that party to impose significant limitations or exclusions of liability. Note that this factor is set out in section 11(4) UCTA; all the other factors mentioned earlier can be found in Schedule 2 UCTA.

One of the peculiarities of UCTA is that it only *requires* the courts to consider these factors when looking at certain types of exemption clause. [You can find more detail on these drafting peculiarities on the companion website, together with details of the Law Commission's proposed reforms in this area.] However, in practice, the courts normally look at these factors whenever UCTA requires them to apply the reasonableness test.

The importance of bargaining power

The courts are generally more willing to find that an exemption clause is unreasonable where it is being relied on against a consumer. This is because consumers are seen as having weak bargaining power. In particular, they are not normally in a position to negotiate changes to the exemption clause and the supplier will generally be in a better position to bear the risk of something going wrong (see, further, Chapter 20, which deals with consumer protection).

In cases involving agreements between businesses, however, the courts have tended to place more emphasis on the need for inequality of bargaining power to justify a finding that a clause is unreasonable under UCTA. This is illustrated by the 'Reality check' textbox on **Watford v Sanderson (2001)**.

The outcome in *Watford v Sanderson* may be contrasted with **St Albans v ICL (1996)**, which also concerned a defective computer system (in this case, the system miscalculated council tax demands sent out by a local authority). Faced with a claim for damages from the local authority for £1.3 million, the supplier, ICL, relied on a clause limiting its liability to £100,000. The judge concluded that there was inequality of bargaining power in this case because most other suppliers imposed similar limitations of liability (so it was unlikely that the local authority

Reality check

Watford v Sanderson (2001)

Equal bargaining power = no help from UCTA

In this case, Watford purchased a computer system from Sanderson. The system did not work properly, causing considerable disruption to Watford's business and Watford eventually decided to purchase an entirely new system. Sanderson relied on an exemption clause limiting its liability to the contract price of just over £100,000 (Watford's claim was for more than £5 million). The Court of Appeal ruled that this clause was reasonable. One of the main reasons for its decision was the fact that Watford had succeeded in negotiating a significant improvement to the contract. This required Sanderson to use its 'best endeavours in allocating appropriate resources to the project to minimise any losses' before it could invoke the limitation of liability. In effect, this meant that Sanderson had to expend a reasonable amount of time and money on resolving the problems with the system before it would be entitled to rely on its exemption clause. The fact that Watford had been able to negotiate such a substantial concession showed that there was equality of bargaining power. The Court of Appeal stressed that where this was the case, the courts should be slow to interfere with what the parties themselves had agreed about how risk should be shared.

could have obtained a better deal elsewhere). ICL had also been able to put pressure on the local authority to sign up to the agreement by threatening to delay the project (which reinforced the judge's view that the local authority was not in a strong bargaining position).

As regards the exemption clause itself, the judge found that the £100,000 limit of liability was much smaller than the loss that the local authority would be likely to suffer if the system did not work properly. ICL also had insurance of £50 million and was clearly in a much better position than the local authority to bear the risk of something going wrong with the computer system.

> **QUESTION 4** Why didn't the Court of Appeal in *Watford v Sanderson* look more closely at issues such as insurance and whether it was reasonable for the customer to bear the risk?

Other reasonableness test factors

Although bargaining power is often an important factor in UCTA cases, it is not always decisive – particularly where the breach of contract in question is fairly serious and the exclusion itself is so wide as to deprive the claimant of any meaningful compensation. For example, in **George Mitchell v Finney Lock Seeds (1983)**, a farmer brought a claim against a seed company for supplying  him with the wrong seed (this had resulted in the farmer losing a cabbage crop that would have been worth over £60,000). The seed company relied on an exemption clause limiting its liability to the price of the seed, which was about £200. The House of Lords ruled that this clause was unreasonable. The main reasons for their decision were as follows:

- The limit of liability was very low when compared with the cost of the damage resulting from the seed company's mistake, which involved a serious case of negligence.
- The seed company could easily have obtained insurance against such mistakes being made.
- When this type of problem had occurred before, the seed company had often offered customers compensation payments that *exceeded* the price of the seed. This suggested it did not regard its own exemption clause as reasonable and implied that it had the resources to meet such claims.

Note that in this case, the court appears to have taken the view that the exemption clause was so destructive of the claimant's rights that equality of bargaining power was not the decisive factor. A further example of this is given in the 'Reality check' textbox on **Messer UK Ltd v Britvic (2002)**.

Reality check

Messer UK Ltd v Britvic (2002)

Bargaining power: not always decisive

In this case, carbon dioxide gas used for fizzy drinks was found to contain small amounts of a harmful chemical called benzene. No one was injured but large quantities of fizzy drinks had to be withdrawn from sale at a cost of several million pounds. The supplier of the gas relied on a clause limiting its liability to the cost of the gas supplied (which was far less than the cost of the product recall). In addition, any claim for gas of defective quality had to be brought within 5 days of delivery. The Court of Appeal ruled that this clause was unreasonable – even though there was equality of bargaining power. The supplier had not done enough to make it clear to its customers that it was seeking to exclude liability for gas even where it was unfit for human consumption (which was a very serious breach of contract). In addition, it might well take longer than 5 days for any contamination to become apparent – and if this requirement were upheld, liability for many claims would be not just limited, but completely excluded. As with the *George Mitchell* case, this is an example of a clause that was very destructive of the claimant's rights; as a result, equality of bargaining power was not the decisive factor.

QUESTION 5 Would the court in *Messer v Britvic* have reached a different conclusion if the exemption clause had contained a more generous limit of liability, such as £500,000, and no time limit on notifying claims?

UCTA and contracts with consumers: a summary

The application of UCTA to contracts where the supplier is a business and the customer is a consumer may be summarised as shown in Table 7.1.

Table 7.1 Application of UCTA to consumers

Type of liability excluded or limited	UCTA reference	Always void?	Other remarks
Death or personal injury due to negligence	Section 2(1)	Yes	—
Loss due to negligence other than personal injury or death	Section 2(2)	No	Subject to reasonableness test*
Loss due to breach of contract	Section 3	No	Subject to reasonableness test*
Loss due to breach of implied terms relating to goods under SGA or SOGASA	Sections 6–7	Yes	—

*Note that, because of consumers' weakness vis-à-vis suppliers, the reasonableness test is generally applied more strictly than is the case with business-to-business contracts.

UCTA and contracts between businesses: a summary

The application of UCTA to contracts involving businesses only (not consumers) may be summarised as shown in Table 7.2.

Table 7.2 Application of UCTA to businesses

Type of liability excluded or limited	UCTA reference	Always void?	Other remarks
Death or personal injury due to negligence	Section 2(1)	Yes	—
Loss due to negligence other than personal injury or death	Section 2(2)	No	Subject to reasonableness test
Loss due to breach of contract	Section 3	No	Only applies if contract is on standard written terms. Subject to reasonableness test
Loss due to breach of implied terms relating to goods under SGA or SOGASA	Sections 6–7	Only as regards attempts to limit/ exclude implied terms relating to title	Attempts to limit/ exclude implied terms other than those relating to title subject to reasonableness test

Answers to in-text questions

QUESTION 1 In order to be properly incorporated, is it always essential for exemption clauses in written contracts to have special attention drawn to them, e.g. by being printed in bold letters?

Not necessarily. In many cases it will be important for the party wishing to rely on the exemption clause to have made at least some attempt to draw attention to it (see discussion of cases such as *Thornton v Shoe Lane Parking* and *Interfoto v Stiletto* in Chapter 6). However, it is possible for exemption clauses to be incorporated in other ways. For example, the other party may have signed the agreement, which will be viewed by the courts as evidence that they have read it and are aware of its contents. Incorporation may also occur by means of a previous course of dealing (see Chapter 6).

QUESTION 2 In *Casson v Ostley*, would it have made any difference had Casson signed the contract?

No. When the courts look at construction, they are considering what a person who had read the agreement would understand from the words used. Since the terms of the agreement were unclear, the signature would not demonstrate that Casson had understood them as excluding Ostley's liability for fires caused by its own negligence; it would only show that Casson was aware of what the terms said. In the actual case itself, Casson accepted that the term had been properly incorporated.

> **QUESTION 3** Can a business or a consumer use section 7 UCTA to challenge an exclusion of liability for breach of section 13 SOGASA (implied term of reasonable skill and care)?

No. Section 7 only applies to the implied terms of SOGASA relating to goods, not services. Only sections 2 and 3 UCTA can be used to challenge such an exclusion. This is another of the peculiarities in the drafting of UCTA, as it is difficult to see why buyers of services should receive less favourable treatment than buyers of goods.

> **QUESTION 4** Why didn't the Court of Appeal in *Watford v Sanderson* look more closely at issues such as insurance and whether it was reasonable for the customer to bear the risk?

The Court of Appeal might have considered these factors in more detail had it been satisfied that there was inequality of bargaining power between the parties. However, in its view, the fact that the customer had managed to secure a significant concession indicated that the exemption clause was reasonable – and if it were not reasonable, it was the fault of the customer for not negotiating a better deal. In *St Albans v ICL*, by contrast, there was more evidence that the customer was in a weaker position. This led the court to look more closely at whether it was reasonable in the circumstances for ICL to limit its liability to £100,000. However, you should not assume that the supplier is always in a better position to insure than the customer. For example, in ***Photo Production v Securicor (1980)***, the House of Lords found that the owner of a factory was in as good a position to take out insurance against fire as the security firm that was guarding the premises (and, as a result, it was perfectly reasonable for the security firm to exclude its liability in the event of a fire). [You can find out more about this case on the companion website.]

> **QUESTION 5** Would the court in *Messer v Britvic* have reached a different conclusion if the exemption clause had contained a more generous limit of liability, such as £500,000, and no time limit on notifying claims?

Yes, in that case, the exemption clause might well have been upheld. Since the parties were found to have had equal bargaining power, a more generous clause would probably have been regarded as reasonable – even though the drinks manufacturer had incurred costs of several times that amount. The figure of £500,000 was discussed by the trial judge in relation to another clause in the contract and he concluded that it would have been a reasonable limit of liability (provided that any time limit on notifying claims was also more generous). The Court of Appeal did not take issue with the trial judge's findings on this point.

Discharge of contracts, performance and remedies for breach

By the end of this chapter, you should be able to explain:

- **The ways in which a contract may effectively come to an end (discharge of contracts)**

- **How the courts decide whether a contract has been properly carried out or whether one of the parties has breached the terms of the contract (performance and breach)**

- **What action may be taken where one of the parties has breached a term of the contract (remedies)**

Introduction

This chapter looks at how the courts decide whether a party has carried out its promises under a contract properly and, if not, what remedies may be available against that party. These topics are key to your understanding of contract law. As we saw in Chapter 3, the real value of a contract to a business is that the promises it contains are legally binding, so action can be taken in the courts if those promises are not met. This chapter explains when it may be possible to take such action and what the courts may do to enforce contracts.

Discharge of contracts

When the parties are no longer under any contractual obligations to one another, the contract is said to be **discharged**. This is an important concept because if a contract has been discharged, then a party to that contract cannot be sued for breach of any of its obligations under that contract (so no contractual remedies will be available). There are a number of ways in which contracts may be discharged.

Discharge by performance

If a person has carried out a promise under a contract properly, this is known as **discharge by performance**. Where there are no further obligations to perform under the contract, then the entire contract is said to be discharged (although as explained in the FAQ textbox, it is often quite difficult to say exactly *when* an entire contract has been completely discharged). Exactly what constitutes performance is discussed in more detail later.

Discharge by agreement

The parties may choose to bring their agreement to an end before its obligations have been fully performed; this is known as **discharge by agreement**. For example, a supplier of clothing based in the USA might appoint a UK firm as its exclusive distributor of its products for 5 years. However, 3 years into the contract, the US firm decides that it wants to appoint another UK firm instead. If the US firm simply terminated the contract with 2 years to go, it could be sued by the UK distributor for breach of contract. Rather than get into a lengthy and potentially expensive legal dispute, it offers the UK firm a substantial compensation payment. Both parties enter into an agreement under which the US firm agrees to pay this sum in return for the UK firm's agreeing to bring the distribution agreement to an end. Both parties would normally agree that their obligations under that contract were discharged (even though the contract had a further 2 years to run). This is known as a **bilateral discharge** (because both parties are giving up rights and neither has performed all its obligations under the contract).

A **unilateral discharge** occurs where one party has already performed all its obligations and the other party wants to be released from its remaining obligations. For example, where a customer has paid a supplier for goods, it will normally have discharged all its obligations – but the supplier is likely to be subject to a number of obligations that will continue for some time after payment has been made, e.g. promises as to the quality of the goods. The supplier can only be discharged from those obligations if it provides some consideration in return for

 FAQ

At what point will a contract be discharged by performance?

As explained already, a contract may be discharged when all its obligations have been carried out. However, in practice, many contracts between businesses will not be fully discharged for some time after the main obligations have been completed. For example, if a supplier of computer equipment has delivered some hardware on time and been paid in full by its customer, the obligations under the contract relating to delivery and payment will have been discharged – but this does not necessarily mean that the contract itself is at an end. The supplier may well have made various promises about the quality of the equipment supplied. It may also have agreed to keep certain information about the customer's business confidential. Although neither of these obligations is likely to last forever, they are likely to remain legally binding for some time after the date of delivery (exactly how long will depend on a variety of matters, such as what the contract says and the circumstances in which it was entered into).

the customer's promise to release it from those remaining obligations, e.g. it would have to pay a sum of money or provide some other benefit to the customer that would qualify as sufficient consideration. Lawyers refer to this as **accord and satisfaction** (accord refers to the customer's agreement to discharge the supplier's obligations and satisfaction to the consideration provided by the supplier).

Discharge by breach

As we saw in Chapter 6, a breach of a term that is a condition of the contract means that the other party may not only sue for damages but can repudiate the contract as well; the whole contract will therefore be discharged by the breach. However, if the term that has been breached is only a warranty, the innocent party may not repudiate the contract (so it will not be discharged) and will normally only be able to sue for damages.

Discharge by frustration

In certain, very limited, circumstances, the courts may be prepared to regard a contract as discharged because – as a result of factors beyond the control of the parties – it has become illegal or virtually impossible to perform the contract as originally envisaged. This is known as **frustration**.

Examples of frustrating events

Frustration may occur in a variety of circumstances, including the following:

- *Supervening illegality*: the courts will not uphold a contract that is illegal (see Chapter 10 for more detail). If a contract was legal to start with but becomes illegal as a result of a change in the law, it will be frustrated. The change in the law is referred to as a **supervening event**, i.e. something that happened after the contract was entered into but before it could be fully performed.

- *Government intervention*: similarly, if the government intervenes to prevent a contract being discharged, e.g. by requisitioning equipment in time of war, the contract may be frustrated.

- *Death, illness or imprisonment*: if the contract can only be performed by a particular individual, then death, illness or imprisonment may result in its being frustrated. For example, in ***Robinson v Davison (1871)***, a piano player was unable to perform due to illness; as a result, the contract for the performance was frustrated.

- *Destruction or unavailability of the subject matter*: if something vital to performance of a contract is destroyed or becomes unavailable, the contract may be frustrated. For example, in ***Taylor v Caldwell (1863)***, a contract for hire of a theatre was frustrated when the theatre burnt down after the contract had been entered into (but before it had been fully performed).

- *Non-occurrence of event*: similarly, if an event that is central to performance of a contract fails to occur, the contract may be frustrated. For example, in ***Krell v Henry (1903)***, a contract for hire of a hotel room to view a procession at the time of the king's coronation was frustrated when the coronation itself had to be postponed; the postponement meant that there was nothing to see from the room, which removed the whole object of the contract. However, in **Herne Bay Steamboat v Hutton (1903)**, the postponement of the coronation did *not* frustrate a contract for hire of a boat to see the British navy, which had assembled to mark the occasion. This was because, in contrast to *Krell v Henry*, postponement did not remove the main object of the contract, which was to see the ships (despite the postponement, the fleet had not dispersed, so it could still be viewed from a boat).

Key characteristics of a frustrating event

There are three common factors in all these situations: (i) the frustrating event occurred after the contract had been entered into; (ii) it was outside the control of the parties; and (iii) it was not dealt with in the contract itself.

For example, in *Taylor v Caldwell*, if the theatre had burnt down *before* the contract was made, the contract would not have been frustrated – because there would have been no contract to frustrate. Instead, the contract would probably have been void for mistake, which is explained in Chapter 9. Similarly, if the owner of the theatre had burnt it down himself in order to claim the insurance money, the courts would not have accepted that the contract had been frustrated because such an act would have been within the control of the owner (and the hirer could have sued him for breach of contract). Finally, the same would have been true if the terms of the contract had dealt with what should happen in the event of a fire; instead of viewing the contract as being frustrated, the courts would have followed what the contract said. Clauses of this type are known as 'force majeure' clauses. [More material on such clauses and on frustration generally can be found on the companion website.]

Frustration: the 'radical change' test

It is not a requirement of frustration that the contract should have become completely impossible to perform; a contract can be frustrated where it is still possible to carry it out in theory but 'the circumstances in which performance is called for would render it a thing radically different from that which was undertaken by the contract...'. This test was developed following the case of **Davis Contractors v Fareham UDC (1956)**, where a firm of builders failed to complete some houses on time owing to a combination of bad weather and labour shortages. The House of Lords ruled that where a contract had become more difficult or expensive to perform, that would not normally be sufficient to invoke frustration. The discussion in the textbox headed '11 September 2001' shows how difficult it can be to show that the 'radical change' test is met in practice.

> **QUESTION 1** Can you think of any situations that would meet the 'radical change' test? Think about some of the established cases of frustration mentioned earlier.

Effects of frustration

Often, a frustrated contract will be only partly performed, e.g. one party may have carried out part of its obligations but may not have been paid by the other party. Under the Law Reform (Frustrated Contracts) Act 1943, however, the courts can order the other party to make a payment corresponding to the benefit it has received (and if a payment has been made in advance but no benefit provided in

Reality check

11 September 2001

Could airlines have invoked frustration after the 9/11 terrorist attacks?

Following the terrorist attacks on the USA on 11 September 2001, many insurers either withdrew terrorism cover from airlines or imposed very significant increases in insurance premiums. This created considerable difficulties for airlines. For example, most airlines registered in the UK are required to have minimum levels of insurance (so it would have been illegal for them to operate without it). Airlines who were not subject to this requirement were still affected by the situation because they rented their planes from aircraft-leasing companies (and the terms of their aircraft leases obliged them to take adequate insurance policies). You might have thought that this would be a situation where the airlines could have refused to honour their contracts with their customers on the basis that those contracts had been frustrated by events beyond their control. However, as the law on frustration currently stands, it could well have been difficult for airlines to succeed with this argument. They might have been able to do so if insurers had withdrawn cover altogether, because this would have made it illegal for many of them to fly. However, it was not *impossible* to obtain insurance – it had simply become a great deal more expensive to do so. This meant that the contracts could still have been performed, although at much greater cost. As we have seen, the mere fact that a contract has become more expensive or difficult to perform is not normally sufficient for the courts to decide that it is frustrated. In fact, the airlines did not need to argue that their contracts with customers had been frustrated because governments stepped in to help provide additional insurance cover for terrorist attacks (at much lower cost to the airlines).

Beams of light commemorating those who died in the 9/11 attack on the World Trade Center

return, the courts can order some or all of the money to be repaid). For example, in **BP Exploration v Hunt (1982)**, a contract for development of an oilfield was frustrated when the Libyan government nationalised its oil industry. Hunt was paid some compensation by the Libyan government, but BP (which had agreed to develop the oil field in return for a 50% share of the revenues) was left out of pocket by $35 million. It was able to claim this sum from Hunt under the 1943 Act.

Performance

As we have seen, one of the means by which a contract can be discharged is by **performance**. A person cannot be successfully sued for breach of his contractual obligations if he can show that he has properly discharged those obligations by performance. It is therefore essential to know what the courts regard as proper performance of a contract.

Performance: the general rule

The general rule is that contracts must be performed strictly in accordance with their terms – although this can sometimes have harsh effects. For example, in **Cutter v Powell (1756)**, Lieutenant Cutter was employed as part of the crew of a ship, but died before the end of the voyage. His contract with the captain, Powell, said that Cutter was obliged to complete the voyage before he would be paid. On behalf of her husband's estate, Cutter's widow brought an action against Powell for breach of his promise to pay for Cutter's services. The court ruled that Powell was not in breach; since Cutter had not fulfilled his obligations under the contract, no payment was due.

In view of the potential harshness of the rule in *Cutter v Powell*, Parliament and the courts have developed a number of ways of alleviating its effects. For example, if Cutter's case were to come before the courts today, his wife would be able to argue that the contract had been frustrated as a result of Cutter's death. His estate would be entitled to payment of a proportion of his salary under the Law Reform (Frustrated Contracts) Act 1943, based on the benefits he had provided to his employer up to the time of his death (see earlier, under the heading 'Discharge by frustration'). Other ways in which the potential harshness of the general rule on performance may be alleviated are explained in the 'Reality check' textbox highlighting **Morse Group Ltd v Cognesis Ltd (2003)** and under following sections.

Divisible contracts

The contract in *Cutter v Powell* was an **entire contract**, i.e. one where payment only became due on completion of all obligations. However, a contract may be a **divisible contract**, i.e. payment is made in a series of instalments, rather than in a single lump sum on completion. This means that if a party fails to do everything he is supposed to do, he is still entitled to be paid those instalments that

Reality check

Morse Group Ltd v Cognesis Ltd (2003)

Failure to perform – whose fault?

If one party prevents another party from performing its obligations, the courts will not normally allow that to be used as a justification for withholding payment. For example, in *Morse Group v Cognesis (2003)*, Cognesis ordered a computer server and a power supply unit from Morse. The power supply unit could not be used as it had not been installed properly. As a result, Cognesis refused to pay for any of the equipment. Eventually, the parties reached an agreement to settle their dispute. This required Morse to install the power supply unit properly and deliver some additional computer equipment. Morse supplied the extra equipment but Cognesis refused to let it install the power supply unit (because by that time, it had decided that it no longer needed the server). It refused to pay Morse, which issued proceedings to enforce payment. Cognesis argued that (as in *Cutter v Powell*) payment was conditional on Morse fulfilling all its obligations under the settlement agreement. Morse argued that it was Cognesis' refusal to allow it to install the PSU that had prevented it fulfilling all its obligations. The judge ruled that Morse was entitled to payment; although, strictly speaking, Morse had not been able to fulfil its obligation to install the power supply unit, this was entirely due to Cognesis' lack of cooperation.

have already become due. For example, in *Morse v Cognesis* (see earlier textbox), the judge noted that Morse's standard terms stated that it did not have to fulfil all its obligations in order to be paid; it was therefore entitled to payment for the additional equipment that Cognesis had ordered on delivery of that equipment (and did not have to wait until it had fulfilled its obligation to install the power supply unit).

> **QUESTION 2** Would it have helped Cutter's wife had the contract not said that payment was conditional on Cutter's completing the voyage?

Substantial performance

The harshness of the rule in *Cutter v Powell* may also be alleviated by the doctrine of **substantial performance**. This prevents a party from refusing to make any payment at all where the other party has carried out the majority of its obligations satisfactorily. For example, in ***Hoenig v Isaacs (1952)***, a customer refused to pay for redecoration of a flat because of a problem with the length of a bookcase and a defective wardrobe door. Since these problems were fairly minor, the court ruled that the decorator was entitled to be paid the remainder of the contract price (£350), less the cost of correcting the problems (about £55). However, it is unlikely that the doctrine of substantial performance would have assisted in *Cutter v Powell*, because at the time of Cutter's death, a substantial part of the voyage (about one-third) still had to be completed.

Acceptance of part-performance

As we have seen, it is possible for a contractual obligation to be discharged by agreement – even where the obligation has not been fully performed (see 'Discharge by agreement', earlier). For example, in *Morse v Cognesis* (see earlier textbox), Cognesis could have agreed that it would accept the server and pay for it but return the power supply unit. By accepting **part-performance** in place of full performance, Cognesis would have released Morse from the obligation to deliver and install the power supply unit (and Morse would have released Cognesis from the obligation to pay for the power supply unit). If Cognesis had refused to pay for the server, it would not have been able to use Morse's failure to install the power supply unit as a justification.

However, the innocent party must be in a position to choose whether to accept the part-performance. For example, in ***Sumpter v Hedges (1898)***, a builder agreed to build a barn but failed to complete it. The customer finished the barn himself, using some of the builder's materials. The builder tried to claim payment for the work that he had done. He argued that the customer was not entitled to refuse payment because he had accepted part-performance of the contract. The court indicated that it might have been prepared to accept this argument if the customer had been offered a choice of continuing with the builder or accepting part-performance. But in fact, the builder had simply abandoned the project, leaving the customer no choice but to finish the work himself. As a result, the builder was not entitled to be paid for the work he had done, although he was able to claim for the cost of the materials that the customer had used (because the customer had a choice as to whether he used those materials or bought his own).

Remedies for breach of contract

Where one party is in breach of a contract, the following remedies may be available to the innocent party (each of these is explained in more detail later):

- *Repudiation*: this remedy allows the innocent party to terminate the contract immediately, but it is only possible if there has been a breach of condition.
- *Damages*: this remedy allows the innocent party to seek financial compensation for loss that it may have suffered as a result of a breach of contract.
- *Equitable remedies*: these include orders made by the court such as injunctions. However, they are generally only available in quite limited circumstances, usually where damages would not be an adequate remedy.

Note that the word **rescission** is sometimes used in cases and some textbooks in place of repudiation. Strictly speaking, this is incorrect; repudiation is a common law remedy, whereas rescission is an equitable remedy requiring an order of court (see Chapter 9).

Time limits for legal action

Under the Limitation Act 1980, legal action cannot be brought in relation to a contract if more than 6 years have gone by since the date of the breach. Normally, this gives parties a reasonable amount of time in which to decide whether to bring a claim. However, this may not be the case where the breach occurred at the very beginning of the contract, but did not become apparent until much later. For example, if a building has not been constructed properly, the breach will have been committed when the building was first put up – but any buyer of the property may not become aware of the problem until much later, quite possibly more than 6 years after buying it. This may mean that the buyer needs to consider other remedies, such as the tort of negligence, where the limitation period runs from the date of awareness of the breach rather than the date of the breach itself.

Repudiation

Repudiation allows the innocent party to terminate (or **repudiate**) the contract with immediate effect. It is only possible where there has been a breach of a condition (which is said to be a 'repudiatory breach'). There is no need to apply to court for permission to exercise this remedy; the innocent party may repudiate by words or conduct, provided that it is clear to the other party that there is an intention to terminate the contract. Following repudiation, the contract is at an end and both parties' obligations are discharged, but the innocent party can still claim damages for losses resulting from the breach.

Breach of condition

We have already seen how the terms implied by the Sale of Goods Act 1979, for example, are regarded as conditions – so breach of them may allow the buyer to reject the goods and repudiate the contract (see Chapter 6). However, it is not

IJS Contractors v DEW Construction

Breach of safety standards – a repudiatory breach?

In *IJS Contractors v DEW Construction (2000)*, the claimant was engaged to refurbish railway stations. Although there was no written contract, the parties had agreed that safety standards were very important. Three of the claimant's staff were found to have smoked marijuana during a tea break. The defendant argued that this could have affected safety and was such a serious breach that it was entitled to repudiate the contract. The

Court of Appeal accepted that there had been a breach of contract, given the importance attached to safety standards. However, the contract had not made it clear that the defendant should have the right to repudiate in these circumstances. It was therefore necessary to look at the effect of the breach. The Court of Appeal noted that the claimant had reacted swiftly by dismissing the staff involved and no evidence had been provided of a danger to the public. In view of this, it could not be said that the breach deprived the defendant of 'substantially the whole benefit of the contract' (as required by the *Hong Kong Fir* case); for example, there was no suggestion that the breach of safety standards meant that refurbishment work could not continue in the manner envisaged by the parties.

always easy to decide whether a term is a condition. Sometimes it is clear from the agreement that the term was particularly important to the parties and that a breach of it (even though it might seem a trivial breach to an outsider) should entitle the innocent party to repudiate (because that is what the agreement says). In cases where the status of the term as a condition is not clear from the agreement, it will depend on the nature and consequences of the breach – as illustrated by the *Hong Kong Fir* case (see Chapter 6) and by **IJS Contractors v Dew Construction (2000)** highlighted in the 'Reality check' textbox.

Problems with repudiation

This last case also illustrates how the innocent party runs a risk when it repudiates a contract. If it turns out that it was not entitled to repudiate (because, for example, the breach was not sufficiently serious to be a breach of condition), the innocent party can be sued for wrongful termination of the contract. In practice, however, other terms of the contract may help to resolve this problem. Many contracts contain express provisions allowing a party to terminate for 'material' breach of any term, not just a condition. Such provisions will often allow the contract to be terminated for less serious breaches. The main difference is that these provisions normally require the innocent party to give the other party a period of time in which to rectify the problem (e.g. 30 days) and the contract is only terminated after expiry of that period. The right to repudiate, by way of contrast, allows a party to terminate the contract with immediate effect.

Affirmation

If a party wishes to repudiate a contract, the courts normally expect that party to do so promptly and not to act in a way that is inconsistent with an intention to terminate the contract. Failure to do so may lead to the innocent party being regarded as having affirmed its willingness to proceed with the contract. Such an

affirmation means the right to repudiate will be lost. See, for example, the case of *Jones v Gallagher* (discussed in Chapter 6), where the court ruled that a couple had lost the right to reject a kitchen because they had delayed too long before rejecting it and had used the kitchen in the meantime.

Equally, there may be situations where an innocent party has a right to repudiate, but would prefer to affirm. However, an innocent party can only do this if it has a legitimate interest in proceeding with the contract. This may cause problems where one party commits an **anticipatory breach** of contract, i.e. it decides that it does not want to proceed with the contract before the innocent party has begun to carry out its obligations. An example is given in the textbox that follows.

Anticipatory breach and affirmation

In *Clea Shipping v Bulk Oil International (1984)*, Bulk Oil decided that it did not want to proceed with an agreement to charter a ship from Clea. Bulk Oil had therefore committed an anticipatory breach. Clea could have repudiated the contract. However, Clea decided to affirm the contract and spent £800,000 on refitting the ship and keeping a crew on standby ready for the charter. The court ruled that an innocent party may only affirm a contract in response to an anticipatory breach of this nature if it has a legitimate interest in proceeding with the contract. In this case, the court noted that after the charter period had ended, Clea had sold the vessel for scrap. It concluded that Clea had decided to proceed with the contract in order to inflate the damages it could claim if the customer refused to pay; this was not a legitimate reason for proceeding. The proper course of action for Clea would have been to repudiate the contract and look for another customer. If none could be found, it would have been able to claim damages from Bulk Oil for its loss of profit on the charter (but not for the costs of carrying out the contract, such as maintaining the crew on standby, since these costs would not have been incurred).

QUESTION 3 In *White & Carter v McGregor (1961)*, a garage owner decided not to proceed with a contract for advertising his business on notices attached to council litterbins. Do you think the innocent party was able to affirm the contract and proceed with it?

Damages

As we have seen, the circumstances in which a party can repudiate a contract tend to be fairly limited. Damages, however, are available in a much wider range of circumstances (whether or not the innocent party has a right to repudiate). Unlike repudiation, however, they can only be obtained by applying to court for an order against the party in breach, requiring financial compensation to be paid to the innocent party.

Damages for breach of contract are intended to put the innocent party in the position it would have been in had the contract been performed properly. However, there are a number of factors that limit the size of damages awards. These are now explained.

Remoteness of damage

Damages may only be claimed for loss that the party in breach either knew about or could reasonably have foreseen at the time the contract was made. This principle, which is known as **remoteness of damage**, was set out in ***Hadley v Baxendale (1854)***, where a mill shaft had to be sent to London to be used as a model for manufacturing a new shaft. There was a delay in returning the shaft, so the mill was out of use for longer than had been expected. The owner of the mill claimed damages for loss of profits over that period. The court ruled that the firm responsible for transporting the shaft was not liable for these losses, because there was nothing to indicate that the mill owner was relying on return of the shaft in order to resume production. This loss was said to be too remote. Another example of the application of these principles is highlighted in the following FAQ textbox.

 FAQ

What sort of damage would *not* be too remote?

A distinction is often made between losses relating to the usual business activities of the innocent party (for which damages can normally be claimed) and losses relating to any unusual activities (for which damages can only be claimed if the party in breach actually knew about them). This is well illustrated by Victoria Laundry v Newman Industries (1949), in which a boiler manufacturer was late delivering a new, larger boiler to a laundry. The manufacturer knew that the laundry was intending to use the boiler to expand its capacity and it knew what kind of business the laundry usually carried out. It was therefore liable to pay damages for the normal additional business that a laundry of that expanded size would have been expected to take on over that period. However, the laundry had also wanted the boiler in order to carry out some dyeing contracts. These were considerably more profitable than the laundry's normal business. The court ruled that the loss of these contracts was too remote to be claimed in damages. This was because the manufacturer had not been made specifically aware of them and could not have foreseen them (because they were not the laundry's usual type of business).

> **QUESTION 4** In the *Victoria Laundry* case, would it have made any difference had the boiler manufacturer been told about the dyeing contracts *after the contract was made*?

Mitigation

A second factor limiting the amount of damages that can be claimed is the duty of the innocent party to pursue **mitigation** of loss. This requires the innocent party to take all reasonable steps to minimise its loss. The principle was set out in

British Westinghouse Electric and Manufacturing Co v Underground Electric Railways Co of London Ltd (1912). It is well illustrated by the case of *Messer v Britvic (2002)*, which has been referred to before in Chapter 7. In that case, carbon dioxide gas supplied by Messer was contaminated with small amounts of a harmful chemical. This led Britvic to withdraw large quantities of its drinks from sale. In acting swiftly to withdraw them, Britvic was complying with its duty to mitigate its loss. Had it failed to act, its losses would probably have been even higher than they were because the damage to its brand and reputation would have led to further lost sales.

> **QUESTION 5** Returning to the topic of remoteness of damage, do you think that lost sales arising from damage to a firm's brand would be too remote?

Causation

A third factor that may limit the amount of damages that can be claimed is the requirement for the claimant to prove beyond reasonable doubt that the loss suffered was actually caused by the breach. This may sound obvious, but it can sometimes be quite difficult to establish. For example, in the *Britvic* case referred to earlier, Britvic argued that – despite its swift action in withdrawing products from sale – it had suffered a certain amount of damage to its brand, which had depressed sales in the period immediately after the product recall. However, there were a number of other possible explanations for this state of affairs. These included poor weather over the summer (leading to lower sales of canned drinks) and the launch of a highly successful new drink, Sunny D, by a competitor. The court was not convinced that the contamination incident was the main cause of the lower sales. As a result, Britvic was unable to pursue the lost sales element of its damages claim, which was worth £6 million (although it did succeed in recovering the costs of the product recall, which were about £2 million).

Loss must be quantifiable

The fourth factor limiting the amount that may be awarded as damages is the rule that any losses being claimed must normally be quantifiable in financial terms. For example, in the *Britvic* case, it was reasonably straightforward to demonstrate the costs of the product recall. However, if Britvic had attempted to claim damages for loss of staff morale, it would have been much more difficult to put a value on this.

Similarly, the courts have traditionally been averse to awarding damages for emotional distress or disappointment, because it is extremely difficult to put a value on a state of mind. However, more recently, the courts have allowed parties to claim damages for distress or disappointment where one of the main aims of the agreement was to provide pleasure, relaxation or peace of mind. This may include contracts for holidays, meals in restaurants or taxi rides. Two examples are outlined in the following case study textbox.

Damages for disappointment or distress

In *Jarvis v Swan Tours (1973)*, a skiing holiday failed dismally to measure up to the description in the brochure. Instead of a lively 'house party' atmosphere, Mr Jarvis was the only person there in the second week. The bar was hardly ever open, the skiing facilities were poor, 'afternoon tea' meant a few crisps and nut cakes and, worst of all, the 'yodelling evening' was well below expectations. In recognition of his disappointment, he was awarded damages equivalent to the full cost of the holiday. In *Farley v Skinner (2001)*, the House of Lords ruled that damages could be claimed from a surveyor who had failed to check the level of aircraft noise affecting a property, despite being specifically asked to do so by the prospective buyer. The House of Lords ruled that the trial judge's award of £10,000 should be upheld, although it acknowledged that it was difficult to put a price on the irritation caused to the buyer by the aircraft noise.

Loss of amenity

Where damages are claimed for **loss of amenity** (e.g. the loss of a facility that the claimant expected to have as a result of the contract), the size of the award must bear some relation to the benefit that it will bring to the claimant. For example, in *Ruxley Electronics & Construction v Forsyth (1995)*, a swimming pool was found to be slightly shallower than the buyer had wanted. Normally, the damages for such a breach would be assessed by reference to the cost of correcting the defect – and in the vast majority of cases, the courts are content to follow this method. However, in this case, the only way to rectify the problem would have been to rebuild the pool at a cost of about £40,000. The House of Lords ruled that such an award would be out of all proportion to the benefit that the claimant would obtain from rebuilding the pool. Instead, the claimant should be awarded a sum to reflect the fact that, although he had a perfectly usable swimming pool, it was not quite as deep as he had wanted. The House of Lords agreed with the trial judge who had awarded him £2500.

Dealing with damages in the contract

It is also possible for parties to include provisions in their contract dealing with damages. For example, a supplier wishing to limit the amount of damages it may have to pay could include exclusion and limitation clauses (provided these comply with the rules outlined in Chapter 7). Equally, a customer wishing to avoid having to go to court to claim damages from a supplier may include a **liquidated damages clause**. Such clauses require the party in breach to pay a specified sum to the other party if there is a breach of contract, so in theory there is no need for the injured party to go to court to have the amount of damages assessed. However, the courts will only enforce liquidated damages clauses if they represent a 'genuine pre-estimate' of the damage likely to be suffered by the injured party. This requires the courts to look at what the parties knew at the time they made the agreement. They must then decide whether the liquidated damages clause was based on a reasonable assessment of the amount that the injured party would stand to lose if there were a breach of contract. The principle was developed in

Reality check

Jeancharm v Barnet FC (2003)

Penalty disallowed

In *Jeancharm v Barnet FC (2003)*, Jeancharm had agreed to supply Barnet FC with football kit. The contract contained a liquidated damages clause stating that, if Barnet failed to pay on time, Jeancharm could claim interest on any outstanding amounts. Although such clauses are quite common, this particular clause imposed an interest rate of about 260% per year, which had the effect of quadrupling the amount owed by Barnet. While Jeancharm had clearly lost out as a result of Barnet's late payment, it was extremely unlikely that it could have earned an interest rate of 260% on the money, had it been paid on time. As a result, the Court of Appeal ruled that the clause did not represent a 'genuine pre-estimate' of Jeancharm's loss (as required by the *Dunlop* case) and could not be enforced. This case also demonstrates that liquidated damages clauses do not necessarily prevent the parties ending up in court; while they may offer a means of claiming compensation without seeking an award of damages from a court, the other party will often challenge the enforceability of the clause on the grounds that it amounts to a penalty.

Like David Beckham at Euro 2004, football kit manufacturer Jeancharm were unable to penalise

Dunlop Pneumatic Tyre Co v New Garage & Motor Co (1915), but a more recent example is outlined in the following 'Reality check' textbox.

Equitable remedies

As explained in Chapter 1, the courts' equitable powers enable them to make orders that would not generally be available under common law (and that alleviate some of the harshness that would result from strict adherence to the common law position). A number of equitable remedies may be available for breach of contract, including:

- *Specific performance*: a court order compelling the party in breach to do something, such as transfer the shares in a limited company.

- *Injunction*: a court order that prohibits the party in breach from doing something, such as not taking any steps to sell the shares in a limited company to anyone else.

The equitable remedy of rescission, which is a court order setting the contract aside, is discussed in more detail in Chapter 9. Unlike damages (which the court is obliged to order, provided the conditions for such an award are met), these remedies are only available where the court believes that it is 'just and equitable' to award them. In particular, the court must normally be satisfied that:

- damages would not be an adequate remedy

- the innocent party has acted without delay and has 'clean hands', i.e. he or she has acted reasonably and honestly
- the equitable remedy will not cause undue hardship or be especially difficult to supervise or enforce.

Damages not an adequate remedy

Imagine that you have agreed to buy a very rare second-hand car, which is the only one in the country. The seller then refuses to hand over the keys and says that he wants to keep the car. An award of damages could compensate you for the money you have had to spend negotiating the agreement and any money you have already paid to the seller. If this were not a very rare car, an award of damages is all that you would be able to obtain, because the courts would expect you to use the damages to go out and find a replacement vehicle (which should not be too difficult). However, in this case, the car is almost unique, so it is likely to be extremely difficult to find a replacement. In these circumstances, the courts may be prepared to make an order for specific performance compelling the seller to honour the agreement and sell the car. The key point to note here is that the situations where damages are not an adequate remedy are fairly limited; the majority of breaches of contract are capable of being compensated financially. An example of an injunction being awarded in a situation where damages were not an adequate remedy is shown in the 'Reality check' textbox below.

Delay and clean hands

In Chapter 1, we saw how equitable rules had their origins in the Court of Chancery, where the judges were clergymen. This resulted in a greater focus on

Reality check

Sainsbury's v British Airways

Damages no substitute for customer loyalty

In **Sainsbury's Supermarkets Ltd v British Airways plc (2002)**, Sainsbury's had an agreement with BA that allowed Sainsbury's customers to exchange their loyalty card points for airmiles. The agreement was exclusive to Sainsbury's (which meant that BA could not offer airmiles to competing supermarkets). Although the agreement was not due to end until March 2002, BA announced in January 2002 that in future it would instead be supplying airmiles to Sainsbury's rival, Tesco – and that Tesco's customers would be able to use points they had acquired *before* March 2002 in order to qualify

for airmiles. Sainsbury's obtained an injunction preventing BA from granting airmiles to customers of Tesco based on points acquired before March 2002. The court ruled that the point of its loyalty scheme was to encourage customers to buy more at Sainsbury's – and its contract with BA had been made on the understanding that BA would not allow other supermarkets, such as Tesco, to offer airmiles to customers in the same way during the term of the agreement. Damages were not considered to be an adequate remedy because it would be quite difficult for Sainsbury's to show exactly what its loss would be; for example, it would be hard to prove beyond reasonable doubt that customers had bought less or had shopped at Tesco as a result of BA's breach. In addition, it was clearly unjust that BA should be paid for provision of airmiles on a non-exclusive basis when it had promised to give Sainsbury's exclusivity.

the moral behaviour of the parties, which is why equitable remedies will only be applied if the person seeking the remedy has acted promptly and behaved fairly; in particular, he must not have contributed to the situation in which he finds himself. By way of illustration, returning to the earlier example of the rare second-hand car, the court might refuse specific performance if there were evidence that the buyer had changed his mind several times about proceeding with the contract and the sale had been delayed for months as a result; in those circumstances, the court might well decide that the buyer only had himself to blame if the seller had decided not to proceed. While the court could not prevent the buyer claiming damages, it might not be prepared to order specific performance.

Supervision and enforcement

The court must also be satisfied that the equitable remedy will not cause undue hardship or be especially difficult to supervise or enforce. For example, if an employee breaches his employment contract, the courts will usually refuse requests for specific performance to compel the employee to go on working. Such an order would normally be viewed as an unreasonable restriction of personal freedom. In some cases, it might also prove difficult to supervise because it could require repeated intervention from the court. This will be the case even where damages would not be an adequate remedy for the employer.

Answers to in-text questions

> **QUESTION 1** Can you think of any situations that would meet the 'radical change' test? Think about some of the established cases of frustration mentioned earlier.

It is possible to draw analogies with some of the earlier cases concerning frustrating events. For instance, in *Krell v Henry*, the postponement of the coronation meant that a contract that was originally intended to be for hire of a viewing point for this event turned into a contract for hire of a hotel room overlooking nothing of any particular significance. It could therefore be said that the frustrating event in this case rendered the obligation to hire the hotel room 'a thing radically different' from what the parties had originally contracted for.

> **QUESTION 2** Would it have helped Cutter's wife had the contract not said that payment was conditional on Cutter's completing the voyage?

Very probably. If Cutter's contract had not made it clear that payment was conditional on completing the voyage, then it would probably have been payable on a weekly or monthly basis; the contract would thus have been divisible and his wife could have claimed payment of all the instalments up to the date of his death.

> **QUESTION 3** In *White & Carter v McGregor (1961)*, a garage owner decided not to proceed with a contract for advertising his business on notices attached to council litterbins. Do you think the innocent party was able to affirm the contract and proceed with it?

Rather surprisingly, the House of Lords decided that the innocent party *was* entitled to proceed. The logic of the decision is difficult to follow, as it is hard to see how the innocent party was pursuing a legitimate purpose in doing so (especially as it could probably have found other customers for its advertising services). It may be that the House of Lords was concerned that a different outcome would have been taken as an encouragement to businesses to commit anticipatory breaches of contract. However, it seems likely that in most situations of this type, the courts will find reasons to avoid having to reach the same outcome as the House of Lords in *White & Carter* and will follow the approach in *Clea Shipping* instead.

> **QUESTION 4** In the *Victoria Laundry* case, would it have made any difference had the boiler manufacturer been told about the dyeing contracts *after the contract was made*?

No – the **test** is what the parties knew or could reasonably have foreseen *at the time the contract was made*. This is because the awareness of the parties at that point may well affect the bargain they make. For example, if the boiler manufacturer had either known or could reasonably have foreseen that the laundry was taking on contracts that were more lucrative than its normal business activities, it might well have insisted on a higher price (owing to the increased risk involved were something to go wrong). This point was underlined more recently by the House of Lords in **Jackson v Royal Bank of Scotland (2004)**, which you can read about on the companion website.

> **QUESTION 5** Returning to the topic of remoteness of damage, do you think that lost sales arising from damage to a firm's brand would be too remote to be claimed as damages?

It is not very hard to see that there will often be a relationship between damage to a brand and lost sales. As a result, such losses would probably be reasonably foreseeable and therefore capable of being claimed as damages. This was particularly so in the *Britvic* case because people in the drinks industry would have been aware of a similar contamination incident involving the French mineral water Perrier, which was generally thought to have caused short-term damage to Perrier's reputation and affected sales of its products. However, just because damages can be claimed as a matter of law does not mean that they will actually be awarded. The claimant must show that there is a causal link between the damage to its reputation and the lost sales. In the *Britvic* case, the court concluded that Britvic's product recall exercise appeared to have been successful in reassuring the public and that its lower than expected sales could be explained by other factors, such as poor weather and competition from other manufacturers.

9 | Validity of contracts (1)

Learning objectives

By the end of this chapter, you should be able to explain:

- **How the validity of a contract may be affected where misleading statements were made before the contract was entered into (misrepresentation)**

- **How the validity may be affected where one or more of the parties entered into the contract based on a fundamental misunderstanding (mistake)**

Introduction

This chapter explores a number of different situations that can affect the validity of a contract – even though the other 'key ingredients' of a legally binding agreement (as explained in Chapters 3, 4 and 5) are present. The effect on the contract varies, depending on the problem with its validity. However, the common feature of all the situations examined in this chapter is that they may affect the ability of parties to enforce their rights under a contract.

Misrepresentation

In Chapter 6, we looked at how a **pre-contractual representation** can sometimes (although not very often) be regarded as a term of the contract – and when answering questions that are concerned with pre-contractual representations, you should always consider this possibility. A more common situation is where misleading statements are made in the course of negotiations but are not incorporated into the contract itself. Although the maker of the statement cannot be sued for breach of contract, the injured party will still be able to make a claim in **misrepresentation**, provided the following conditions are met:

- A reasonable person in the position of the injured party would have regarded the representation as one that was based on facts, rather than a mere expression of opinion (with no basis in fact).
- The representation was false.
- The injured party believed it to be true.
- The representation was one of the reasons why the injured party entered into the agreement.

A recent example – Nelson Group Services v BG plc (2002) – is highlighted in the 'Reality check' textbox.

What is a representation?

As we have seen, a statement made in negotiations (such as the sales forecasts in *Nelson v BG*) may amount to misrepresentation. The statement can be written or oral. But words are not necessarily required; a representation may also be made by the conduct of the parties.

For example, in **Spice Girls v Aprilia World Service (2002)**, the Spice Girls pop group agreed to appear in an advertising campaign by a scooter manufacturer, Aprilia. Although the Spice Girls knew that one of the group, Geri Halliwell, would shortly be leaving, they proceeded to attend a photo shoot and sent a fax saying that they were 'fully committed' to the agreement (which was only signed after the photo shoot). Geri Halliwell's departure

© ROBERT ERIC/CORBIS SYGMA

Calm before the storm: the Spice Girls at the Aprilia photo shoot

meant that Aprilia would only be able to make limited use of the photos, because once she had left they would be out of date. Aprilia argued that the conduct of the Spice Girls in turning up to the photo shoot and not informing it that Geri Halliwell was leaving amounted to misrepresentation.

Reality check

Nelson Group Services v BG plc

Misleading statements in negotiations

In *Nelson Group Services v BG plc (2002)*, Nelson had purchased a business from BG (formerly British Gas). During negotiations, BG provided various sales forecasts, which led Nelson to believe that the business would achieve certain levels of profitability. In fact, actual sales were well below these forecasts, leaving Nelson with a shortfall of about £1.7 million. Nelson could not sue BG in contract because the sales forecasts were not incorporated into the agreement as terms; they were merely pre-contractual representations. The Court of Appeal ruled that the misleading sales forecasts had been a major factor in persuading Nelson to enter into the contract in the first place; Nelson was therefore able to claim damages against BG based on misrepresentation.

FAQ

Change of circumstance

If the seller of a business makes a statement about the number of customers that is true at the time, but later becomes untrue, is the seller obliged to correct its statement?

In **With v O'Flanagan (1936)**, a doctor wishing to sell his practice provided the buyer with figures indicating the income that the practice could be expected to generate. However, by the time the practice was sold, the number of patients had dropped substantially, which meant that the practice was worth far less than suggested by the original figures. The court ruled that the change in circumstances was so significant that the doctor was obliged to correct his original statement – and his failure to do so amounted to a misrepresentation (like the Spice Girls, he continued to act as if all were well with the business, when, clearly, it was not).

As a general rule, remaining silent or doing nothing is not enough to amount to a representation; some positive act must be involved. The Court of Appeal ruled that the requirement for a positive act was fulfilled in the *Spice Girls* case because, although the group remained silent on the subject of Geri Halliwell's departure, their actions (such as attending the photo shoot) told a different story; they gave the impression that she would be remaining with the group long enough for Aprilia to make reasonable use of promotional materials featuring all five members.

Representation of fact, not opinion

Lawyers often say that in order to prove misrepresentation, the injured party must be able to point to a misleading statement of fact, not opinion. However, this does not mean that misrepresentation is confined to statements that are purely factual. What the courts are really looking for is a statement that is made in such a way that it appears to have some basis in fact. For example, in *Nelson v BG plc* (see earlier), it was clearly impossible for BG to present the sales forecasts as 'facts' in the strict sense of the term, since they related to matters in the future *that* it could not know for certain. Nevertheless, the Court of Appeal ruled that in view of BG's knowledge of the business, Nelson was entitled to assume that the forecasts must have been based on facts (e.g. past sales figures) and should therefore be reasonably reliable.

Where, by the same token, the person making the statement has no real expertise, the courts will normally be less willing to view it as a representation of fact. For example, in **Bisset v Wilkinson (1927)**, the seller of a farm stated that it could support 2000 sheep (there was no suggestion that the seller had deliberately set out to mislead the buyer). In fact, the seller had no experience of sheep farming and the buyer knew this; as a result, the buyer was not justified in viewing the seller's statement as a representation of fact (it was merely a statement of opinion based on nothing more than the seller's best guess).

QUESTION 1 In *Bisset v Wilkinson (1927)*, would it have made any difference if the seller, despite not having any experience of sheep farming, knew that 2000 sheep was probably too many?

Sykes v Taylor-Rose

Sellers gave honest answers about 'House of Horror'

In **Sykes v Taylor-Rose (2004)**, Mr and Mrs Sykes discovered that their house had been the site of a gruesome murder. They claimed that the sellers had made a false statement when they answered 'No' to the question, 'Is there any other information which you think the buyer might have a right to know?' on the seller's property information form. The Court of Appeal ruled that this answer was not a false representation. If the question had been 'Are you aware of any crimes which have been committed at the property?' then clearly, the answer 'No' would have been false. However, the question asked whether *the sellers thought* that the buyers had a legal right to know about the murder (not whether the buyers actually had such a right). The sellers had taken legal advice on the subject and honestly believed that no such right existed; 'No' was therefore the correct response.

Representation was false

It goes almost without saying that the representation must be false; if it was accurate, then the 'injured' party has nothing to complain about. However, the *Sykes* case highlighted in the 'Reality check' textbox shows that in some situations, there may be room for debate as to whether a representation was false or not.

Injured party believed representation was true

The courts take the view that if the injured party knew that a representation was false, he should never have allowed it to influence his decision to enter the contract (and cannot therefore claim in misrepresentation). However, parties are not generally expected to check the truth of statements made to them unless there is good reason to doubt their reliability. For example, in **Redgrave v Hurd (1881)**, a solicitor bought a legal practice on the basis of a false statement about how much the business was worth. The fact that he had refused an opportunity to look at the accounts (which would have revealed that the statement had been false) made no difference.

QUESTION 2 In *Redgrave v Hurd (1881)*, would it have made any difference had the buyer been sent copies of the accounts but had not bothered to read them?

Representation induced a contract

Having demonstrated that false representations of fact were made, the injured party must then prove that those representations were one of the reasons why he entered into the contract. Many claims for misrepresentation fail as a result of this requirement. For example, in **Attwood v Small (1836)**, the court was not convinced that the purchasers of a mine had relied on false statements about the capacity of the mine, as they had commissioned their own experts to produce a report on the matter; as a result, the purchasers could not claim in misrepresentation.

However, where a representation has been relied on, it does not have to be the only reason or even the main reason for entering into the contract; it may be one of several reasons why the agreement was made. In ***Edgington v Fitzmaurice (1885)***, an investor bought debentures in a company, partly on the basis of statements in a prospectus (which turned out to be false) and partly as a result of his own mistaken belief about the terms of the debentures. The investor's mistaken belief about the terms (which was entirely his own fault) did not prevent him from pursuing a remedy for misrepresentation based on the statements in the prospectus.

Remedies

The following remedies are available for misrepresentation:

- *Rescission*: this is an equitable remedy that allows the court to order the contract to be set aside and restore the parties to the position they were in before the contract was entered into. The court may also order the repayment of any money that has changed hands or the return of property. However, since the remedy is equitable, the precise contents of the order will vary depending on what the court considers to be a just outcome. In practice, it is relatively rare for the courts to order rescission and there are many well-established circumstances in which they will refuse to do so, e.g. where it is impossible to restore the parties to their pre-contract positions, where there is delay in seeking rescission or where the claimant appears to have affirmed the contract. [You can find out more about these on the companion website.]

- *Damages*: the injured party can seek a financial award designed to compensate it for its loss. Damages for misrepresentation are based on the tort of deceit. Unlike damages for breach of contract (see Chapter 8), they are only designed to put the injured party back in the position it would have been before the contract was entered into; they cannot, for example, be used to claim loss of profits that the injured party had expected to make if the representation had been accurate.

Precisely which remedy is available depends on the type of misrepresentation involved:

- *Fraudulent*: if the person responsible for the misrepresentation knows that it is untrue or made it with a reckless disregard for the truth, this will be regarded as **fraudulent misrepresentation**: see ***Derry v Peek (1889)***. The injured party can seek both rescission and damages.

- *Negligent*: if the misrepresentation is not fraudulent, but the person responsible for it is unable to show that he believed it to be true and had reasonable grounds for that belief, this will be regarded as **negligent misrepresentation**: section 2(1) of the Misrepresentation Act 1967. The injured party can seek both rescission and damages. In theory the claimant can claim the same level of damages as a claimant alleging fraudulent misrepresentation. In practice though, the courts generally award a slightly lower sum in recognition of the fact that the misrepresentation was not made fraudulently. Having said that, negligent misrepresentation is significantly easier to prove than fraudulent misrepresentation (see the FAQ textbox).

- *Innocent*: if the misrepresentation does not fall into these categories (i.e. the person responsible for it is not at fault), it will be regarded as innocent. The injured party can seek rescission, although damages may be awarded if the court will not order rescission (the level of damages is likely to be relatively low because the person responsible was not at fault).

Why is negligent misrepresentation easier to prove than fraudulent misrepresentation?

A negligent misrepresentation is significantly easier to establish than a fraudulent one because section 2(1) of the Misrepresentation Act 1967 reverses the burden of proof. This means that once the claimant has shown that a misrepresentation was made, it is up to the defendant to prove that he believed the representation to be true and had reasonable grounds for that belief. Case law suggests that the courts expect defendants to go to some lengths before they can say that they have 'reasonable grounds for belief'. For example, in *Howard Marine and Dredging Co Ltd v A Ogden & Sons (1978)*, the defendants provided incorrect figures when asked about the carrying capacity of a barge. They argued that they had reasonable grounds for believing that the figures were true because they obtained them from an official register. However, the Court of Appeal ruled that they should have checked the figures with their head office as well.

Mistake

Where one or more of the parties entered into a contract based on a misunderstanding of some factual issue (and the party in question is not to blame for that misunderstanding), the courts may decide that the contract is void for **mistake**.

For example, if a business had agreed to sell a factory to one of its competitors but – unknown to either party – the factory had burned down half an hour before the contract was signed, the courts would probably conclude that the agreement was void. This is because the parties entered into it on a completely false assumption (i.e. that the factory still existed) that was of central importance to the contract (i.e. without the factory, there is only a derelict patch of land to sell – so the agreement bears no relation to what the parties thought they had agreed at the time). Similarly, in *Couturier v Hastie (1856)*, the House of Lords ruled that a claim for the price of some corn could not succeed because – at the time of the agreement – the particular consignment of corn was no longer available (the corn had already been sold to another buyer).

Where both parties are mistaken in the same way about the same issue, lawyers say that there has been a **common mistake**. Where only one party is mistaken, this is known as **unilateral mistake**.

Mistake of fact

This chapter is mainly concerned with **mistakes of fact**. This is where the contract was entered into based on some mistaken belief relating to a factual matter, such as the example just given about the contract for sale of a factory that was no longer in existence at the time of the contract. It is also possible for a contract to be affected by a mistaken belief about the law, but as will be explained later in this section, a **mistake of law** does not have the same effect as a mistake of fact.

Effect of mistake of fact

If the court concludes that there has been a mistake of fact, the entire contract is void, i.e. it is treated as if it never existed and neither party was ever under any contractual obligations. The effects of this can be quite harsh. For example, if one party has paid the other money, it cannot claim it back (even where it has received no benefit in return).

Until fairly recently, it was believed that the courts could, in certain situations, use their equitable powers to achieve a just outcome (e.g. by ordering the repayment of money). However, in *Great Peace Shipping v Tsavliris Salvage (2002)* (see case study), the Court of Appeal ruled that equitable remedies are not available where there has been a mistake of fact. The Court of Appeal recognised that in some cases, this could result in a harsh outcome but said that it was for Parliament, not the courts, to correct any unfairness. The only mistakes where equitable remedies are relevant are considered later under the heading 'Other types of mistake'.

Mistake and frustration

In Chapter 8, we looked at how a contract may be discharged as a result of frustration. Mistake of fact is often confused with frustration, as it too may allow the parties to be released from their contractual obligations. However, there are two key differences:

- Mistake of fact is only relevant when looking at circumstances at the time the contract was entered into (whereas frustration is concerned with circumstances that arose afterwards).

Great Peace Shipping v Tsavliris Salvage (2002)

Tsavliris Salvage needed to pick up the crew from a ship called the *Cape Providence*, which had broken down. It chartered a ship from Great Peace in the mistaken belief that the ship was close to the *Cape Providence*. In fact, the Great Peace ship was not as close as Tsavliris had believed. Tsavliris argued that it did not have to proceed with the contract because it had entered into it on the basis of a fundamentally mistaken belief about the ship's position. The Court of Appeal said that although Tsavliris had clearly been mistaken, the mistake was not so fundamental as to defeat the purpose of the contract; in particular, it noted that the Great Peace ship was close enough for it to have been used to pick up the crew (so there was no question of Great Peace having taken advantage of an obvious error by Tsavliris). The Court of Appeal also noted that Tsavliris could easily have protected itself against the consequences of its mistake by obtaining a warranty from Great Peace about the correct position of the ship. This would have allowed it to claim damages for the fact that it had cost more money and taken longer than expected to pick up the crew of the *Cape Providence*. In reaching this conclusion, the Court of Appeal overruled one of its own earlier decisions (*Solle v Butcher (1949)*) on the grounds that it was wrong in law. [You can find out more about this earlier case on the companion website.]

- If a contract has been entered into based on a mistake of fact, it is void from the time that it was entered into (where a contract has been frustrated, however, it will only be void from the time of the frustrating event).

Mistakes of fact: subject matter

We have already seen how a contract can be void if one or more of the parties is mistaken about the *existence* of the subject matter of the contract (see *Couturier v Hastie* and the example given at the start of this section concerning a contract for purchase of a factory that had burnt down before the agreement was made). This is one type of **mistake as to subject matter**. It is also possible for a contract to be void for a mistake as to the quality of the subject matter. This may apply where one or both of the parties is mistaken about a feature of what they are buying or selling or the nature of what they are agreeing to do. For example, in *Great Peace Shipping v Tsvaliris* (see earlier), the subject matter of the contract was the Great Peace ship itself. The dispute was concerned with whether the ship was in a particular position; this was an aspect of the *quality* of the subject matter, rather than its existence.

Mistakes as to quality seldom result in the contract being void at common law. As illustrated by the *Great Peace* case, the courts normally expect the party that is concerned about the quality of the subject matter to protect themselves against the possibility that they may be mistaken by obtaining a warranty about the quality of the subject matter. This point was considered by the House of Lords in ***Bell v Lever Brothers (1932)*** highlighted in the case study textbox (and the Court of Appeal's decision in the *Great Peace* case was based on this ruling).

Bell v Lever Brothers (1932)

Lever Brothers agreed to pay Bell £30,000 as compensation for early termination of his employment contract. Later on, however, Lever Brothers discovered that Bell had broken company rules, which meant that he could have been dismissed without payment. The company argued that the contract was void for mistake, because it had entered into it on the false assumption that Bell had a good employment record (and could not therefore be dismissed for breach of contract). The House of Lords ruled that a mistake as to quality could only make the contract void if it fundamentally altered the 'identity of the subject matter'. In this case, the subject matter of the contract was Bell's rights arising out of his employment with Lever Brothers; the agreement was for Lever Brothers to 'buy out' those rights so that Bell's employment would be terminated. The mistake had not prevented those rights being 'bought out'; it had merely affected the value that Lever Brothers had put on those rights. As such, it could not be viewed as a mistake that had fundamentally altered the subject matter of the contract. In addition, Lever Brothers could have protected itself against the consequences of its mistake by obtaining a warranty from Bell that he had not broken company rules.

QUESTION 3 Why wasn't the mistake in *Bell v Lever Brothers* regarded as a mistake of law? After all, surely the whole case revolved around a legal issue, namely whether Bell could have successfully sued Lever Brothers for early termination of his employment contract?

Mistake of fact: identity

Mistake as to identity may occur where a person believes they are dealing with one person when they are, in fact, dealing with someone else. For example, in **Cundy v Lindsay (1878)**, a man called Blenkarn pretended to be a representative of Blenkiron & Son and persuaded Lindsay to sell him some handkerchiefs. Blenkarn sold most of them to Cundy, but failed to pay Lindsay and then disappeared. The court needed to decide whether the contract between Blenkarn and Lindsay was void for mistake. If it were void, then Cundy could be required to return the handkerchiefs to Lindsay. The court ruled that the contract was void because (i) Lindsay had made a mistake about the identity of the person it was contracting with; and (ii) that mistake was fundamental to its decision to enter into the contract (i.e. Lindsay only agreed to accept payment later because it thought that it was dealing with the firm of Blenkiron & Son; it knew this firm existed and knew that it was reputable).

By contrast, in **Kings Norton Metal Co Ltd v Edridge, Merrett & Co Ltd (1897)**, the sellers were persuaded to part with goods by an individual who appeared to be a representative of a respectable firm. Unlike Blenkiron & Son in *Cundy v Lindsay*, the firm did not exist and the sellers had not heard of it before. The court ruled that the contract was *not* void for mistake. This was because the mistake in this case concerned the apparent attributes of the person the sellers were dealing with; the issue of identity was not crucial because the sellers would have made the contract with anyone who appeared sufficiently respectable.

QUESTION 4 In the *Kings Norton* case, would it have made any difference had the firm actually existed, even though it was not known to the sellers?

Mistake of fact: terms

Mistake as to terms may occur where a person enters an agreement in the belief that they have agreed one thing, but the agreement says something different. For example, in **Hartog v Colin & Shields (1939)**, the sellers offered various animal skins by the pound when they had intended to offer them by the piece. This meant that the skins were being sold at an absurdly low price. The court decided that the buyer must have been aware of the mistake and was effectively seeking to take advantage of it. In those circumstances, the contract was void for mistake. The possible application of the *Hartog* case to pricing mistakes on the worldwide web is considered in the 'Reality check' textbox on 'Kodak and Argos'.

Reality check

Kodak and Argos

Pricing mistakes on the web

In 1999 the website of the retailer Argos appeared to be offering very generous discounts, including TV sets that normally cost £299 at the bargain price of £2.99. Argos received hundreds of emails placing orders for the goods and sent automatic emails in reply. It then refused to fulfil these orders, arguing that the prices were a mistake. Although many customers complained, none of these disputes reached the courts. Had they done so, it is quite possible that Argos could have successfully relied on *Hartog v Colin & Shields*, because the mistake would have been obvious to most people and the customers were effectively trying to take advantage of it. In 2002 a similar website pricing error led to Kodak receiving hundreds of orders for digital cameras

actually costing £329 that were priced at £100. As with Argos, Kodak had sent automated replies to the emails. Unlike Argos, Kodak decided to supply the cameras at the advertised price, incurring an estimated £2 million loss. Had it refused to supply them, it might well have faced a more difficult task than Argos in convincing a court that any contracts with customers should be regarded as void for mistake; the price was certainly good value, but it was not so low as to be obviously absurd.

Mistake of fact: non est factum

Where a person signs a document believing it to be something fundamentally different from what it really is, they may be able to argue that the resulting contract is void for mistake. This type of mistake is known as **non est factum**, which is Latin for 'it is not my deed'. However, like most types of factual mistake, non est factum is quite difficult to establish. For example, in **Saunders v Anglia Building Society (1970)**, an elderly woman signed a document believing that it would make her nephew owner of her house, so that he could mortgage it in order to raise money for his business. In fact, the document made her nephew's business partner the owner. However, since he also proceeded to take out a mortgage in order to raise money for the business, the House of Lords took the view that the actual agreement was not fundamentally different from the one that the elderly woman thought she had signed. They also ruled that, even though she had lost her glasses and could not read the document, she should have asked someone else to check the paperwork before signing it.

Other types of mistake

So far in this chapter we have been considering mistakes of fact, where the effect of the mistake is to render the contract void (and no equitable remedies are available). However, there are a number of other types of mistake that do not affect the validity of the contract as such, but which may allow the parties to seek equitable remedies to prevent an unjust result:

- *Rectification*: where the court is convinced that that the terms of the contract do not reflect the intentions of the parties at the time they made their agreement, it may use its equitable powers to order the agreement to be corrected. This is known as **rectification**. For example, in **Hurst Stores v ML Europe (2004)**, ML Europe made significant changes to a draft contract just before signature, without drawing attention to them. Hurst believed that the final contract was in the same form as the latest draft it had been sent and signed the contract. The Court of Appeal ruled that ML Europe must have known that Hurst had been unaware of the changes; it therefore ordered the contract to be changed back to the position in the latest draft.

- *Mistakes of law*: where one or more of the parties enters into the agreement based on a fundamental misunderstanding of the law, the court may use its equitable powers to achieve a just outcome. For example, in **Kleinwort Benson v Lincoln City Council (1998)**, the House of Lords found that Kleinwort had entered into investment contracts with local authorities based on a mistake of law. It used its equitable powers to order the local authorities to return the money they had been paid by the bank, otherwise the local authorities would have been unjustly enriched.

You can find out more about both these types of mistake on the companion website.

Answers to in-text questions

> **QUESTION 1** In *Bisset v Wilkinson (1927)*, would it have made any difference if the seller, despite not having any experience of sheep farming, knew that 2000 sheep was probably too many?

Possibly. If there were evidence of fraud, the court would probably be inclined to regard the statement as one of fact in view of the seriousness of the seller's misconduct. The buyer would have to prove that the seller had deliberately set out to mislead him or had displayed a reckless disregard for the truth of the statement. However, in the absence of fraud, knowledge on the part of the seller that the estimate was probably too high would not necessarily make any difference. This is because the courts are concerned not so much with what the seller knew, but with what the buyer knew (or could reasonably have assumed) about the seller's knowledge. In *Bisset v Wilkinson*, the buyer knew that neither the seller nor any of the previous farm owners had ever used it for sheep, so anything the seller said about sheep farming had to be viewed with a degree of scepticism.

> **QUESTION 2** In *Redgrave v Hurd (1881)*, would it have made any difference had the buyer been sent copies of the accounts but had not bothered to read them?

Much would depend on whether the court thought that it was reasonable to expect the buyer to read the accounts. In practice, most business purchases do not proceed without the purchaser doing at least some 'due diligence' (e.g. inspecting the accounts of the business etc.). As a result, there would probably be an expectation in many cases that the buyer would look at the accounts. This would probably make it harder for the buyer to convince the court that he had relied on the misrepresentation (see under the earlier heading 'Representation induced the contract'). For example, in **Infiniteland v Artisan Contracting Limited (2005)**, the buyer of a company alleged that the seller had made misleading statements about the company's finances. However, as part of its due diligence, the buyer had received (and would normally have been expected to read) accounting documentation that should have revealed the true state of the company's profitability. This was one of the reasons why the court was not convinced by the buyer's claims that it had relied solely on the statements by the seller.

> **QUESTION 3** Why wasn't the mistake in *Bell v Lever Brothers* regarded as a mistake of law? After all, surely the whole case revolved around a legal issue, namely whether Bell could have successfully sued Lever Brothers for early termination of his employment contract?

The mistake in *Bell v Lever Brothers* was concerned with a question of *fact*, not law, namely whether Bell had broken company rules. Lever Brothers believed that he had not, leading them to believe – mistakenly – that unless they paid him off, he might well sue them for early termination of his contract. But this mistaken belief about the legal position flowed from the mistaken belief about the factual issue of Bell's employment record.

> **QUESTION 4** In the *Kings Norton* case, would it have made any difference had the firm actually existed, although it was not known to the sellers?

No. In **Phillips v Brooks (1919)**, a man pretended to be Sir George Bullough and gave the address of the real Sir George Bullough, which the seller was able to check. However, unlike the situation in *Cundy v Lindsay*, the seller had never heard of the real Sir George Bullough. As a result, the court ruled that his mistake was primarily related to the attributes of the person he thought he was dealing with, i.e. he thought that a person calling himself 'Sir George Bullough' must be respectable. This was not sufficient and the contract was not void for mistake.

10 | Validity of contracts (2)

By the end of this chapter, you should be able to explain:

Learning objectives

- **How the validity of a contract may be affected where the contract was entered into as a result of threats or abuse of a position of trust (duress and undue influence)**

- **How the validity is affected where the contract is against the law (illegality)**

- **How the validity is affected when one of the persons making the contract did not have the capacity to do so (incapacity)**

Introduction

As in the previous chapter, this chapter explores different situations that can affect the validity of a contract – even though the other 'key ingredients' of a legally binding agreement (as explained in Chapters 3, 4 and 5) are present.

Duress and undue influence

The validity of a contract may be affected if it has been entered into as a result of threats of some kind (**duress**) or because one of the parties has unfairly exploited its relationship with the other party (**undue influence**). If either of these factors is present, the courts may conclude that one of the parties did not enter into the contract of its own free will.

Effect of duress and undue influence

The effect of duress or undue influence is normally to make the contract **voidable**, i.e. if the innocent party wishes to be released from its obligations, it can ask the court to set the contract aside. Where a contract is void, on the other hand, neither party has any choice in the matter; even if the innocent party wants to proceed with the contract, it cannot enforce the contract against the other party.

However, duress and undue influence render contracts voidable by different routes. Duress is based on the *common law*; it allows contracts to be set aside because that is the remedy that the courts have traditionally applied in such cases. Undue influence is based on *equitable principles*; when the innocent party asks the court to set the contract aside, it is seeking the equitable remedy of rescission (the same remedy as for misrepresentation).

This may seem a rather technical distinction, but it is important to use the correct terminology when discussing duress and undue influence, because their legal origins are very different. A more practical consequence of the distinction is that in cases of undue influence, other equitable remedies may be available besides rescission (although rescission is the most common). For example, in some situations, merely setting the contract aside might result in an unjust outcome; if so, the courts may use their equitable powers to make additional orders (e.g. requiring the return of money that has been paid).

Physical duress

If a person has entered into a contract as a result of violence or the threat of such violence, the contract may be voidable for physical duress. For example, in **Barton v Armstrong (1975)**, Barton, who was managing director of an Australian company, agreed to buy shares from Armstrong, who was chairman of the same company. The price of the shares was very favourable to Armstrong. The court ruled that the contract could be set aside because Armstrong had threatened to have Barton killed unless he signed the agreement. This meant that Barton did not sign the contract of this own free will; he was coerced into doing so.

Economic duress

Until relatively recently, the courts did not recognise any form of duress other than physical duress. It is now possible to ask a court to set a contract aside because it was entered into as a result of some form of non-physical, economic pressure (economic duress). However, this is more difficult to establish than physical duress and the courts are generally reluctant to intervene in all but the most extreme of situations. An example is given in the following 'Reality check' textbox that follows.

Reality check

Atlas Express v Kafco (1989)

Economic duress

In **Atlas Express v Kafco (1989)**, a delivery firm (Atlas) threatened to withdraw its services unless its customer, Kafco, a small company that made baskets, agreed to a price rise. The threat was made in the run-up to Christmas, when it would have been extremely difficult for Kafco to make alternative arrangements. It also stood to lose an important contract to supply Woolworths if the deliveries were not made. The court ruled that Kafco's agreement to the price rise had been obtained by economic duress.

The test for economic duress

In **Pao On v Lau Yiu Long (1979)**, the House of Lords ruled that in order to establish economic duress, two key conditions must be fulfilled:

* *Illegitimate pressure*: some form of illegitimate pressure must have been applied. For example, in the *Kafco* case, the delivery firm had threatened to break its contractual obligations without justification, which would have had a very serious adverse effect on its customer. More recently, in **CTN Cash & Carry Ltd v Gallaher Ltd (1994)**, the Court of Appeal ruled that the illegitimate pressure does not have to consist of an illegal act (such as a threat to break a contract). However, in order to be illegitimate, the conduct must be fairly extreme and needs to go some way beyond hard-headed business tactics.

* *No practical alternative*: a reasonable person in the position of the victim would have had no practical alternative but to give in to the pressure. For example, in the *Kafco* case, the customer could in theory have attempted to find other delivery firms. However, it was the run-up to Christmas when most delivery firms were already quite busy. As a small firm with limited resources, which could not afford significant disruption to its deliveries at this time, the customer had no practical alternative but to accept the price rise.

QUESTION 1 A company is not satisfied with the work done by one of its suppliers. It threatens to withhold payment unless the supplier agrees to carry out additional work. If the supplier agrees, has the agreement been obtained by economic duress?

Undue influence

Where one person has exploited their relationship with another person in order to persuade them to make an agreement, the court may use its equitable powers to set the contract aside on grounds of undue influence. It is rare for businesses to be the victims of undue influence; the victim is normally an individual and the undue influence usually involves exploiting that person's emotional or intellectual vulnerabilities. For example, in **Williams v Bayley (1866)**, an elderly man was told by some moneylenders that unless he guaranteed his son's debts, they would see to it that the son was prosecuted for fraud. The father agreed, because he did not want his son to go to prison. The court set the contract aside.

There are two types of undue influence – actual and presumed.

Actual undue influence

To establish **actual undue influence**, the party wishing to set the contract aside must prove the following:

* *Dominance*: there must be a relationship of dominance that puts the other party in a position of power or authority, allowing them to influence the victim. For example, in *Williams v Bayley*, the moneylenders were in a position to exercise considerable leverage over the father by exploiting his emotional weaknesses.

- *Influence*: the victim would not have entered into the contract without the influence exercised by the other party. For example, in *Williams v Bayley*, the father clearly felt that he had no option but to do what the moneylenders had asked him.

In contrast to duress, the victim does not need to show that a reasonable person in his position would have acted in the same way. Whereas the test for duress is *objective*, i.e. it involves looking at how a reasonable person in the victim's position would have behaved, the test for undue influence focuses on the *subjective* perceptions of the victim (which are not required to be reasonable). Neither is it necessary to show (as in economic duress) that there was no practical alternative; all that matters is that the victim would not have entered into the contract without the undue influence.

Presumed undue influence

Presumed undue influence arises where there is a relationship of trust and confidence between the parties. The courts take the view that relationships of this kind carry such potential for abuse that undue influence will be presumed, unless the alleged wrongdoer can show that the contract was freely entered into by the victim. This means that a victim of presumed undue influence only needs to prove that:

- there was a relationship of trust and confidence
- the relevant contract was 'manifestly disadvantageous' to him.

In some cases, the victim may not even have to prove the first point, because there are some relationships where the courts accept that a relationship of trust and confidence must exist, e.g. solicitor–client, parent–child, doctor–patient etc. The alleged wrongdoer can normally only be certain of defeating the presumption of undue influence if it can show that the victim was told to seek independent advice. This is illustrated by the case highlighted in the textbox that follows.

You can find out more about duress and undue influence on the companion website.

Presumed undue influence: the importance of independent advice

In *Lloyds Bank v Bundy (1975)*, a farmer and his son had banked with Lloyds for many years, with the result that a relationship of trust and confidence had built up between them. The bank lent money to the son and the farmer agreed to offer his house as security for the loan. The court ruled that the farmer had looked to the bank for advice as to whether it was sensible for him to do this, but the bank had a clear conflict of interest when it came to advising him (because it was in the bank's interest to have the farmer's house as security for the loan). The bank's failure to recommend that the farmer seek independent advice meant that it could not defeat the presumption that it had exercised undue influence on the farmer. The court therefore agreed to set the contract aside. However, note that banker–client is not one of those relationships where the courts automatically assume that a relationship of trust and confidence exists. This case was unusual in that the farmer had quite a close relationship with his bank going back many years, but in most cases involving banks there is no relationship of trust and confidence.

Illegality

There are two types of illegality that may affect the enforceability of a contract:

- *Illegal purpose*: where the *purpose* of a contract is illegal, the courts will not uphold it and neither party can enforce it (even if one party did not realise that the contract was illegal or will lose money or property as a result).
- *Illegal performance*: where the contract itself is legal, but it has been carried out in an illegal *manner* (e.g. because one party has committed a criminal offence in carrying it out), the courts will not allow the party responsible for the illegal performance to enforce the contract, but the innocent party may enforce it.

Contracts for an illegal purpose

Some contracts are illegal because they are prohibited by statute. For example, the Competition Act 1998 prohibits agreements between businesses that significantly restrict competition within the UK (or a substantial part of the UK). An agreement between a manufacturer and a retailer requiring the retailer not to sell goods below the manufacturer's recommended retail price (RRP) would normally be regarded as illegal under the Act. If the manufacturer discovered that the retailer had been selling goods for less than RRP and sued it for damages, the court would not uphold the agreement and the manufacturer's claim would fail. Price fixing of this type could also lead to the manufacturer being fined by the Office of Fair Trading (see Chapter 2). You can find out more about competition law in Chapter 12 in the discussion of breach of statutory duty and on the companion website.

Contracts may also be illegal because of the common law. For example, in **Parkinson v College of Ambulance Ltd and Harrison (1925)**, a charity was given £3000 in return for a promise that it would arrange for the donor to be given a knighthood. There was no statute saying that such an agreement was illegal. However, the court ruled that the agreement was against **public policy** because it involved a promise by the charity to corrupt public officials. When Parkinson failed to obtain his knighthood and sued for return of the money, the court refused to allow the agreement to be enforced. Another example of contracts that are illegal on grounds of public policy is provided by the common law doctrine of **restraint of trade**, which is discussed next.

> **QUESTION 2** The sales director of a company pays a bribe to a purchasing manager who works for one of its customers. In return for the bribe, the purchasing manager ensures that his employer signs a contract to buy a large quantity of the first company's products. Is the agreement between the two companies illegal?

Restraint of trade

Among other things, restraint of trade limits the extent to which businesses can prevent ex-employees from working for competitors (other aspects of employment contracts are discussed in Chapter 21). It is common for employers to include certain restrictions in their contracts with employees. These are often referred to as **restrictive covenants.** Typically, they aim to prevent the employee from doing some or all of the following, both during their employment and for a period after their employment has come to an end:

- working for a competitor of the employer
- setting up a business that competes with the employer's business
- contacting customers of the employer with a view to taking their business away from the employer
- contacting employees of the employer with a view to persuading them to work for him
- using or disclosing any trade secrets of the employer's business.

The courts will only enforce such restrictive covenants if the following conditions are met:

- The clause protects a legitimate interest of the employer.
- The clause goes no further than is reasonably necessary to protect that legitimate interest.
- It is in the public interest to enforce the clause.

These rules are known as the doctrine of restraint of trade. A clause that is in restraint of trade is regarded as having an illegal purpose and cannot be enforced.

Legitimate interests and reasonableness

While the employee is still working for the employer, the courts will normally be prepared to uphold most of the restrictions just outlined. For example, working for a competitor could give rise to serious conflicts of interest for the employee, which would tend to undermine the key relationship of trust and confidence with the employer. However, once the employee has stopped working for the employer, it is rare for the courts to allow the employer to prevent ex-employees from working for competitors for an indefinite period (even though the employer may have a legitimate interest in upholding the restriction).

FAQ

To what extent can ex-employees be prevented from working for competitors?

An employer may be concerned about an ex-employee working for a competitor because the ex-employee has knowledge or expertise that could benefit the competitor, e.g. the employee has dealt with customers in a particular area (and could try to use his relationship with those customers to the competitor's advantage). While it may be legitimate for the employer to seek to protect his customers from such 'poaching', this will not usually justify a blanket restriction on the employee working for a competitor. The restriction must normally be confined to the particular area in which those customers were located; if it goes further than this, it is likely to be unreasonable. Similarly, the restriction should only last as long as the employer reasonably needs to deal with any disruption caused to customer relationships by the departure of the employee, e.g. by recruiting a new employee to manage those customers and reassuring them that they will continue to receive the same levels of service. In most cases, this should not take more than 6–12 months, so longer periods are unlikely to be regarded as reasonable.

Reality check

Anstalt v Hayek

Inventor should be free to invent

In **Anstalt v Hayek (2002)**, Anstalt and various associated companies tried to enforce a restrictive covenant preventing an ex-employee, Hayek, from competing with it. While working for Anstalt, Hayek had invented a mechanical ventilator used for medical purposes (the patents to which were owned and exploited by Anstalt and its associated companies). After he left his employment with Anstalt, Hayek developed a new ventilator and set up his own business to sell it in competition with his existing invention. Anstalt and its associated companies tried to enforce a restrictive covenant that prevented Hayek competing with them on a worldwide basis for so long as they continued to manufacture and sell ventilators. The Court of Appeal ruled that Anstalt and its associated companies were entitled to use patent rights to prevent Hayek using certain aspects of his old invention in his new product. However, the restrictive covenant attempted to prevent Hayek's applying his inventive skills to develop new, superior ventilators, which could be of considerable benefit to society. The Court of Appeal ruled that it was against public policy for an inventor's activities to be restricted in this manner. As a result, the restrictive covenant could not be enforced.

Public policy considerations

Even where the employer has a legitimate interest to protect and the restrictive covenant goes no further than is reasonable to protect that interest, the courts may still refuse to uphold the clause on grounds of public policy. For example, in **Herbert Morris Ltd v Saxelby (1916)**, the court refused to enforce a 7-year restrictive covenant on an engineer who had been employed by a hoisting machinery firm. This was not only much longer than was justified to protect the employer's legitimate interests but would have prevented the engineer from earning his living and using his skills for the benefit of society for a very lengthy period indeed. Another example of this approach is highlighted in the 'Reality check' textbox on *Anstalt v Hayek (2002)*. [More cases on restraint of trade can be found on the companion website.]

> **QUESTION 3** Restraint of trade can also apply to agreements between businesses that restrict competition, but its importance in regulating such activities has decreased in recent years. Why do you think this is? (Clue: think about the legislation discussed earlier in this section.)

Severance

Contracts often contain many different clauses and it is rare for them all to be illegal. In such cases, the courts may rule that the illegal portion of the contract can be 'severed' and the remainder of the contract can be upheld; this is known as **severance**. However, the courts must be satisfied that the remainder of the agreement continues to make sense (both grammatically and in terms of continuing to reflect the parties' original intentions) if the illegal portions are removed.

For example, in **Attwood v Lamont (1920)**, a restrictive covenant was imposed on a former employee of a tailor, which prevented him working as a tailor, dressmaker, general draper, milliner, hatter, haberdasher, gentlemen's, ladies' or children's outfitter within 10 miles of his former employer's shop. The geographical area was reasonable but the scope of the restriction was not, because it went beyond working as a tailor to include other businesses that did not compete with the former employer's business. In theory, the court could have ruled that the words 'dressmaker, general draper' and so on should be severed. However, it concluded that the clause had to be read as a single restriction and taken in its entirety – so severance of parts of the clause was not possible. (See also the FAQ textbox.)

Lawful contracts that are illegally performed

A perfectly lawful contract may become illegal if it is performed in an unlawful manner. For example, in **Birkett v Acorn Business Machines Ltd (1999)**, Birkett needed to obtain finance to fund the purchase of a photocopier from Acorn. Both parties knew that the finance company, Mercury Assist, would only provide finance if the supply agreement was for telecommunications equipment. They therefore entered into an agreement that said that the Acorn would provide a facsimile–photocopier. There was nothing illegal about this agreement. The illegality came about because instead of providing a facsimile–photocopier, Acorn had (with Birkett's agreement) supplied a normal photocopier. This failure to perform the contract properly meant that Mercury Assist was the victim of a fraud designed to deceive it into providing finance. The Court of Appeal ruled that the illegality in the performance of the contract meant that Birkett could not sue Acorn for other breaches of that contract.

Reform

The Law Commission has stated that the existing law on illegality is 'unnecessarily complex, may result in unjust decisions, and [is] in many respects obscure'. At the time of writing, it was consulting on possible reforms that would give courts greater discretion to produce a just outcome in cases involving illegality. [You can find out more about these proposals on the companion website.]

 FAQ

Severance: the impact in practice

Is it possible to draft agreements in a way that avoids the problems with severance encountered in Attwood v Lamont?

Lawyers often draft restrictive covenants so that they consist of several separate promises. For example, in a case such as *Attwood v Lamont*, they would probably have separated the promise not to compete as a tailor from the promise not to compete as 'dressmaker, general draper, etc.'. This would have made it clear that the restriction on working as a tailor was separate from the restriction on working in other, similar jobs (thus potentially allowing the court to sever the second restriction while leaving the first restriction in place).

Capacity

A contract will not normally be enforceable if one of the parties did not have the legal power to make it. Lawyers refer to a person's ability to make contracts as their **capacity**. The general rule is that if it should have been obvious to one party that the other party did not have capacity, the contract will not be enforceable. For example, if a person is obviously so drunk that they do not know what they are doing, they will not be regarded as having the necessary capacity to make a contract – and any contract they have made will not be legally binding. However, once the drunk person has sobered up, any agreement they made while drunk could become binding if they **ratify** it (i.e. if they confirm that they did intend to be legally bound, even though they were drunk at the time).

A similar approach is adopted where an employee signs a contract on behalf of a company; as a general rule, the other party is entitled to assume that the employee has authority to sign the contract unless it was unusual for an employee in that position to sign contracts of that type. The law on capacity and authority in relation to contracts made by companies is discussed in more detail in Part 5. This chapter concentrates on capacity of individuals making contracts for themselves (rather than on behalf of a business).

Mentally ill or mentally handicapped people

The approach to the mentally ill or mentally handicapped is similar to the approach to drunks, i.e. if it should have been obvious to the other party that the person they were dealing with does not have capacity to make a contract, any agreement made will not be binding. However, unlike a drunk, a person who is mentally ill or mentally handicapped will not normally be able to ratify a contract (although this is not impossible, e.g. where a person recovers fully from a bout of mental illness, they could still ratify an agreement made during the period of illness).

Special protection is accorded to people who have been put under the protection of the court or 'sectioned'. Where someone has been sectioned, no contract they make will be binding – even if it was not obvious to the other party that the person did not have the necessary capacity.

Minors

Special rules apply to **minors** – i.e. people under 18. These rules are primarily designed to protect under 18 year olds from being exploited by businesses. If a minor wants to enforce his contractual rights against a business, he will normally be allowed to do so and the courts will treat the contract as valid. But if a minor decides that he does not want to be bound by a contract, the general rule (subject to a number of exceptions) is that a business will not be able to enforce it.

Minors and contracts for necessaries

In **Nash v Inman (1908)**, a tailor supplied 11 'fancy waistcoats' to a minor, who
failed to pay for them. The court ruled that minors could be forced to pay up if
the goods were **necessaries**. Although the name 'necessaries' suggests that it
would only cover things that a minor actually needs in order simply to survive,
such as food or very basic clothing (not fancy waistcoats), it can cover other
items, depending on the social standing of the minor. For example, in *Nash v
Inman*, the court said that fancy waistcoats could be regarded as necessaries, as the
minor was the son of an architect and his social standing was such that people
would expect him to be reasonably well dressed. However, as he already had
plenty of waistcoats, the court ruled that he did not actually need them at the
time, so they could not be regarded as necessaries.

The definition of 'necessaries' has now been codified in section 3 of the Sale of
the Goods Act 1979 as goods or services that are suitable:

- 'to the condition in life of the minor'
- 'to his actual requirements at the time of sale and delivery'.

Unless *both* conditions are met, businesses will not be allowed to enforce payment. Where a minor is liable to pay for necessaries, the Sale of Goods Act 1979
states that he or she is only obliged to pay a 'reasonable price' (this rule is
designed to protect minors from being charged exorbitantly high prices).

Minors Contracts Act 1987

Although *Nash v Inman* and the Sale of Goods Act 1979 remove some of the
unfairness that can be produced by the law on contracts with minors, they still
allow minors to get away without paying if the goods are not necessaries (and
normally the minor will be able to keep the goods). Section 3 of the Minors
Contracts Act 1987, however, allows businesses to ask the courts to make an order
for the return of their property if a minor refuses to pay. This applies whether or
not the property would amount to 'necessaries'. The courts will agree to this provided that it is 'just and equitable' to do so. For example, if the business has taken
advantage of the minor, it is unlikely that a court will grant such a request.
However, the courts can only order return of the property if it is still in the
minor's possession. If the minor has sold it, he or she can be ordered to hand over
the proceeds of sale – but if the minor has spent the money or consumed the
goods, then the Minors Contracts Act will not help.

> **QUESTION 4** How can businesses protect themselves against minors who refuse to pay?

Minors and contracts of employment, education or apprenticeship

In addition to contracts for necessaries, the courts will also allow businesses to enforce contracts of employment, education of apprenticeship – but only where the contract as a whole is beneficial to the minor. For example, in **De Francesco v Barnum (1890)**, the court refused to enforce a contract for a minor to be an apprentice dancer because it was very unfavourable to her (it was very poorly paid and contained very harsh conditions, such as a requirement not to marry for 7 years). However, in **Doyle v White City Stadium Ltd (1935)**, a boxing contract with a minor was enforceable. This was because, although it contained some provisions that were not in the minor's favour, the contract as a whole was beneficial to him, since it helped him on his way to becoming a professional boxer.

Answers to in-text questions

> **QUESTION 1** A company is not satisfied with the work done by one of its suppliers. It threatens to withhold payment unless the supplier agrees to carry out additional work. If the supplier agrees, has the agreement been obtained by economic duress?

It depends on the circumstances. If the supplier has failed to fulfil its contractual obligations, the contract may well allow the customer to withhold payment – in which case, the customer's threat would be perfectly lawful. If the contract did not permit this, it could be a breach of contract for the customer to refuse to pay. But in order to amount to 'illegitimate pressure', the threat needs to go further than hard-headed commercial tactics. In a situation where the supplier appeared to be at fault, the courts would probably view a threat of non-payment by the customer as nothing more than a hard-headed commercial response (even if carrying out the threat would involve a breach of contract). If, however, the customer has no justification whatsoever for withholding payment, then the threat could amount to duress – but only if the supplier had no practical alternative but to go along with it (and in practice, there may well be several practical alternatives). A further point to consider here is whether any agreement by the supplier to do additional work is supported by consideration from the customer; if the customer is not promising anything in return, the courts may not uphold the agreement (see Chapter 5, in particular the discussion of *Williams v Roffey*).

> **QUESTION 2** The sales director of a company pays a bribe to a purchasing manager who works for one of its customers. In return for the bribe, the purchasing manager ensures that his employer signs an agreement to buy a large quantity of the first company's products. Is the agreement between the two companies illegal?

It is important to distinguish between illegal contracts and perfectly legal contracts that arise because of an illegal act. In this case, there is nothing illegal about the contract between the two companies for supply of products – this is a perfectly normal agreement of the type that businesses enter into every day. If there is an agreement with an illegal purpose here, it is the agreement between the two individuals concerning the payment of a bribe. While the companies concerned could not use illegality to avoid performing the contract for supply of products, they could probably sue the individuals to recover the bribe and any losses they have suffered as a result of entering into a contract that may not represent the best commercial deal for them.

> **QUESTION 3** Restraint of trade can also apply to agreements between businesses that restrict competition, but its importance in regulating such activities has decreased in recent years. Why do you think this is? (Clue: think about the legislation discussed earlier in this section.)

There is substantial overlap between the doctrine of restraint of trade and the Competition Act 1998, which is discussed at the beginning of the section on illegality. While this legislation has not displaced the doctrine of restraint of trade altogether, lawyers advising businesses on any reasonably significant transaction now tend to consider whether any restrictions on competition are enforceable under the Competition Act before they consider restraint of trade. However, the Competition Act only applies to agreements that have a *significant* adverse effect on competition. Restrictions agreed between quite small businesses or restrictions imposed on employees generally have too small an impact to fall within its scope; however, these agreements may still fall within the doctrine of restraint of trade.

> **QUESTION 4** How can businesses protect themselves against minors who refuse to pay?

In practice, it is very much up to businesses to look out for themselves when dealing with minors. However, there are practical ways in which they can protect themselves against minors who refuse to pay. For example, a business selling mobile phones to minors would be well advised to sell only 'pay-as-you-go' models (because these require an upfront payment) or to obtain a guarantee from the minor's parents (which can be enforced under the Minors Contracts Act).

Website summary

The book's website contains the following material in respect of Part 2:

- PowerPoint slides containing relevant information from each chapter to help with revision
- Four additional questions with answers per chapter
- Quiz containing 10 multiple-choice questions for each part
- Biannual update bulletins to the book, which will consist of brief details of any major common law, statutory and constitutional developments affecting the currency of the book

PART THREE

Tort

In Part 2, we examined how the contractual activities of individuals and businesses are determined by the law of contract. These contractual obligations are freely undertaken, but English law also provides for civil obligations to arise through the application of the law of tort. Under tort law, there is a general duty not to intentionally or negligently commit certain acts or omissions that will cause harm or damage to another. The most important tort illustrating the existence of such a duty is *negligence*, a tort that impacts significantly on the activities of individuals, businesses, public authorities and other organisations and whose modern origins stem from the House of Lords decision in the famous case of **Donoghue v Stevenson (1932)**.

Another significant feature of the law of tort, particularly in respect of its impact on businesses, is how it provides for employers to be held liable for acts of employees done in the course of employment. Imposing liability on employers in this way avoids the difficulties that would arise were claimants only able to bring claims against individual employees, as such employees would be unlikely to have the resources to meet the costs of such claims.

In Part 3, the following aspects of the law of tort are covered:

- **The general principles of liability in tort (Chapter 11)**

- **The nature and scope of liability in negligence (Chapter 11)**

- **The liability of individuals and businesses for other torts, such as nuisance and occupiers' liability (Chapter 12)**

- **The liability of employers for the acts of employees under the doctrine of vicarious liability (Chapter 12)**

General principles of liability in tort and the tort of negligence

Learning objectives

By the end of this chapter, you should be able to explain:

- **The distinction between a contractual liability and a liability in tort**
- **How businesses can be liable in tort as a consequence of their activities**
- **How a person can bring an action in the tort of negligence**

Introduction

The chapters in Part 2 explained how contracts are formed, enforced and ended. The two chapters in this part explain a closely related area of law, the law of tort.

Whereas the law of contract deals with obligations freely undertaken by agreement, tort deals with obligations imposed on us in a wider sense. For example, where a business fails to pay for goods it has bought, that business is in breach of a contractual duty. If, by the same token, a business's activity disturbs a neighbour's peace and quiet, it is in breach of a duty owed to others generally and could be sued in the tort of nuisance. So a tort can be defined as a civil wrong (excluding a breach of contract) that gives rise to a claim for damages or another remedy.

General principles of liability in tort

In tort law, the general duty imposed is to not intentionally or negligently do things (or omit to do things) that will cause legally recognised damage to another. There are torts, however, as we shall see later, where liability does not require any fault on the part of anyone involved or that do not require the need to prove that any damage was caused. The two most important examples of torts relevant to businesses are negligence and nuisance. In this chapter, we shall be examining the tort of negligence. Nuisance is dealt with in the next chapter, along with other torts likely to affect the activities of businesses such as nuisance, occupiers' liability and the economic torts.

Duty of care

After contractual liability, the tort of negligence is the most important form of civil action likely to affect businesses and individuals. In order for a claimant to succeed in a claim in negligence, it will be necessary for him to show that he was owed a legal **duty of care**, that the defendant breached that duty and that the failure to take the requisite degree of care caused the claimant's loss or harm. Many cases relate to individuals, but the same principles apply where a business is involved. We shall see later what conditions result in a duty of care being owed.

Defences to an action

Where a claimant has established the ingredients for an action in tort, such as negligence, his claim still may not succeed, for he may find that the defendant is able to rely on a defence to the commission of the tort. In negligence, for instance, where a claimant has partly contributed to his injuries, a defendant can plead **contributory negligence** on the part of the claimant. Although not a complete defence, a successful plea of contributory negligence can lead to a reduction in damages the defendant may have to pay the claimant.

Time limits

The Limitation Act 1980 states that the general time limit on actions in tort is 6 years from the date on which cause of action started (the same time limit, therefore, as for breach of contract). Where, however, the claim is based on negligence, nuisance or **breach of duty** in respect of any personal injuries, the claim period is 3 years from either the date on which it occurred or the date that the injury is known by the claimant to be attributable to another person's act or omission. This is in line with claims brought under the Consumer Protection Act (CPA) 1987 in respect of a defective product causing personal injuries, although no claims under the CPA 1987 can be brought where the product has been in circulation for more than 10 years. The CPA 1987 provides for a no-fault system of liability

 FAQ

What is the purpose of tort law?

The purpose of tort law is to resolve disputes arising from the conflicting personal, property and economic interests of individuals and organisations. In so doing damages may be awarded to those whose interests have been harmed by others. In deciding the amount of damages, the court will award a sum that is enough to place that person in the position they would have been in had the tort not occurred. A range of torts have been created to protect against:

- personal injury/damage arising from negligence (the tort of *negligence*)
- damage to reputation (the tort of *defamation*)
- infringement of personal freedom (the torts of *assault*, *battery* and *false imprisonment*)
- wrongful interference with ownership and enjoyment of property (the torts of *trespass*, *conversion* and *nuisance*)
- wrongful interference with commercial interests (the tort of *passing off*).

for producers of defective goods. There is, therefore, no requirement for the claimant to establish negligence on the part of the defendant. As the CPA 1987 is a measure of consumer protection, its provisions are covered in Chapter 20 on consumer law.

Tort and other forms of liability

Tort and contract

Although a tort can be distinguished from a breach of contract, both branches of law may be involved in a single situation. For example, a manufacturer of dangerous or defective goods may be liable in negligence to the party harmed by those goods and in contract law to a party to whom he sold them. Where the injured party was the purchaser, that person could bring an action in contract and tort.

Tort and criminal law

A tort may also amount to a crime. For example, a manufacturer of dangerous goods may incur criminal as well as tortious liability. Similarly, in a factory accident, an employer could be prosecuted by the Health and Safety Executive under health and safety legislation and could also be sued in tort by the injured party.

Types of liability in tort

There are two forms of liability in tort – primary liability and secondary liability. Both of these have an impact on businesses. Primary liability is where a person who commits a tort can be sued individually or jointly with others; for example, a builder and foreman could be held jointly liable for negligently causing injury through bad workmanship and supervision. An example of secondary liability is where a business (e.g. a sole trader, a partnership or a company) is liable for the torts of its employees. This form of secondary liability is known as *vicarious liability*, a legal doctrine under which an employer is liable for the torts of its employees commited during the course of employment. We will be covering vicarious liability in the next chapter.

 FAQ

In view of the high potential for tort claims in the business world, how important is insurance to a business?

With the law of tort, insurance plays a vital role in business management. While some insurance is compulsory, e.g. employer's public liability insurance and vehicle third-party insurance, other insurance is not, and serious consideration needs to be given to the risk of inadequate insurance. For businesses engaged in providing professional services, such as solicitors, accountants and architects, it may be a condition of membership of a professional body that professional indemnity insurance is taken out in order to cover the business in the event of a claim of professional negligence.

Another feature of insurance is that where a business is insured, the insurance company is likely to 'step into its shoes' in the event of legal action, as it is the insurance company that will foot the bill for any successful action against the business. This would mean that where the manufacturer wanted to settle, it could not do so without the insurer's agreement.

The tort of negligence

Negligence, as a tort, is a breach of a legal duty of care that results in damage caused to another. Most situations in which negligence arises are in a non-contractual setting, e.g. a motorist causing harm to a fellow road user or an employee injuring a fellow employee at a place of work. Not all careless conduct, however, is actionable and what is required is a breach of a legal duty to take care that results in damage to the claimant.

The key ingredients to a successful action in negligence are that:

1 The defendant owed the claimant a legal duty of care.
2 There was a breach of that duty.
3 The breach of duty caused the claimant's loss and the damage suffered by the claimant was of a foreseeable kind.

These ingredients often overlap and cannot always be kept apart, but before examining them in detail, we can see how they operate in practice by reference to the following 'Reality check' textbox.

Reality check

A fictional example of a manufacturer's liability in negligence

Lactophil purchases production line machinery for the manufacture of a new range of 'Greek' yoghurt. Lactophil got a good deal on the equipment because the equipment manufacturer was new to the market and was prepared to undercut competing equipment manufacturers. But, due to a design fault, pipes in the equipment became corroded and lubricant contaminated the yoghurt. Lactophil incurred expenses in (i) putting it right, (ii) recalling and disposing of large quantities of the contaminated yoghurt and (iii) lost orders. The machinery was not purchased directly from the manufacturer but from a distributor, which has since become insolvent, so any contractual claim against the distributor would be worthless and there is no privity of contract with the equipment manufacturer. However, the law of tort allows Lactophil to sue the equipment manufacturer in negligence.

Lactophil's negligence claim, referring back to the three 'key' ingredients, can be applied as follows.

Duty of care?

1 The manufacturer of the equipment is likely to be regarded as owing a duty of care to end users of its machinery, based on the neighbour principle in *Donoghue v Stevenson (1932)* where the claimant obtained a contaminated drink from a friend but successfully sued the manufacturer of the drink.

Breach of the duty?

2 As regards breach of duty, the courts would expect the equipment manufacturer to meet the standards of a reasonable manufacturer of similar equipment. So the fact that the manufacturer was inexperienced in producing this type of equipment would not necessarily excuse the design fault relating to the pipes. A court would ask whether a reasonable manufacturer would have detected the problem. If the answer is yes, then the manufacturer is likely to be in breach.

Did the breach cause the loss and was the loss foreseeable?

3 Lactophil has to show that the breach of duty led to the damage. So, for example, if Lactophil

continued over

failed to follow the equipment manufacturer's instructions properly on cleaning the pipes and it is this that led to the contamination, that might break the chain of causation, even if there is in fact a design fault that might have led to the contamination. Also, Lactophil would only be able to claim for damage that was of a foreseeable kind. This means that the courts do not allow recovery for all the losses of a claimant – only those losses that are not considered 'too remote'. In this case, the cost of repairing the machine and disposing of the contaminated yoghurt would be recoverable but probably not the cost of lost orders as **economic loss** generally is not recoverable in negligence.

QUESTION 1 Suppose Lactophil had purchased the yoghurt-making equipment from the manufacturer of the equipment and not the distributor, could Lactophil have sued the manufacturer for breach of contract as well as in the tort of negligence?

Duty of care

Prior to 1932 the courts took a cautious approach toward actions for negligence and a duty only existed within limited categories such as occupiers of premises and visitors, users of the public highway and skilled tradesmen and their clients.

Donoghue v Stevenson (1932)

The manufacturer of ginger beer sold ginger beer in opaque bottles to a cafe owner in Paisley, near Glasgow. A bottle was sold to a customer who gave it to Mrs Donoghue to drink. She claimed that the bottle contained the decomposed remains of a snail and she alleged that she became seriously ill as a result of drinking the contents of the bottle. She sued the manufacturer in negligence. The House of Lords held that the manufacturers did owe a duty to take care to ensure that the bottle did not contain any noxious matter. In formulating the 'neighbour principle', Lord Atkin said:

> You must take reasonable care to avoid acts or omissions which you can reasonably foresee would be likely to injure your neighbour. Who, then, in law is my neighbour? The answer seems to be those persons who are so closely and directly affected by my act that I ought reasonably to have them in contemplation as being so affected when I am directing my mind to the acts or omissions which are called in question.

The 'neighbour principle' and the foreseeability of damage

In 1932, the landmark case of *Donoghue v Stevenson* moved away from this notion of a 'duty situation' and towards what subsequently became known as the 'neighbour principle'. The reasoning (or *ratio*) of the case was that a manufacturer owes a duty of care to the end user of his products. More significantly, in the context of the development of the tort of negligence, the case decided as part of a wider *ratio* that the tort of negligence was not tied down by existing precedent and that a duty of care is owed by everyone to their 'neighbour'.

In *Donoghue v Stevenson*, the consumer of the product was the 'neighbour' of the manufacturer and sued in negligence for her illness. Lord Atkin based the 'neighbour principle' on reasonable foresight. Liability in negligence since this landmark case has arisen in a wide variety of situations, such as motorists causing harm to fellow road users and employers failing to provide a safe system of work in the workplace. In **Haley v London Electricity Board (1965)**, the claimant fell into a hole in the pavement left by the defendant working on the street. The precautions taken by the defendant were sufficient for a sighted person, but the claimant was blind. He was injured when he fell into the trench. The court held that there was a duty of care owed to a blind person as they were within the category of people who should have been in the foresight of the defendant as someone likely to walk the streets.

> **QUESTION 2** If a motorist failed to have motor insurance and, as a result of negligent driving, caused harm to a pedestrian, would the pedestrian be prevented from bringing a claim against the driver?

It is probably true to say that many matters might be reasonably foreseeable, e.g. psychiatric illness suffered by a witness to a horrific accident or loss of profits sustained by a business following the forced closure of a factory. The law, however, does not always allow recovery by such victims. In **Bourhill v Young (1943)** a woman who was pregnant suffered **nervous shock** after attending the scene of a motorcycle accident. She went to the scene after hearing the impact of the collision from a distance of 50 metres away as she was alighting from a tram. She later suffered a miscarriage. Her action failed as the court considered her to be outside the immediate impact of the accident. Her loss was not a reasonably foreseeable consequence of the motorcyclist's negligence.

Since the case of *Donoghue v Stevenson (1932)*, the 'neighbour principle' has been refined and the current position is to be found in **Caparo Industries plc v Dickman (1990)** where the House of Lords laid down a threefold test to be applied in order to see whether a duty of care exists. In addition to reasonable foresight, whether a duty of care exists depends on the existence of a close and proximate relationship between the parties and whether it is fair, just and reasonable to impose a duty.

Proximity

While closely related to the matter of foresight, *proximity* refers to the nature of the relationship between the claimant and the defendant. This has played a significant role in determining the existence of a duty in cases not involving physical harm to the claimant or damage to the claimant's property. In these cases different considerations apply. For instance, in a case of economic loss arising from negligent advice, there is a need for a 'special relationship' to exist between the person giving the advice and the person receiving it. In the case of psychiatric harm suffered by a witness of an accident, there is a need for a 'close relationship of love and affection'. Both these areas are discussed later.

The 'floodgates' factor

What is 'fair, just and reasonable' is a factor used by the courts as a means of addressing the *'floodgates'* argument, i.e. the courts ask whether, if a duty of care were to be imposed, would it lead to the opening of a 'floodgate' of claims. To limit this, the courts, looking at considerations of public policy, have applied a third constraint on the existence of a duty of care, namely, whether in the circumstances it is fair, just and reasonable to impose a duty. However, it is important to consider the impact of the Human Rights Act 1998 in this area – see ***Osman v UK (2000)*** and ***Z v UK (2001)***. Consider ***Hill v Chief Constable of Yorkshire (1987)***.

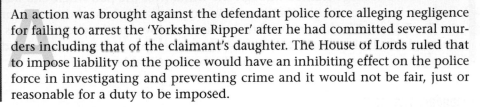

Hill v Chief Constable of Yorkshire (1987)

An action was brought against the defendant police force alleging negligence for failing to arrest the 'Yorkshire Ripper' after he had committed several murders including that of the claimant's daughter. The House of Lords ruled that to impose liability on the police would have an inhibiting effect on the police force in investigating and preventing crime and it would not be fair, just or reasonable for a duty to be imposed.

Cases like *Donoghue v Stevenson (1932)* and *Haley v LEB (1965)* are a straightforward application of a duty of care to a situation involving physical injury. Similarly, the courts have no difficulty in applying the same principles to cases involving damage to a claimant's property. There are, however, cases involving different types of loss that the courts have had to deal with and it to these that we now turn to. It should be borne in mind that such cases can have impact on businesses either because a business is the party committing or suffering the harm or because a business has 'stepped into the shoes' of one of the parties in its capacity as an insurer.

Duty of care and psychiatric harm (nervous shock)

Psychiatric harm (or nervous shock) is a term used in law to describe the incidence of a recognised psychiatric illness caused by the negligence of the defendant. A recognised psychiatric injury must be proved to have occurred, i.e. some form of psychiatric illness, such as post-traumatic stress disorder (PTSD). Damages for 'ordinary' grief, sorrow or distress are not recoverable. The law demands that the claimant must prove that psychiatric injury was a reasonably foreseeable consequence of the defendant's negligence, i.e. a bystander of reasonable fortitude would have suffered psychiatric illness.

Most of the case law on nervous shock revolves around employees in the workplace or individuals witnessing horrific events and involve two categories of victim. The first category comprises victims who suffer physical harm and psychiatric harm. Psychiatric harm as a consequence of physical harm is recoverable, applying the general principles of negligence. The second category comprises victims who suffer psychiatric injury alone (or *pure* nervous shock). Of the second category, victims who suffer psychiatric injury after having been put in personal danger of physical harm are known as primary victims. Victims who suffer psychiatric injury after witnessing injury to others are known as secondary victims. To recover damages for nervous shock as a secondary victim is more difficult. This might sound complicated but the cases that follow should enable you to understand the distinction between the two categories.

Primary victims

Where the claimant suffers psychiatric harm, as a result of reasonably fearing for his or her own safety, damages are recoverable, so long as the claimant is within the area of reasonably forseeable physical risk. This is illustrated in the following case study.

In Dulieu v White (1901) a publican's wife suffered extreme shock when a horse-drawn carriage crashed through the window of the pub where she was working. She miscarried her baby as a consequence and claimed damages for the shock she suffered. It was held that a duty was owed in the circumstances. Although she had not suffered physical harm, she feared that she would and damages for the resultant nervous shock were recoverable.

Secondary victims

Recovery of damages for pure nervous shock as a secondary victim depends on whether the nervous shock suffered by the claimant was foreseeable due to proximity (such as the claimant witnessing the event through their own unaided senses) and the relationship that the claimant bears to the injured person (such as parent and child or spouse and spouse). For example, in the case of *Hambrook v Stokes (1925)*, a lorry careered out of control towards an area where a mother knew her children to be. She suffered nervous shock and had a miscarriage. Her action succeeded. There was a relationship of parent and child and she had witnessed the incident with her own unaided senses.

The law was developed further by the House of Lords' decision in *McLoughlin v O'Brien (1983)*, where the victim's family was involved in a car accident that resulted in the death of one of her children, serious injury to two others and injury and shock to her husband. She did not witness the accident, having been two miles away at the time, but was told to come to the casualty department. On arriving at the hospital, she discovered that her family was still covered in dirt and blood and her son was screaming in pain and fear. She suffered nervous shock and sued the defendant. Her action was successful since (i) despite her not witnessing the accident, she had experienced the immediate aftermath of the accident, (ii) she experienced it with her own senses and (iii) she, with her close 'blood tie', was part of a category of persons for which shock was foreseeable.

The Hillsborough disaster

These factors of proximity and relationship were developed subsequently in *Alcock v Chief Constable of South Yorkshire (1991)*, a case arising from the Hillsborough disaster in which 95 football supporters died (see the 'Reality check' textbox).

Reality check

The Hillsborough disaster – Alcock v Chief Constable of South Yorkshire (1991)

In 1989, at the semi-final of the FA Cup at Hillsborough, Sheffield, prior to the start of the match between Liverpool and Nottingham Forest, a policing error directed too many Liverpool fans into a single enclosure. This, coupled with the fact that the fans were entering the ground late, meant that there was a surge of fans into the enclosure. Fans at the front were crushed against the metal barrier fencing and unable to escape. Ninety-five fans lost their lives and a further 400 needed hospital treatment.

Claims brought on behalf of those suffering physical injury or death were settled out of court, but there remained primary and secondary victims who had suffered nervous shock. The primary victims were those, including rescuers, who were involved in the incident and who suffered psychiatric illness (this is discussed in **White v Chief Constable of South Yorkshire (1998)**). The secondary victims, who represented the largest category, witnessed the incident (at the ground, on the television, on the radio) and suffered nervous shock as a result.

The House of Lords held that in order for the secondary victims to recover for pure nervous shock they would have to show that they must have (i) sufficiently close ties of love and affection with the person endangered or harmed; (ii) been present at the accident or immediate aftermath; and (iii) perceived directly the events of the accident or its immediate aftermath.

There was a range of secondary victims in the *Alcock* case but none satisfied these criteria. Unsuccessful litigants included:

- brothers and brothers-in-law of those killed and physically injured who were found on the facts not to have exhibited a close tie of love and affection

- a sibling who identified a brother 8 hours after the incident was considered not to be in the immediate aftermath

- people in the football ground and outside the ground and those watching on the television who were not considered to have experienced the incident at close enough hand.

The distinction between primary and secondary victims was developed in **White v Chief Constable of South Yorkshire (1998)**, which was another case arising from the Hillsborough disaster. In the *White* case, there were four claimant police officers. Some of them had dealt directly with the victims, giving cardio-pulmonary resuscitation, lifting the dead and dying over the fencing and carrying the dead bodies from the scene to a temporary mortuary. They argued that either the police, as their employers, owed them a duty of care as employees or that the police owed them a duty of care as rescuers. In addition, they argued that, given their close involvement with the tragedy, the policemen were primary victims and, therefore, not subject to the restrictions set out in *Alcock* that applied to secondary victims. In reversing the Court of Appeal decision, the House of Lords rejected their claim. Primary victims were restricted to those physically injured or in danger of being physically injured. Rescuers, whether professional or voluntary, and employees witnessing such events must, in the absence of being a primary victim, satisfy the criteria set out in the *Alcock* case.

Relevance of nervous shock to business

The relevance for businesses of the case law on nervous shock is that businesses can be responsible for accidents and may have liability to people other than those who suffer physical injuries as a direct result. In connection with recent rail accidents, Network Rail (fomerly Railtrack) has paid significant sums in compensation, based essentially on its liability in tort. Any extension of liability to people suffering nervous shock means that the premiums paid by businesses for liability insurance would be higher than would otherwise be the case.

Liability for negligent misstatements

You may recall from Chapter 9, on the validity of contracts, that a party that is induced to enter into a contract on the basis of a false statement of fact has an action for rescission of the contract and damages against the other party. There may, however, be circumstances where a party relies on a misleading statement where there is no contract between the person making the statement (the adviser) and the person relying on the statement (the advisee). In these circumstances, the advisee as claimant would need to establish liability for **negligent misstatement** under tort law.

The courts were once reluctant to find a rule that a defendant who negligently makes a false statement is liable if the claimant foreseeably suffers loss as the result of the statement. This was because it was thought that to some extent different considerations applied to words than to acts. Until the decision in ***Hedley Byrne & Co Ltd v Heller & Partners Ltd (1964)*** (see below), the courts did not award damages for negligent statement causing financial loss to a claimant unless the statement constituted a breach of contract or amounted to a misrepresentation, or the defendant was in breach of a fiduciary duty owed to the claimant (such as the formal relationship of trust between solicitor and client or accountant and client).

After *Hedley Byrne* the courts were prepared to make an award of damages for a negligent statement in circumstances where a 'special relationship' could be said to exist, so that a duty of care would arise between the maker of the statement and the person receiving the information.

Hedley Byrne & Co Ltd v Heller & Partners Ltd (1964)

Advertising agents were worried about the financial status of a client, Easipower, and they sought a statement from their bank about its financial security. A good reference was received from the client's bank, subject to an exclusion clause covering any inaccuracies. The advertising agents relied on the statement and lost a large sum of money when Easipower became insolvent. The House of Lords held that the exclusion clause operated to deny recovery, but had it not existed, the client's bank would have owed the advertising agents a duty of care because there was a 'special relationship' between the parties and reasonable reliance had been placed on the statement by the advertising agents.

In *Hedley Byrne*, the House of Lords did not define what was meant by a 'special relationship'. However, subsequent case law has shown that there is a need for an adviser to have given information or advice in circumstances where he knows or should have known that it was likely to be relied on by the recipient or another person. The typical scenario is where advice is given in the context of a business or professional relationship by a skilled and experienced person. However, it is possible for social exchange to give rise to a duty provided it is clear that carefully considered advice is being sought and is relied on.

In **Caparo Industries plc v Dickman (1990)**, the House of Lords reviewed the meaning of a 'special relationship' in respect of negligent advice and defined the extent of an auditor's duty of care in tort. The facts are discussed in the case study textbox.

The House of Lords in *Caparo* held that the requirements for a duty of care to exist are the same as for an action based on negligent acts, namely:

1 Was the damage or loss a reasonably foreseeable result of the activity?
2 Was there a 'close and direct relationship of proximity' between the claimant and the defendant?
3 Was it 'fair, just and reasonable' to impose a duty of care?

As a general principle developed from this case, the House of Lords held that where a defendant gives advice or information *and* they were fully aware of the purpose of the advice *and* were aware of the nature of the transaction that the claimant had in mind, a duty of care is owed. In contrast, where a statement or advice was given that is in general circulation and it could be foreseen that a person might rely on it for a variety of purposes, none of which the adviser would have any particular reason to contemplate, a duty of care would not be owed.

Disclaimers

You may recall from the facts of the *Hedley Byrne* case that the use of a disclaimer protected the bank from liability for any negligent advice. The case arose before the passing of the Unfair Contract Terms Act (UCTA) 1977 and any similar exemption clause would now be subject to the provisions of the UCTA 1977. Under the UCTA 1977, a person in the course of business cannot exclude liability, in any contract or notice, for financial loss, including damage to property, unless he can show the clause to be reasonable. In **Smith v Eric S Bush (1990); Harris v**

Caparo plc v Dickman (1990)

The defendants were auditors of the accounts of a public company and produced annual accounts in accordance with their duty under the Companies Act 1985. The claimants were existing shareholders of the company who relied on the company's audited accounts to purchase more shares in order to take over the company. The takeover was not a success and the claimants lost a considerable amount of money. They accused the auditors of negligently auditing the accounts. The House of Lords held that the extent of any duty of care owed by auditors was to existing shareholders as a whole insofar as they could use the accounts for purposes associated with their role in the company. The duty did not extend to individual shareholders for matters the purpose of which could not be ascertained at the time of the giving of the advice – i.e. the future purchase of further shares.

FAQ

What type of businesses may be liable for negligent misstatement?

Lawyers, financial advisers, surveyors, accountants and management consultants might be considered obvious examples, but any business can be liable where it makes a statement that it knows others will be likely to rely on. In *Spring v Guardian Assurance (1994)*, a reference was given about an ex-employee stating that he had little integrity and was involved in selling unsuitable insurance products to clients. This was an honest belief when written. The ex-employee sued, claiming that they owed him a duty of care not to write careless references. The House of Lords held that the employer does owe a duty of care to employees and ex-employees to not cause economic loss by writing careless references. The principle in *Hedley Byrne* was not restricted to negligent advice or information given to someone but could be extended to cover comments made *about* someone.

Wyre District Council (1990), the House of Lords ruled that a clause in a contract excluding a surveyor or valuer from liability for a negligent survey or valuation was unreasonable and could not be relied on. It would be unfair for a person claiming professional expertise to exclude liability for failing to provide such expertise where he would know or ought to know that the purchaser of the property would rely on him.

Liability for economic loss

Pure economic loss is loss suffered by the claimant that is not linked to personal injury or injury to property. An example is a loss of profits suffered by a business. Apart from a couple of special cases, the courts do not allow recovery for pure economic loss. This is because recovery of pure financial loss would lead to difficult problems of limiting the extent of liability and would impose an immense burden on the defendant. The exception to this rule is to be found in the *Hedley Byrne* case, as we saw earlier, where financial loss emanating from negligent words or advice, as opposed to negligent acts, is recoverable.

Although pure economic loss is not recoverable, damages for consequential economic loss can be recovered. The distinction between the two is illustrated in **Spartan Steel and Alloys Ltd v Martin & Co Ltd (1972)** (see case study textbox), where the claimant claimed for two different types of loss of profit.

Breach of duty

Once the claimant has shown that the defendant owed him a duty of care, he must prove that there was a breach of the duty of care. Whether there is a breach of duty is judged by reference to the **reasonable man** and the question to be asked is whether, in the circumstances, the defendant achieved the standard expected of the reasonable man. Where the defendant's conduct fails to pass this test, he is said to be in breach of his duty of care. The standard of care expected to be shown is objectively assessed. In **Nettleship v Weston (1971)**, for example, the court held that a learner driver was expected to exhibit the same degree of skill as an experienced driver. However, in relation to skilled persons, the standard of care is judged by what an ordinary skilled person in that job or profession would have done – see **Bolam v Friern Hospital Management Committee (1957)**, which was concerned with the standard expected of the reasonable doctor.

Spartan Steel and Alloys Ltd v Martin & Co Ltd (1972)

The claimant operated a steel smelting factory and the defendant's employees cut through the main electricity cable while digging up the road. As a result of the loss of power, three kinds of damage were suffered: (i) physical damage to the machinery; (ii) the cost representing the loss of the profit of the melt that was in the machinery at the time of the accident (i.e. consequential economic loss); and (iii) the cost representing the loss of profit on four further melts that the claimant was unable to start until the machinery was repaired (i.e. pure economic loss). It was held that, despite all three types of loss being reasonably foreseeable, only the loss arising from the physical damage and the consequential economic loss were recoverable. The loss of profit from the four further melts were not recoverable as that loss did not flow from the claimant's physical loss.

It is important to be clear that cases on breach of duty serve only as illustrations. It is for a court to decide on the facts whether, in the circumstances, a duty of care has been breached and, in arriving at a decision, a court can take into account several factors. These factors are as follows:

- the degree of risk to the claimant created by the defendant's conduct
- the seriousness of the harm that the claimant may suffer
- the social utility of the defendant's action
- the expense and practicability of taking precautions against the risk.

Degree of risk to the claimant created by the defendant's conduct

Whether the defendant can be judged to have taken reasonable care depends on the degree of risk. The court will consider the likelihood of injury against the seriousness of the injury that is risked. The greater the risk of injury the more unreasonable it would be not to take precautions. In **Bolton v Stone (1951)**, a batsman, who hit a cricket ball out of a village cricket ground and struck the claimant in the road, was judged not to be in breach of duty because the risk had been small. The ground was surrounded by a fence 17 feet high, the part of the fence the ball had crossed was a considerable distance from the wicket (100 metres) and a cricket ball had been hit out of the ground only six times in 30 years. The limited likelihood of injury did not demand more be done than was done.

Seriousness of the harm that the claimant may suffer

A reasonable person would be, or ought to be, influenced not only by the greater or lesser probability of an accident occurring but also by the gravity of the consequences if an accident did occur. In **Paris v Stepney Borough Council (1951)**, the claimant was a one-eyed employee of the defendant council who had lost an eye in a previous work related incident. He was a mechanic who regularly inspected and repaired council vehicles. The work involved welding, which exposed employees to some risk of eye injury, although not enough normally to warrant the issue of protective goggles. While inspecting the underside of a vehicle, a piece of metal entered his good eye and blinded him.

The defendant council was held liable. The risk of injury to the particular claimant was severe, as the loss of an eye was graver for a one-eyed person than it was for a two-eyed person.

Social utility of the defendant's action

The reasonableness of the defendant's conduct will also depend on the proportion that the risk bears to the object to be attained, e.g. the saving of life or limb justifies taking risks that would not be permissible in the case of an ordinary commercial enterprise. In **Watt v Hertfordshire County Council (1954)**, a fireman was injured by an unsecured jack while in a vehicle not designed to carry such a heavy jack. The jack was needed to save the life of a woman who was trapped under a heavy car. The fireman's action failed. The importance of the objective of saving the woman's life outweighed the extra risk undertaken.

> **QUESTION 3** Can any driver of an emergency vehicle be excused from negligent driving?

Expense and practicability of taking precautions against the risk

The risk has to be weighed against the measures necessary to eliminate it. The greater risk, the less the weight should be given to the questions of cost of taking precautionary measures in terms of time or money. In **Latimer v AEC Ltd (1953)**, the defendant's factory became flooded after a rainstorm and water mixed with oil on the factory floor. Sawdust was spread on the floor but the claimant slipped on an uncovered patch. It was held that the defendant had taken all reasonable precautions and was not in breach of duty. Closing the factory would have been costly and out of proportion to the risk.

Causation and remoteness of damage

Once a duty of care has been shown to exist and the duty has been breached, the final element of a claim is that of **causation** and **remoteness of damage**. Causation requires that the claimant establish that the breach of the duty owed

 FAQ

Who must prove 'negligence'?

The burden of proof, as with the other elements of an action in negligence, is on the claimant. Proving a breach of duty, however, may in practice be very difficult. The claimant, if injured, may not recall what happened, or witnesses may be non-existent or evidence may be destroyed. However, where the cause of the accident lies solely within the knowledge of the defendant who caused it, the maxim *res ipsa loquitor* (the thing speaks for itself) may be raised and applied by the courts. This means that where there was no explanation for what had happened and there was an apparent lack of care, the defendant is considered to be best placed, having control of the situation, to advise the court on how it happened. Under these circumstances, the onus is on the defendant to *disprove* negligence.

In **Scott v London & St Katherine's Docks (1865)**, the claimant had been hit by bags of flour that had fallen from a window of a warehouse the defendant occupied. It was held that the facts 'spoke for themselves' and, on application of the principle, the onus was on the defendant to provide an explanation for the falling flour. He was unable to do so and he was held liable.

In Barnett v Chelsea and Kensington Hospital Management Committee (1969)

Three night watchmen, one of whom was the claimant's husband, arrived at a hospital early in the morning complaining of vomiting after drinking tea. The nurse on duty consulted with a doctor by phone who advised that the man go home and consult his own doctor. Later the same day, the claimant's husband died of arsenic poisoning. A claim of negligence was brought but the action failed. There had been a clear breach of duty by the doctor failing to examine the patient but the breach had not caused death. The claimant's husband would have died from the level of arsenic already in his body.

by the defendant caused or contributed to the claimant's injury or damage, i.e. *but for* the defendant's conduct, the damage to the claimant would not have occurred. This has become known as the 'but for' test. Remoteness of damage is concerned with the consequences for which the defendant should be liable.

Causation

In order to succeed in his action, the claimant must be able to prove a causal connection between the breach and the damage suffered (see the *Barnett* case study textbox).

What can break the chain of causation?

Where the chain of events is broken by an independent or new act intervening between the wrongful act and the resulting damage (called a **novus actus interveniens**), over which the defendant has no control, causation cannot be shown, for the chain of causation is broken. Such an act must be an independent or new act in the sense that it is unconnected with the initial act. Where it is something that happens as a consequence of the initial breach, or is a foreseeable event arising from the breach and so intrinsically bound up with it, then the defendant will remain liable. This is sometimes difficult to distinguish (see the *Lamb* case study textbox to help you grasp the principle involved).

Lamb v Camden London Borough Council (1981)

The defendants negligently damaged a water main, which flooded the claimant's house. The house was vacated for repairs but squatters moved in and damaged the property further. It was held that the defendant not liable for the squatters' damage because of the unlikeliness of the event and because it was not the duty of the defendant to keep squatters out. The damaged state of the house was as a result of the 'intervening act' of the squatters moving in.

Is the 'but for' test applied in all cases of causation?

In some cases, such as the *McGhee* and *Fairchild* cases that follow, the 'but for' test does not work in favour of the claimant because it is not possible to show that the defendant's conduct caused the claimant's loss. However, not to allow recovery in these cases, which are based on exceptional circumstances, would be seen as causing an injustice. So, to avoid the claimant going uncompensated, the House of Lords has developed alternative approaches to the issue of causation. In **McGhee v National Coal Board (1972)**, the claimant worked in very hot and dirty conditions in a brick kiln. No showers were provided and he could not get clean until he got home from work. He later contracted dermatitis. The claimant could not prove that showering before leaving work would have prevented his condition but, as medical evidence showed that a lack of showers increased greatly his chances of obtaining dermatitis, the House of Lords held the defendant was liable. In **Fairchild v Glenhaven Funeral Services Ltd (2002)** the 'but for' test did not benefit the claimants who contracted mesothelioma, a form of cancer, from working for more than one employer in the asbestos industry, as it could not be established that a particular employer's asbestos fibre or fibres caused the claimants' illness. The House of Lords ruled that the approach in McGhee was to be adopted on the basis that all the employers had increased materially the claimants' chances of contracting the condition and not to allow recovery would have been unjust.

Remoteness of damage

As well as establishing a causal connection between the breach of duty and the damage suffered, the claimant must also show that the damage was not too remote a consequence of the defendant's negligent act and that the damage resulted from the type of risk that the defendant created. The test is one of reasonable foreseeability, as illustrated in the *Overseas Tankships* case study.

Overseas Tankships (UK) Ltd v Morts Dock & Engineering Co Ltd, *The Wagonmound* (1961)

The defendants negligently spilled oil from a ship called *The Wagonmound* into Sydney Harbour. The oil spread to the claimant's wharf where welding was taking place. The claimants were assured that the oil would not ignite and resumed welding. However, molten metal fell onto cotton waste floating in the harbour. This ignited the waste and this set fire to the oil. The fire spread to the wharf and the rest of the harbour causing substantial damage. It was held that the defendants were only liable for the fouling caused by the oil and not for the fire damage to the wharf. As the oil had a high ignition point, it could not reasonably be foreseen that it would ignite on water.

Hughes v Lord Advocate (1963)

Post Office employees negligently left open a manhole cover and two boys climbed down it. The manhole had a striped tent over it and was surrounded by paraffin lamps. One of these lamps was taken by one of the boys into the hole and, after dropping it, he suffered severe burns when it ignited flammable vapours in the manhole causing an explosion. Their action was successful. The type of damage, i.e. harm by burning, could have been foreseen by the reasonable man – in this case where boys had access to burning paraffin lamps. The fact that the burns were caused by an explosion, which was unforeseeable, did not prevent the action succeeding.

As we can see in the *Hughes* case study, although the damage must be of a type that is within the class of risk created, neither the precise extent of the damage nor the precise manner of its infliction need be foreseeable.

The eggshell skull rule

It does not matter if the claimant's damage is aggravated by some physical peculiarity he has, provided that the injury is within the class of risk created. The principle in these situations is that the defendant 'takes his victim as he finds him'. Also known as the **eggshell skull rule**, this principle states that where negligent liability is established, it is no defence to complain that the extent of damage suffered is high because the average person would not have been so severely injured. Consider the *Smith* case study.

Defences

Once a claim in tort has been brought, the defendant may wish to avoid or limit the extent of his liability by raising a defence. There are a range of defences available. Some are general to all torts, e.g. mistake, inevitable accident and necessity, while others are specific to certain torts, e.g. the defence of 'privilege' in defamation. Three general defences have a particular application in negligence and these are: (i) illegality, (ii) **volenti non fit injuria** (consent) (which are complete defences) and (iii) contributory negligence (which is a partial defence).

In Smith v Leech Brain & Co (1962)

A worker had molten metal splash on his lip while at work. He suffered a minor burn, which was foreseeable. However, he had a pre-cancerous skin condition, unknown to anybody, which, when burned by the metal, triggered cancer, from which he died. His widow sued successfully in negligence, relying on the eggshell skull rule. It was no defence to argue that her husband was more likely to suffer harm than someone without such a pre-existing condition.

Complete defences

Illegality This complete defence is raised and used as an aspect of public policy and precludes someone engaged in an illegal activity from being able to sue successfully in tort. This defence has little relevance to businesses and tends to be applied in cases involving criminal conduct.

Volenti non injuria (consent) *Volenti non fit injuria* (meaning 'no injury is done to a consenting party') is another example of a complete defence to a tort. The nature of the defence is that there is deemed to be no injury done to the claimant because the alleged victim has consented to the risk involved. The courts, in assessing whether a claimant consented, adopt an objective test, i.e. was the behaviour of the claimant such that it was reasonable to think that they had consented.

For the defence to succeed, it must be shown that the claimant assented to the risk and that such consent was freely given. Just having knowledge of the risk is not enough, as can be seen in the following case.

ICI v Shatwell (1965)

The claimant and his brother, James, were experienced shot-firers employed by ICI and were told not to engage in unsafe practices when testing detonators. They ignored the warnings and tested the detonators without taking the appropriate precautions, including failing to retreat to a shelter. In an explosion, the claimant was injured. He sued ICI, as being vicariously liable for the acts of his brother. The action was unsuccessful as the defence of consent was available to James' conduct. ICI was not vicariously liable.

The defence of consent has been used in a number of sporting cases, where a participant or spectator has suffered harm as the result of a sporting activity. The leading case is ***Wooldridge v Sumner (1963)***.

Wooldridge v Sumner (1963)

The claimant was a photographer at a horse show, taking photographs from the edge of the arena. As a result of an error in judgement, the defendant failed to turn his horse and hit the claimant, injuring him. The claimant's action was unsuccessful. It was held that the defendant had made an error of judgement and had not disregarded the safety of others by his actions. A person attending a sports event takes the risk of any damage caused to him, unless a reckless disregard of his safety has occurred.

The use of consent as a defence has become less frequent since the Unfair Contract Terms Act 1977 (UCTA) was passed. The act prevents the exclusion of liability, in any contract or notice, for death or personal injury due to negligence.

Partial defences

Contributory negligence Unlike the two previous defences, contributory negligence is not a complete defence but a partial defence. The nature of the defence is that a claimant should not be entitled to receive a full entitlement of damages where they have contributed to their own injury or damage.

Under the Law Reform (Contributory Negligence) Act 1945 damages are reduced by the court in proportion to the claimant's own share of responsibility. It is not necessary that the claimant owed a duty of care or was negligent. What is required is that the claimant failed to take proper care for his own safety and contributed to his own injury or damage. The defence of contributory negligence has led to a reduction in damages of 25% for motorists not wearing seatbelts where negligently injured by other motorists and 15% for motorcyclists not wearing crash helmets. In *Capps v Miller (1989)*, a 10% reduction in damages was imposed on a motorcyclist failing to secure the straps of his motorcycle helmet.

QUESTION 4 If I fail to wear a seatbelt and I am injured as a result of another person's negligent driving, does that failure amount to contributory negligence?

Answers to in-text questions

QUESTION 1 Suppose Lactophil had purchased the yoghurt-making equipment from the manufacturer of the equipment and not the distributor, could Lactophil have sued the manufacturer for breach of contract as well as in the tort of negligence?

Yes, as there can be concurrent liability in contract and tort, although the rules relating to the recovery of damages are not always the same.

QUESTION 2 If a motorist failed to have motor insurance and, as a result of negligent driving, caused harm to a pedestrian, would the pedestrian be prevented from bringing a claim against the driver?

The absence of insurance does not prevent the pedestrian, or any other victim, from suing the motorist in negligence. The principles of liability are not dependent on one party being insured. However, the presence of insurance does ensure, to the extent of available cover, that the victim does not go uncompensated where, for example, the motorist has insufficient resources to meet the victim's claim.

> **QUESTION 3** Can any driver of an emergency vehicle be excused from negligent driving?

No, only if the court is satisfied that the social utility of the driver's act, as balanced against other factors, if relevant, outweighed the risk involved.

> **QUESTION 4** If I fail to wear a seatbelt and I am injured as a result of another person's negligent driving, does that failure amount to contributory negligence?

No. It is not the act of failing to wear a seatbelt that is determining of contributory negligence, but whether the failure to wear the seatbelt in circumstances where it should have been worn, would have prevented, or lessened the extent of, your injuries.

12 | Other business-related torts and vicarious liability

By the end of this chapter, you should be able to explain:

- **How businesses can be held liable in respect of torts other than negligence, such as nuisance, occupiers' liability and the economic torts**
- **How businesses can be held liable for torts committed by their employees**

Introduction

The purpose of this chapter is to show how businesses and their activities can lead to liability in torts other than negligence. The most significant of these are nuisance, occupiers' liability and the economic torts.

Businesses and individuals may be liable directly for the commission of a tort, but a business, as an employer, can also be held liable for the acts of employees and this chapter will be examining the extent of that liability under the doctrine of vicarious liability. Not all tortious acts of an employee cause the employer to be held liable, for a distinction has to be drawn between an act of the employee that is done in the **course of employment** and an act of an employee that is an independent act.

Other business-related torts

Nuisance

The tort of nuisance can be divided into two categories: private nuisance and public nuisance. Private nuisance has greater importance for businesses than public nuisance.

Private nuisance

Private nuisance is a tort that attempts to balance conflicting interests in land use. The interests of a factory owner differ from his neighbour in adjoining residential property as do those of an old people's home with a night-club next door. These matters are regulated by planning and pollution controls, noise legislation, local bye-laws and restrictive covenants on the sale of land. But where these legal and administrative controls fail in an individual case, the injured party may bring a civil action for private nuisance. The case in the 'Reality check' textbox below, for example, was concerned with residents of a tower block who complained that television reception was unlawfully interfered with by the development of Canary Wharf in the docklands area of London.

Definition of nuisance Private nuisance is defined as unreasonable interference with a person's use or enjoyment of land. Because the law is trying to reconcile the conflicting interests of the parties, it is more concerned with the impact of the interference on the victim rather than the intention of the party who caused it. For example, a court might decide that the smell from a pig farm is a nuisance to a neighbour despite the farmer's efforts to control it.

To some extent, nuisance appears to overlap with negligence. For example, in ***Leakey v National Trust (1980)***, the defendants allowed a mound of earth to slip onto the claimant's land. Although the claimant sued in nuisance, an action could have been brought in negligence. The defendants knew that the mound was liable to cracking and slipping but refused to carry out any repairs. Generally, an isolated act amounts to negligence while a continuing state of affairs is considered a nuisance. In ***Canary Wharf Ltd v Hunter (1997)***, the House of Lords stated that nuisance affects rights, use and enjoyment in land whereas negligence deals with conduct affecting people generally.

Unreasonable interference The interference may cause physical damage to property (e.g. fumes from a factory that damage plants and trees) or may encroach on

Reality check

Interference with television reception – Hunter v Canary Wharf Ltd (1997)

The claimants were residents in a block of flats who discovered that the development of Canary Wharf in London by the defendant caused interference with television reception, in particular the construction of a 250-metre high, steel-clad tower. The House of Lords ruled that only those with rights in land, such as owners and tenants in common, could bring a claim in nuisance and that interference with a television signal (as with blocking a view) by the construction of a building did not amount to an actionable nuisance. The interests of the residents had to be balanced with the interests of other land users who wished to develop their land by constructing buildings.

The interests of the latter were held to prevail in this case. The House of Lords did stress that such activities can be controlled by planning laws or contractual agreements, but there was no breach of such laws or obligations in this case.

Canary Wharf, London

property (as in the *Leakey* case just examined) or it may simply interfere with enjoyment (e.g. loud music).

The interference must be unreasonable. The courts have not allowed slight or trivial interference to justify a claim, such as crying children, and interference that may be reasonable in one locality may not be in another. A nuisance in a residential area is not the same as a nuisance in an industrial area, although interference may still be unreasonable in an area where industry already interferes with the enjoyment of property.

The duration of the nuisance is also a factor in determining liability. The sound of cement mixers, pneumatic drills and pile drivers may amount to a nuisance over a long period but may not be in the short term.

Defences to nuisance The defendant can avoid liability if he can show that the nuisance was caused by an 'Act of God', i.e. a storm, earthquake or other natural disaster. However, he must show that he did not know of it or could not reasonably know of it or that he took reasonable steps to end it. In **Goldman v Hargrave (1967)**, the defendant was held liable for damage where he failed to put out a fire caused by lightening striking a tree on his land. The fire spread to a neighbour's land and it was held that the fire on the defendant's land could have been put out by the use of water at an earlier stage.

It is also a defence to show that the nuisance was authorised by statute. In **Allen v Gulf Oil Refining Ltd (1981)**, the defendants, sued in nuisance for operating an oil refinery, successfully argued that they were authorised to do so by statute.

Who can sue and be sued? Any party who has an interest in the land affected by the nuisance can sue. This will be the occupier, who may or may not be the owner, so that, for example, a landlord not in occupation can sue where the nuisance causes lasting damage to his property. The occupier, is liable for a nuisance originating on the land, whether or not he caused it, provided he knew or ought to have known of the nuisance and failed to take reasonable steps to stop it. In **Canary Wharf Ltd v Hunter (1997)**, the House of Lords ruled that in that case only owners and tenants in common could bring a claim in nuisance in respect of the interference with a television signal.

Remedies for private nuisance As the victim wants the nuisance stopped, he will seek an *injunction*. An injunction is a discretionary remedy issued by a court that

FAQ

Is it a defence to show that an activity has taken place over a very long period of time?

The defendant can claim that he has a legal right to pursue an activity after 20 years, but time only runs from when it became a nuisance, not from when the activity began. In **Miller v Jackson (1977)** the claimant bought a new house by a cricket field on which the game had been played for nearly 70 years. The claimant brought an action for nuisance 4 years after purchase because cricket balls were frequently hit onto his land. His claim was successful as it was held that the 20-year defence ran from the time that the house was purchased, not from when the activity began. This case also shows that it is no defence that the claimant moved to the nuisance and, by so doing, consented to it.

restrains someone from committing or continuing to commit an unlawful act. In awarding an injunction the court must weigh not only the interests of the claimant and defendant but also the wider community. Damages can be awarded instead of an injunction to compensate for personal injury, damage to property and economic loss, as in negligence. An alternative is for the claimant to abate the nuisance, which means that the claimant can enter the defendant's premises in order to stop the nuisance The claimant must give notice of entry to the defendant's property (except in an emergency) and must do no more than is necessary in bringing the nuisance to an end.

Public nuisance

Public nuisance, as the name suggests, is concerned with acts that affect the comfort and convenience of the public generally. It is not concerned with the individual enjoyment of land. Public nuisance is also a crime and covers a wide range of acts from public health to obstructing the highway. To some extent, it has been superseded in modern times by statutory offences on public health and safety. A person may only sue in the tort of public nuisance where that person has suffered special damage beyond that incurred by the public generally. For example, where an unlawful obstruction of the highway impeded access to business premises, the owner of the premises would be able to sue, as this would set him apart from the harm generally suffered by others.

The rule in Rylands v Fletcher (1866)

Closely related to nuisance is the rule in **Rylands v Fletcher (1866)**, a form of liability named after the case in which it was established. Although often regarded as a separate form of liability, the House of Lords in **Cambridge Water Co v Eastern Counties Leather (1994)** and **Transco plc v Stockport Metropolitan Borough Council (2004)** considered that the rule in *Rylands v Fletcher* is to be regarded as a species of nuisance and not a separate form of liability.

The rule in *Rylands v Fletcher* (see the case study textbox below) was developed in order to render strictly liable those who brought things onto their property that were not natural to it and that escaped and caused injury or damage to others. It was particularly suited to an increasingly industrialised society and the hazards that might result from industrial activities. The rule in *Rylands v Fletcher* differs from negligence because the defendant's negligence does not have to be proved and, unlike nuisance, it is concerned with dangerous things that escape rather than with the acts of individuals.

Rylands v Fletcher (1866)

The claimant's mine was flooded as a result of inadequate measures by the defendant to shore up shafts on his land near a reservoir that was being built for him. Water escaped from the defendant's mineshaft to an adjoining mineshaft on a neighbour's land. The defendant had not been negligent but the House of Lords held the defendant liable on the principle that where he brings something onto his land and it escapes, he does so at his peril.

Cambridge Water Co v Eastern Counties Leather (1994)

The defendant used a solvent in its tanning business. The solvent escaped from containers and seeped into the ground beneath the works. The solvent percolated eventually into the water supply, polluting the claimant's borehole and the claimant was forced to abandon the borehole and develop new water supplies. The House of Lords held that the claimant's claim for compensation in accordance with the rule in *Rylands v Fletcher* should fail on the ground that, although the storage of solvents was a non-natural use of land, the defendant could not reasonably have foreseen that the spillage of solvent over time would contaminate the water supply.

'Dangerous things' would include chemicals and explosives, but for liability to exist there must be an escape. For example, where chemicals do not leak onto adjoining land from a factory, but injure an employee working in the factory, liability would be in negligence. Where, however, they leak onto land and injure the owner or damage his property, that person can sue under the rule in *Rylands v Fletcher*. As with negligence, any loss suffered by the owner of the adjoining land must be foreseeable and the test for foreseeability is the same as for negligence (see Chapter 11). This is seen in the *Cambridge Water Co* case above.

There is no liability in the tort for the escape of something that is 'natural' to the land. Defining this term, however, has caused problems, as can be seen in the *Transco* case below. Escaping flames from a house fire are natural but not if they come from a flammable liquid brought onto the property.

Defences to Rylands v Fletcher

There are defences to the rule in *Rylands v Fletcher (1866)* and these are similar to the defences to an action in nuisance. The defendant can plead 'Act of God', act of a stranger, consent and, more importantly, statutory authority. Public or private bodies, such as gas and water undertakings, for example, have statutory authority to bring non-natural and potentially dangerous substances onto land.

Transco plc v Stockport Metropolitan Borough Council (2004)

The claimant brought an action against the defendant council to recover the costs of remedial action to a gas main that had been left exposed and unsupported by the collapse of an embankment. The cause of the collapse of the embankment was a leak of water from a pipe connecting the mains supply to tanks in the basement of a block of flats owned by the defendant. The fracture in the pipe was undetected for a considerable period of time and a considerable amount of water escaped from the pipe and found its way to the embankment, which became saturated and collapsed. The House of Lords held that the defendant was not liable under the rule in *Rylands v Fletcher* as the defendant had not brought onto its land anything likely to cause danger or mischief if it escaped. In piping water to the flats, the defendant council was acting as an ordinary user of land.

Occupiers' liability

As buildings can be a danger to those who enter them, particularly factories and other similar business premises, the occupier of the premises owes a **duty of care** to those who visit such buildings. This tort is obviously important in the business world and is a risk normally covered by appropriate public liability insurance to cover injuries and harm to third parties. The Occupiers' Liability Act (OLA) 1957 and the OLA 1984 set out the nature and extent of that liability towards persons who are either lawful visitors or non-lawful visitors (i.e. trespassers). The occupier is not necessarily the owner. It is the person who has control of the premises and he or she may be a tenant or a manager.

The OLA 1957 states that an occupier owes a duty of care towards all lawful visitors. A person who enters premises with the express permission of the occupier is a lawful visitor, as are those who have a contractual right to be there, such as employees. Permission may be implied where, for instance, a trader or other person enters to transact business. Permission can also be withdrawn and, where appropriate, the visitor must be given a reasonable time to leave before being ejected. Permission can be confined to visiting at certain times and for certain purposes and for certain parts of the building.

Liability is not confined to indoor places, for premises can include outdoor spaces that are under the control of the occupier. An example relating to outdoor spaces arose in the *Gwilliam* case considered in the 'Reality check' textbox below, in respect of hospital grounds, although on the facts there was no finding of liability in this case.

Are trespassers owed a duty of care?

Persons who enter premises without permission or statutory authority are non-lawful visitors (or trespassers). Before the OLA 1984, no duty of care was owed to trespassers, although there was a duty not to injure them deliberately or recklessly. The OLA 1984, however, places on the occupier a duty of care where:

 Reality check

Gwilliam v West Hertfordshire Hospital NHS Trust (2002)

A hospital trust was not held liable in this case, but the case shows that holding a fair in the grounds of a hospital does constitute premises for the purposes of the OLA 1957 and that members of the public visiting such events are entitled to assume that the trust as occupier has taken care towards their welfare.

In this case, a hospital trust was holding a fund-raising fair and contracted with an **independent contractor** to set up a 'splat wall', the hospital trust checking that the contractor carried public liability insurance. A visitor suffered harm as a result of the negligence of the contractor setting up the wall. The contractor had insufficient resources to meet the claimant's claim and its insurance had lapsed 4 days before the fair began. The claimant brought proceedings against the hospital trust on the ground that, as owner of the premises, they had a duty to take care, by ensuring that the contractor was competent. The Court of Appeal held that the hospital trust was not liable as it had made the necessary checks to ensure the contractor was competent by checking that the contractor had insurance at the time of engagement.

- He knows or has reasonable grounds to believe that a danger exists.
- He knows or has reasonable grounds to believe that non-lawful visitors may come into its vicinity.
- The risk is one in which he can reasonably be expected to provide protection.

A higher duty of care is owed towards children.

The current position as regards trespassers is well illustrated in the 'Reality check' textbox below highlighting **_Tomlinson v Congleton Borough Council (2003)_**. As in this case, occupiers may attempt to avoid liability by means of warning notices. However, such notices are subject to the provisions of the Unfair Contract Terms Act 1977, which limits the occupier's right by contract or notice to avoid liability for injury to persons and damage to property.

Breach of statutory duty

As the general rules of contract have been supplemented by legislation (for example the Contracts (Rights of Third Parties) Act 1999), so the ordinary principles of negligence have been given a more detailed statutory form in respect of particular situations. In the employer/employee relationship, for example, legislation sets out an employer's responsibilities in health and safety, such as imposing criminal liability on employers for the fencing of machinery. Similarly, special legal regimes affecting businesses can be found in the Defective Premises Act 1972 and, in the case of manufacturers' liability, in the Consumer Protection Act 1987 (which we look at in Chapter 20, on consumer law).

Reality check

Diving into a shallow lake in a public park – Tomlinson v Congleton Borough Council (2003)

The claimant, a trespasser, dived into shallow water in a lake in a public park that was owned by the defendant council. He became paralysed after striking his head on a rocky outcrop. The lake was a flooded quarry and there were signs prohibiting swimming and warning that it was dangerous. The claimant was aware that swimming was prohibited, but argued that, as the defendant knew that people swam in the lake, it could have done more in deterring swimming by, for example, making the lake look unattractive. The House of Lords held that the defendant was

not liable as, under the OLA 1984, the state of the premises were not dangerous and the risk was an obvious one for adults to be free to take.

Failure to comply with these statutes may lead to a criminal prosecution, but, in some cases, an injured party may pursue a civil action and sue in tort for **breach of statutory duty**. Not all statutes, however, provide for such a right of action and whether civil liability can arise from a breach of statutory duty depends on ascertaining from the statutory enactment the intention of Parliament. An example can be found in s41 of the Consumer Protection Act 1987, which provides expressly for a civil right of action in the event of a failure by a defendant to comply with the criminal provisions of Part II of the Act relating to consumer safety. A number of other examples can be found in health and safety legislation and in relation to competition law.

Economic torts

These torts are concerned with the intentional infliction of economic loss. The law attempts to balance the need to prevent undue economic harm to businesses with the need to allow fair competition in the business world, even if the competition sometimes comes from the employees of the business. There is much in statute and case law that encourages economic competition, but businesses that suffer adversely from competition have no legal claim against the victors. The economic torts do, however, provide civil remedies for certain forms of business malpractice. Much of this area of the law of tort has been overtaken or supplemented by statute law on fair trading and competition law, such as the Competition Act 1998, which prohibits certain anti-competitive activities such as **restrictive trade practices** and **cartels**. Nevertheless, there is a need to consider the rights given in tort to those whose business or contracts suffer at the hands of third parties, although only brief coverage of some of the more important economic torts will be provided in this chapter.

Competition law

Competition law is designed to ensure that businesses do not undermine the economic benefits of a market economy by, for example, agreeing not to compete with one another on key terms such as price. As explained in Chapter 8, such agreements are illegal under the Competition Act 1998. Where the agreement affects trade between member states of the EU, it may also be illegal under Article 81 of the EU Treaty (on which the UK Competition Act 1998 is based). Under English law, a business that infringes the Competition Act 1998 or Article 81 commits a breach of statutory duty. It can therefore be sued in tort by other businesses that have suffered loss as a result of that breach (see **Crehan v Inntrepreneur Pub Co (2004)**). This is illustrated by the example in the 'Reality check' textbox entitled 'The vitamins cartel'.

Inducing a breach of contract

Where A induces B to break a contract with C, privity of contract prevents C suing A and any claim in contract law C may have will be against B. However, it is possible for C to sue A in the tort of inducing a breach of contract. In **Lumley v Gye (1853)**, a third party persuaded an opera singer to breach her contract with her first employer and work for him. He was held liable in tort to the singer's first employer.

Interference with the performance of a commercial contract may also lead to liability. In **Torquay Hotel Co Ltd v Cousins (1969)**, it was held that the defen-

Reality check

The vitamins cartel

Vitamins suppliers made to pay for an illegal cartel

In November 2001 the European Commission, which is responsible for enforcing Article 81, imposed fines totalling €850 million (over £500 million) on various suppliers of vitamins (for use in both human and animal food products) that had operated an illegal price-fixing agreement or *cartel*. As a result of the cartel, many customers of those suppliers had to pay more for vitamins than they would have done had the cartel members been competing with one another (since competition would have forced down the price). At the time of writing, a number of purchasers had brought actions for damages In

the English courts against the vitamins suppliers in order to recover their loss. These actions are based on the tort of breach of statutory duty (the relevant statute in this case being Article 81). If the claimants are successful, in addition to the fines payable to the European Commission, the defendants may have to pay substantial damages, as the cartel was in existence for many years.

dants who sought to prevent delivery of oil to the claimants with whom they had an industrial dispute could be liable in tort.

The key conditions for the tort of procuring a breach of contract were set out in **Greig v Insole (1978)**, as follows:

- direct interference or indirect interference (if coupled with unlawful means)
- knowledge of the contract
- an intention to interfere with the contract.

It must be shown that there was a specific, subjective intention to interfere, in that the unlawful conduct has to be aimed at the contract (**Mainstream Properties Ltd v Young (2005)**). However, it is not necessary for the defendant to have detailed knowledge of the terms of the contract whose breach he induced. In **Merkur Island Shipping Corp v Laughton (1983)**, a seamen's union had refused to load or unload a ship, knowing that this would interfere generally with contracts between the owner of the ship and others, such as charterers and owners of cargo. The union was held liable.

Intimidation

Intimidation involves the use of unlawful threats by one party against another party so as to influence his behaviour. It can also involve one party threatening another party with a view to influencing that party's actions against a third party.

In **Rookes v Barnard (1964)**, the claimant, an employee of BOAC, an airline, resigned from a draughtsmen's union. The defendants, who were union officials, threatened BOAC that they would call a strike if the claimant was not dismissed. As the union had a closed shop agreement with BOAC, the airline dismissed the claimant. The defendants were held liable for intimidating the airline into breaching its contract with the claimant.

Conspiracy

Conspiracy is defined as an agreement of two or more persons to do an unlawful act or a lawful act by unlawful means, resulting in damage to the claimant. Where the parties combine to inflict economic damage on the claimant, they may be liable in tort.

In **Quinn v Leathem (1901)**, the defendant sought to have his staff join a union. The union said that the defendant would have to dismiss them and replace them with union members. The defendant refused and the union persuaded some of the defendant's customers not to deal with the defendant. It was held that the union was liable in conspiracy as its purpose was to injure the defendant.

Passing off

The tort of passing off is committed where a business attempts to pass off its goods or services as those of another. The tort exists to protect the good name and reputation of a business. Anyone who uses the trademark or trade name of a competitor in order to deceive is liable in the tort, but a claimant does not have to prove that damage has been suffered. In the *Warnink* case (see case study below), Dutch manufacturers of a drink called advocaat protected the name 'Advocaat' from its use by an English firm. The 'key ingredients' of this tort are set out in the case study.

Another example can be found in **Reckitt & Coleman Products Ltd v Borden Inc (1988)**. In this case, the claimant sold lemon juice called 'Jif' in a plastic lemon-shaped container. The defendant's product looked very similar and could barely be distinguished from the claimant's product. The claimant succeeded in his action against the defendant. The tort of passing off can also occur in relation to the internet.

The tort of passing off differs from trademark infringement (which is an unauthorised use of a registered trademark) as passing off is concerned with *unregistered* trademark rights. Protection of registered trademarks is dealt with by the Trade Marks Act 1994, which enables a claimant to bring an action for an infringement of a registered trademark.

Breach of confidence

This area of law gives limited protection to privacy in private and business life. Where one party confides information to another, a legal duty may be created not to reveal that information to anyone else. A duty of confidence can arise informally

Warnink BV v J Townend & Sons (Hull) Limited (1979)

In this case, Lord Diplock described the ingredients of the tort as follows:

(1) A misrepresentation, (2) made by a trade or in the course of trade, (3) to prospective customers of his or ultimate consumers of goods or services supplied by him (4) which is calculated to injure the business or goodwill of another trader in the sense that this is a reasonably foreseeable consequence and (5) which causes actual damage to a business or goodwill of the trader by whom the action is brought or ... will probably do so.

(such as that between friends, family members and business colleagues), by a term of a contract (such as a **contract of employment**) or by the operation of law. A common example of a duty of confidence arising by the operation of law is through the existence of a **fiduciary** relationship between parties dealing with one another, such as solicitor and client or doctor and patient.

Liability will arise where the following criteria are satisfied:

- The claimant expressly or impliedly reveals confidential information to another person.
- A relationship of trust exists between the parties or is created as a result, so that it becomes apparent that the information is private and that it will be kept confidential.
- The confidant makes use of the information or passes it to a third party.
- The claimant as a consequence suffers damage.

Where a claimant's action is successful, economic damage is recoverable as is loss of privacy and any distress suffered by the claimant. Liability, however, can be avoided where the defendant can show that it was in the public interest to reveal the information.

Confidential information and the Data Protection Act

In respect of confidential information, additional protection is provided by the Data Protection Act (DPA) 1998. The Act is of particular relevance to businesses as businesses are likely to hold 'personal information' about their suppliers and customers (as well as their employees) and the Act is designed to prevent unauthorised access to, or disclosure of, such information. Under the DPA 1998, holders of data must be registered as a data user and an individual is entitled to compensation from a data user for any damage or distress suffered as a result of any loss, damage, destruction, disclosure or access to his personal data. More information on data protection can be found on the website www.dataprotection.gov.uk.

Vicarious liability

Introduction

Vicarious liability is a legal doctrine whereby an employer is liable to a claimant for the tortious acts of employees committed in the course of employment. Most businesses are likely to be aware that they are liable for the authorised acts of their employees, as it is they who have employed the employee to act on their behalf. What many businesses may not realise, however, is that under the doctrine of various liability, they can also be held liable for unauthorised acts of employees or their improper acts of, for the application of the doctrine is not restricted to authorised acts of employees.

Various explanations have been put forward to justify the existence of the doctrine, but the most likely explanation is the concept of group liability. A collection of individuals in the form of an enterprise has more funds available to meet liability. If individual employees had to bear the liability for their torts alone, they would be forced to take out insurance. The considerable premium for this would presumably be reflected in a need for higher wages, so that the employer would be indirectly paying the premium. Further, the process of separately insuring numerous employees would not only be uneconomic but would require a statutory system of enforcement in the interests of the injured party. By the same token, if the enterprise bears the costs of insurance, the costs and any losses are borne in small amounts by customers of the enterprise, the claimant suffering harm is guaranteed recovery for his or her loss and the employee responsible, whose personal fault may be slight, avoids the financial consequences of being sued in tort.

It is appropriate, therefore, that the employer carries public liability insurance and, in fact, is required to do so by the Employers Liability (Compulsory Insurance) Act 1969. Other business insurance is available, such as product liability insurance and, in the case of professional advisers, such as solicitors and accountants, professional indemnity insurance. It is likely to be a condition of membership of a professional body that members of such bodies take out professional indemnity insurance.

What is needed to establish vicarious liability?

There are two factors. In order for an employer to be held liable for the acts of his employees:

- There must be a contract of employment (or service) between the employer and employee.
- Any tortious act needs to have been committed in the course of employment.

Contract of employment

The employee must be serving under a contract of employment or service, as an employer's liability does not extend to an independent contractor, i.e. a self-employed person. An employee works under a contract of employment, whereas an independent contractor works under a contract for services. In deciding whether a worker is under a contract of service, the courts have developed a series of tests to establish the nature of the relationship between an employer and an employee.

Traditionally, the courts followed a control test, i.e. where an employer told the worker what to do and how to do it, the latter was considered an employee.

FAQ

Does the doctrine of vicarious liability excuse the employee from liability?

Despite the existence of the doctrine of vicarious liability, an employee can be held liable for any torts he commits, for suing an employer under the doctrine provides for an additional, not an alternative, defendant. In **Merrett v Babb (2001)**, for example, a surveyor, who was employed by a firm of surveyors, was held liable for errors in a valuation that he conducted and signed in his name in the course of employment. He was liable to pay damages of £23,000 to the claimant. Although the firm would have been held liable under the doctrine of vicarious liability, the claimant was unable to sue the surveyor's employer as the firm had gone bust and there was no run-off insurance cover for the business.

However, this test, although suitable to small businesses with an unskilled workforce, has little relevance to specialist employees in large enterprises, where employers are likely to have minimal control over such employees as computer programmers, production mangers, engineers and accountants in instructing them on how to do their jobs. This led to the development of the integration (or organisation) test, as used by Lord Denning in **Stevenson, Jordan & Harrison Ltd v MacDonald & Evans (1952)**. Lord Denning considered that the test should be whether the worker was fully integrated into the employer's organisation. Where the employee was part and parcel of the business, the worker was an employee. However, where integration begins and ends is not always clear and more recently the courts have balanced the different factors involved and decided the nature of the relationship on the basis of a multiple test. With this approach, the courts examine a range of factors to see whether the relationship is one of employer and employee or hirer and independent contractor. Such factors include the payment of tax and national insurance, entitlement to holiday and sick pay and who supplies any tools and equipment. Whether an employee is called self-employed or not, however, is not necessarily a determining or conclusive factor. The distinction between employee and independent contractor is analysed in the *Ready Mixed Concrete* case below.

Borrowed employees The issue of vicarious liability is complicated where employees are *lent* to other employers and it may be uncertain which employer should be responsible for the actions of an employee. The general position is that there is a heavy burden on the general and permanent employer that it must shift in order to avoid responsibility for the acts of its employees.

In **Mersey Docks and Harbour Board v Coggins & Griffith Ltd (1947)**, an employer employed a crane operator but lent him and the crane to another employer. During the secondment, it was agreed between the two employers that the employee should be an employee of the second employer, but that he should be paid by the first employer who retained a power of dismissal. While unloading some goods, the employee negligently injured the claimant. Although the second employer told the crane driver what to do and when to do it, he could not tell him *how* to do it. The court held that the first employer, as the general and permanent employer, was liable to the claimant. On the facts, the first employer had not discharged the burden of remaining responsible for the employee.

Ready Mixed Concrete (South East) Ltd v Ministry of Pensions and National Insurance (1968)

The contract between a driver employed to carry concrete and the company described him as an independent contractor. He undertook to carry goods only for the company in a vehicle that he would buy on hire purchase from the company. He was to wear the company uniform, paint the vehicle in the colours of the company and bear any running and repair costs. If he was ill, he was allowed to hire a substitute. The court declared that many of the driver's duties were more like a contract of carriage than a contract of service. The ownership of the assets, the chance of profit and the risk of loss were the responsibility of the driver and not the company. Further, the driver paid his own tax and national insurance contributions. The court held that, although the driver was subject to a high degree of control, he was an independent contractor.

It was significant in this case that the employee was lent with complicated machinery, since in such cases it is easier to infer that the burden has not shifted. Had the employee been lent on a labour-only basis, the burden would have been easier to shift.

In *Viasystems (Tyneside) Ltd v Thermal Transfer (Northern) Ltd (2005)*, the Court of Appeal to ok the view that, in some circumstances, where two employers retain equal control of an employee, both employers could be held vicariously liable.

> QUESTION 1 To what extent do you consider that a temporary worker on the 'books' of an agency, such as a secretary, is an employee of the agency or of any business that uses the services of a temp?

Course of employment

Where a third party has been injured by a tort committed by an employee, whether action can be taken against the employer depends on whether the employee was acting in the course of employment or performing an independent act outside the course of employment. Acts that are expressly authorised by the employer clearly come within the employee's course of employment, but acts that appear to be unauthorised pose more of a dilemma.

In deciding whether a particular act of the employee is within the employee's course of employment, the courts have traditionally made reference to the employee's 'sphere of employment'. Under this approach, an employer can be held liable for unauthorised acts, as well as authorised acts, of the employee, provided that the unauthorised act is so connected with an act that he has been authorised to do (expressly or impliedly) that they might be regarded as ways, albeit improper ways, of doing that job. Acts that are incidental to the employee's duties are also part of the sphere of employment. On the other hand, where the unauthorised and wrongful act of the employee is not so connected with the authorised act as to be a way of doing it, but is an independent act, the employer is not responsible, for in such a case the employee has gone outside the course of employment. More recently in *Lister v Hesley Hall Ltd (2001)*, the House of Lords held that liability is based on whether the employee's act is 'closely connected' with his employment. Although a broader approach, it is unlikely that cases decided under the 'sphere of employment' test would result in a different conclusion.

It is a question of fact as to whether the particular act of an employee comes within the employee's course of employment or remains outside it. The act in question does not necessarily depend on the employee being negligent, for the doctrine of vicarious liability extends to other tortious acts committed by an employee. In some cases, an employer can be held liable in connection with criminal acts of an employee.

Civil liability

Employees acting within the course of employment The following two cases are examples where the court found employees to be acting within the course of employment.

Century Insurance Co Ltd v Northern Ireland Road Transport Board (1942)

In this case, a driver of a petrol tanker lit a cigarette on the premises of a garage where the contents of the tanker were being delivered. On discarding the match, a fire ensued and substantial damage arose from the resulting explosion. The company was held vicariously liable for the act of the driver. Although he was acting improperly, he was acting within the course of his employment, for the act of delivering the petrol, albeit in a negligent manner, was an act in connection with his employer's business.

Kay v ITW Ltd (1967)

An employee was authorised to move obstacles out of the way of other vehicles in a garage belonging to the employer, but no instructions were given as to how he could move such vehicles. In driving a five-ton lorry out of the way, he damaged the claimant's property through careless driving. His employer was held liable to the claimant, for the act of the employee was part of doing something he was authorised to do, i.e. the general act of moving vehicles causing an obstruction.

Employees acting independently The next two cases demonstrate how acts of an employee were held to be independent acts, for which the employer bore no responsibility.

Hilton Thomas Burton (Rhodes) Ltd (1961)

In this case, workmen were allowed to use their employer's van, as they were working in a country area. One lunchtime, they set off for a cafe seven miles away, changed their minds on the way and drove back. During the return journey, one workman was killed due to the negligent driving of a colleague. The court held that the journey had nothing to do with their employer's business, neither was it incidental to it, and the employer was therefore not vicariously liable.

Beard v London General Omnibus Company (1900)

A bus conductor negligently drove a bus while parked at the bus terminal, causing damage. The action against the employer failed as driving a bus, as opposed to acting as conductor, was not something he was employed to do.

What distinguishes these last two cases from the first two is that, although in the *Century Insurance* and *Kay* cases the employees had acted improperly, their acts were acts that came within the employees' sphere of employment, whereas in the *Hilton* and *Beard* cases, the employees were acting *outside* their sphere of employment. Their acts were neither authorised nor an improper way of doing an authorised job.

What if an employee commits a tort when doing something expressly forbidden by the employer? A related area is where an employee does something in contravention of a prohibition imposed on the employee by the employer. Generally, where an employee acts in a way that has been forbidden by an employer, the employer will not be liable, if the restriction relates to what the employee is employed to do. Where the restriction on the employee, however, does not relate to what is done, but on the way or mode in which an act is done, the employer can be held liable, for such an act comes within the sphere of employment.

In **Twine v Bean's Express (1946)**, drivers employed by the defendant were prohibited from giving lifts. A driver gave a lift to the claimant who was injured in an accident. The court held that the defendant was not vicariously liable for the negligence of the driver for the employee was doing something unconnected with his job. By contrast, in **Limpus v London General Omnibus Co (1862)**, bus drivers were specifically told not to race each other on their routes. Two drivers failed to heed the warning and the claimant's horses were injured as a result of the negligent driving of one or both of the drivers. The bus company, the drivers' employer, was held vicariously liable, for, although they drove in a prohibited manner, their act amounted to an improper mode of performing an authorised act and not an independent act taking them outside the course of employment. Another example can be found in the **Rose v Plenty (1976)** case study.

Criminal liability

As a general rule an employer is not vicariously liable for the crimes of his employees, although statute has created some exceptions. However, where an employee abuses a position of trust to commit a crime as well as committing a tort, the employer will assume vicarious liability for the tort. The doctrine of vicarious liability parallels the liability of a principal for the acts of an agent in the law of agency (see Chapter 22, on agency). Cases such as **Lloyd v Grace, Smith & Co (1912)** and **Morris v CW Martin (1965)**, which are now summarised, are examples of vicarious liability of an employer in tort as well as liability of a principal for the acts of an agent acting within the scope of their actual or apparent authority. In both cases, the employer was held vicariously liable for acts of which he neither knew nor approved.

In *Morris v CW Martin & Sons Ltd (1965)*, an employee of a subcontracting cleaning firm stole the claimant's fur coat while it was in the subcontractor's possession. Although the employee has committed a dishonest act, the company was held vicariously liable for the act of the employee whose duty was to look after the claimant's property. In *Lloyd v Grace, Smith & Co (1912)*, an employer, a firm

Rose v Plenty (1976)

Drivers of a dairy's milk floats were expressly prohibited from giving lifts to members of the public during the course of their rounds. One of the dairy's drivers gave a lift to a 13-year-old boy in return for the boy collecting moneys due from customers of the dairy. Owing to the driver's negligent driving, the boy fell off the float and was injured. The act of the driver, although prohibited, was held to be within the driver's course of employment. He was performing his job, albeit in an improper way. The collection of moneys due from customers was an act in connection with the business of the employer.

of solicitors, was held liable to the claimant in the tort of deceit in connection with a fraudulent transaction carried out by a clerk of the firm. The clerk worked unsupervised and he had persuaded the client, an elderly widow to sell her cottage through him to increase her income. He arranged for her to execute two documents, which, unknown to her, transferred the property into his name. It was held that the act, although fraudulent, came within his job of handling conveyancing transactions. Although he was not expected to carry out such transactions in a fraudulent manner, he was nonetheless doing a job he was employed to do.

Liability of an employer can extend to violent criminal acts committed by an employee, provided the act was done in the course of the employee's employment. In **Poland v John Parr and Sons (1926)**, the driver of a cart was held to be acting within the course of his employment in striking a boy who the driver had suspected of attempting to pilfer goods from the back of the cart. He had an implied duty to look after his employer's property and, so long as his acts could not be described as excessive, he was fulfilling that duty. More recently, in **Lister v Hesley Hall Ltd (2001)**, the House of Lords held that a warden in charge of a boys' boarding school who had abused sexually boys while in his care, caused his employer to be vicariously liable. Although his act was a criminal act, he was in a position of trust and his acts were so closely connected with his employment that it would be fair and just to hold his employer vicariously liable.

Primary liability of an employer

As we have seen, an employer is not responsible for the torts of an independent contractor. The employer, by definition, cannot be vicariously liable for such torts, since an independent contractor is not an employee. However, the employer may

FAQ

Where an employer is held vicariously liable, can the employer sue the employee in order to recover his losses toward the claimant?

While the employer may be vicariously liable for the wrongs committed by his employees in the course of employment, the employer can seek an indemnity from the employee concerned. In **Lister v Romford Ice and Cold Storage Co Ltd (1957)**, an employee was employed as a lorry driver by the defendant and drove a lorry with his father as his 'mate'. After an accident, the employee's father sued successfully the defendant for injuries suffered by him as a result of the employee's negligent driving. Subsequently, the defendant sued the employee for breach of contract, alleging that the employee's contract of employment contained an implied term that he was to use reasonable care and skill in the performance of his duties. The court held that there was such an implied term and the defendant, as employer, was able to recover damages from the employee.

The indemnity an employer is entitled to, however, is unlikely to be pursued for a number of reasons. It is likely that it would have an adverse effect on employee relations and the employee is unlikely to have the funding to indemnify an employer. It is also likely that the employer's insurance company would take over any action under its rights of subrogation before the employer had an opportunity to consider its course of action, and the general practice of insurance companies is not to pursue employees in these circumstances. A right of subrogation means that the insurance company has the right to 'step into the shoes' of the insured party where the insurance contract allows for this.

incur primary liability for a breach of duty where, for example, he had been negligent in engaging the services of an independent contractor. In addition, certain legal duties, such as those found in health and safety legislation, cannot be delegated and liability will follow where care is not taken in respect of such duties.

It is also open to a claimant to sue directly an employer on the basis that the employer had been negligent in failing to provide a safe system of work or in failing to provide adequate training or supervision of its employees.

Answer to in-text question

> **QUESTION 1** To what extent do you consider that a temporary worker on the 'books' of an agency, such as a secretary, is an employee of the agency or of any business that uses the services of a temp?

This issue has been a difficult one for the courts to resolve. Unlike *Mersey Docks and Harbour Board v Coggins & Griffith Ltd (1947)*, it could not be said that a 'temp' is an employee of the agency or a business that engages their services. A more likely conclusion is that a temporary worker is to be regarded as an independent contractor, although tax and national insurance deductions are likely to be made by one of the two 'employers'. For some guidance see **Carmichael v National Power plc (1999)**; **Montgomery v Johnson Underwood Ltd (2001)**; and **Dacas v Brook Street Bureau (UK) Ltd (2004)**.

Website summary

The book's website contains the following material in respect of Part 3:

- PowerPoint slides containing relevant information from each chapter to help with revision
- Four additional questions with answers per chapter
- Quiz containing 10 multiple-choice questions for each part
- Biannual update bulletins to the book, which will consist of brief details of any major common law, statutory and constitutional developments affecting the currency of the book

PART FOUR

Company law

In the preceding chapters, we considered the rights and obligations of individuals and businesses in contract law and under the law of tort. In Part 4, we examine a body of law that affects a particular type of business, namely an incorporated company. The main source of company law is legislation, principally the Companies Act 1985, which consolidated several past Companies Acts. In addition to legislation, there is a body of law developed by the courts, which has provided additional fundamental principles relating to companies, such as duties of directors and shareholder protection.

Company legislation is both enabling and regulatory. It is enabling in that it allows for the formation of a distinct corporate body. The regulatory function relates to the conditions that have to be met for the purpose of incorporation and for the protection of various groups involved with a company. These groups include shareholders, directors, employees, creditors and parties contracting with companies, such as customers and suppliers.

Recently, company law has undergone a process of wide-scale reform, aimed at modernising company law, particularly for private companies. At present, the Company Law Reform Bill 2005 is going through Parliament, but any new Companies Act is unlikely to be implemented before 2007.

In Part 4, the following areas of company law are covered:

- **Formation of companies and a comparison with other forms of business associations (Chapter 13)**
- **Significance and consequences of incorporation (Chapter 14)**
- **Capital of a company (Chapter 15)**
- **Management of a company (Chapter 16)**
- **Directors' duties (Chapter 17)**
- **Shareholder protection (Chapter 18)**
- **Corporate insolvency (Chapter 19)**

13 | Business associations

Learning objectives

By the end of this chapter, you should be able to explain:

- The different forms of association that exist for the running of a business

- The law relating to general partnerships and limited liability partnerships

- The different types of company and how a company can be formed

Introduction

There are mainly four types of business association that can be used as a means of running a business. These are a sole trader, an ordinary **partnership**, a **limited liability partnership** and an incorporated company. At first sight and mainly because of its implied personal guarantee of protection against bankruptcy, the idea of forming a company appears attractive to people intending to become self-employed. However, there are many reasons why people choose a form of business association different from that of a company and it is likely that the real purpose of forming a company is to allow the growth of a business by means of introducing new capital from outside sources. The choice of business association is likely to depend on size, convenience and taxation and the larger the business enterprise, the more likely a company will be formed.

Sole traders

A sole trader represents the simplest form of carrying on a business. It involves a natural person, as distinct from an artificial legal person such as a **registered company**, carrying on business as an individual. This person owns the assets of the business and employs others to assist him, either as employees or independent contractors. He will be liable for acts he authorises his employees or agents to carry out. The use of a business name does not create a new entity or person in law.

There are no formalities in setting up this form of business but HM Revenue and Customs will need to know the date of commencement of business and proper accounts must be kept to enable the profits of the business to be calculated for income tax and capital gains tax purposes. Where relevant, HM Revenue and Customs will need to be informed for the purpose of the imposition of value-added tax and excise duties.

Partnerships

A partnership comprises two or more persons coming together to run a business. There are three types of partnership recognised in English law – an ordinary partnership as defined by the Partnership Act 1890; a publicly registered limited partnership formed under the Limited Partnerships Act 1907; and a limited liability partnership formed under the Limited Liability Partnership Acts 2000. An ordinary or general partnership is the most common type of partnership. The second type is rare, while the limited liability partnership represents a new type of business association with features common to a registered company and an ordinary partnership.

Ordinary partnerships

This is defined by the Partnership Act (PA) 1890 as 'the relationship which subsists between persons carrying on business in common with a view to profit' (s1(1) PA 1890). This relationship requires pre-existing persons, recognised by the law, whether human or artificial, with whom will vest the rights and liabilities of the business. The use of a separate business name by the partners does not change the relationship or create a new legal entity, but it does allow the partnership the convenience of suing and being sued in the partnership name.

Until December 2002 unless an exempt partnership, there was a restriction of 20 on the number of partners who could comprise a partnership. Exempt partnerships were professional firms such as accountants and solicitors. From December 2002 the restriction was removed and any number of persons may form a partnership.

The partners relate to each other according to their agreement, express or implied, and therefore the principles of contract law that we looked at in Part 2 operate in relation to the agreement as they would to contracts generally. In the absence of an agreement, the rights of the partners will be implied largely under the PA 1890. For instance, the PA 1890 provides that property brought into the firm is partnership property, as is any property bought with money belonging to the firm. However, it is possible for a partnership to use property that belongs to one of the partners.

In forming a partnership, it is strongly advisable, for the partners' benefit, for a written partnership agreement (often referred to as a partnership deed or articles) to be drawn up. This is to enable the partners to turn to the terms of the agreement in the event of a dispute. The types of thing that may be found in a partnership agreement are as follow:

- partners' names and business name
- nature of the business or profession and business address

FAQ

Can any agreement between individuals preparing a business venture amount to a partnership for the purpose of the PA 1890?

Where two or more persons decide to form a business venture but, due to differences decide not to continue the venture, an issue arises as to whether the relationship constitutes a partnership, if work has been carried out or expense incurred.

In **Khan v Mia (2000)** the House of Lords ruled that five individuals who were planning to set up a business running a restaurant and who took preliminary steps were acting as a partnership although trading had not commenced. Finding premises and buying furniture and linen with a view to making a profit constituted a partnership. The House of Lords stressed that whether or not parties who proposed to enter into a business venture had entered into one was a question of fact for the trial judge. In this case, the individuals had transacted business of a joint venture.

Other indications as to whether a partnership is in existence are provided by the PA 1890. For example, in the absence of evidence to the contrary, a person who receives a share of any profits is considered a partner. However, the PA 1890 provides a list of circumstances where a person sharing profits is presumed not to be a partner, e.g. taking a share of profits as a salary or as payment for the **goodwill** of a business. Further, joint or common ownership of property is not to be taken as creating a partnership, neither does the sharing of gross returns. But these are no more than indications.

- the amount contributed by each partner and the arrangements governing any necessary increases of capital
- preparation and auditing of annual accounts
- method of apportioning profits and drawing on accounts
- duration of the partnership (e.g. for a fixed number of years, or until retirement or on the death of a partner) and the arrangements for continuation by survivors
- arrangements for dissolution of the partnership, whether voluntary, on retirement or by death
- method of valuation and division of assets for contributions to net losses on dissolution
- collection of debts, banking and bookkeeping arrangement
- employment of staff
- whether unanimity, or a majority view, is required on matters of management
- agreements by partners not to set up in competition within a certain area
- provision for arbitration in the event of dispute
- sharing of profits and losses
- exclusion, if relevant, of sleeping partners from participating in partnership management
- division of responsibility.

Relationship between the partners

Rights of partners

Subject to express provision to the contrary in the partnership agreement, the rights of partners are set out in s24 PA 1890. The main rights partners enjoy are as follows:

- To share equally in the capital and profits of the business. Where the partnership agreement is silent on the matter, the facts of the case can provide evidence of a contrary intention.
- To be indemnified by the firm for any liabilities incurred or payments made in the course of the firm's business.
- To take part in the management of the business. A silent or sleeping partner is a partner who has been excluded expressly by the partnership agreement from acting in the management of the partnership. A partner is not entitled to receive any salary for acting in the partnership business unless otherwise agreed.
- To have access to the firm's books, which are kept usually at the firm's principal place of business.
- To prevent the admission of a new partner or to prevent any change in the nature of the partnership business.

Duties of partners

The fiduciary nature of the partnership relationship is based on a duty to act with loyalty and in good faith. Similar considerations apply to directors of companies and employees, as discussed in Chapters 17 and 21, respectively. In addition to the general fiduciary duties, there are a number of specific duties laid down in ss28–30 PA 1890.

Duty of disclosure Under s28 PA 1890 partners must render true accounts and full information in relation to all things affecting the partnership to the other partners or their legal representatives. In *Law v Law (1905)*, William and James Law were partners in a woollen manufacturing business. William took little part in the running of the business. Later, James bought William's share of the business for £21,000 without disclosing the full nature of the partnership's assets. The Court of Appeal held that the purchasing partner, who knew more of the partnership business, was under a duty to supply the selling partner with all the material facts relating to the partnership assets. Therefore, the contract could be set aside.

Duty to account Section 29 PA 1980 provides that partners must account to the firm for any benefit obtained, without consent, from any transaction concerning the partnership, its property, its name or its business connection. In *Bentley v Craven (1853)*, Craven was in partnership with three others in a sugar refinery business and acted as the firm's buyer. He bought sugar on his own account at a discount and later sold it to the partnership at a market rate. In making a profit, he did not declare his interest to the other partners. It was held that he was liable to account to the firm for the profit he made.

Duty not to compete Under s30 PA 1890, a partner competing with the partnership business, without the consent of the other partners, is liable to account to the partnership for any profits made in the course of that business.

FAQ

Can a partner be expelled from a partnership for wrongdoing?

Section 25 PA 1890 provides that a majority of the partners cannot expel another partner unless a power of expulsion is contained in the partnership. Where such a power is included, it must be exercised in good faith. In **Blisset v Daniel (1853)** the court held that the partners had not acted in good faith in expelling a partner as the power of expulsion was being used as a means of obtaining the expelled partner's share of the partnership at a discount. In **Green v Howell (1910)**, however, it was held that expelling a partner without giving him an opportunity to explain his actions was not acting in bad faith as diverting profits from the partnership was a flagrant breach of his duties.

Relationship between partners and third parties

The PA 1890 covers the relationship of the members of a partnership to outsiders who deal with the partnership and the extent to which the partnership and the partners are liable for the actions of individual partners. In essence, what needs to be considered is the extent to which a partner can be held liable to a third party in tort and contract.

Authority of partners to bind the firm

Section 5 PA 1890 declares that every partner is an agent of the firm for the purpose of the partnership's business and that the acts of a partner done in the usual way of the firm's business shall bind the firm and the partner, unless the partner in question has no authority to so act and the third party knows this or does not know or believe him to be a partner. Each partner, therefore, has the power to bind co-partners and make them liable on business transactions. The partnership agreement, however, may expressly seek to limit the powers of particular partners. The effect of such limitations on third parties depends on the circumstances of each case, so that a firm may be liable to a third party where the other partners have not expressly approved the action, but the partner concerned acted within the usual scope of the firm's business. Where however, the third party had actual knowledge of a partner's lack of authority, the partnership is not bound by the transaction, although the partnership can ratify an authorised contract of a partner. (See the textbox case study on **Mercantile Credit v Garrod (1962)**.)

A similar example can be found in *United Bank of Kuwait v Hammoud (1988)*. In this case, a firm of solicitors was held, by virtue of s5 PA 1890, bound to a guarantee given by a salaried partner in connection with a bank loan given to a client of the firm, the client later disappearing without repaying the loan to the bank. The salaried partner had actual authority to represent himself as being a practising solicitor and the guarantee was given in the context of an underlying transaction that was part of the usual business of a solicitor.

Partners are presumed to have authority to enter into the following transactions:

- to sell the firm's goods
- to buy goods of a kind normally required by the firm
- to hire employees

Mercantile Credit v Garrod (1962)

P and his sleeping partner, G, formed a partnership for the purpose of letting garages and carrying out motor repairs, but expressly excluding in their agreement the buying and selling of cars. P, without G's knowledge purported to sell a car to which he had no title to Mercantile Credit, a finance house, for £700. In holding that G was liable, the court dismissed the argument that the transaction was not binding because of the exclusion of buying and selling cars in the partnership agreement, preferring instead to look at the matter from what was apparent to the outside world in general. Here, P was doing an act of a kind carried on by persons trading as a garage, as any third party, in the absence of knowledge to the contrary, would believe.

- to receive payment of debts due to the partnership
- to pay debts owed by the partnership and to draw cheques for that purpose
- to employ a solicitor to act for the firm in defence of an action or in pursuit of a debt.

These implied powers apply equally to trading and non-trading partnerships. Partners in trading firms have the following additional implied powers:

- to accept, draw, issue or endorse bills of exchange or other negotiable instruments on behalf of the firm
- to borrow money on the credit of the firm
- to pledge the firm's goods as security for borrowed money.

Contractual and tortious liability

Under the PA 1890, all partners, including silent partners, are liable for contractual and other wrongs to the full extent of their assets. Liability is joint and several. However, this does not apply where a partner is a member of a publicly registered limited partnership and who does not participate in the management of the business (Limited Partnerships Act 1907). Such partnerships, however, are rare.

Under s9 PA 1890, the liability of partners as regards debts or contracts is joint and several so that a judgment obtained against one partner does not prevent action against other partners in order to recover all that is owed. Liability under the PA 1890 was joint, but became joint and several with the passing of the Civil Liability (Contributions) Act 1978.

Under s10 PA 1890, the liability of partners with regard to torts or other wrongs committed in the ordinary course of the partnership business is joint and several. In such a situation, there is no bar on taking successive actions against partners

Hamlyn v Houston and Co (1905)

One of the partners in a firm, whose job was to obtain information on competitors, bribed a clerk employed by a rival firm, in order to get confidential information about the rival firm's business. The rival firm sued the other partners of the firm in order to recover the loss it suffered as a consequence. It was held that, although the partner has used illegal methods to extract the information, the other partners were liable for the tortious act of inducing a breach of contract, as the partner had acted within the scope of the firm's business, which was to obtain information.

in order to recover all that is due. The wrongful act must have been committed in the ordinary course of partnership business or with the express approval of all the partners. Where a tort is committed outside the ordinary course of business, the partner responsible is liable. (See the textbox case study above on **Hamlyn v Houston and Co (1905)**.

In another example, **Dubai Aluminium Co Ltd v Salaam (2003)**, the House of Lords held that s10 PA 1890 includes equitable wrongs committed by a partner in the course of partnership business such as in respect of liability arising out of a fraudulent act.

Liability of incoming and outgoing partners

A person who is admitted into an existing firm is not liable to creditors of the firm for anything done before they became a partner (s17 PA 1890). The new partner can, however, assume such responsibility by way of novation, which is an arrangement whereby a retiring partner is discharged from an existing liability, which is assumed by the newly constituted partnership. Novation is an agreement involving the retiring partner, the partner of new firm and the existing creditors. Creditors do not have to accept a novation and a creditor may hold a retired partner responsible for any debts due at the time of his retirement, although the new firm may agree to indemnify the retiring partner against any such claims. The estate of a deceased person is only liable for debts or obligations arising before death. Where someone deals with a partnership after a change in membership, they are entitled to treat all the apparent members of the old firm as being members, until they receive notice of any change in membership.

Dissolution of a partnership

As a partnership is based on agreement, the agreement can provide for the partnership to be brought to an end. However, unless otherwise stated in the partnership agreement, ss31–34 PA 1890 provides for the automatic dissolution of a partnership on the following grounds:

- the expiry of a fixed term or the completion of a specified enterprise
- the giving of notice
- the death or bankruptcy of any partner
- where a partner's share becomes subject to a charge under s23 PA 1890, the other partners can choose to dissolve the partnership
- illegality.

Although the occurrence of any of the first three grounds will bring the partnership to an end, it is usual for a partnership agreement to provide for the continuation of the business under the control of the remaining partners.

The occurrence of events making the continuation of the partnership illegal is illustrated by the facts of **Hudgell, Yeates and Co v Watson (1978)**. In that case, one of the partners of a three-partner firm forgot to renew his practice certificate and was not legally entitled to act as a solicitor. It was held that the failure to renew the practice certificate brought the partnership to an end, although a new partnership came into existence between the other two members of the old firm.

Under s35 PA 1890, a court may order the dissolution of the partnership in the following circumstances:

- where a partner becomes a patient under the Mental Health Act 1983
- where a partner suffers some other permanent incapacity
- where a partner engages in an activity prejudicial to the business
- where a partner persistently breaches the partnership agreement
- where the business can only be carried on at a loss
- where it is just and equitable to do so.

The just and equitable ground is similar to s122(1)g Insolvency Act (IA) 1986, which provides for a winding up of a company on the same basis, in particular, small, private companies that are run like partnerships (called 'quasi-partnerships'). The application of s122(1)g IA 1986 to companies is covered in Chapter 18.

On dissolution of a firm, the value of the partnership property is realised and the proceeds are applied in the following order:

- in paying debts to outsiders
- in paying to the partners any advance made to the firm beyond their capital contribution
- in paying the capital contribution of the individual partners.

Any residue is divided between the partners in the same proportion as they shared in profits.

Limited liability partnerships

Under the Limited Liability Partnerships Act 2000 (LLPA), it is possible to create a different form of business association, called a limited liability partnership. Under the LLPA 2000, a limited liability partnership becomes a corporate body with a legal personality separate from that of its members. As such the members of a limited liability partnership will not ordinarily become liable for its debts. In practice, limited liability partnership is likely to have features similar to an ordinary partnership. However, under s1 LLPA 2000, the law relating to ordinary partnerships does not apply to limited liability partnerships. To be incorporated, a limited liability partnership needs to be registered with the **registrar of companies** at Companies House.

A participant in a limited liability partnership is known as a **member**, not a partner, and it is possible for companies to be members of a limited liability partnership. A limited liability partnership may engage in any kind of business, as, unlike a registered company, there is no requirement for a limited liability partnership to have an objects clause. The profits of a limited liability partnership are not subject to corporation tax and the members of a limited liability partnership are taxed on profits in the same way as partners in an ordinary partnership. As a limited liability partnership is a corporate body, a limited liability partnership will not be dissolved on one of the members leaving the limited liability partnership.

The law relating to limited liability partnerships is to be found in the LLPA 2000 and in the form of secondary legislation, principally the Limited Liability Partnership Regulations (LLPR) 2001, which apply provisions of the Companies Act (CA) 1985, the Company Directors Disqualification Act (CDDA) 1986 and the Insolvency Act (IA) 1986 to limited liability partnerships.

Formation of a limited liability partnership

A limited liability partnership is created by registration with the registrar of companies. Once the registrar has registered a limited liability partnership and issued a certificate of incorporation a new corporate body, with a legal personality of its own, is created. Section 2(1) LLPA 2000 provides that:

- Two or more persons associated for carrying on a lawful business with a view to profit must have subscribed their names to an incorporation document, which is to be delivered to the registrar of companies.

- A statement that the requirements of s2 LLPA 2000 have been complied with is also delivered to the registrar of companies. This statement must be made by one of the subscribers to the incorporation document or by a solicitor who was engaged in the formation of the limited liability partnership.

The incorporation document is to be in a form approved by the registrar of companies and to state the following matters: the name of the limited liability partnership; whether the **registered office** is in England, Wales or Scotland; the address of the limited liability partnership; the names and addresses of all the members on **incorporation**; and a statement of who the designated members are or a statement that all members of the limited liability partnership, at any time, are to be designated members.

Members and designated members

Section 4(1) LLPA 2000 provides that the members of a limited liability partnership are the persons who subscribed to the incorporation document. Section 4(2) LLPA 2000 provides that any other person may become a member by agreement with all existing members and s4(3) LLPA 2000 provides that a person may cease to be a member either by agreement with the other members or by giving reasonable notice to the other members. A member who has died, or become dissolved in the case of a corporate member, ceases to be a member.

The LLPA 2000 provides for two members to become designated members who are responsible for the limited liability partnership complying with the administrative requirements as laid down by the LLPR 2001. Under s8(2) LLPA 2000 where there is no designated member, or only one designated member, every member of the limited liability partnership becomes a designated member. A person who ceases to be a member of a limited liability partnership ceases to be a designated member.

Designated members have certain specific duties such as signing the limited liability partnership's accounts and delivering them to the registrar, giving the registrar notice that a limited liability partnership has changed its name and giving the registrar notice of designated members. The rules on approval and removal of auditors, on filing an annual return and on filing of accounts are essentially the same as those that apply to a **limited company**.

Unlike a private company, there cannot be a single-member limited liability partnership, so s24 CA 1985 applies to limited liability partnerships. This means that where a limited liability partnership carries on business with one member for more than 6 months, that member becomes liable for debts incurred while he was the only member.

Contractual liability

Section 6(1) LLPA 2000 provides that every member of a limited liability partnership is an agent of the limited liability partnership and therefore a limited liability partnership will be bound by a contract entered into by an agent with authority to make it. However, under s6(2) LLPA 2000, a limited liability partnership is not bound by anything done by a member in dealing with a person where (i) the member in fact has no authority to act for the limited liability partnership by doing that thing and (ii) the person knows that he has no authority or does not know or believe him to be a member of the limited liability partnership.

Section 36C CA 1985 applies to limited liability partnerships, as it does to companies, so a person making a pre-incorporation contract on behalf of a limited liability partnership will be liable on it. Under s5(2) LLPA 2000, an agreement made between the subscribers to the incorporation document, before the incorporation of a limited liability partnership, may impose obligations on the limited liability partnership to take effect at any time after its incorporation.

Liability in tort

Under s4(4) LLPA 2000 a limited liability partnership is liable for any wrongful act or omission of a member committed during the course of the business of the limited liability partnership or with the authority of the limited liability partnership. Where a member is liable for any wrongful act or omission, the limited liability partnership will be liable equally.

Members' relationship with each other

Section 5(1) LLPA 2000 provides that the mutual rights and duties of the members of a limited liability partnership shall be governed by agreement between the members or by agreement with the limited liability partnership. It is likely therefore that members of a limited liability partnership will have a relationship based on similar terms to that found in an ordinary partnership.

In the absence of any agreement, the default provisions contained in regulation 7 LLPR 2001 will apply. These are similar to the default provisions set out in s24 PA 1890 as they apply to ordinary partnerships and these provisions show therefore how the nature of the relationship of members of a limited liability partnership is similar to that of partners of an ordinary partnership. Similarly, regulation 8 LLPR 2001 provides that no majority of a limited liability partnership can expel a member unless a power to do so has been conferred by express agreement between the members. Where a member is expelled, the power of expulsion, as we saw with ordinary partnerships, must be exercised in good faith for the benefit of the limited liability partnership.

Minority protection

Under s122(1) Insolvency Act 1986 (IA) a member can petition the court for a winding-up order on the ground that it is just and equitable and s459 CA 1985 enables a member to petition the court for relief on the ground of unfair prejudice. It is likely that a common ground of conduct caught by these two provisions is *wrongful exclusion* from management. However, unlike company law where similar provisions are used, mainly in respect of small, private companies, members of a limited liability partnership may by unanimous agreement exclude the right contained in s459 (1) CA 1985 for such period as they agree (s459(1A) CA 1985).

The circumstances in which the Department of Trade and Industry can investigate a company's affairs apply also to a limited liability partnership. Such an investigation can arise where a court orders an investigation or where at least 20 members of a limited liability partnership demand it.

Reality check

Why was the Limited Liability Partnership Acts 2000 introduced?

The LLPA 2000 introduced a new form of business association for the running of a business. The Act was brought about partly in response to concerns expressed by the accounting profession in respect of the cost in settling professional negligence claims where damages were higher than the cover provided by professional indemnity insurance. The accounting bodies were looking for a form of business structure that possessed the convenience of running a business as a partnership but benefiting from incorporated status, as existed in other jurisdictions.

On the passing of the LLPA 2000, the Act introduced a limited liability partnership as a legal entity, so that in the event of any third-party action, the limited liability partnership and not the members would become liable for any contractual or tortious wrong.

The process of formation of a limited liability partnership is similar to that of a registered company in that registration at Companies House is required before a limited liability partnership can come into existence. Under the LLPA 2000, members can choose to retain the arrangement of an ordinary partnership but the Act, in conjunction with the LLPR 2001, requires compliance with certain administrative requirements, such as registering particulars of members, making annual returns and filing accounts. Therefore, the legislation governing limited liability partnerships imposes a regulatory burden on the members of a limited liability partnership and fines can be imposed in the event of default. In case of persistent non-compliance, a member can be disqualified from being a member of a limited liability partnership or a director of a company, by the provisions of the CDDA1986.

In respect of the legal profession, out of 100 firms of solicitors surveyed in 2004, 14 were discovered to have converted to the status of a limited liability partnership, including a number of major law firms, such as Eversheds, Allen & Overy and Clifford Chance. The main reasons for so doing were on the same basis as expressed by the accounting profession. However, some firms have chosen not to convert to the status of a limited liability partnership, citing reasons of confidentiality and convenience. In other professions, firms of architects and surveyors have converted from an ordinary partnership to a limited liability partnership.

A limited liability partnership has advantages in terms of liability, but it may not be the answer for all businesses that want to use a partnership structure.

Winding up

The IA 1986 applies to limited liability partnerships in the same way that it applies to companies and, as a limited liability partnership is a corporate body, it is the limited liability partnership that will be liable for its debts and not generally, therefore, the members of the limited liability partnership. However, as with company law, the wrongful trading and fraudulent trading provisions under ss213 and 214 IA 1986 apply to members of a limited liability partnership so that a court can order a member to contribute to the assets of a limited liability partnership in the event of a winding up. Members can also be made liable under ss74 and 214A IA 1986. Section 74 IA 1986 provides that members of a limited liability partnership can agree to assume liability for the company's debts. Under s214A IA 1986 a member or shadow member who, within 2 years of the commencement of winding up, withdrew limited liability partnership property while having reasonable grounds for believing either that the limited liability partnership could not pay its debts or would have been unable to pay its debts once the property had been withdrawn, can be ordered by a court to pay such a contribution to the limited liability partnership's assets as the court thinks proper. The court will make the order only if the member knew or ought to have known, at the time of the relevant withdrawal, that the limited liability partnership had no reasonable prospect of avoiding going into insolvent liquidation.

Disqualification of members

The CDDA 1986 applies to both members and shadow members of a limited liability partnership, so that a person disqualified from being either a director of a company or a member of a limited liability partnership will be disqualified from being a director of any company or a member of any limited liability partnership. A person who acts as a limited liability partnership member in breach of a disqualification order commits a criminal offence and can be liable without limit for the limited liability partnership's debts. The application of the CDDA 1986 to delinquent directors is dealt with in Chapter 16, on company management.

Incorporated companies

An incorporated company is an artificial legal person with an entity that is separate and distinct from its members. The most common form of incorporated company is a registered company, but other types of company exist, such as a chartered company and a **statutory company**. The law relating to the formation and running of companies is to be found in the CA 1985, the CA 1989 and case law. The CA 1985 is the principal piece of legislation governing companies, but it should be noted that the CA 1985 will contain a number of modifications when the Company Law Reform Bill 2005 is passed. The stated aim of the Department of Trade and Industry in promoting the bill is to provide a more flexible regulatory regime for companies choosing to register and trade in the UK, particularly **private companies**, for which some aspects of the CA 1985 and CA 1989 are seen as imposing an unnecessary burden. The bill will also be codifying some aspects of case law, such as directors' duties, which are based at present on the common law and equity.

Types of company

There are three types of company that can be incorporated. These are chartered companies, statutory companies and registered companies. Registered companies are the most common and may be either public companies or private companies.

Chartered companies

Chartered companies are created by the Crown under prerogative powers or special statutory powers. Examples are the BBC and some public schools and universities. Professional bodies such as the Institute of Chartered Accountants and the Chartered Association of Certified Accountants are also chartered companies.

Statutory companies

Statutory companies are formed by a special Act of Parliament with rights and liabilities and special powers created by appropriate legislation. Examples were the former public utilities that have been replaced by public limited companies following privatisation legislation, e.g. the Royal Mail is one such public corporation.

Registered companies

Registered companies are the most common type of incorporated company. They are either formed under the CA 1985 or were created under a former CA. Any registered company formed before or after 1985 is governed by the CA 1985. Registered companies can be either public companies or private companies.

Public companies

Section 1(3) CA 1985 defines a public company as one limited by shares whose **memorandum of association** states that the company is a public company and that has complied with the statutory requirements regarding registration. It must have the words 'public limited company' (or plc) at the end of its name (or the Welsh equivalent).

A public company needs at least two members and two directors and one secretary, the last with professional qualifications, although it is proposed in the Company Law Reform Bill 2005 that a public company may be formed by one member. A public company's authorised share capital, i.e., the amount of capital it is allowed to issue, must be at least £50,000, of which, on allotment of the shares, at least one-quarter of the nominal value of the shares and the whole of any premium has been received by the company. As a public company raises capital from the public by issuing shares or debentures, it is subject to stricter controls than other companies.

'Limited' refers to the liability of the members and not to the company itself, which must always discharge its liabilities, assets permitting. Therefore, with a limited company with a share capital, a member's liability is limited to the value of his shareholding. Once a member has paid the company for his shares, including any uncalled capital, his liability is discharged.

Under s117 CA 1985, a public company may not commence business or borrow money until the registrar of companies has issued a trading certificate. However, the need for this certificate is rare as it is unusual for a company to incorporate as a public company. It is more common to incorporate as a private company and float as a public company at a later stage.

FAQ

What is the difference between a 'listed' company and a 'quoted' company?

Both types of company are public companies. A listed company is a public company that has its shares listed on the official list of the Stock Exchange and is subject to the Stock Exchange Listing Rules and to regulation by the Financial Services Authority. A quoted company is a public company, but whose shares are traded on another stock market, such as the Alternative Investment Market. Such companies are also subject to regulation by market rules and the Financial Services Authority. The role of the Financial Services Authority in respect of company law is that it acts as the Listing Authority and has responsibility for the investigation of suspected cases of insider dealing and market manipulation.

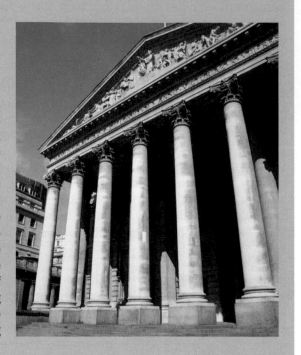

Private companies

The CA 1985 defines a private company as any company that is not a public company (s1(3) CA 1985). By virtue of s1(3A) CA 1985, a private limited company can be formed by one person. There are different types of private company, but the most common is a private company limited by shares.

A company limited by shares

This is the most common form of registered company. The members will only be liable to the amount unpaid, if any, on their shares should the company go into liquidation. At least one director (s282 CA 1985) and a **company secretary** (s283 CA 1985) are required, although in the Company Law Reform Bill 2005, it is proposed that it will no longer be necessary for a private company to have a company secretary. A sole director may not also be the company secretary (s283 CA 1985). Shares in a private company are transferred privately, any restrictions on transfer being commonly found in the company's **articles of association**.

A company limited by guarantee

In relation to a company limited by guarantee, members' liability is incurred on the liquidation of the company and is limited to a guaranteed amount found in the company's memorandum of association. The amount is usually a nominal sum, in practice, frequently £1. At least one director is required (s282 CA 1985) and the company must have a company secretary who may not be the sole director (s283 CA 1985).

Examples of companies limited by guarantee are trade protection societies; social and athletic clubs; and concerns not intended to make a profit. A number of universities are run as private companies limited by guarantee.

Unlimited companies

Section 1(2) CA 1985 provides that a registered company may be a company not having any limit on the liability of its members – an **unlimited company**. However, although unlimited companies do not have to file accounts with the registrar of companies, which keeps their affairs private, they are rare, as members do not have the protection of limited liability.

Small and medium-sized companies

Companies can be categorised in relation to their size. This is important as it can have a bearing on whether a company needs to comply with the administrative requirements of company legislation such as the need to submit accounts or to appoint an auditor.

Whether a company can be defined as small or medium sized depends on turnover, the value of the company's balance sheet and the number of employees it has, as follows (two of the following requirements must be satisfied):

	Small	*Medium*
Turnover	Not more than £5.6m	Not more than £22.8m
Balance sheet	Not more than £2.8m	Not more than £11.4m
Number of employees	Not more than 50	Not more than 250

FAQ

What is meant by a group of companies?

A group of companies exists where two or more companies are in the relationship of 'holding' and 'subsidiary' to each other. Section 736 CA 1985 provides that a company is a subsidiary of a, holding company, where the holding company:

- holds a majority of the voting rights in it

- is a member of it and has the right to appoint or remove a majority of its board of directors

- is a member of it and controls alone a majority of the voting rights in it or if it is a

subsidiary of another company which is itself a subsidiary of the holding company.

Therefore, a company is a wholly owned subsidiary of another company where it has no members except that other or that other's wholly owned subsidiaries or persons acting on its behalf.

In relation to accounting requirements, s258 CA 1985 defines the relationship of parent company and **subsidiary company** in a similar way but makes additional reference to the parent company exercising a dominant influence over the subsidiary company. Under s229 CA 1985, a group is required to be treated as a separate entity in relation to group accounting provisions.

Community interest companies

A community interest company is a new type of company provided for by the Companies (Audit, Investigations and Community Enterprise) Act 2004, which is designed for social enterprises that want to use their profits and assets for the benefit of the community, such as environmental protection and community transport. They are not charitable companies as, unlike a charitable company, a community interest company can provide returns for investors. However, a community interest company has mainly social objectives and any surplus is to be mainly reinvested for that purpose and not as a means of maximising profits for its shareholders. There is also a restriction on distributing profits and assets to the members of the company, as assets are to be used principally to benefit the community.

Community interest companies can be registered as private or public companies and can be registered as a company limited by shares or by guarantee.

Registration of companies

Registration procedure

Section 1 CA 1985 provides that any two or more persons associated for a lawful purpose may form an incorporated company, with or without limited liability, by subscribing their names to (and signing) a document called a memorandum of association and by complying with certain other requirements of the CA 1985.

Application for registration is made by delivering certain documents to the registrar of companies. These documents are:

- **memorandum of association** (s10(1) CA 1985)
- **articles of association**, if any (s10(1) CA 1985)
- a statement signed by or on behalf of the subscribers to the memorandum containing the names and particulars of the directors and secretary and a consent signed by each of them consenting to act in the relevant capacity (ss10(1)(3) CA 1985)
- a similar statement specifying the situation of the company's registered office (s10(6) CA 1985)
- a statutory declaration by a solicitor engaged in the formation of the company or by a person named as the director or secretary to the effect that the requirements of the CA 1985 have been complied with (s12(3) CA 1985).

Where the memorandum delivered to the registrar under s10 CA 1985 states that the company is to be a public company, the amount of the share capital with which the company proposes to be registered must not be less than the authorised minimum, which is £50,000 (s11 CA 1985).

The nature and scope of the memorandum and articles of association is discussed in Chapter 14.

Under the Companies Act 1985 (Electronic Communications) Order 2000, it is possible to register a company by delivering the particulars of registration in electronic form. It is also possible for the administrative requirements of the CA 1985 to be complied with by using electronic communication and the Company Law Reform Bill 2005 proposes to enhance the provisions relating to electronic communication. The Bill also proposes to make significant changes to the constitutional arrangement of a company.

Fees

Section 708 CA 1985 provides that the secretary of state shall have power by regulations made by statutory instrument to require the payment to the registrar of certain fees. The registration fee for a new company, is currently £20 (£15 for electronic incorporation). In addition, there may also be costs incurred for professional services and the preparation of the relevant documents, for example, where use is made of a company formation agent.

Duty of the registrar and effect of registration

Where the registrar of companies is satisfied that all the requirements of the CA 1985 in respect of registration have been complied with, he must retain and register the memorandum and articles (if any), although he may accept the s12(3) declaration as sufficient evidence of compliance.

On registering the memorandum, the registrar must allocate to the company a registered number and grant a certificate that the company is incorporated and, where appropriate, that the company is limited or that the company is a public company.

A certificate of incorporation is conclusive evidence that all the registration requirements have been complied with and the company has been duly registered (s13(7) CA 1985). The certificate of incorporation is dated by the registrar and the company is incorporated as from that date (s13(3) CA 1985). In ***Jubilee Cotton Mills Ltd v Lewis (1924)***, this was taken as meaning from the first moment of that day.

Business names

The Business Names Act (BNA) 1985 deals with the use of business names by those engaged in a business, whether a sole trader, a partnership or a registered company.

Sections 2 and 3 BNA 1985 provide that a business name (or **company name** or limited liability partnership name) must not be one likely to give the impression that the business is connected with Her Majesty's government or with any local authority, or contain any words or expression for which approval is required, unless such approval has been obtained.

Under s4 BNA 1985, where a person carries on business in a name other than his own, that person must state in legible characters on all business documents and negotiable instruments the name of the owner of the business and an address at which documents may be served. Such business documents include, for example, invoices and receipts, such as a till receipt. The particulars of ownership must also appear in a prominent position where it may easily be read by customers or suppliers in any premises where business is carried on. An example would be a high street shop, as that is a common place for customer transactions to take place.

Section 7 BNA 1985 provides a criminal sanction for breach of the provisions of the Act, while s5 BNA 1985 states that a breach of s4 BNA 1985 enables a court to dismiss any civil proceedings brought by an owner of a business against a customer unless the owner obtains a court order.

The provisions of the BNA 1985 relating to business or trading names are different from the provisions of the CA 1985 that relate to the use of words as part of the registered name of a company. These provisions are dealt with in Chapter 15.

The Company Law Reform Bill 2005 proposes making some changes to the BNA 1985, particularly in relation to companies.

FAQ

> **QUESTION 1** What do you think is the purpose of s4 BNA 1985? Who do you consider is intended to be protected by the section?

What are the advantages and disadvantages of running a business as an ordinary partnership or a registered company?

The answer is one based on convenience and financial and legal risk. A partnership as recognised by the Partnership Act 1890 enables the affairs of the business to be run with minimal administrative regulation. Other than ensuring that accounts are prepared for taxation purposes, there are few administrative requirements. A registered company, by way of contrast, needs to comply with the requirements of company legislation such as the maintaining of registers and the filing of accounts and returns. A failure to comply can lead to the officers responsible, usually the directors and/or the company secretary, being subject to default fines and in cases of persistent non-compliance, can lead to a director being disqualified from holding office as director under the Company Directors Disqualification Act 1986.

Tax burdens for a company may be more complicated because, unlike the individual partners of a firm, a company's income is taxed as corporation tax, with directors' salaries and shareholders' dividends subject to income tax. The requirements of the Companies Act 1985 also mean that a company's affairs are made public. A company's filed accounts and returns can be inspected at Companies House on the payment of a search fee. The company's register of charges and names and addresses of its directors can also be consulted. A partnership's affairs can be kept private and known only between the partners.

The main advantage that incorporators of a company have over a partnership is that the company is a separate legal entity distinct from its members and directors and can enter into contracts in its own right. Should the company be in breach of contract, action by a third party is taken against the company and not individual directors or shareholders of the company. If the company has insufficient assets to meet a claim, the third party cannot ordinarily sue the directors or shareholders personally. By contrast, the Partnership Act 1890 provides that acts of each partner done in the usual course of the firm's business bind each partner and the firm, and liability in respect of contractual and tortious wrongs attracts personal liability.

Financial considerations in respect of companies and partnerships are broadly similar. A small private small with a small asset base is unlikely to be in position to grant security in the form of fixed or floating charges. In early years, capital for a partnership or a company is likely to be based on the personal capital of either the partners or the director/shareholders. Alternatively, loans from banking institutions can be obtained but it is possible that a bank will seek a personal guarantee in connection with the loan in the event of default. It is therefore a matter of contract law and not company law as to whether and to what extent the director/shareholder is liable in respect of a personal guarantee.

In relation to liability for tax, the position in respect of income tax and capital gains tax is broadly similar whether the business is run as a partnership, sole trader or registered company, assuming the business is a small one.

Answer to in-text question

> **QUESTION 1** What do you think is the purpose of s4 BNA 1985? Who do you consider is intended to be protected by the section?

The purpose of s4 BNA 1985 is to protect customers of a business, so that in the event of a legal dispute arising between a customer and a business, compliance with the section enables the customer, if necessary, to discover the name of the owner of the business and an address at which legal documents can be served. A trading name is not sufficient for this purpose, as a trading name does not constitute a legal entity that can be sued.

14 | Incorporation

Learning objectives

By the end of this chapter, you should be able to explain:

- **The nature of corporate personality and the circumstances in which the veil of incorporation may be disregarded**

- **The role and duties of promoters and the effect of any pre-incorporation contract**

- **The nature and scope of a company's memorandum and articles of association**

Introduction

In the previous chapter, we looked at different types of business association that people can use as a means of running a business. One of these is a registered company and the remaining chapters of this part of the book are devoted to a detailed consideration of the principles that govern the regulation of companies and the conduct of those involved with companies, such as directors and shareholders. We start this process by examining the consequences of incorporation. This involves examining more closely the concept of corporate personality and the means by which, in limited circumstances, the veil of incorporation can be disregarded, such as in the case of 'sham' companies or fraudulent or wrongful trading. We shall also be looking at the role of promoters. Promoters (or incorporators) are the people responsible for setting up a company. Their activities are subject to company law, for they owe duties to the company, as directors do, and they can be held liable on any pre-incorporation contracts. A pre-incorporation contract is a contract entered into by a person on behalf of a company, such as a promoter, before that company has come into existence.

We conclude this chapter by considering, once a company has been incorporated, the nature and scope of a company's constitution in the form of the **memorandum of association** and the **articles of association.**

Corporate personality

As we saw in the previous chapter, a **company** is a separate legal entity, distinct from those who form it or are its members. On **incorporation**, a company becomes a legal person, albeit an artificial legal person, having rights and duties of its own. As with natural legal persons, a company may enter into contracts and it may sue and be sued and its existence is maintained though members may die or are removed or replaced. This should be contrasted with a **partnership**, where, if a partner dies, retires or goes bankrupt, the partnership's existence comes to an end, although, in practice, the business will usually continue under the remaining partners.

The leading case illustrating the nature of corporate personality is the House of Lords decision in ***Salomon v A Salomon & Co Ltd (1978)*** (see textbox below).

A further illustration of the principle of *Salomon v A Salomon & Co Ltd (1897)* can be found in ***Lee v Lee's Air Farming Ltd (1960)***. Lee formed a company, Lee's Air Farming Ltd, for the purpose of aerial crop spraying. Lee was the controlling shareholder and governing **director** of the company. He was also appointed as the company's chief pilot. In 1956, Lee was killed in an air crash during the course of crop spraying. His widow claimed compensation from the company in accordance with New Zealand legislation, which provided for compensation to widows of employees in the event of death or personal injuries sustained during the course of employment. The court held that Lee's widow *was* entitled to compensation. In applying *Salomon v A Salomon & Co Ltd*, Lee was considered an employee within the legislation, because he and the company were separate legal persons. Both parties could enter into a contract of employment – one as employer, the other as employee, even though Lee represented the employer.

Salomon v A Salomon & Co Ltd (1897)

Salomon was a manufacturer of leather boots. He later transferred the business to a newly incorporated company in which Salomon, his wife and five children subscribed to one share each. Payment to Salomon for the business was through issuing him a further 20,000 £1 shares and £10,000 in debentures issued by the company and secured by a floating charge against the company's assets. This made Salomon a secured creditor. A year later, the company went into liquidation with debts to unsecured creditors amounting to £8000 and company assets worth £6000. The unsecured creditors claimed the assets ahead of Salomon, arguing that Salomon could not by his status as secured creditor have priority over them as the company and Salomon were 'the one and the same'. The House of Lords disagreed and held that, as the company was a separate entity, distinct from Salomon, the debentures were valid and Salomon was entitled to the assets owing to his security.

As the principle of corporate personality is a well-established part of company law, it is unlikely that third parties dealing with a company will get caught out?

A consequence of forming a company is to enable a business person to run his or her affairs through the medium of a company and to be shielded from the effects of any losses on company contracts. Third parties dealing with companies need to be aware that individuals behind the company do not bear any responsibility for any losses sustained by a third party in its dealings with the company. This applies equally to any harm or loss a third party suffers as a result of losses in tort. A recent example of corporate personality in respect of a company's liability in tort can be found in *Williams v Natural Life*
Health Foods Ltd (1998). In this case, the claimants entered into a franchise scheme operated by N Ltd, the original defendants, relying on statements contained in N Ltd's marketing brochure and financial projections. The advice given proved to be misleading and the claimants made a loss of over £38,000. During the course of legal proceedings, N Ltd went into liquidation and the claimants sought to make M, the company's managing director and principal shareholder, liable. M's expertise had been highlighted in the brochure and he had played a prominent part in producing the projections. The House of Lords held that the claimants' contract was with N Ltd, not M, and any action in contract or tort could only lie against the company. M could not be held liable in the tort of negligence unless, which was absent in this case, there was an assumption of personal liability based on principles laid down in *Hedley Byrne v Heller (1964)*. M was therefore protected and the claimant had a worthless claim against an insolvent company.

Lifting the veil of incorporation

Although the cases examined so far show that there is a corporate shield between a company and its members, in some circumstances the veil of incorporation is lifted in order to enable the individuals 'hiding' behind the veil to be attacked or for the human and commercial reality to be exposed. **Lifting the veil** of incorporation can be done by the courts or in accordance with statute.

Intervention by the courts

Trading with the enemy In *Daimler Co Ltd v Continental Tyre & Rubber Co Ltd (1916)*, at the outbreak of war with Germany, the court looked at the nationality of **company members** of a British-registered company in order to see if they were enemy aliens. The company was registered in Britain with a British **registered office**. The court, however, was prepared to lift the veil of incorporation to see who was in control of the company's affairs and, on so doing, discovered that the members and directors of the company were German nationals. As a consequence, the court ruled that the company could not maintain proceedings brought against another company as that would amount to trading with the enemy.

Sham companies Where a company is formed as a means of enabling a person to avoid a personal obligation, that may be a ground for a court to ignore the existence of the company (see the *Gilford Motor* case study textbox).

Another example can be found in *Trustor AB v Smallbone (No 2) (2001)*. In this case, the managing director of the claimant company in breach of duty

Gilford Motor Co Ltd v Horne (1933)

The claimant company was a manufacturer of vehicles and supplier of spare parts. The defendant was the managing director of the company whose contract of employment contained a restrictive covenant preventing him from soliciting the claimant's customers during his employment and afterwards. On the termination of his employment, the defendant set up a limited company trading in the same line of business. The claimant sought an injunction against the ex-employee and the company he formed. The injunction was granted. The creation of the company was simply a sham designed to enable the defendant to avoid his obligations under the covenant.

transferred substantial sums belonging to the claimant to I Ltd, a company controlled by the managing director. The claimant claimed that it could bring proceedings against I Ltd for recovery of the transferred funds, on the basis that I Ltd was a façade, set up as a vehicle for receiving the funds transferred by the managing director in breach of duty. It was held that the claimant's action could succeed, as I Ltd was a façade, designed to conceal the true facts and to avoid the obligations imposed on the managing director.

Not all cases of pleading a sham company are successful. In **Ord v Belhaven Pubs Ltd** *(1998)*, the Court of Appeal held the defendant company, B Ltd, could not be construed as a mere façade in respect of the transfer of its assets as part of a restructuring within a group of companies. The transfer was undertaken without any intention to prejudice the claimants who were suing the defendant company. The motive for the reconstruction had been based on an understandable business decision, which had been undertaken as a consequence of a decline in the property market. Where a strong economic unity existed between companies within a group of companies, this was not necessarily a ground for lifting the veil of incorporation. This was also the view of the Court of Appeal in **Adams v Cape Industries plc** *(1990)*.

Groups of companies Where groups of companies exist, e.g. in the form of a parent company with several subsidiary companies, each company is to be treated as a legal entity and the act of one company within the group is not to be treated as a an act of another company within the group (as we just saw in *Ord v Belhaven Pubs Ltd (1998)*). However, it is possible to hold that, within a group of companies, one company is an agent of another. In **Firestone Tyre & Rubber Co Ltd v Lewellin (1957)** nearly all the income of an English wholly owned **subsidiary company** was forwarded to the American parent company. It was held by the House of Lords that the English company was acting as agent for the parent company, which was conducting its business in England through the subsidiary and it was therefore liable to pay UK tax.

Legislation For taxation purposes, holding companies of groups of companies are required to keep group accounts, despite the separate legal personality of every member in the group. Other legislation, such as the CA 1985, imposes liability on members or directors for acts of the company, for example, a sole member of a company is liable for debts incurred by the company where he allows the company to carry on business with only one member for more than 6 months (s24 CA 1985). This provision does not apply to single-member, private companies (s24A CA 1985). Similarly, under s349 CA 1985 where an officer of a company or a person on its behalf signs or authorises to be signed on behalf of the company any bill of exchange, promissory note, endorsement, cheque or order for money or goods in which the company's name is not mentioned, he is liable to a fine and, further, becomes liable to the holder of the cheque, etc., for the amount stated, unless it is duly paid by the company.

Another example of personal liability can be found in the Insolvency Act (IA) 1986. Under the IA 1986, directors can be held liable to make a contribution to the assets of an insolvent company where their conduct preceding insolvency amounted to either **fraudulent trading** (s213 IA 1985) or **wrongful trading** (s214 IA 1986). As fraudulent or wrongful trading arise in the context of the insolvency of a company, these provisions are dealt with in Chapter 19.

Limited liability of members

Limited liability means that the liability of members, either as shareholders or guarantors, is limited to the value of their shareholding or the amount of the guarantee. It is not the liability of the company that is limited. The company's liability remains unlimited, at least to the extent that it has assets to meet claims made against it.

FAQ

Can a company be held criminally liable?

As a company is a legal person separate from its members, companies were considered originally to be outside the ambit of criminal law, apart from strict liability offences, because a company could not have mens rea, i.e. a guilty mind, nor could a company be punished. However, the courts developed the doctrine of identification as a means of enabling companies to be held liable for certain criminal offences. Under the doctrine, persons who control or manage the affairs of the company are regarded as the company and, where they are acting in the capacity of controlling officers, the company is identified with their acts and their state of mind. In *R v ICR Haulage Ltd (1944)* a company, its managing director and others were charged with conspiracy to defraud and the state of mind of the managing director was imputed to the company.

The doctrine of identification refers to controlling officers. There is no clear test for determining whether someone is acting as a controlling officer. In *Tesco Supermarkets Ltd v Nattrass (1972)*, it was held by the House of Lords that a shop manager was a mere servant or agent and could not be regarded as representing the controlling mind of the company. It is the directors of a company who are more likely to be taken as representing the controlling mind of the company.

The 'directing mind and will' test may not always be appropriate in determining the criminal liability of companies. In *Meridian Global Funds Management Asia Ltd v Securities Commission (1995)* Lord Hoffman stated that it was a question of construction as to whether a particular rule, such as one found in statute, requires that knowledge of an individual should be attributed to the company and that individual may not necessarily represent the company's directing mind and will.

Promotion of a company

Before a company can be formed, some person or persons must form an intention and take the necessary steps to carry that intention into operation. Such a person is called a **promoter**.

The word promoter has never been clearly defined either by the judiciary or by legislation, despite the fact that it is used frequently in decisions and statutes. In ***Twycross v Grant (1877)***, Cockburn LJ said that a promoter is one 'who undertakes to form a company with reference to a given project and to set it going, and who takes the necessary steps to accomplish that purpose'. Promoters would certainly be persons who give instructions for the preparation and registration of the memorandum and articles, issue prospectuses, negotiate contracts for the purchase of property by the company and to obtain the directors. Often a promoter is a prospective director and a company can act as a promoter in promoting another company.

Legal position of promoters

A promoter is not an agent for the company he is forming, for a company cannot have an agent before it comes into existence. Neither is he a trustee, but from the moment he acts with the new company in mind he stands in a fiduciary position towards the company. This means that, although there is nothing wrong in a promoter making a profit out of the promotion of a company, such as where the promoter sells property to the company, he must disclose any profit he has made, to either an independent board of directors or the existing and prospective shareholders.

Disclosure to an independent board of directors may be difficult to comply with, since promoters are often the first directors of the company. Where there is not disclosure to an independent board, disclosure must be made to the shareholders, through listing particulars or a prospectus. In ***Salomon v A Salomon & Co Ltd (1897)***, **Salomon** sold his business to a company he had promoted. The business was sold at an overvaluation and he made a profit. However, he was not liable to account for the profit, as the profit was disclosed to his family who were the other shareholders.

The remedies available to a company for breach of duty by a promoter enable the company to rescind the contract, i.e. return the property and recover the purchase price or to claim the secret profit that the promoter has made. The right of rescission may be lost where the parties cannot be restored to their original position, for instance, where the company has sold the property to another party who has acted in good faith. In such cases, the company is likely to pursue the alternative remedy of account of profit.

Disqualification of promoters

The Company Directors Disqualification Act 1986 provides that, where a person has been convicted of an indictable offence in connection with the promotion or formation of a company, the court may make an order that, unless he obtains leave of the court, that person shall not be a director or liquidator of a company or be concerned in the promotion of a company for up to 15 years.

Pre-incorporation contracts

In the case of a **private company**, contracts are classified as either pre-incorporation or post-incorporation. In respect of a public company, because of the provisions of s117 CA 1985 a post-incorporation contract may, after incorporation, be entered into before or after the trading certificate is issued by the **registrar of companies**. Section 117(8) CA 1985 provides that a failure to obtain a trading certificate does not affect the validity of any transaction entered into by the company, but where the company enters into a transaction before the certificate has been issued and fails to comply with its obligations within 21 days from being called on to do so, the directors are jointly and severally liable to indemnify the other party in respect of any loss he has suffered by reason of the company's failure.

In respect of pre-incorporation contracts, where a promoter enters into a contract with a third party on behalf of an unformed company, the question of whether the promoter is bound to the contract is determined by s36C CA 1985, which states:

> A contract which purports to be made by or on behalf of a company at a time when the company has not been formed has effect, subject to any agreement to the contrary, as one made with the person purporting to act for the company or as agent for it, and he is personally liable on the contract accordingly.

Section 36C CA 1985 provides therefore that, unless there is an agreement to the contrary, a promoter or agent is liable in respect of any pre-incorporation contract. The company is not liable because it was not in existence at the time the contract was entered into. The section was considered by Lord Denning in **Phonogram Ltd v Lane (1982)**, highlighted in the case study.

Phonogram Ltd v Lane (1982)

A group of pop artists were intending to perform under the name 'Cheap Mean and Nasty' and a company, Fragile Management Limited, was to be formed to manage them. The group manager, Lane, entered into negotiations with P Ltd, under which, in anticipation of an album, P Ltd agreed to provide £12,000 in two equal instalments, one of which was paid, to finance the group. The cheque for £6000 sent to Lane was accompanied by a letter stating that, if the contract were not completed within a certain period, 'you will undertake to pay us £6000'. Lane was asked to sign a copy of the letter and return it to P Ltd, which he did, signing 'for and behalf of Fragile Management Ltd'. The album was not produced, Fragile Management Ltd was never formed and the £6000 was not repaid. An issue arose at to who was liable to repay the sum. As it was established that Fragile Management Ltd could not be sued since the company had never come into existence, the question then arose as to whether Lane was personally liable under the contract. Lord Denning's view was that, even without s36C CA, Lane was liable. The letter was, in effect, the contract and 'you will undertake ...' meant Lane, the person. Lord Denning also considered s36C and thought that it covered the present case. Lane had made the contract on behalf of Fragile Management Ltd at a time when it had not been formed and he purported to make it on behalf of the company. Therefore, he was liable on the contract.

In ***Braymist Ltd v Wise Finance Ltd (2002)***, the court held that a promoter or third party acting on behalf of an unformed company was able to obtain the benefits of a pre-incorporation contract as well as be liable under such a contract.

It should also be remembered that under the Contracts (Rights of Third Parties) Act 1999, as discussed in Chapter 5, depending on the construction of the contract, it is possible for rights to be conferred on a company that has not come into existence.

QUESTION 1 Why would a promoter run the risk of incurring personal liability by entering into a contract on behalf of a company before it became incorporated?

Constitution of a company

As part of a process of streamlining company law, a number of changes to the constitutional arrangement of a company have been proposed in the Company Law Reform Bill 2005. When the Bill is passed these changes will take effect for new and existing companies. At present, the constitution of a company is based on two documents:

- The **memorandum of association**, which regulates the company's external affairs and informs persons dealing with the company what it is formed to do and the amount of capital it has.

- The **articles of association**, which regulate the company's internal affairs, such as matters relating to the issuing of **shares**, the holding and proceedings of meetings, voting rights and dividends.

If there is a conflict between the two documents, the memorandum prevails, but the articles may be looked at to explain any ambiguities in the memorandum. In relation to matters that can be dealt with by either the memorandum or the articles, where the memorandum is silent on a matter, reference can be made to the articles.

QUESTION 2 Where might you be able to obtain a copy of a company's memorandum and articles of association?

Memorandum of association

Section 2 CA 1985 provides that the memorandum of association of a company limited by shares must state the following:

- **company name**
- whether the company's registered office is to be situated in England and Wales or Scotland
- company's objects
- that the liability of its members is limited
- the amount of share capital with which the company proposes to be registered and the division of share capital into shares of a fixed amount.

The memorandum of a public company must further state that it is to be a public company (s1(3) CA 1985) and the memorandum can contain other clauses in addition to those required by the CA 1985. The memorandum must be signed by each subscriber in the presence of at least one witness who must attest the signature (s2(6) CA 1985).

Only one subscriber is required where the company is to be a private **limited company** but the memorandum of a public company or an **unlimited company** must have at least two subscribers (s1 CA 1985).

The name clause

A company may have two different names: a corporate name, which is the registered name of the company, and a business or trading name.

The provisions about corporate names, such as words that may be used, are to be found in ss25–34 CA 1985. For instance, under regulations passed under s29 CA 1985, the consent of the secretary of state would be required if the registered name is to include the words 'National', 'England', 'Council', or 'Society', etc. The Company Law Reform Bill 2005 contains proposals that strengthen these provisions by preventing the use of words or symbols that might mislead or deceive customers.

The CA 1985 provides that the name of a limited company must end with the words 'public limited company' or 'limited' or, as is more usual, the abbreviation of 'plc' or 'ltd'. Where the **registered company** is to be situated in Wales, the equivalent in Welsh is permitted. An exception applies to private companies limited by guarantee, which are charitable companies, such as some universities. These companies can dispense with the word 'limited' or the abbreviation 'ltd'.

You may recall from Chapter 12, that where a company is registered with a name too similar to that of another previously registered, that company can seek redress through an action in the tort of *passing off* and where the use of the name is likely to deceive the public, an injunction may be granted to restrain its use.

The provisions about business names are located in the Business Names Act 1985 and the significance of the use of a business name was looked at in Chapter 13.

Registered office clause

Section 287(1) CA 1985 provides that a company shall at all times have a registered office. This is important, as there must be an address where legal documents can be served. The CA 1985 provides that the following registers and documents are to be kept at the registered office:

- register of members (s353 CA 1985)
- register of debenture holders, if any (s190 CA 1985)
- company's register of charges (s411 CA 1985)
- minute book of **general meetings** (s383 CA 1985)
- register of directors and **company secretary** (s288 CA 1985)
- register of directors' interests in shares and debentures of the company or associated company (s325 CA 1985)
- register by a public company of substantial interests in shares (s211 CA 1985 CA)
- directors' service contracts (s318 CA 1985).

A companies registered office, however, is not necessarily the same as its head office, which is the centre of control of its affairs.

The objects clause

The memorandum of association of a company is required to state the objects that the company is formed to pursue. Prior to reform of the doctrine of **ultra vires**, the significance of the objects clause lay in relation to a company's capacity to enter into transactions with third parties. The CA 1985, as amended by the CA 1989, however, abolished the doctrine of ultra vires to the extent that the presence of the objects clause has limited effect on the position of third parties in its dealings with a company (s35 CA 1985).

Abolition of ultra vires The effect of the virtual abolition of the doctrine of ultra vires is that a company generally has the requisite capacity to enter into contracts, but, unlike a limited liability partnership, a company does not have unlimited capacity to enter into contracts, although the Company Law Reform Bill 2005 proposes that a company, unless it decides to the contrary, does not have to have an objects clause.

The scope of the ultra vires doctrine is further limited by s3A and s4 CA 1985. By virtue of s4 CA 1985 (subject to a right of rejection under s5 Ca 1985) a company can, by the passing of a **special resolution**, alter its objects and under s3A CA 1985, where the company's memorandum states that the object of the company is to carry on business as a 'general commercial company', the company can carry on any trade or business whatsoever and can do all such things that are incidental or conducive thereto.

FAQ

Why was the doctrine of ultra vires abolished?

A registered company must have an objects clause in its memorandum of association and the doctrine of ultra vires was designed as a means of protecting shareholders and creditors of the company by ensuring that company resources were not dissipated through ventures not authorised by its memorandum. In *Ashbury Railway Carriage & Iron Co v Riche (1875)*, the purchase of a concession for the construction of a railway in Belgium was held not within the company's objects clause, which provided for the manufacture of railway carriages and wagons, not whole railway systems. The contract, which was causing financial difficulties to the company, was held to be ultra vires the company and, as a consequence, void and unenforceable.

A consequence of the doctrine of ultra vires, however, was that it caused undue hardship to third parties who might be unaware that the company was acting ultra vires. Even where a third party had a copy of the company's memorandum of association, it might not understand its significance or be certain whether the particular transaction fell within or outside the company's objects clause. The position was made more unsatisfactory by the doctrine of constructive notice, whereby anyone dealing with the company was deemed to have knowledge of the company's memorandum and articles of association.

To offset the hardship of the ultra vires doctrine caused to third parties, changes were introduced by s9 European Communities Act 1972 (later becoming s35 CA 1985) but these changes proved unsatisfactory and the doctrine was abolished effectively by CA 1989 by the insertion of a new s35 into the CA 1985. Under s35(1) CA 1985 an act of a company cannot be questioned on the ground of a lack of corporate capacity and therefore where an act of a company is beyond the company's objects, it becomes binding and effective.

Under current company law, however, the doctrine of ultra vires may have a role to play, as a proposed ultra vires act can be challenged by a shareholder seeking an injunction, and ultra vires acts that come within s 322A CA 1985 (as set out later) are not valid but voidable.

An issue related closely to the doctrine of ultra vires is where a company act is within its powers but beyond the powers of the directors. Such an act is also binding, by virtue of s35A CA 1985, which provides that a third party, acting in good faith, can assume that there is no limitation on the board's powers to bind the company or those authorised by the board.

For external purposes, therefore, it can be seen that the doctrine of ultra vires has been abolished. However, s35 CA 1985 does provide a measure of shareholder protection. Directors are under a duty to observe the company's memorandum (s35(3) CA 1985) and a company can take action against the directors for failing to so do, but establishing breach of s35(3) CA 1985 might require an assessment of the past rules developed under the doctrine of ultra vires. To this extent, the doctrine may still have a role to play in company law. The company is not compelled to take action against the directors and s35(3) CA 1985 provides that the directors may be relieved of liability for breach of duty by the passing of a special resolution by the general meeting. A further measure of protection to shareholders is provided by s35(2) CA 1985. Under s35(2) CA 1985, a shareholder can seek an injunction preventing the company from entering into a proposed ultra vires act, but obtaining relief in the case of a minority shareholder is limited, as the company by the passing of a special resolution can ratify an ultra vires act (s35(3) CA 1985) and the granting of an injunction is subject to 'any legal obligation arising'. Similar provisions exist in s35A CA 1985.

Ultra vires and voidable contracts The doctrine of ultra vires may also play a part in relation to contracts between the company and a director of the company that are beyond the company's or the board's powers. Section 322A CA 1985 provides that where a third party to a transaction with a company is a director of that company, or its holding company, or is connected to the director, and the transaction is beyond the powers of the company or of the board of directors under the company's constitution, the contract becomes voidable at the instance of the company. The section further provides that the third party or the directors who authorised the transaction are liable to indemnify the company for any loss or damage resulting from the transaction and to account to the company for any gain made from the transaction. To this extent the doctrine of ultra vires may be relevant, as whether a particular transaction is caught by s322A CA 1985 may require an assessment of the objects clause to see whether the act is within or outside the company's powers. However, as with ss35(2) and (3), the length and breadth of a company's objects clause may suggest that very few transactions are likely to be considered ultra vires for these purposes.

The capital clause

The memorandum of association of a company limited by shares must state the amount of the company's **share capital** and its division into shares of fixed amounts. Shares must have a fixed value that will be as the promoters or directors decide. As we shall see in Chapter 15, this fixed value is called the par or nominal value. In the capital clause, the amount of capital stated is the nominal or authorised capital. Once a share is allotted, the shareholder will be able to sell it at its market value.

Optional clauses in the memorandum

In addition to those clauses that must be contained in the memorandum, other clauses may be included, the most common being special rights for different classes of shareholder. The non-compulsory clauses can be altered in accordance with s17 CA 1985, which provides for alteration by the passing of a special resolution. Dissentient members can object in the same way as they can in respect of an alteration to the objects clause. Section 17 CA 1985 does not apply where the memorandum provides for or prohibits an alteration, neither does it apply to **class rights**, which are rights that a particular type of shareholder enjoys. Further, s17 CA 1985 is subject to s16 CA 1985, which is discussed later in relation to the articles of association.

Articles of association

Nature of the articles

The articles of association of a company concern its internal management and regulate the rights of its members. They deal with such matters as the transfer of shares, declaration of dividends, the holding of meetings and the appointment, removal and powers of the directors. Specimen articles of association are provided by the Companies (Tables A to F) Regulations 1985, with Table A the most common as that is the one that is designed for a public or private company limited by shares.

Section 8(1) CA 1985 gives a general permission for a company to adopt the whole or any part of Table A and s8(2) CA 1985 states that, where a company is registered without articles, Table A will apply. The section also provides that, where articles are registered, Table A will apply unless it is excluded or modified. Exclusion can be by express word to that effect in the articles, while modification can be expressed or implied. Express modification would occur where the articles state that Table A will apply with certain alterations and implied modification where the articles are inconsistent with Table A.

Legal effect of the memorandum and the articles

A number of disputes have arisen between members and companies in respect of the terms of the articles of association. Such disputes have been based on either the legal effect of the company's constitution or where the articles have been altered.

Section 14 CA 1985 provides that the memorandum and articles, when registered, binds the company and its members, so that each member is bound to observe the provisions of the memorandum and the articles. Section 14 CA 1985, therefore, gives contractual status to the company's constitution. This 'special contract' or 's14 contract', as it is sometimes referred to, has been interpreted by the courts in the following way:

- The memorandum and the articles constitute a contract between the company and each member.
- The articles constitute a contract between individual members.
- The articles constitute a contract where they affect the member in the capacity of member and not in some other capacity. This means that so-called 'outsider rights' cannot generally be enforced by the articles.

These three interpretations are flushed out, respectively, in the following case studies.

Hickman v Kent or Romney Marsh Sheepbreeders Association (1915)

The articles of the company provided for disputes between the company and members to be referred to arbitration. Action was brought by a member on the basis that the company had refused to register certain of his sheep for breeding purposes for which he claimed damages. It was held that the company was entitled to have the court proceedings stayed. The articles amounted to a binding contract between the company and the member to refer disputes to arbitration.

Rayfield v Hands (1958)

The articles of a private company provided that 'every member who intends to transfer his shares shall inform the directors who *will* take the said shares equally between them at a fair value'. The claimant held 725 fully paid shares of £1 each and he asked the three directors of the company, who each held one share, to buy them, but they refused. It was held that the directors were bound to take the shares. The relevant article constituted a binding contract between the directors, as members, and the claimant, as member, in respect of his rights as a member.

Eley v Positive Security Life Assurance Co Ltd (1876)

The articles of a company contained a clause appointing E, a shareholder, as solicitor of the company. The company ceased to employ him as solicitor and E brought an action for breach of contract. The Court of Appeal held that E's action failed because there was no contract between the company and E under the articles. He was an 'outsider', acting in his capacity as a solicitor. Although he was a member, he could not enforce the articles since the articles gave him rights in his capacity as solicitor, not as shareholder.

By contrast to the *Eley* case, in **Pender v Lushington (1877)**, the court held that a member was entitled to enforce an article giving him a personal right to vote at general meetings. The company was compelled to record his vote, as his right to vote affected him in his capacity as member.

FAQ

Are there any circumstances where outsider rights can be enforced?

Despite the rule against the enforcement of outsider rights, it does appear that outsider rights may be enforceable in some circumstances, for instance, where a director's contract of employment is inferred from the conduct of the parties, the terms of service being based on the articles. In *Re New British Iron Co ex parte Beckwith (1898)*, B was employed as a director of the company without an express service contract, relying for his remuneration on the company's articles, which provided for directors pay at £1000 per annum. On the company going into liquidation, B claimed for arrears. It was held that, although the articles did not constitute a contract between the company and B in his capacity as director, he was entitled to the fees as he had accepted office and worked on the basis of the articles. There was an implied contract between the parties, with the articles representing the terms of that contract.

Alternatively, although a company cannot be prevented from altering its articles, where there is an express contract, the company can be held liable in damages where an alteration of the articles results in the breach of that contract. In *Southern Foundries (1926) Ltd v Shirlaw (1940),* the House of Lords held that the claimant's contract as managing director contained an implied term that the article making him director would not be altered. Since it *had* been altered, there was a breach of contract and the company was liable. The claimant was awarded £12,000 in damages for wrongful dismissal.

Alteration of articles of association

A company has the power to alter its articles of association. This is provided for by s9 CA 1985, which provides that subject to the provisions of the CA 1985 and to the conditions contained in its memorandum, a company may by special resolution alter its articles of association.

The power to alter the articles may not be taken away or limited in any way, neither will any attempt to require the articles to be altered in any way other than by a special resolution be valid, although informal consent or an agreement of all the members can make an alteration effective. The alteration becomes effective from the time that the special resolution is passed, except where it is conditional on the happening of some event and an alteration of the articles cannot have retrospective effect.

Section 380 CA 1985 requires a copy of the special resolution to be forwarded to the registrar within 15 days after the resolution has been passed and, where articles have been registered, for a copy of the resolution.

Although a company may alter its articles, there are a number of restrictions imposed on a company's power of alteration. The most common ground is that any alteration must be in good faith for the benefit of the company as a whole. This represents one of the few occasions where restraint is placed on how shareholders vote. Whether the alteration is for the benefit of the company as a whole is a matter for the members to decide and the court will intervene only if no reasonable person could consider it so. Where an alteration is in good faith for the benefit of the company as a whole, it is immaterial that it prejudices the minority, although there must be no unfair discrimination between the majority and minority shareholders. The *Dafen Tinplate* and *Sidebottom* case studies contain examples of where an alteration was held invalid and valid, respectively.

Dafen Tinplate Co Ltd v Llanelly Steel Co (1907) Ltd (1920)

The defendant company was in the business of selling steel and supplying steel to member companies, although there was no contract to that effect. In 1912 the claimant company, who was a member of the defendant company, decided to purchase its steel from another company in which it had an interest. In response, the defendant company proposed to alter its articles with the effect of expelling the claimant company as a member, the alteration providing that the defendant company could by ordinary resolution require any member to sell his shares to other members, at a fair price fixed by the directors. The claimant company sought a declaration that the alteration was invalid.

The court held that, in the circumstances of the case, the alteration could not be allowed. The power inserted into the articles was a *bare power of expulsion* and could be used to expel any member, including a member who was not acting to the detriment of the company.

Sidebottom v Kershaw, Leese & Co (1920)

The defendant company altered its articles to empower the directors to require any member who carried on a business competing with that of the company, to sell his shares at a fair price to persons nominated by the directors. The claimant company was a member of the defendant company and ran steel mills in competition with it. The claimant brought an action challenging the validity of the alteration of the articles. The Court of Appeal held that the alteration was valid as the evidence showed that the claimant might cause the defendant company loss by information that he received as a member and the power was restricted to expulsion for competing. The alteration was for the benefit of the company as a whole.

Where the alteration involves class rights, additional measures will apply, affording protection to dissenting shareholders. Although a company might only issue one class of shares, giving the holders the same rights, it is common practice for companies to issue shares with different rights. Preference shares, for example, may have priority rights over ordinary shares with respect to dividends or the repayment of capital, and shares can carry different voting rights. It is usual for class rights to attach to particular shares and for these rights to be provided for in the articles of association. The procedure for altering class rights is set out in ss125–127 CA 1985 and the procedure depends on where the rights are set out (e.g. in the memorandum or the articles) and whether there is a procedure for altering the rights.

Answers to in-text questions

> **QUESTION 1** Why would a promoter run the risk of incurring personal liability by entering into a contract on behalf of a company before it became incorporated?

Apart from promoters being unaware of the consequences of a pre-incorporation contract, it is for commercial reasons that a promoter may choose not to wait for a company to come into existence. The opportunity to secure a deal before incorporation may outweigh the potential pitfall of incurring personal liability in the event of non-performance or wrongful performance of the contract.

> **QUESTION 2** Where might you be able to obtain a copy of a company's memorandum and articles of association?

Companies House, as s10 CA 1985 requires a company's memorandum and articles of association to be submitted to the registrar of companies. The memorandum and articles of association are public documents and, on payment of a search fee, are open to inspection.

By the end of this chapter, you should be able to explain:

- **What is meant by a company's capital and the need for a company to maintain its capital**
- **The difference between share capital and loan capital**
- **The priorities of creditors in the event of a winding up of a company**

Introduction

As with any other business, a company requires capital in order to finance its trading activities. Capital comprises **share capital**, i.e. money raised from investors, and loan capital, i.e. money raised from lenders such as banks and other financial institutions.

Capital is the fund that creditors of the company ultimately look to for payment of their debts and it is a fundamental principle of company law that a company maintains its capital for the protection of creditors, both existing and future. The significance of the capital rules for a business is that many creditors are businesses and, as with other creditors, it is in their interests that a company maintains its capital.

Loan capital is represented principally in the form of **debentures** issued by a company in respect of loans from banks and other lending institutions. Debentures are likely to be secured by a charge over a company's assets and, as such, represent a valuable form of security for a creditor, particularly where the company becomes insolvent and there is a need for competing creditor claims to be resolved.

Share capital

A **share** represents the interest of a shareholder in a company measured by a sum of money. A share is 'a unit of measurement of a person's interest in and their liability to the company' (***Borland's Trustee v Steel***

Brothers & Co Ltd (1901)). There are various meanings of share capital and some of the most common are as follows:

- *Nominal share capital* represents the unit value of the shares that a company is allowed to issue. It is also called the authorised share capital and is specified in the capital clause in the **memorandum of association**. The nominal value of the share normally fixes the amount that the shareholder is required to contribute to the assets of the company. Shareholders must pay at least the full nominal value of any shares issued to them, as shares must not be issued at a discount (s100 CA 1985).

- *Allotted share capital* refers to shares that have been issued or allotted to shareholders. A company is not obliged to allot all its authorised share capital. You may recall from Chapter 13 that public companies must have a minimum issued capital of £50,000 of which one-quarter is allotted and paid up (s11 CA 1985).

- *Called-up capital* represents that amount of the issued shares that have been paid for by the shareholders. Where a company, for example, issues a share for £1 and charges £1 for the share, that share has been issued 'at par' or at its nominal value. The company may then **call** on the shareholder to pay some or all of the £1 owed for the share. Where the shareholder pays the amount called it is known as paid-up share capital and shares may be fully paid up, as is frequently the case, or partly paid up. Any amount of the purchase price of the share that is not required by the company is uncalled capital.

- Where a company is able to sell its shares for more than the par or nominal value this is known as a *premium*. If, for example, the shares had a nominal value of £1 and were sold for £1.50, the amount over and above the nominal value would be known as a 'premium'. Where the company issues shares at a premium, the holders of those shares will be liable to pay the amount owed over and above the nominal value. The excess must be kept in a separate, capitalised account, known as a 'share premium account' (s130 CA 1985).

Shares

A share represents a package of rights and forms property in itself known as a *chose* or *thing in action*. These are intangible rights that entitle the shareholder to certain benefits. A shareholder usually has three main rights:

- the right to vote at general meetings
- the right to receive **dividends**
- the right to a return of capital when the company is wound up, or when the capital is reduced by returning assets to the members or cancelling their liability.

Section 370 CA 1985 provides that, in the absence of a provision to the contrary in the articles, voting at general meetings is on the basis of one vote for each share or £10 of stock held.

There is a presumption that, as between shareholders, there is equality, so that where a company issues shares to its members, they acquire equal rights and are subject to the same liabilities. The presumption, however, can be displaced by an express provision to the contrary, giving different rights to different classes of shares.

Types of share

The creation of different classes of share can be achieved by the memorandum, the **articles of association** or some other means, such as an ordinary resolution increasing the company's capital under s121 CA 1985. Some of the more common classes of shares are ordinary shares and preference shares.

Ordinary shares

Ordinary shares constitute the usual type of share in a company and generally form the greatest proportion of the capital. Ordinary shares entitle the holders to the greater portion of the net profit of the company, after payment of any fixed dividend on any preference shares. Where the preference shareholders have priority as to a return of capital on liquidation, the ordinary shares will be entitled normally to all the surplus assets. Ordinary shares usually give the holder a right to attend and vote at general meetings, but some companies issue ordinary shares with no voting rights, usually designated 'A' shares.

Preference shares

These are shares the issue of which is authorised by the memorandum or articles. They carry a right to a preferred final dividend. This means that the dividend payable is fixed and is payable before the ordinary shareholders receive a dividend. There is a presumption that preference shares are cumulative. This means that, where in any year, the company does not declare a dividend it must carry the arrears forward (or accumulate them) from year to year until they are paid and that is before the ordinary shareholders receive any dividend. Where the preference shares are non-cumulative, and the company does not declare a dividend on the preference shares in any particular year, the investors will not receive any dividend for that year.

Preference shares often carry different voting rights from ordinary shares and sometimes they carry no votes at all.

Issuing shares

Directors are generally not allowed to issue shares without the authority of the members of the company or in accordance with the articles. In practice, it is usual for the directors to be granted general authority to issue shares in the company, as long as that authority does not extend beyond a period of 5 years (s80 CA 1985), although private companies may waive the 5-year period on the passing of an elective resolution (s80A CA 1985).

 FAQ

What is meant by a bonus issue and a rights issue?

These are terms that often appear in the pages of the business press. Where a company is able to capitalise some part of its profits, as part of an accounting exercise, it may choose a **bonus issue** of shares. These are shares given by a company to a member usually in proportion to the member's existing holding and for which no fresh consideration is required. The value of shareholder's shares remains the same, the shareholders simply obtain more shares than before. A **rights issue**, by way of contrast, is a right given to an existing shareholder to subscribe for further shares, usually, at a discount. The exercise of a **pre-emption right** therefore enables a shareholder to retain their shareholding in the company without its being diluted by the company offering shares to the public.

Dividends

A dividend may be defined as a proportion, either fixed or variable, of the company's assets legally available for dividend and divided among the members in proportion to their shareholding. In the absence of anything to the contrary in the articles, shareholders cannot insist on a dividend being paid. It is the directors who recommend the amount of dividend and, as dividends are essentially paid out of profits, where no profits are made, or none is distributable, no dividend will be declared. Article 102, Table A provides that the company in general meeting may not declare a dividend higher than that recommended by the directors.

Membership of a company

As it is members of a company who agree to contribute towards the capital of the company, in order to become a member of a company, two conditions must be satisfied (s22 CA 1985):

- the person has agreed to become a member
- the person has his or her name recorded on the register of members.

Agreeing to membership There are six ways of agreeing to membership of a company through the acquisition of shares:

1 subscribing to the memorandum of association
2 an allotment of shares
3 a transfer of shares
4 holding a share warrant
5 estoppel
6 transmission.

The first four ways require the express consent of the individual. The other two ways occur by operation of law. Estoppel arises as a result of conduct on the part of the member. Transmission occurs on the death or bankruptcy of a member, enabling the trustee in bankruptcy or personal representatives to become members. The Company Law Reform Bill 2005 proposes to make it easier for trustees in bankruptcy and personal representatives to become members.

> **QUESTION 1** Do you know anyone, perhaps a friend or a member of your family, who is a shareholder of a company? Do you know how they acquired their shares?

Register of members Section 352 CA 1985 obliges every company to keep a register of members, which must contain the following information:

- names and addresses of the members
- date on which each person was registered as a member
- date on which any person ceased to be a member.

Section 356 CA 1985 provides that the register shall be open for inspection during business hours (subject to such reasonable restrictions as the company in general meeting may impose, but so that no less than 2 hours each day is available) by members for free and by any other person for a small fee.

Termination of membership This occurs where the name of a former member is removed from the register. The most common circumstances where this occurs is on a transfer of shares, death or insolvency of a shareholder and following a winding up and dissolution of a company.

Maintenance of capital

It is a principle of company law that the share capital of a company must be maintained so that creditors have a right to see that a company's capital is not dissipated unlawfully. As such, there are a number of rules ensuring that companies maintain their share capital so that they have assets from which to pay creditors should the need arise. The rules may seem complicated, but the important thing to remember is that the rules are designed to provide a measure of creditor protection, whether those creditors are customers, employees, or as is more likely the case, other businesses. The rules vary as between public and private companies. Greater safeguards exist for public companies and it is proposed in the Company Law Reform Bill 2005 to lessen the burden for private companies by providing for the abolition of some of the rules relating to private companies.

Company purchasing its own shares

It is illegal for a company to acquire its own shares, except as provided for by the CA 1985 (s143(1) CA 1985). Where a company purports to act in contravention of s143(1) CA 1985, the company is liable to a fine and every officer of the company, who is in default, is liable to imprisonment or a fine, or both, and the purported acquisition is void (s143(2) CA). This provision re-enforces the rule in **Trevor v Whitworth (1888)** (see case study), for a company cannot be a shareholder of itself.

The general prohibition is, however, subject to certain qualifications and it may be necessary, subject to strict safeguards, particularly for public companies, to enable a company to purchase or redeem its shares in some circumstances.

Financial assistance

Section 151 CA 1985 makes it illegal for a company or any of its subsidiaries to provide **financial assistance** to any person to enable them to buy shares in the company. The section applies to both direct and indirect assistance and does not depend on whether the assistance was given before or after the share purchase. Financial assistance is defined widely by s152 CA 1985 and includes gifts, loans and any other transactions that allow the purchaser of the shares to use the company's assets to pay for the shares.

Trevor v Whitworth (1888)

The articles of association of a company allowed the company to purchase its own shares where requested to do so by a member. One member exercised this option, but the company went into liquidation before it had fully paid for the shares. The shareholder took an action against the liquidators to recover the amount outstanding. The House of Lords held that the action failed.

Section 153 CA 1985, however, provides for exceptions to the application of s151 CA 1985. Lending in the ordinary course of business, for instance, is not prohibited, neither is assistance provided for employees' share schemes. The most significant exception, however, is that provided under s153(1) 1985, which allows the company to finance share purchases as long as it is done in good faith and in the pursuit of some larger purpose. Exceptions to the general rule are also to be found in relation to private companies (ss155–158 CA 1985). Private companies are allowed to provide financial assistance, as long as it does not come out of the company's capital but from profits available for distribution.

The criminal penalties for a breach of s151 CA 1985 are a fine for the company and a fine and/or imprisonment for every officer who is in default, usually the directors and company secretary of the company. The effect on the transaction is that it becomes unenforceable (**Heald v O'Connor (1971)**) and the directors responsible can be held liable for breach of duty. In addition, any third party, who received corporate property in circumstances where they are held accountable, can be held liable as a constructive trustee (**Selangor United Rubber Estates Ltd v Cradock (1968)**). A constructive trustee is someone who has come across misapplied funds in circumstances where it is unjust or inequitable for that person to keep those funds.

An example of unlawful financial assistance arose in **Brady v Brady (1989)**, a case involving a number of family-run, private companies featured in the 'Reality check' textbox.

Dividends

Under s263 (1) CA 1985, a company may not make a distribution except out of profits available for the purpose. Section 263 (1) CA 1985 applies to all companies, public and private, although private companies will be able to pay dividends out of capital on the passing of the Company Law Reform Bill 2005.

With some minor exceptions, distribution is defined as 'every description of distribution of a company's assets to members of the company, whether in cash or otherwise'.

Directors who knowingly pay dividends out of capital are liable to the company to replace any money so paid out (**Re Exchange Banking Co, Flitcroft's Case (1882); Bairstow v Queen Moat Houses plc (2001)**). Section 277 CA 1985 provides that shareholders who receive payments, with reasonable grounds to know that they are made in breach of the rules, shall be liable to repay the amount received to the company. In *Bairstow v Queen Moat Houses plc (2001)*, the directors were held liable to account for £27 million in respect of unlawful dividends paid to shareholders.

Unauthorised return of capital

A company is not permitted to make an unauthorised return of capital to its members. In **Re Halt Garage Ltd (1982)**, the court held that the payment of remuneration to a director/shareholder of a small, private company who was unable to continue as director owing to illness, was not genuine and amounted to a disguised return of capital to that person in their capacity as shareholder.

Reality check

Use of financial assistance to resolve a dispute within a family-controlled group of companies – Brady v Brady (1989)

Two brothers, who were caught up in a bitter family dispute, ran a group of companies. After some time they decided that the family rift would never heal and that their business interests should be divided in two. This involved a complicated scheme of reconstruction, whereby assets of one company were transferred to another. It was admitted that this would involve a discharge of liability incurred by the purchase of shares in one of the other companies in the group and, as such, this appeared to be an infringement of s151 CA 1985. It was argued, however, before the court that the principal purpose of this transaction was to resolve the deadlock and bitterness between the brothers and therefore there was no breach of s151.

The House of Lords held that the transaction was on the face of it illegal, since, although the intention was to resolve a conflict between family members, this provided simply a reason for the purpose of giving financial assistance to purchase shares in the company.

The brothers were, however, allowed to complete the transaction, since, as private companies, they fell within the exception provided by s155 CA 1985.

Cases such as *Brady v Brady (1989)* demonstrate how costly for private companies restructuring schemes can be, given the need for considerable professional and legal advice. In fact, it is perhaps surprising that the legal advice given in this case did not reveal that the scheme was allowable under s155 CA 1985.

It is partly for these reasons, that, on the passing of the Company Law Reform Bill 2005, the prohibition against private companies providing financial assistance will be abolished. This will mean that the exceptions to s151 CA 1985 for private companies will also become redundant. Private companies like those in *Brady v Brady (1989)* will no longer be prevented from giving financial assistance as a means of genuinely solving a conflict, and substantial costs incurred as a result will be avoided. For reasons of market confidence and investor protection, the rules will remain in place for public companies.

Reduction of capital

A company may by the passing of a special resolution reduce its capital if authorised by the articles, subject to court approval (**authorised capital**). The provisions are found in ss135–137 CA 1985 and include provisions intended to safeguard the interests of creditors and minority shareholders. The procedures under which companies may reduce the amount of their issued share capital are set out in s135 CA 1985. Section 135 states that a company may reduce its capital in any way, where so authorised in its articles, by the passing of a special resolution. Any proposal to reduce a company's capital is subject to confirmation by the court (s136 CA 1985) on such terms as it thinks fit (s137 CA 1985). In considering any capital reduction scheme, the court will take into account the interests of the members and creditors of the company and the general public.

Loan capital

Companies usually acquire the capital they need to engage in their particular business through the issue of shares. It is, however, common practice for companies to borrow money to finance their activities, in particular from banks and other lending institutions. The memorandum of association of companies is likely to contain an express power allowing the company to borrow money, but where the memorandum is silent on the matter, a power to borrow money will be implied as being incidental to the conduct of the business of any trading company. The articles of association may limit the borrowing powers of the directors, to whom the general power to borrow is delegated, but as a consequence of s35A CA 1985, an outsider acting in good faith is not affected by a limitation on the board's powers or those authorised by the board. Section 35A CA 1985 was examined, along with s35 CA 1985, in Chapter 14, in relation to a company's capacity to enter into transactions with others.

Ian Hodgson/Reuters/Corbis

Malcolm Glazier's takeover of Manchester United was funded by substantial loans

Debentures and charges

A debenture is a document that creates or acknowledges a debt due from a company, such as a loan from a bank. It is usually but not always given with a charge over the company's assets by way of security. A debenture is defined by s744 CA 1985 as including debenture stock, bonds and other securities of a company (but not shares) whether constituting a charge on the assets of the company or not.

A debenture does not refer to any security that may have been given in relation to the loan, but in practice the use of the term 'debenture' is extended to cover the loan itself and usually designates a secured loan, as opposed to an unse-

FAQ

What are the differences between a debenture and a share?

Although issuing shares and debentures represents ways of raising capital, there are some important distinctions to be made between the two and these are as follows:

Debentures	Shares
Debenture holders are creditors of the company	Shareholders are members of the company
As creditors, debenture holders receive interest on their loans	Shareholders receive dividends
Debenture holders are entitled to receive interest whether the company is profitable or not and payment can be made out of capital	Dividends must not be paid out of capital
Debentures may be issued at a discount, that is, at less than their nominal value	Shares cannot be issued at a discount and the company must receive the equivalent to the nominal value of the shares

cured one. Similarly, the words 'debenture holder' and 'charge holder' are used interchangeably when referring to a secured creditor.

Where the lender is given security, the security does not give the lender any interest in the company but represents a claim against the company and the relationship between the company and the lender is one of debtor and creditor.

There are two types of charge (fixed and floating) that can be granted over a company's assets as a means of providing security.

Fixed charge

A fixed charge is a mortgage of ascertained and definite property, such as land and buildings, and prevents a company from realising the property without the consent of the charge holder. A fixed charge may be legal or equitable. Where, for example, a company charges land and premises to a bank by means of a mortgage, the bank has a fixed legal charge over that property. The bank will obtain the title deeds to the property, which effectively precludes the company from dealing with the property without the knowledge and consent of the bank. A fixed equitable charge is less formal and can be achieved by the deposit of title deeds. A fixed charge holder does not claim against the general assets of the company on winding up, he claims against the asset that is represented by the charge. Where the same asset has been used as security for a further loan, a question of priority will arise. As a fixed charge prevents the company from dealing with the charged asset without the consent of the charge holder, it is an inappropriate form of security for assets that are changing constantly such as stock in trade. Otherwise, a company would be unable to deal freely with the goods without the prior approval of the charge holders, which would prevent the company from carrying out its business activities.

Floating charge

There is no statutory definition of a floating charge and what the parties call a particular charge is not conclusive evidence of its status, but the courts have identified certain factors that are likely to be present if a charge is to be classified as a floating charge. In *Illingworth v Houldsworth (1904)*, a floating charge was described as a charge over a class of assets, both present and future, which, in the ordinary course of business, changes from time to time and which leaves the company free to deal with the charged asset in the ordinary course of its business. Assets, therefore, that are typically the subject matter of a floating charge are stock in trade and goods in production, although in *Re Panama, New Zealand and Australian Royal Mail Co (1870)*, it was held that a company could grant a floating charge over the company's entire undertaking. The advantage to a company of a floating charge is to enable the company to deal with its property without the need to seek the approval of the charge holders.

A floating charge does not attach to any specific property of the company until it crystallises through the act or default of the company in relation to the loan. This is the moment when all the assets subject to the charge become fixed, the company cannot deal with those assets and the debenture holder can extract the necessary assets, through the appointment of a receiver to enforce the loan. The most common forms of **crystallisation** are the winding up of the company or the appointment of a receiver by the charge holder. These are examples of a company becoming insolvent, something we shall be returning to in Chapter 19,

Reality check

The use of a company's book debts as a form of security – fixed charge or floating charge?

National Westminster Bank plc v Spectrum Plus Ltd (2005)

A *book debt* may be the subject matter of either a fixed charge or a floating charge. A book debt is money owed to a company from its customers and can represent a valuable asset to be used as security by a company. Whether a book debt is the subject matter of a fixed or floating charge depends on whether there are any restrictions on how the company can deal with the debts as the debts become extinguished. The normal position as stated in *Re Brightlife Ltd (1987)* is that book debts are the subject mater of a floating charge as the value of a company's book debts are likely to be constantly changing and the company is able to use moneys collected from extinguished book debts in the ordinary course of business. Where, however, for example, a company must place money collected from extinguished book debt in a separate bank account and may not use that money in the ordinary course of business without obtaining the consent of the charge holder, the charge created over the book debts is a fixed charge.

This is what National Westminster Bank was attempting to rely on in *National Westminster Bank plc v Spectrum Plus Ltd (2005)*, where the House of Lords restated the general position that in the absence of any restrictions, charges on book debts are regarded as floating charges. The House of Lords also confirmed the view of the Privy Council in *Agnew v Commissioner of Inland Revenue (2001)* that a charge that states that it is a fixed charge over uncollected book debts and a floating charge over collected book debts is a floating charge, not a partly fixed charge and a partly floating charge. The facts of the *Spectrum Plus* case were that a debenture, which was expressed as a fixed charge, required the proceeds of a company's book debts to be paid into the company's bank account and that the company was not at liberty to factor or sell its book debts. The charge, however, placed no restriction on the use that could be made of the balance on the account as moneys collected were paid in. The House of Lords held the charge was a floating charge. The fact that the charge was expressed as a fixed charge did not prevent the company drawing on the account.

where we shall be examining more closely the nature of different forms of corporate insolvency such as receivership and liquidation.

Reservation of title clauses

A reservation of title, or retention of ownership, clause is a device used by sellers of goods in contracts of sale, where the seller reserves title (or ownership) in the goods until he has received payment from the buyer in full. Where the company becomes insolvent without having paid for the goods supplied, the trade creditor will rank as an unsecured creditor, the goods supplied forming part of the general assets of the company to be used for meeting the claims of secured creditors holding a floating charge or creditors possessing a preferential debt. However, the trade creditor will be able to recover the goods, at the expense of other creditors, if he can rely on a reservation of title clause.

Not all these clauses (sometimes referred to as *Romalpa* clauses, after the name of the case cited in the following case study) are effective. The success or otherwise of the operation of the clause depends on the wording of the clause and what has happened to the goods. Further, some clauses have been attacked by the courts on the grounds that they amount to a floating charge and therefore void if not registered under the CA 1985.

Aluminium Industries Vaassen BV v Romalpa Aluminium Ltd (1976)

A Dutch company supplied aluminium foil to the defendant company. It was a term of the contract that ownership of the foil was not to transfer until the price had been paid in full. The company went into liquidation before the foil had been paid for in full. The insolvent company's assets included unmixed foil on the company's premises. The court held that the Dutch company could reclaim the unmixed foil ahead of the company's secured and unsecured creditors. The property in the foil had not passed to the company.

Similar clauses in other cases, however, have not been successfully relied on. In **Borden (UK) Ltd v Scottish Timber Products Ltd (1981)**, the reservation of title clause was held ineffective as the goods supplied, resin, had been lost and destroyed in the course of manufacture, the resin having been used in the manufacture of chipboard. A similar result was reached in **Re Peachdart Ltd (1984)**, where leather had been supplied and used in the manufacture of handbags. In **Hendy Lennox (Industrial Engines) Ltd v Grahame Puttick Ltd (1984)**, however, the trade creditor was able to recover his goods as the engines supplied and bolted to the company's generators retained their identity and could be removed intact.

A reservation of title clause is unlikely to protect a trade creditor where the supplied goods were sold and the trade creditor is claiming the proceeds of sale of those goods. Another part of the trade creditor's claim in the *Romalpa* case related to proceeds of sale of unmixed aluminium foil. This was held to be successful owing to another part of the term of the contract that compelled the company to retain any proceeds of sale of the original goods supplied on the creditor's behalf. Subsequent authority, however, have applied such clauses more restrictively or held that a term of the contract relating to proceeds of sale will constitute a charge over the insolvent company's property and, as set out later, charges granted by a company over its property must be registered under the CA 1985. In **Re Andrabell Ltd (1984)**, a trade creditor attempted to claim the proceeds of sale of travel bags that he had supplied. His claim failed as the relevant term in his contract amounted to a charge that was void for non-registration.

An interesting use of a *Romalpa* clause is to be found in **Armour v Thyssen AG (1990)**. In that case, the creditor was able to rely on an 'all moneys' clause, which can be described as a variation on a standard reservation of title clause. The clause provided that ownership did not pass in the goods supplied to the buyer until all moneys outstanding from other contracts between the parties had been paid. Although the immediate goods had been paid for, the House of Lords ruled that ownership had not passed in the goods as there were outstanding moneys in relation to other contracts between the buyer and the seller.

Registration of charges

Section 399 CA 1985 provides that the registration of prescribed particulars of charges must be made with the registrar of companies. Registrable charges, as defined by s396 CA 1985, include charges on land (e.g. a mortgage), any floating charge and any charge on a company's book debts or intellectual property.

Where a charge is not registered within 21 days of its creation, it becomes void (s399 CA 1985) as against a liquidator or creditor of the company, although the obligation to pay remains valid as an unsecured debt and that the money provided becomes immediately payable (s407 CA 1985). Under s404 CA 1985, the court has the power to permit late registration. In allowing late registration, the court can impose such terms and conditions as it considers 'just and expedient'. Parties who lent money to the company and received security for their loans will be protected and will not be affected by creditors obtaining rights following any late registration.

In addition to registration at Companies House, companies are required to maintain a register of all charges on their property (s401 CA 1985). Such a register has to be made available for inspection by members and creditors of the company.

The registration of company charges (and security interests generally) has been subject to review, although, to date, none of the changes proposed in respect of company charges has been implemented. The report of the Company Law Review Steering Group (2001) and the Law Commission (2002), for instance, favoured a notice system similar to that found in the USA, where there is no particular time for registration of a charge before it ceases to be valid. Any priority, as such, would date from filing notice, not from creation. The changes to the system of registration of charges contained in the CA 1989, but which were not implemented, are proposed to be abolished by the Company Law Reform Bill 2005.

Priority of creditors

Where a company goes into liquidation, the liquidator will need to rank the creditors in accordance with the priority of their claims and, where a company's liabilities are greater than its assets, it becomes important to ascertain which of the creditors will be satisfied and which will remain unsatisfied, in full or in part. The priority of creditors depends on a number of rules and these are set out as follows:

- A fixed charge ranks over any floating charge including any earlier floating charge. This is because it is the nature of a floating charge that a company retains the freedom to grant further security over its assets in the ordinary course of business and this includes the company having the right to grant fixed charges (*Wheatley v Silkstone and Haigh Moor Coal Co (1885)*). As such, fixed charge holders, whether the fixed charge is created before or after a floating charge, take priority over the holder of the floating charge.

- Where there is more than one floating charge, such holders rank in accordance with creation and it is immaterial if the second floating charge holder is given priority by the instrument creating the charge (*Re Benjamin Cope & Sons Ltd (1914)*). Fixed charges also rank on creation.

- Where the earlier charge prohibits the company from granting priority to any later charges, a subsequent fixed charge holder will take priority over the earlier floating charge, unless the subsequent fixed charge holder has notice of the prohibition (*Re Castell & Brown Ltd (1898)*; *English & Scottish Mercantile Investment Co v Brunton (1892)*). These clauses are known as negative pledge clauses. Mere registration of such a clause (as opposed to the charge) at Companies House as part of the particulars of registration does not constitute effective notice.

- A registered floating charge ranks ahead of any unregistered charge and it is immaterial that the holder of the later charge has notice of the unregistered security (*Re Monolithic Building Co (1915)*).

- **Preferential debts**: s175 Insolvency Act (IA) 1986 gives preferential status to certain unsecured creditors with such creditors ranking in priority to all creditors except fixed charge holders. Creditors with preferential debts include HM Revenue of Customs and company employees for unpaid wages up to £800, including any outstanding and accrued holiday entitlement. Preferential creditors rank equally among themselves. In respect of any insolvency after 15 September 2003, the Crown loses its preference by virtue of a change to the Insolvency Act 1986 brought about by the Enterprise Act (EA) 2002. The EA 2002 provides a reform of corporate insolvency law in order to facilitate a 'rescue culture' for failing companies. The changes introduced by the EA 2002 are examined further in Chapter 19.

- *Unsecured creditors* come after the claims of the secured creditors and the preferential creditors have been met. However, in respect of new insolvencies from 15 September 2003, under s176A IA 1986 (as inserted by the EA 2002), the secretary of state may, by order, prescribe a part of the property that would otherwise be payable to floating charge holders to be reserved for unsecured creditors. Where a company's net assets are more than £10,000, the amount a liquidator must set aside for the unsecured creditors ahead of the floating charge holders is 50% of the first £50,000 and 20% of any assets above that value up to a maximum of £600,000. Where the value of the company's net assets is below £10,000, the liquidator does not have to make such a distribution if he considers that the costs of making such a distribution would be disproportionate to the benefits.

- *Deferred creditors*, i.e. shareholders with unpaid dividend claims, are paid after the claims of the secured and unsecured creditors have been met.

In the event of a surplus, the members are entitled to a return of their capital in accordance with the provisions of the articles of association. Thereafter, any surplus is distributed to the members in accordance with the rights stated in the articles or other documents.

The costs and expenses of a liquidation and the liquidator are paid after the payment of any fixed charge holder and out of the floating charge assets in the hands of an administrative receiver (s175 Insolvency Act 1986). An exhaustive list of recoverable expenses is to be found in the Insolvency Rules 1986.

Finally, we need to note the position of a trade creditor who is able to rely on a reservation of title clause. Such a creditor will be able to recover his goods without their becoming part of the general assets of the company to meet the claims of other creditors.

Reality check

How the relationship between charge holders and preferential creditors works in practice – National Westminster Bank plc v Spectrum Plus Ltd (2005) revisited

In this case, the company had gone into liquidation owing £165,407 to National Westminster Bank. The company's liquidator had collected £113,000 in respect of book debts, i.e. money owing to the company. The company's unsecured creditors included preferential creditors who were claiming £16,000. As the House of Lords held that the charge over book debts was only a floating charge, the preferential creditors were entitled to be paid out of the proceeds in priority to the bank under s175 IA 1986. The bank, you will recall, submitted that the debenture created a fixed charge on book debts.

As the bank lost its claim that the charge was a fixed charge, the preferential creditors ranked ahead of the bank. The bank's charge was a floating charge. This meant that of the £113,000 collected by the liquidator, £16,000 had to be set aside for the preference creditors. The bank was entitled to £97,000, not £113,000, as it ranked below the preferential creditors. Had the bank succeeded in its claim that its charge was a fixed charge, it would have been entitled to £113,000 as preferential creditors do not rank ahead of fixed charge holders.

FAQ

Although a form of security, are there any disadvantages associated with a creditor holding a floating charge?

Where a company decides to borrow money in order to expand its business, any creditor is likely to require security. Companies have two forms of security they can deploy: fixed charges, that is, a charge over a specified asset or property; or floating charges, that is, a charge over a class of asset that is likely to be changing, such as stock in trade. Both types of charge are subject to registration and, if not registered, are void (s395(1) CA 1985), although the underlying debt remains valid and becomes immediately repayable (s395(2) CA). Both types of charge may be set aside where the company goes into insolvent liquidation within a statutory period of the charge being created and the charge was designed to prefer one creditor over another (s239 IA 986 (IA)). To this extent, floating charges are not treated any differently from a fixed charge.

However, the floating charge is not always treated equally and there may be disadvantages in a creditor holding a floating charge in the event of a company's insolvency. A floating charge holder, although ranking ahead of unsecured creditors, ranks below fixed charge holders and creditors with preferential debts (although, in respect of insolvencies after 15 September 2003, the Crown loses its preference). There may therefore be insufficient assets to meet the claims of the floating charge holder. Further, the claims of a trade creditor who holds a reservation of title clause will mean that the goods retained by the trade creditor will not become part of the general assets of the company to meet the claims of the floating charge holder. In addition, floating charges can be declared invalid if caught by s245 IA 1986. Section 245 IA 1986 provides that a floating charge created within 12 months of the onset of insolvency (the period is 2 years where the creditor is a connected person) is invalid, except to the extent of any money paid to the company after the creation of the charge and in consideration for the charge.

Further disadvantages of possessing a floating charge can be found in the EA 2002, which introduced changes to the IA 1986 as part of a reform of corporate insolvency law, with effect from 15 September 2003. From this date, a floating charge holder in relation to floating charges created after that date will no longer be able to appoint an administrative receiver in order to realise the company's assets that were the subject of the floating charge. This is to encourage administration as the preferred route for insolvent companies and, while a company is in administration, creditors' claims may not be pursued. Administration as a form of corporate insolvency is dealt with in Chapter 19. Another feature of the EA 2002 is that, with effect from 15 September 2003, a liquidator can set aside a certain amount of the company's assets that would otherwise be realised to satisfy the claims of the floating charge holder, to meet the claims of unsecured creditors.

Avoidance of charges

Certain rules are designed to prevent certain creditors being given a preference where insolvency of the company granting the charge is imminent.

Section 245 Insolvency Act 1986 (IA) provides that any floating charge created within 12 months of a liquidation of an administration order is void unless (i) it relates to the supply of new monies, goods or services or (ii) the company was solvent immediately after the creation of the charge. Further, floating charge created in favour of a director of the company or an associated person is void, where it was created within 24 months of liquidation, regardless of the state of insolvency.

Sections 238–244 IA 1986 provide that any charge made by a company within 6 months of liquidation (or 2 years where the creditor is a connected person) is void where it amounts to a preference of any of the company's creditors and any transaction made within a 2-year period of insolvency is void if it is part of a transaction at an undervalue.

Answer to in-text question

QUESTION 1 Do you know anyone, perhaps a friend or a member of your family, who is a shareholder of a company? Do you know how they acquired their shares?

The most common way a person can acquire shares is by purchasing shares in a public company using the services of a stockbroker. Individual share ownership has become more popular following the privatisation programme of the former nationalised public utility companies and employee share schemes. However, the vast majority of shareholders of public companies are City institutions and pension funds.

16 | Company management

By the end of this chapter, you should be able to explain:

Learning objectives

- **The division of powers between shareholders and directors of a company**
- **The nature of a director's appointment**
- **The role of the company secretary and company auditors**
- **The importance and nature of company meetings**

Introduction

As a company is an artificial legal person, it can enter into transactions and make decisions in its own right. However, a company can only do this through the actions of natural legal persons, in the form of either the members (usually, the shareholders) or the directors of the company. Where a company has corporate members or directors, these companies in turn will be governed by individuals.

Whether the power to enter into transactions lies with the shareholders or the directors of the company will depend on the company's **articles of association**, which is likely to give day-to-day responsibility for the company to the board of directors. An example of such an article is to be found in Table A, the model, statutory form of articles that most companies adopt either in full or in part. Where Table A has not been adopted, it is likely that the company's articles provide for the directors to govern the company, as shareholders are not interested usually in managing the company on a day-to-day basis. Their interests are likely to be in connection with improved company performance, as reflected in increased dividends and an increase in the value of their shareholding.

The administrative side of a company's business is in the hands of the **company secretary**, an officer of the company that every company must have (although, in order to ease the burden on private companies, the Company Law Reform Bill 2005 proposes that a private company does not have to appoint a company secretary). The general task of a company secretary is to ensure due compliance with the formalities of the running of a company. In relation to public companies, the role of the company secretary has become an increasingly important one, as in addition to dealing with the administrative matters of company legislation, the company secretary is expected to show that the company has complied with the Combined Code on Corporate Governance. Media attention relating to executive pay, golden handshakes (particularly for failing executive directors) and the social responsibility of companies, have contributed to a considerable debate on the way in which companies are governed. As a consequence, since 1993, public companies have been subject to a code of practice dealing with such matters as the independence of the board of directors, auditing and the setting of executive directors' remuneration. The code has been revised on a number of occasions and is known as the Combined Code. It is appended to the Stock Exchange Listing Rules. Public companies that fail to comply with its provisions have to explain the reasons for non-compliance in their annual reports, as presented to the company's shareholders.

Another important aspect of company management and a measure of investor protection is the role of the company **auditor** in ensuring that a company's accounts give a true and fair view of the company's affairs. The role of company auditors has been subject to a great deal of scrutiny following a number of high-profile cases involving financial scandal or massive corporate failure, such as Barings Bank, Polly Peck International, BCCI and, in America, Enron and WorldCom.

Division of powers

To determine the distribution of powers within a company between the **general meeting** (i.e. the members) and the board of directors, we need to look at the company's articles of association, for example, the adopted Table A. Art 70, Table A provides that subject to the provisions of the CA 1985, the memorandum and the articles and to any directions given by **special resolution**, the business of the company shall be managed by the directors, who may exercise all the powers of the company. These powers do not have to be exercised exclusively by the board, for Art 72, Table A, for example permits the board of directors to delegate its powers to a committee, a managing director or an **executive director**. Further, the power of management would include the power to delegate tasks to subordinates, such as senior managers, etc.

The effect of Art 70, Table A is that the board of directors is given a wide-ranging power to manage the company's business and little managerial control is retained by the shareholders other than through special resolutions and certain powers conferred by statute. Even where a special resolution is given in accordance with Art 70, Art 70 states that it cannot invalidate a prior act of the board of directors. An example illustrating a conflict between shareholders and directors relating to the exercise of a corporate power can be found in *Automatic Self-Cleansing Filter Syndicate Co v Cuninghame (1906)* (see case study).

Despite the existence of Art 70, Table A, the general meeting can act in certain circumstances, although, in practice, shareholders may be faced with some difficulties in pursuing these courses of action. There are various circumstances in which shareholders can act.

Automatic Self-Cleansing Filter Syndicate Co v Cuninghame (1906)

The company's articles of association contained a provision similar to Art 70, Table A and which provided that the management of the company vested in the directors who could exercise all the powers of the company, except any act that was in contravention of an **extraordinary resolution** of the shareholders of the company. At a general meeting, the shareholders passed an **ordinary resolution** ordering the directors to sell the company's assets to another company. The directors refused to comply with the resolution, believing that it was not in the best interests of the company.

The court held that in the absence of an extraordinary resolution, as set out in the company's articles, a decision whether to sell the company's assets was a matter for the board of directors and not the shareholders.

Default powers

Where the board is unable to act, the general meeting is able to exercise a residual or default power. In **Barron v Potter (1914)**, the company's articles of association gave a power to the board of directors to appoint an additional director, but owing to differences between the existing directors – they refused to talk to one another – no meeting of the board could be held for this purpose. The company in general meeting chose to act on the power by passing an ordinary resolution. The court held that, in these circumstances, where the board was in deadlock, the general meeting retained the power to make an appointment.

Removal of directors

Under s303 CA 1985, a director may be removed before the expiration of his period of office by an ordinary resolution of the company, regardless of anything to the contrary in the articles of association or any contract between the company and the director. There may, however, be a number of financial and legal constraints in pursuing this course of action, depending on whether the director concerned is a director of a public company or a private company. These constraints can be identified as follows:

- A director cannot be prevented from pursuing a claim for compensation under s303(5) CA 1985, for termination of appointment. An example would be a director of a public company serving under a fixed-term contract, who may be entitled to substantial compensation should his fixed-term contract come to a premature end.

- Relief may be available under ss459–461 CA 1985 for conduct termed **unfair prejudice** on the basis of wrongful exclusion from management, where the dismissed director was also a shareholder and had a legitimate expectation of employment as a director. This remedy is more appropriate for a director who is a shareholder of a private company, as we shall see in Chapter 18.

- The director, where he is a shareholder, particularly of a private company, may be able to benefit from a weighted **voting** right contained in the company's articles of association. An example of such a clause can be seen in **Bushell v Faith (1970)** (see case study).

Reality check

Confidentiality orders – Huntingdon Life Sciences

Company legislation requires that the names and addresses of directors (and company secretaries) are kept in the company's register of directors and secretaries (s288 CA 1985) and in the company's records at Companies House (s10 CA 1985). This is to enable interested parties such as law enforcement authorities the means of locating company directors, in order, for instance, to serve legal documents. Since April 2002 under s723B–F CA 1985, a director or company secretary can apply to the secretary of state for a confidentiality order, so that the residential address of a director, although provided, is not made available for inspection by the public or members of the company. The secretary of state can grant a confidentiality order where he thinks that the availability of the applicant's residential address creates a serious risk that the individual or someone who lives with the applicant the will be subjected to violence or intimidation.

Confidentiality orders were introduced as a result of government concerns at protestors targeting directors and employees of companies engaged in activities to which protest groups objected. In the case of Huntingdon Life Sciences, directors and employees of the company, as well as personnel of businesses who contracted with Huntingdon Life Sciences were intimidated or assaulted outside their homes, or their property was damaged by protestors objecting to the company's use of animals for medical research. Huntingdon Life Sciences was one of the companies that had lobbied the government for the introduction of confidentiality orders, as a means of protecting its directors. However, confidentiality orders do not have retrospective effect. Where a confidentiality order has been made, a service address, at which legal documents can be served, has to be provided and made available.

The Company Law Reform Bill 2005 proposes that directors can use a service address in order to satisfy the requirements of s10 CA 1985.

© TOUHIG SION/CORBIS SYGMA

A peaceful protest against Huntingdon Life Sciences

director fails to obtain a share qualification, or ceases to hold it, he must vacate his office and continuing to act as a director renders him liable to a fine (s291 CA 1985).

Vacation of office

Section 303 CA 1985 provides that a director may be removed before the expiration of his period of office by an ordinary resolution of the company regardless of anything to the contrary in the articles of association or in any agreement between the company and the director. The ordinary resolution must come with **special notice**, i.e. 28 days notice must be given to the company and the director is entitled to be heard at the relevant meeting. In addition, the director may be entitled to compensation for termination of appointment under s303(5) CA 1985.

The articles of association usually provide for the automatic vacation of office in the event of certain circumstances. For example, Art 81, Table A provides for the vacation of office in the event of bankruptcy, mental disorder or absence from board meetings without permission for more than 6 months. Loss of office can occur in other ways, e.g. a failure to obtain or ceasing to hold a share qualification and in most cases of a winding up of a company. For delinquent directors, directors can be disqualified from holding office under the Company Directors Disqualification Act (CDDA) 1986, (see the 'Reality check' textbox).

Where a director acts in contravention of a disqualification order or undertaking, s15 CDDA 1986 provides that the director is liable for any debts incurred while disqualified and s19 CDDA 1986 provides a remedy against directors where, in the course of a liquidation, money or other property has been misapplied or retained, or there has been misfeasance or breach of duty. Section 11 CDDA 1986 prohibits an undischarged bankrupt from acting as a director of a company or being involved in its promotion, formation or management.

An example of proceedings taken under the CDDA 1986 arose out of the collapse of Barings Bank in 1995. The bank collapsed in 1995 owing to the unauthorised trading activities of Nick Leeson, an employee, who was based in

 Reality check

How the Company Directors Disqualification Act 1986 deals with rogue directors

The CDDA 1986 was introduced as a means of preventing directors from abusing the corporate form and to protect the public from directors deemed unfit to govern a company. You may recall from earlier chapters that the principle of corporate personality protects a director or shareholder from the claims of creditors, as such claims must be pursued against the company. Where the company becomes insolvent, a director or shareholder remains protected and, although, in certain circumstances proceedings can be taken against delinquent directors under the IA 1986 for fraudulent or wrongful trading, these provisions do not prevent a director from acting as a director of another company. Under the CDDA 1986, however, a court can impose a period of disqualification up to a maximum period of 15 years on a delinquent director or other person.

The court is given the power under the CDDA 1986 to make an order against a person that he or she shall not, without leave of the court, be a director of a company or be concerned or take part in the promotion, formation or management of a company. There are a number of grounds on which an order can be made, such as where a person is convicted of an indictable offence in connection with the promotion, formation, management or liquidation of a company (s2 CDDA 1986) or where a person is in persistent breach of the companies legislation in respect of filing of accounts and other documentary requirements (s3 CDDA 1986). The most important ground, however, is contained in s6 CDDA 1986, which provides that a court must make a disqualification order against a person where it is satisfied that the person has been a director of a company that has become insolvent and that his conduct as a director makes him unfit to be concerned in the management of a company. The minimum period of disqualification under s6 CDDA 1986 is 2 years and the maximum period is 15 years. Schedule 1 to the CDDA 1986 lists the matters to which the court is to have regard when determining whether a person's conduct makes him unfit to be concerned in the management of a company and these include any breach of duty by the director and, where the company has become insolvent, the extent of the director's responsibility for the company's insolvency.

A director can also be disqualified from holding office under s10 CDDA 1986, where he has been held liable for fraudulent trading (under s213 IA 1986) or wrongful trading (under s214 IA 1986).

Singapore. The result was massive losses. In *Barings Bank plc (No 5) (2000)*, disqualification orders were sought against three of its former directors based in London, including B. It was alleged that they had been guilty of serious failures of management in relation to Leeson's activities, including, specifically, leaving Leeson in sole control of the dealing and settlement offices in Singapore, ignoring an internal audit recommendation that the roles be separated and failing to institute internal management controls. The Court of Appeal upheld the 6-year disqualification order imposed on B. B had failed to take reasonable steps to ensure that Leeson's trading activities were conducted properly. B's conduct involved a serious abdication of responsibility by a senior director of the main operating subsidiary of a major public company.

The number of disqualification orders that have been imposed on directors between April 2001 and March 2004, as notified to Companies House, is as follows:

- 1 April 2001 – 31 March 2002: 2063
- 1 April 2002 – 31 March 2003: 1911
- 1 April 2003 – 31 March 2004: 1710

Court proceedings involving a disqualification order can be lengthy and costly and to overcome this, the CDDA 1986, following an amendment introduced by the Insolvency Act 2000, provides that the secretary of state can accept an undertaking from a director to consent to a period of disqualification where it is 'expedient in the public interest'.

In addition to the CDDA 1986, a director can be disqualified from holding office under s216 Insolvency Act 1986 (IA). Section 216 IA 1986 is aimed at tackling 'phoenix companies', i.e. where directors of an insolvent company form a new company to purchase the old business and run the new company on similar lines to the old company, but leave creditors with claims only against the old company. The effect of s216 IA 1986 is that a person who was a director or a shadow director of an insolvent company within 12 months before it went into liquidation is prohibited, except with leave of the court, from being a director or concerned in the management of a company that uses a name the same as, or suggesting an association with, the company that has gone into liquidation. A failure to comply is an offence, punishable by a fine or imprisonment or both, and renders the person responsible for the company's debts.

FAQ

What type of conduct determines the length of a period of disqualification?

In *Re Sevenoaks Stationers (Retail) Ltd (1991)* the Court of Appeal imposed a 5-year disqualification order on a director and laid down some guidelines for the operation of the CDDA 1986 by providing for the division of the potential 15-year disqualification under the CDDA 1986 into three tiers. The court suggested that the top tier of disqualification for periods over 10 years should be reserved for the most serious of cases, such as the director who has already had a ban imposed on him and incurs another. The middle tier of 6 to 10 years should be used where the case is serious but falls short of the top tier and the minimum tariff of 2 to 5 years should be used where, although disqualification is mandatory, the case is not very serious.

Directors' remuneration

Directors of companies are not entitled to be paid unless this is expressly provided for, such as by the articles of association. An example is Art 82, Table A, which provides for remuneration to be fixed in general meeting. In the absence of ratification by the company, it is misfeasance on the part of a director to take remuneration in excess of the provision made. The Directors' Remuneration Report Regulations 2002 provide that information about the remuneration of a public company's directors must be disclosed in its annual accounts and reports.

Directors' service contracts

It is common practice for executive directors to have a contract of service, a copy of which the company must keep in accordance with s318 CA 1985. Under s319 CA 1985 a director's contract of employment, which includes contracts of service, as well as contracts for services (e.g. a consultancy agreement) exceeding 5 years in length requires the prior approval of the company in general meeting. In practice, however, due to the provisions of the Combined Code, contracts of service for directors of public companies are usually of 1-year duration. This provision was designed to reduce the amount of compensation a director would be entitled to on early termination of appointment should he serve under a longer contract, although compensation can be substantial where the director is entitled to a year's notice of termination.

Company secretary

The company secretary is an officer of the company who has an important role to play in relation to the company complying with the administrative requirements of company legislation, although the Company Law Reform Bill 2005 proposes that for private companies, so long as the requirements of the CA 1985 are complied with, it is not necessary for a company secretary to be appointed.

Section 283 CA 1985 provides that every company shall have a company secretary and that a sole director shall not also be the company secretary. A company is permitted to have joint company secretaries under s290 CA 1985. Art 99, Table A provides that, subject to the provisions of the CA 1985, the company secretary shall be appointed by the directors for such term and at such remuneration as they may think fit and any secretary so appointed may be removed by them. The duties of company secretaries are set by the board of directors and therefore vary from company to company, but, as an officer of the company, the company secretary will be responsible for ensuring that the company complies with company legislation, so that:

- necessary registers are established and properly maintained
- all annual returns required to be lodged with the registrar of companies are prepared and filed within the appropriate time limits
- meetings of the shareholders and directors are organised
- documents are signed
- in respect of public companies, the company complies with the provisions of the Combined Code of the Stock Exchange Listing Rules.

FAQ

Does a company secretary have authority to enter into contracts on the company's behalf?

In **Barnett, Hoares & Co v South London Tramways Co (1887)**, it was said that a company secretary was a mere servant, who no person could assume had any **authority** to represent the company. However, in **Panorama Developments (Guildford) Ltd v Fidelis Furnishing Fabrics Ltd (1971)**, Lord Denning recognised that a company secretary has become a much more important person, who is an officer of the company with extensive duties and responsibilities. In that case, the company secretary hired cars on the company's behalf, signing relevant car hire documentation as company secretary and informing the car hire company that the cars were to be used for chauffeuring clients. He used the cars for private purposes and the company refused to pay the car hire charges, claiming that the company secretary had no authority to make the contract on the company's behalf. The court held the company was liable to pay, as the company secretary had acted within the scope of his usual authority. The court considered that a company secretary is entitled to sign contracts concerned with the administrative side of the company's affairs, such as employing staff and hiring cars.

Qualifications of a company secretary

The company secretary of a private company does not need to hold any formal qualification, but s286 CA 1985 provides that it shall be the duty of the directors of a public company to take reasonable steps to ensure that the company secretary has the requisite knowledge and experience and:

- held the office of company secretary on 22 December 1980
- had been the secretary of a public company for at least 3 out of the 5 years preceding his appointment as secretary
- is a member of the Institute of Chartered Accountants (ICA), the Chartered Association of Certified Accounts, the Institute of Chartered Secretaries and Administrators (ICSA), the Chartered Institute of Management Accountants, the Chartered Institute of Public Finance and Accountancy or the Chartered Association of Certified Accountants
- is a barrister or solicitor.

> **QUESTION 2** Do you think a company secretary would have the authority to enter into a commercial contract on a company's behalf, such as the buying and selling of goods?

Auditors

An audit is a process, carried out mainly on behalf of the shareholders of a company, that examines the records and systems used to prepare the accounts of a company, in order to establish whether those accounts give a true and fair view of the company's affairs. Although employed by the company, auditors represent the interests of the shareholders, by ensuring that the company is being run on a proper basis. Auditors have the right of access to the company's books and accounts and officers of the company are required to provide such information and explanations as the auditors consider necessary. Auditors powers have been strengthened recently by the passing of the Companies (Audit, Investigations and Community Enterprise) Act 2004 – an Act which also aims to improve the reliability of financial reporting and the independence of auditors.

Appointment

Section 384(1) CA 1985 requires every company to appoint an auditor, or auditors, unless it is a dormant company, i.e. a company that is a 'small', private company having had no 'significant accounting transaction' since the end of the previous financial year.

The law relating to the eligibility for appointment as company auditor is contained in the CA 1989. A person is eligible for appointment as a company auditor where that person is a member of a recognised supervisory body, such as the Institute of Chartered Accountants or the Association of Chartered Certified Accountants, and is eligible for the appointment under the rules of that body. An individual or a firm may be appointed a company auditor, but an auditor must be independent of the company.

The appointment of auditors is made initially by the directors and the auditor remains in post until the end of the first general meeting before which the accounts are laid. Subsequent appointments are made by the general meeting, although a private company may elect to dispense with the requirement to appoint auditors annually. Where directors fail to appoint the first auditors, the company in general meeting can make the appointment and where no auditors are appointed, the secretary of state can appoint a person to act as auditor.

Remuneration

Where the company in general meeting appoints auditors, the company in general meeting shall fix the remuneration. Where the directors appoint, or the secretary of state appoints the auditors, the directors or the secretary of state shall fix the remuneration (s390A CA 1985).

Removal

A company may, by ordinary resolution, remove an auditor before the expiration of his office, despite any agreement to the contrary (s391 CA 1985). Special notice of the resolution must be given and notice must also be provided within 14 days to the registrar of companies. The auditor of a company who is to be removed or not reappointed is entitled to make written representations and require these to be circulated or have them read out at the general meeting (s391A CA 1985).

Resignation

An auditor may resign his office by depositing a notice in writing at the company's registered office (s392 CA 1985), but the notice is not effective unless it contains either a statement that there are no circumstances connected with his resignation that he considers should be brought to the notice of the company's members or creditors or a statement identifying such circumstances. Once an effective notice has been given, the company must within 14 days file a copy with the registrar of companies and, in the event of the second type of statement, the auditor can require the company to call a meeting to allow an explanation of those circumstances to be given to the shareholders (s392A CA 1985).

Company meetings

The holding of meetings is an important part of a company's business, as it enables the company to conduct that part of its business that requires the passing of resolutions in accordance with company legislation and its constitution. The holding of meetings also represents a form of shareholder protection in that meetings enable shareholders to receive information relating to company performance and to have an opportunity to question the directors of the company. Meetings do not have to take place in person. In **Byng v London Life Assurance Ltd (1990)**, it was held that it was possible to have a validly held meeting without all the members being present so long as an effective audio or visual link was provided.

Following the passing of the Electronic Communications Act 2000, a company may choose to use electronic means in order to communicate with members and Table A has been modified accordingly. This means, for example, that a company may send proxies and notices electronically and board meetings may be held through telephone or video conferencing.

The Company Law Reform Bill 2005 proposes to make changes to the law governing meetings. The most significant of these are set out at the

Following the *Byng* case, there is a wide range of possibilities for the location of the holding of meetings

end of the chapter. They are designed at simplifying the law relating to company meetings so as to offer companies and shareholders increased flexibility in how they can take decisions.

Types of meeting

There are two types of meeting that shareholders of a company can attend – an **annual general meeting** and an **extraordinary general meeting**. In addition, shareholders can attend a class meeting at which shareholders of a particular class of shares, such as preference shareholders, attend alone.

Annual general meeting

By virtue of s366 CA 1985, every company is required to hold an annual general meeting every calendar year, subject to a maximum period of 15 months between meetings. Under s366A CA 1985, private companies, subject to approval by a unanimous vote, can dispense with the holding of an annual general meeting and, under s381A CA 1985, it is no longer necessary for a private company to convene a general meeting where the members have unanimously signed a **written resolution** setting out a particular course of action.

Extraordinary general meeting

An extraordinary general meeting is any meeting other than an annual general meeting. Extraordinary general meetings are usually called by the directors, but members holding 10% of the voting shares may requisition such a meeting in accordance with s368(1) CA 1985 (as detailed later).

Calling of meetings

The right to convene meetings is largely the responsibility of the directors, e.g. as provided for in Art 37, Table A. However, s368(1) CA 1985 provides a method by which members holding not less than one-tenth of the company's paid-up capital or, where the company does not have a share capital, one-tenth of the total voting rights, may make a requisition for a meeting. The requisitionists must state the object of the meeting and the directors must convene it. Where the directors have not done so within 21 days, the requisitionists may do so, as long as it is within 3 months of the requisition. A similar provision is contained within s370 CA 1985.

Meetings can also be called in the following circumstances:

- Directors of public companies are required under s142 CA 1985 to call a meeting where there has been a serious loss of capital.

- By a resigning auditor of a company under s392A CA 1985, who can require the directors to convene a meeting in order to explain the reason for the auditor's resignation.

- Under s367 CA 1985, the secretary of state may, on the application of any member, call a meeting of a company where it has failed to hold an annual general meeting as required under s366 CA 1985.

- The court may order a meeting under s371 CA 1985 where it is impracticable to call a meeting and on such terms as the court thinks fit. This method of calling an annual general meeting was used by the directors of Huntingdon Life Sciences (see 'Reality check' textbox), a company we highlighted earlier.

 Reality check

Huntingdon Life Sciences revisited

In a particular year, it was discovered that the company could not hold an annual general meeting owing to the disruptive activities of activist shareholders, who had intimidated owners of buildings from allowing the company's annual general meeting to be held. The company was prosecuted and convicted for failing to hold an annual general meeting. Later, the company made an application under s371 CA 1985. The court ordered an annual general meeting to be held at the company's premises on terms that two of the company's directors were the only persons entitled to attend the meeting and that shareholders could act only through proxy, who were to be the two directors. The annual general meeting took place without incident.

Notice of meetings

Proper and adequate notice must be sent to all those who are entitled to attend any meeting, although the precise nature of the notice is governed by the articles of association. Adequate notice of the content of any resolution must be sent to members, so that they can decide whether to attend the meeting or to appoint a **proxy** to vote in line with their instructions. In ***Baillie v Oriental Telephone Co Ltd (1915)***, the Court of Appeal held that notice of an extraordinary meeting had failed to give sufficiently full and frank disclosure of resolutions relating to the remuneration of the directors, which was substantial.

Section 369 CA 1985 provides that the minimum period of notice is 21 days for an annual general meeting and 14 days for all other meetings, except those called to consider a special resolution, which require 21 days' notice. Shorter notice is permissible in the case of an annual general meeting, where all the members entitled to attend agree and, in the case of any other meeting, where holders of 95% (or 90% in the case of private companies by means of an **elective resolution**) of the nominal value of the voting shares agree.

The directors decide usually which motions will be put to the company in the general meeting. Members, however, may set the agenda where they have requisitioned an annual general meeting in accordance with s368 CA 1985. In relation to an annual general meeting, s376 CA provides that members, representing not less than one-twentieth of the total voting rights, or 100 or more members holding shares in the company on which there has been paid up an average sum of not less than £100 per member, can, by written requisition, compel the company to give notice to members of any resolution that may properly be moved and that they intend to move at the annual general meeting. The Company Law Reform Bill 2005 proposes to reduce the level of notice.

Types of resolution

There are three types of resolution applicable to all companies, although private companies can also pass written and elective resolutions.

Ordinary resolution

An ordinary resolution requires a simple majority of those voting. Notice in relation to an ordinary resolution depends on the type of meeting at which it is proposed (s369 CA 1985). For an AGM, the notice period is 21 days and 14 days for an EGM, although, in relation to an ordinary resolution to remove a director under s303 CA 1985, the company must be given special notice of 28 days.

Special resolution

A **special resolution** is one that has been passed by a majority of not less than three-quarters at a general meeting, of which not less than 21 days' notice has been given, such notice having specified the intention to propose the resolution as a special resolution (s378(2) of the CA 1985). The 21-day notice period may be shortened, as with extraordinary resolutions, under s368 of the CA 1985. Examples of company legislation requiring a special resolution are in relation to an alteration of the objects clause (s4 CA 1985), ratification of an ultra vires act (s35 CA 1985), an alteration of the articles of association (s9 CA 1985), a change of company name (s28 CA 1985) and a reduction of capital (s135 CA 1985). In addition, as we saw earlier, shareholders wishing to give directions to the directors, in accordance with Art 70, Table A, must pass a special resolution to that effect.

QUESTION 3 Is there an advantage for a minority shareholder possessing 26% of the shares in a company?

Extraordinary resolution

Section 378(1) CA 1985 provides that an extraordinary resolution is one passed by a three-quarters' majority of votes cast at a meeting convened by a notice specifying the intention to propose such a resolution. As no period of notice is stated in s378 CA 1985, unless the articles provide for a longer period, the minimum period of notice will be 14 days, as laid down for extraordinary general meetings, or 21 days for AGMs (s369 CA 1985). An example can be found in connection with s84 Insolvency Act 1986, which provides for the voluntary winding up of a company on the basis of insolvency.

Written resolution

Section 381A CA 1985 enables a private company to dispense with the need to call meetings or give notice for resolutions, by the passing of a written resolution. Anything which might be done by resolution in a general meeting or class meeting may be done by resolution in writing, signed by, or on behalf of, all members who would be entitled to attend and vote at such a meeting. The company is required to keep a record of any written resolutions but resolutions for the removal of directors or auditors before expiry of their term of office cannot be the subject of written resolutions.

Elective resolution

Under s379A CA 1985, a private company may dispense with certain procedural requirements of the Companies Act 1985 by passing an elective resolution to that effect. These are in relation to providing directors with permanent authority to allot shares (s80A CA 1985), dispensing with laying accounts and reports before a general meeting (s252 CA 1985), dispensing with the holding of annual general meetings (s366A CA 1985), reducing the majority required to consent to short notice of a meeting (s369 CA 1985) and dispensing with the annual appointment of auditors (s386 CA 1985).

An elective resolution requires 21 days' notice to be given of the meeting at which it is to be proposed, although members may agree unanimously to dispense with the notice requirement. An elective resolution requires unanimity of all members entitled to attend and vote. An elective resolution may be revoked by an ordinary resolution.

Proceedings of meetings

Section 370 CA 1985 provides that the minimum number of persons that must be present at a meeting is two, unless the articles provide otherwise. Art 41, Table A sets the **quorum** at two, who must be *continuously* present at the meeting. A meeting of one person, however, is possible in relation to a class meeting of one shareholder, a private company with only one member or as ordered by the secretary of state or a court. In respect of a sole-member company, s322B CA 1985 requires any contract between a single-member private company and a member–director of the same company to be in writing or contained in the **minutes** of the board of directors. A failure to comply can render the person liable to a fine.

A resolution is decided by a show of hands, unless a poll is demanded. On a show of hands, every member has one vote. In a poll, it is usual for each share to carry a vote.

Section 372 CA 1985 provides that any member of a company who is entitled to attend and vote at a meeting may appoint another person as their proxy, that is, to act as their agent in exercising their voting right. Every notice of a meeting must state a member's right to appoint a proxy and, although the articles may require notice of the appointment of a proxy to be given to the company, they may not require more than 48 hours' notice. Proxies have no right to speak at meetings of public companies, but they may speak at a meeting of a private company and they are allowed only to vote in regard to a poll.

Section 370 CA 1985 provides that any member of the company may act as chairman, unless the articles state otherwise, such as Art 42, Table A, which provides that the chairman of the board of directors, or some other nominated director, shall act as chairman. The chairman is responsible for taking the meeting through the agenda, for putting matters to the vote and for keeping order. He can adjourn the meeting with the consent of, or where instructed to do so by, the meeting and the articles provide usually for the chairman to have a casting vote (such as Art 88, Table A).

Section 382 CA 1985 requires that minutes of all general meetings and directors' meetings must be kept by the company. Members have a right to inspect the minutes of general meetings but not the minutes of directors' meetings.

Reform

The law relating to meetings is complicated and contains a number of provisions of the CA 1985 and CA 1989 that are more applicable to public companies than private companies. The Company Law Reform Bill 2005 proposes to make it easier for small, private companies to transact business in respect of the procedure relating to meetings. The bill also proposes to reform the law relating to meetings for all companies as a means of enhancing shareholder protection. The most significant changes proposed by the bill are as follows:

- Extraordinary resolutions and elective resolutions to be abolished.
- The notice period for any meeting to be 14 days unless the company's constitution states otherwise.
- Written resolutions to be passed by a majority of all eligible votes rather than the unanimous consent of all shareholders as currently required.
- The default majority required to agree a shorter notice period at a private company to be reduced from 95% to 90%.
- Section 370 CA 1985 to be repealed.
- Members of private and public companies to have the right to appoint more than one proxy, and proxies, whether of private or public company members, to be able to attend, speak, vote on a show of hands or a poll and demand a poll.
- Public companies will be required to hold an annual general meeting within 6 months of the end of their accounting year. This is expected to enable shareholders to call the directors to account at an earlier period compared to the current position.

- A quoted, public company to be allowed a 15-day *holding period* after the annual accounts have been published. During this period, members have the right to requisition a resolution for the meeting at which the accounts are to be laid, such as the annual general meeting.
- Abolition of s367 CA 1985 (the right of the Secretary of State to call a meeting).

Answers to in-text questions

> **QUESTION 1** Suppose the wrongdoers control the board of directors and the general meeting of a company. How likely is it that action would be taken by the company against the wrongdoers in such a situation?

It would be very unlikely that wrongdoers who controlled the board of directors and the general meeting of a company would decide on the company's behalf to sue themselves. In such a situation, company law provides for a minority shareholder to sue the wrongdoers, but only where the conduct of the wrongdoers amounts to a 'fraud on the minority'. This is discussed in Chapter 18 on shareholder protection.

> **QUESTION 2** Do you think a company secretary would have the authority to enter into a commercial contract on a company's behalf, such as the buying and selling of goods?

Unless a company secretary has express authority to enter into a commercial contract on behalf of a company, it is unlikely that a company secretary would have authority to bind a company to such a transaction.

> **QUESTION 3** Is there an advantage for a minority shareholder possessing 26% of the shares in a company?

Although such a shareholder would be unable to prevent the passing of an ordinary resolution, he would be in a position to block a special resolution. This can be an important part of a minority shareholder's armoury as important aspects of a company's business cannot be achieved without a special resolution, such as an alteration of the articles of association. This is known as negative control, i.e. the consent of a shareholder with a 26% shareholding would be required in order to pass any special resolution at a general meeting of the company.

By the end of this chapter, you should be able to explain:

- **The importance of directors' duties**

- **The nature and scope of the no-conflict rule, the proper purpose rule and the requirement to act in good faith**

- **The remedies available to the company for breach of duty and the means by which a director can be relieved from liability**

- **The means by which third parties who have assisted In a director's breach of duty can be held liable**

Introduction

In practice, a company's **articles of association** are likely to give day-to-day responsibility of the company to the board of directors and not its members such as the shareholders. An example can be found in Art 70, Table A, the statutory model of articles of association, where Art 70 gives a wide power of management to the board of directors. Shareholders' main interests are likely to be in connection with company performance with a view to increased dividends and enhanced share value. Given that **directors** are responsible for managing company assets, safeguards have evolved to protect the company from directors abusing their powers or position of trust. These safeguards are reflected in the form of duties imposed on directors by both the common law and equity. Under the common law, directors are expected to exercise care and skill in the performance of their duties. In equity, because of the position of trust they hold, directors owe **fiduciary** duties to the company. These equitable duties are based on notions of loyalty and good faith, and similar duties are owed by employees towards their employers, as can be seen in Chapter 21. An example of how these duties operate in respect of directors can be in seen in the 'Reality check' textbox, which is concerned with a case arising out of the creation of the Eden Project in Cornwall.

Reality check

Ball v Eden Project Ltd (2002)

In the 1990s Jonathan Ball helped to set up the Eden Project, a major visitor and research centre in Cornwall. The project was later run by a charitable trust, which formed an operating company, Eden Project Ltd, to run the business, with Ball appointed as one of the directors of the company. An ongoing dispute arose between Ball and the company in respect of money that Ball considered was owing to him for his efforts in connection with the project. In 1997 Ball registered in his own name the mark 'Eden Project'. In 2000 Ball left the company and issued proceedings against the company, seeking compensation to which he believed he was entitled. The company issued a counterclaim, claiming that Ball had breached his fiduciary duty in registering the Eden Project mark in his name. The High Court agreed with the company, stating that, despite Ball's claim for compensation, that did not entitle him to register the company's mark in his own name and depriving the company of the use of its property. Ball's duty as director of the company should have been to exploit the Eden Project mark for the company's and not his own benefit and to enable the company to earn profits as a result of goodwill that the mark would have generated over time.

The Eden Project, Cornwall

The case demonstrates that a company as a separate legal entity can own assets, including intellectual property rights such as copyright and trademarks. Directors are under a duty to manage the company's assets for the company's benefit and not to use them for their own purposes. It may be possible for a director to exploit corporate property, but the director must obtain the company's consent. This is something Ball failed to do and presumably something he was unlikely to obtain given the nature of his relationship with the company.

To whom duties are owed?

The fiduciary and common law duties imposed on directors are owed to the company, i.e. the shareholders as a body corporate, and not to individual shareholders, employees or creditors of the company. In **Percival v Wright (1902)**, certain shareholders approached the directors and asked if they would purchase their shares. Negotiations took place but the directors failed to mention that a takeover bid had been made for the company, which affected the price of the shares. The court held that the directors were not liable for breach of duty, as any duty they owed was owed to the body of shareholders and not to any individual shareholder.

The decision might have been different if there had been a special relationship of trust between the directors or a relationship of agency between the directors and the shareholders. The principle that directors owe their duties to the company is illustrated further in ***Peskin v Anderson (2001)*** (see case study), which concerned former shareholders of the RAC who did not benefit from a share of the proceeds of sale on the disposal of the RAC's motoring business.

Peskin v Anderson (2001)

The claimants were former members of the RAC, a club owned by RAC Ltd. On ceasing to be members of the club in 1995, the claimants also ceased to be shareholders of RAC Ltd, by virtue of the company's articles of association, but, under club rules, former members could reapply for membership within 3 years of resigning. In 1998 RAC Ltd disposed of its motoring services business with members of the club each receiving over £34,000. The claimants claimed that the directors of RAC Ltd, who were also committee members of the club, had failed to advise them of the proposed sale of the motoring business before they resigned their membership. Applying the general principle of *Percival v Wright (1902)*, the court held that fiduciary duties are owed by directors to the company they serve and not to individual shareholders, unless some special relationship between the directors and the shareholders exists, which is capable of generating fiduciary obligations, such as a duty of disclosure. No such obligation however arose from the facts of the case.

FAQ

Why do directors owe duties to the companies they serve?

A company, as a separate legal entity, is capable of owning property and entering into legal arrangements. Its actions, however, are dependent on the intervention of individuals acting on its behalf. Such individuals will be either the shareholders (the members) of the company or the board of directors. In practice, it is to the directors that the company turns for day-to-day decision making and for the protection of its assets and interests. It is for this reason that duties have evolved treating directors like trustees of the company's property, so that directors are under an obligation of good faith and loyalty when acting individually or collectively. This means that directors must not place themselves in a position of conflict, such as receiving a bribe or inducement from a contracting third party or misappropriating a company asset. Should a director breach one of these duties, it is for the company to decide whether or not to take action against the director, for these duties are owed to the company and not the shareholders of the company.

With reference to the *Eden Project* case, we can see that Ball had breached a fiduciary duty by misusing a corporate asset and not acting for the company's interests. The Eden Project mark did not belong to him, but to the company, and his duty was to avoid exploiting the mark for his own benefit.

Fiduciary duties of directors

A fiduciary is someone who has undertaken to act for and on behalf of another in a particular matter in circumstances that give rise to a relationship of trust and confidence. A fiduciary, therefore, is a person who is bound to act for another's benefit, for example, agent to principal, solicitor to client and director to company. Fiduciaries have duties imposed on them by equity for the protection of the persons for whom they act. Directors are not trustees but they do occupy a fiduciary position towards the company whose board they form. Three, sometimes overlapping, fiduciary duties can be identified:

- the no-conflict rule
- the duty to act bona fide (i.e. in good faith) in the interests of the company
- the proper purpose rule.

The no-conflict rule

A director is under an obligation not to allow a conflict of interest to arise between his duty to the company and his own personal interest. An example is a director having an interest in a company contract, such as where the director has received an inducement from the other party to the contract or where the director has entered into a contract with the company, such as selling his own property. In ***Aberdeen Railway Co v Blaikie Bros (1854)***, a conflict of interest arose where a director, unknown to his company, was a senior partner of the other party to a contract involving the company.

The no-conflict rule operates in two ways:

- contracts involving the company in which a director has an interest
- misuse of corporate property.

Contracts involving the company in which the director has an interest

We talk about a director having an interest in a company contract in the sense that a director may be connected with the other party to the contract or that he has received an inducement in connection with the contract, such as a bribe. Where a director is in a position of conflict, the company can pursue the following remedies:

- rescission of the contract
- account for profit
- damages.

Rescission of the contract Any contract or proposed contract in which a director has an interest is voidable at the instance of the company. As we saw in Chapter 9, unlike a void contract, which is void and unenforceable from the outset, a voidable contract is one that gives the aggrieved party, the company in this case, the option of avoiding the contract. This is the remedy the court granted the company in *Aberdeen Railway Company v Blaikie Bros (1854)*, where the company entered into a contract with a firm for the manufacture and supply of iron chairs, a contract that the company later attempted to avoid. The contract was held to be voidable at the instance of the company as one of its directors was a senior partner in the firm, the other contracting party.

Account for profit The company can compel the director to account for any secret profit he has made, e.g. a bonus, commission or inducement received from the other contracting party. The rule applies regardless of whether the company rescinds or affirms the contract. Alternatively, the company may choose to allow the director to keep the profit, again, regardless of whether rescission or affirmation of the contract has taken place.

In **Boston Deep Sea Fishing Co v Ansell (1888)**, a director of BDSF entered into a contract on the company's behalf with a shipbuilder for the building of fishing vessels, for which the director, unknown to the company, was to receive a commission paid by the shipbuilder. It was held that the director was liable to account to BDSF for the commission received. By being awarded with a bonus from the other contracting party, he had placed himself in a position of conflict.

Damages The company can seek compensation from the director for any loss sustained as a result of entering into the contract in which the director has an interest, but the company cannot claim damages and the secret profit – it must elect between the two. In **Mahesan v Malaysian Government Officers' Co-operative Housing Society (1979)**, a manager of a housing society agreed with a third party for the housing society to purchase a piece of land from the third party for £900,000, £500,000 more than its true market value. The third party gave the manager a commission of £120,000. On discovering these events, the housing society claimed from the manager the secret profit and damages covering its loss, the loss being the difference between the price paid for the land and its true value. The court held that the housing society had a remedy against the manager for breach of the no-conflict rule, but would have to choose between the secret profit and damages.

> **QUESTION 1** Which remedy do you think the society would choose and why?

The no-conflict rule is applied strictly by the courts and liability can arise whether a conflict of interest arose intentionally or innocently. In addition, s317 CA 1985 places a statutory duty of disclosure on directors. The section provides that a director who is directly or indirectly interested in a contract or proposed contract must declare the nature of any interest at a meeting of the directors. A failure to comply with the section will render the director liable to a fine. This is a criminal sanction and is a separate matter from the general equitable rules that non-disclosure would bring into play. The provision applies to 'one-person' companies, so that in **Neptune (Vehicle Washing Equipment) Ltd v Fitzgerald (1996)**, it was held that the sole director of a company had failed to disclose his interest in a contract with the company at a board meeting of the company – a meeting at which he was the only director in attendance.

Other relief

Despite the strict application of the no-conflict rule, a director may be able to obtain relief from liability for breach of the no-conflict rule either by **ratification** or by complying with the company's **articles of association**.

Ratification A company in **general meeting**, i.e. the members, can ratify the contract and/or allow the director to retain any secret profit made. Where the general meeting does so ratify, in the absence of fraud or oppression, an interested director who is a shareholder of the company, can exercise his vote as shareholder.

North-West Transportation Co v Beatty (1887)

A company agreed to purchase a steamship from one of the directors, who held the majority of the shares in the company. At a general meeting, against the wishes of the minority shareholders, a resolution was passed approving the contract. The court held that, in the absence of fraud or oppression, the interested director was able as shareholder to exercise his votes in securing the resolution. There was no evidence of fraud on the minority as the company was in genuine need of the replacement vessel, the vessel concerned met the company's requirements and the price paid was not an unreasonable one. (Fraud on a minority as a form of shareholder protection is examined in detail in Chapter 18.)

Articles of association An alternative to ratification is for the director to rely on Art 85, Table A or a similar provision in the company's articles of association. Art 85 provides that as long as a director has disclosed to the board the nature and extent of any material interest of his, he may be party to, or otherwise interested in, any transaction with the company and shall not be accountable to the company for any benefit he derives. In addition, no such transaction is liable to be avoided on the ground of such interest or benefit.

Fair dealing provisions

In addition to the general equitable rules, there are a number of statutory provisions relating to contracts between directors and the company they serve. These fair dealing provisions, which also apply to a **shadow director**, are contained in Part X Companies Act 1985. They prohibit certain types of contract entered into by a director with a company, for which a range of criminal and civil penalties apply. Such contracts include the acquisition of shares in, or debentures, of the company, loans beyond an amount of £5000 and 'substantial property transactions'. The prohibition relating to debentures and shares applies to spouses and children. Directors are also under a duty to notify the company within 5 days of acquiring or disposing of any beneficial interest in the shares of the company or of a company in a group of companies. Following the recommendations of the Company Law Reform (2001), some minor modifications to these provisions have been made by the Company Law Reform Bill 2005.

Misuse of corporate property

A director is under an obligation not to misappropriate corporate property, such as corporate know-how and opportunities and benefits derived from company contracts. Should he do so, he can be compelled to account for any secret profit made from the contract. As we saw earlier in respect of the first part of the no-conflict rule, this aspect of the no-conflict rule is also applied strictly. It is immaterial that the company could not obtain the profit, neither does liability depend on fraud or the absence of good faith. The two cases that follow serve to illustrate the point.

Cook v Deeks (1916)

The Toronto Construction Company had built up considerable goodwill with the Canadian Pacific Railway (CPR) as a result of the satisfactory performance of contracts for the laying of railway lines. Three of the four directors were negotiating with CPR for an extension to an existing line but, prior to completion of the contract, took the contract in their own names. At a meeting of the company, the three directors, who were the majority shareholders, passed a **resolution** to the effect that the company had no interest in the contract and consenting to the directors taking the contract. On an action brought in the company's name by the fourth director in his capacity as minority shareholder, the Privy Council held that the benefit of the contract belonged to the company and the directors had to account for the profit made.

Regal (Hastings) Ltd v Gulliver (1942)

Regal owned a cinema in Hastings and the directors wanted to purchase two other cinemas in the area with a view to selling all three together. For this purpose, they formed a subsidiary company (Amalgamated) with a share capital of £5000 to purchase the two cinemas, but Regal was unable to pay for more than 2000 of the 5000 £1 shares in the subsidiary. Four of the five directors agreed to purchase the balance of the shares. Later, the proposal to sell the three cinemas was abandoned and replaced by an agreement for the shares in both Regal and Amalgamated to be sold. On selling the Amalgamated shares, each director made a profit of £2.80 per share. Regal, under new control, sought to make the former directors liable for the profit they had made. The House of Lords held that, although the directors had acted honestly, they were liable for breach of duty as it was only through their knowledge and position as directors that they were able to obtain the opportunity to acquire the shares.

In **Cooks v Deeks (1916)** and **Regal (Hastings) Ltd v Gulliver (1942)**, it can be seen that both companies were pursuing actively the benefit of a contract. In *Cook v Deeks*, the company was deprived of the opportunity by the actions of the directors. In *Regal (Hastings) Ltd v Gulliver*, the company was only able to gain the benefit of a contract by virtue of the financial assistance provided by the directors. In both cases, the directors were held liable to account for the profit they made.

In **Industrial Developments Consultants Ltd v Cooley (1972)**, the court held that the claimant company, IDC, was entitled to recover a profit made by a director on the contract that IDC was unlikely to obtain. In that case, the **managing director**, an architect, of IDC was involved actively in negotiations with the Eastern Gas Board, endeavouring to secure for IDC consultancy contracts in connection with the construction of four depots. In the course of negotiations, EGB made it clear that it did not wish to deal with a firm or company of consultants but rather with a private architect. Shortly afterwards, Cooley was offered the work in his private capacity, but before taking up the contract gained release from his employment with IDC by claiming that he was in ill health. The court held that the director's action amounted to diverting a maturing business opportunity that rightly belonged to the company and he was liable to account for the whole of the benefits derived from the contract, even though IDC had only a minimal chance of obtaining the contract itself.

Relief from liability

A director may be relieved from liability for a misuse of corporate property by seeking approval from the company in general meeting. In *Regal Hastings Ltd v Gulliver (1942)*, Lord Russell stated that the directors could have protected themselves by seeking ratification, antecedent or subsequent, of their actions. In *Cook v Deeks (1916)*, however, the court held that ratification could not avail the directors of their liability to account for the profit they had made in breach of their duty.

> QUESTION 2 Why do you think in *Cook v Deeks (1916)* the court took the view that the directors' actions could not be condoned by the general meeting?

To act bona fide in the interests of the company

Directors of a company must act bona fide (i.e. in good faith) in what they consider, and not what a court may consider, is in the interests of the company. A director of a company that obtains its property by misuse of his powers is regarded as a constructive trustee of that property. Any contract made between the company and a director may be rescinded and the directors, as constructive trustees, liable to replace any of the company's money they have used improperly. The facts of *Cook v Deeks (1916)* provide an example of directors acting in bad faith. In that case, in diverting a contractual opportunity away from the company they served, they had failed to consider the interests of the company.

To act in the interests of the company means acting in the interests of the shareholders as a whole, such as balancing the interests of current members with those of future shareholders. Recent case law and statutory developments suggest that creditors' interests, where relevant, may also in some circumstances have to be taken into account by directors when making an assessment of what is in the interests of the company. In **West Mercia Safetywear Ltd (in liq) v Dodds (1988)**, the court held that duty to act bona fide in the interests of the company, where the company was insolvent, included the directors having to consider the interests of creditors. However, the duty to act in good faith is owed to the company, not to the creditors of the company.

The proper purpose rule

Where the directors have acted bona fide in the interests of the company, there is a further constraint in that they must not exercise their powers for a purpose different from that for which the powers were conferred on them. However, unlike acting in bad faith, acting for an improper purpose may be ratified by the company in general meeting.

Hogg v Cramphorn (1967)

The directors of a company had a power under the articles to issue new shares. In order to defeat a proposed takeover bid for the company by an outsider, the directors allotted new shares with special **voting** rights to trustees on behalf of company employees. The court held that although the directors had believed honestly that it was not in the company's interest for the outsider to gain control of the company, nonetheless they had used their powers of allotting new shares for an improper purpose, namely to defeat the outsider's bid. The decision whether to approve the bid was a matter for the existing shareholders. At a subsequent general meeting of the company, the shareholders approved the action of the directors.

To avoid similar cases to *Hogg v Cramphorn* arising, the CA 1985 provides that an allotment of shares by directors must be authorised by the company, such authority (unless a private company) not to exceed a period of 5 years (ss80 and 80A CA 1985).

> **QUESTION 3** What might be an accepted proper exercise of the power to allot shares?

FAQ

Can a director be prevented from competing with his company?

It is generally stated that a director cannot be restrained from competing with the company he serves. This was the position established in *London & Mashonaland Ltd v New Mashonaland Ltd (1891)* and *Bell v Lever Bros (1932)*. However, a director competing with the company runs the risk of breaching the no-conflict rule or breaching his contract of service should the contract contain a clause prohibiting the director from having a competing interest or other directorships. In *Thomas Marshall Ltd v Guinle (1978)* a company was granted an injunction preventing a director from using lists of customer names and trade secrets in connection with a rival company he set up while working for the company. By using such information, he was in breach of his service contract, which prohibited him from so acting.

However, not all actions restraining directors from competing are successful. In *Balston Ltd v Headline Filters Ltd (1990)*, for example, it was held that the general fiduciary duties of a director do not prevent a director, while a director, from forming an intention to set up in competition or from taking preliminary steps to forward such an intention, provided that, while the directorship continued, there was no competitive tendering or actual trading. In *Coleman Taymar Ltd v Oakes (2001)*, however, the court held that the director's actions, in indirectly purchasing unwanted equipment belonging to the company while employed by the company, went beyond the taking of preliminary steps towards the commencement of his competing business.

Duties of care and skill

Traditionally, the courts have been reluctant to impose rigorous standards of care and skill on directors, partly because shareholders choose their own directors and partly because the imposition of higher standards might involve a judicial assessment of management decision making, something the courts have been reluctant to undertake in company law. However, following recent statutory enactments, notably s214 of the Insolvency Act (IA) 1986 and the Company Disqualification of Directors Act (CDDA) 1986, it may be that higher standards are to be required of directors in the future. In *Norman v Theodore Goddard (1991)* and *Re D'Jan of London (1994)*, the court accepted that the standard laid down in s214 IA 1986 in respect of wrongful trading applied generally to directors. In *Re Barings plc (No 5) (2000)*, the court held that in the context of an application for a disqualification order under the CDDA 1986, directors had both collectively and individually a continuing duty to acquire and maintain a sufficient knowledge and understanding of the company's business to enable them to properly discharge their duties as directors.

The starting point of the duties of care and skill is *Re City Equitable Fire Insurance Co (1925)*, and the three propositions of Romer J.

Re City Equitable Fire Insurance Co Ltd (1925)

The liquidator of the company discovered substantial losses caused partly by the fraudulent activities of the company chairman who had been convicted and sentenced. The liquidator brought an action against other directors alleging negligence in respect of losses caused by investments and loans initiated by the chairman who had been left with the management of the company's affairs. The court held that the directors could not be held liable on the grounds of a clause contained in the company's articles that exempted them from liability other then for wilful neglect or default. However, in providing a summary of the common law, Romer J stated that, in ascertaining the duties a director is appointed to perform, it will be necessary to take into account the nature of the company's business, the size of the company and the manner by which its work is distributed between directors and other officers. He put forward three propositions:

1 A director need not exhibit in the performance of his duties a greater degree of skill than may reasonably be expected from a person of his knowledge and experience.

2 A director is not bound to give continuous attention to the affairs of his company. His duties are of an intermittent nature to be performed at periodical board meetings and at meetings of any committee of the board on which he happens to be placed. He is not, however, bound to attend all such meetings, although he ought to attend whenever in the circumstances he is reasonably able to do so.

3 In respect of all duties that, having regard to the exigencies of business and the articles of association, may properly be left to some other official, a director is, in absence of grounds for suspicion, justified in trusting that official to perform such duties honestly.

A more recent case applying the duties of care and skill is ***Dorchester Finance Co Ltd v Stebbing (1989)***. The company had one **executive director** and two **non-executive directors**, each having considerable accountancy and business experience. The day-to-day running of the company was left to Stebbing, the executive director, with the non-executive directors visiting the company's offices in order to sign blank cheques for Stebbing to use against the company's account. Later, the company sued all the directors for negligence, claiming damages for losses it suffered as a result of S's actions. The court held that the directors had been negligent. A director must show such skill as may reasonably be expected from a person with his knowledge and experience and must take such care as an ordinary man might be expected to take in his own affairs. The court drew no distinction between standards applying to executive and non-executive directors.

The company in general meeting can ratify a director's breach of duty of care and skill, subject to any fraud on the minority. In ***Pavlides v Jensen (1956)***, the court held that it was open to the shareholders to approve the directors' act of selling an asbestos mine belonging to the company at a gross undervalue.

Liability of third parties

As directors owe fiduciary duties to the company, it follows that, where there is a fraudulent or dishonest breach of such a duty and company property is misapplied, anyone who receives such property with knowledge of the breach of duty will be liable in damages to the company. Such persons are held liable on the basis that they are considered to be a constructive trustee. A constructive trust is a trust that arises by operation of law, where a person acquires property that he is not entitled to retain. A third party can be held liable on the basis of 'knowing receipt' or 'knowing assistance'. Knowing assistance is where a third party assists dishonestly in a director's breach of duty, while knowing receipt is where a third party comes in receipt of company property with knowledge of the director's breach of duty.

> **QUESTION 4** In what circumstances do you think it might be advantageous for a company to sue a third party who has participated in a director's breach of duty?

Statutory provisions

Apart from the fair dealing provisions of Part X CA 1985, which we looked at earlier, there are other statutory provisions relating to directors' duties. These include ss310 and 727 CA 1985.

Section 310 CA 1985

Section 310 CA 1985 states that any provision, whether in the articles of association or in a contract with the company, exempting a director from liability for breach or duty or indemnifying him against such liability, is void. The provision

Is there a case for codifying the duties of directors?

Apart from the fair dealing provisions, directors' duties are based on case law and not statute. Law reformers have suggested that better compliance by directors with these duties might be better served if the various case law duties were codified in statute. As part of the Department of Trade and Industry's review of company law, the Company Law Review (2001) proposed that there should be a statutory statement of directors' duties and that directors should be made aware that, in promoting the company's success for the benefit of its membership as a whole, they must take account of long-term as well as short-term consequences and that they must recognise the importance of relations with employees, suppliers, customers and the community. These recommendations have made their way into the Company Law Reform Bill 2005 and the common law and equitable duties that directors owe a company are to be codified. By codifying the duties, it is hoped that directors will become more aware of their responsibilities towards the companies they serve.

was introduced to prevent directors avoiding liability on the basis of an exemption clause contained in a company's articles of association, as we saw in *Re City Equitable Fire Insurance Co Ltd (1925)*. However, under s310(3) CA 1985, a company is permitted to purchase insurance cover for its directors in the event of legal proceedings being taken or liability being established against a director. A company can also pay a director's defence costs as they are incurred (Companies (Audit, Investigations and Community Enterprise) Act 2004).

Section 727 CA 1985

Under s727 CA 1985, a court may grant relief to a director from liability for a breach of duty where it appears to the court that a director has acted honestly and reasonably and ought fairly to be excused. In ***Selangor Rubber Estates Co Ltd v Cradock (1968)***, it was held that the directors of a public company who disposed of virtually all its assets without regard for minority shareholders, and who did so under the sole direction of the majority shareholder who appointed them to the board, did not act reasonably and could not be relieved.

Reform

Following the recommendations of the Law Commission (1999) and the Company Law Review (2001), the Company Law Reform Bill 2005 contains a proposal to codify directors' duties, both at common law and in equity. This is intended to clarify the duties directors owe and to make directors more aware of their responsibilities.

Answers to in-text questions

> QUESTION 1 Which remedy do you think the society would choose and why?

Damages, as this would represent a greater amount than the secret profit made by the agent.

> QUESTION 2 Why do you think in *Cook v Deeks (1916)* the court took the view that the directors' actions could not be condoned by the general meeting?

As the three directors in *Cook v Deeks (1916)* held 75% of the shares in the company, they were able as shareholders to pass a resolution at a general meeting approving their actions. The court held the ratification to be ineffective as it amounted to a misappropriation of a corporate asset to the controllers of the company.

> QUESTION 3 What might be an accepted proper exercise of the power to allot shares?

The courts have held that a proper exercise of the power to allot new shares is for the raising of capital.

> QUESTION 4 In what circumstances do you think it might be advantageous for a company to sue a third party who has participated in a director's breach of duty?

The most likely reason for a company to sue a third party is where the director has become insolvent or has disappeared. A corporate third party is more likely to have the resources or insurance cover to meet the claim of the company.

Learning objectives

By the end of this chapter, you should be able to explain:

- The concept of majority rule and the rule in *Foss v Harbottle (1843)*

- The nature and scope of shareholder protection at common law and the difficulties faced by minority shareholders in bringing derivative claims against corporate wrongdoers

- The nature and scope of statutory protection for minority shareholders, in particular, relief for unfair prejudicial conduct

Introduction

It is not easy for a minority shareholder to bring legal proceedings against alleged wrongdoers either personally or on behalf of the company. First, it may be difficult for a shareholder to obtain sufficient evidence to support legal action. Second, a shareholder may have to consider the time and cost involved in bringing legal proceedings. Third, on bringing a claim, he might be faced with the courts' traditional reluctance to interfere with the business of a company.

A dissatisfied shareholder's best course of action might be to withdraw his investment by selling his shares. This should be fairly straightforward where the company is a public company, but, in a private company, he may have difficulty in finding a willing purchaser of his shares or he may discover that he is bound by restrictions in the company's articles as to the transfer of shares.

Should a shareholder decide to take legal proceedings, there are three types of claim that can be pursued. These are:

- a **personal claim**, where some personal individual right has been infringed

- a **representative claim**, where a shareholder is acting on behalf of a group of shareholders in connection with an infringement of some personal right common to that group

- a **derivative claim**, where the wrongdoers are in control of the company and are preventing improperly the company from suing.

A derivative claim will only be permitted in exceptional circumstances, for the proper claimant to bring an action for a wrong done to the company is the company and not any individual shareholder. This is known as the rule in ***Foss v Harbottle (1843)***.

Alternative action for an aggrieved shareholder is through statute, either by seeking relief under ss459–461 Companies Act 1985, where the company's affairs have been conducted in an unfairly prejudicial manner, or by petitioning the court under s122(1)(g) Insolvency Act 1986 for **winding up** on the **just and equitable ground**. These statutory provisions are dealt with later in the chapter. The first thing to consider is the protection available to a minority shareholder at common law.

Majority rule

The rule in Foss v Harbottle (1843)

The court will not ordinarily intervene in a matter that it is competent for the company to settle or, in the case of an irregularity, to ratify or condone by its own internal procedure (see case study below). Where there is a wrong done to the company, it is for the company as a legal entity to decide whether to sue and this is seen as a matter of **majority rule**.

Another example is to be found in ***MacDougall v Gardiner (1975)***, where a minority shareholder brought an action for a declaration from the court that the chairman's conduct in adjourning a **general meeting** without holding a poll was improper. The Court of Appeal rejected the claim on the basis that if the conduct of the chairman were wrong, that was a matter of internal management for which the company and not individual shareholders could decide whether or not to sue.

> **QUESTION 1** Noting what was said in Chapter 16 on the division of powers, would a decision by a company to instigate legal proceedings lie with the board of directors or the general meeting?

Foss v Harbottle (1843)

Two shareholders of a company took proceedings against the directors of the company to account for losses sustained by the company in buying land at a price greater than its true value. The court held that the shareholders' action failed as the proper claimant to take action was the company in its corporate character and there was nothing preventing it from taking legal proceedings if it thought fit to do so.

FAQ

What is the rationale for the rule in Foss v Harbottle (1843)?

The clearest advantage to the rule is for the avoidance of multiplicity of legal claims so as to prevent company resources in terms of money and time being engaged in litigation. However, a major disadvantage of the rule is where alleged wrongdoers are in control of the company, either of the board of directors, the general meeting or, as most likely, both. It is for this reason that a number of exceptions to the rule in *Foss v Harbottle (1843)* have been developed. Some of these can be properly described as exceptions to the rule, while others are simply instances where the rule cannot operate.

Exceptions to the rule in Foss v Harbottle (1843)

Ultra vires acts

The doctrine of **ultra vires** was examined in Chapter 14. By virtue of s35(1) CA 1985, the doctrine has been abolished in respect of the capacity of corporations to enter into transactions. However, it is possible under s35(2) CA 1985 for a shareholder to seek an injunction to prevent the company from entering into a *proposed* ultra vires act, although such actions are likely to be rare as majority shareholders can ratify an ultra vires act by passing a **special resolution** and it must be shown in any event that the proposed act was beyond the powers of the company.

Where, alternatively, an aggrieved shareholder is seeking compensation on the company's behalf for a loss caused to the company by the directors entering into an ultra vires transaction, he will be prevented from so doing by one of the following:

- the rule in *Foss v Harbottle (1843)*
- the passing of a special resolution under s35(3) CA, relieving the directors of liability
- a decision of other, independent shareholders for proceedings not to be brought, as was the ruling of the court in **Smith v Croft (No 2) (1987)**, a case to which we shall return later.

There are provisions similar to s35 CA 1985 in s35A CA 1985 relating to acts that are beyond the board of directors' powers.

Special majorities

A company cannot act on the passing of an **ordinary resolution** where statute or the company's articles of association require a **resolution** passed by a special majority (see the **Edwards v Halliwell (1950)** case study).

Infringement of a shareholder's personal right

Where there has been a wrong done to a shareholder and not the company, a shareholder can bring a personal claim for infringement of a personal right. Personal rights arise from the articles of association, statute or the terms of a shareholder agreement. However, only a limited number of personal rights

Edwards v Halliwell (1950)

The rules of a trade union, similar to a company's articles of association, provided that any increase in members' contributions could only be made after a two-thirds' majority had been obtained in a ballot of the members. At a meeting of members, a bare majority passed a resolution increasing members' contributions without holding a ballot. Two members of the union sought a declaration that the resolution was invalid. It was held that, as the matter was not a mere irregularity of internal management, but a matter of substance and tainted with oppression, the court would grant the claimants relief as an exception to the rule in *Foss v Harbottle*. The rule in *Foss v Harbottle* did not apply to matters that required a special majority and where only a bare majority had been obtained.

arising from the articles have been recognised by the courts, e.g. the right to have a vote at meetings recorded by the company (as in **Pender v Lushington (1877)**) and the right to receive a dividend in cash (as in **Wood v Odessa Water Works (1889)**).

FAQ

Can a shareholder bring a personal claim for the loss in the value of his shares caused by the damage suffered to the company by the conduct of a wrongdoer?

In **Stein v Blake (1998)** and **Johnson v Gore Wood & Co (2001)**, it was held that a shareholder cannot maintain such an action, as the shareholder's loss is merely a reflection of the loss suffered by the company and should the company succeed in its action against the wrongdoers, the shareholder should no longer suffer a loss in the value of his shareholding. In *Stein v Blake (1998)*, the claimant owned half the shares in a number of companies. The defendant owned the other half and was sole director of the companies. The claimant alleged that the defendant had misappropriated assets from the companies and the claimant brought a personal claim, claiming damages for the loss in value of his shares in the companies resulting from the misappropriated assets. The companies were subsequently placed into liquidation, but no action was brought by the liquidators against the defendant. The Court of Appeal held that claimant could not recover from the defendant, as the loss caused to the claimant was only a reflection of the companies' loss and the companies were the proper claimants to bring legal proceedings against the defendant. Similarly, in *Johnson v Gore Wood & Co (2001)*, the House of Lords held that the claimant's claim in respect of the diminution in value of his pension and shareholding in the company should be struck out, as this was merely a reflection of the company's loss.

However, in **Giles v Rhind (2003)**, the Court of Appeal held that where the company was unable to bring an action because of the conduct of the wrongdoer, the reflective loss rule did not apply and, therefore, so long as a shareholder had a separate cause of action, he could bring a personal action in such circumstances.

Fraud on the minority

Where wrongdoers, who have caused the harm to the company, control the company, a minority shareholder can bring a derivative claim against the wrongdoers, with the company joined to the proceedings. The injured party will normally be the company and should an action be successful the benefit of such proceedings, such as an award of damages, will go to the company and not the shareholder bringing the claim. An aggrieved shareholder needs to establish two things in order to come within the exception, namely:

- fraud and
- wrongdoer control.

Fraud denotes some form of misuse or abuse of power, such as an expropriation of corporate assets or an act of bad faith. However, not all wrongdoers' conduct amounts to a misuse or abuse of power. Examples of what may or may not amount to such conduct can be illustrated with reference to decided cases, as follows.

Misappropriation of corporate property A misappropriation of corporate property by the majority cannot be condoned by a company. In **Menier v Hooper's Telegraph Works Ltd (1874)**, E Ltd, whose majority shareholder was H Ltd, held a government licence for the laying of a transatlantic telegraph cable. H Ltd transferred the government licence from E Ltd to another company, in connection with which, H Ltd was able to make a profit. In order to prevent E Ltd taking action for the loss of the licence, H Ltd passed a resolution at a general meeting putting E Ltd into liquidation. M, a minority shareholder in E Ltd, brought a representative action against H Ltd. The court upheld M's claim for an account of profit on the sale of the cable. Where the majority shareholder's purpose was to gain a benefit at the expense of the minority, the court may be prepared to intervene in order to protect the latter, by allowing the minority to bring a derivative claim. In this case, the majority shareholder had obtained certain advantages by dealing with something which was the property of the company.

> **QUESTION 2** Another example of a case involving a misappropriation of corporate assets is *Cook v Deeks (1916)*, a case we looked at in Chapter 17. In that case, how did the wrongdoers, who were directors and shareholders of the company, attempt to prevent action being taken against them and was it effective?

Negligence Negligence on the part of the controllers does not amount to fraud. However, this is not the case where the wrongdoers benefit from their negligent conduct (see the **Pavlides v Jensen (1956)** case study).

By contrast, in **Daniels v Daniels (1975)**, the minority shareholders of a company brought a successful action against the directors, who were the majority shareholders of the company, for authorising the sale of company land to one of their own at a price alleged to be well below its market value. The land was sold for £4250 and, 4 years later, was resold by the director for £120,000. It was held that the action could be taken by the minority shareholders as the action of the directors, although based on negligence and not fraud, conferred a personal benefit.

Pavlides v Jensen (1956)

A minority shareholder in TAC Ltd sought to bring an action on behalf of himself and other shareholders, claiming damages against the directors. He alleged that the directors had been negligent in selling an asbestos mine in Cyprus for £182,000 when its market value was nearer £1m. The majority shareholder in TAC was another company, the directors of which were also the directors of TAC. The court held that the action could not be maintained because the sale of the mine did not involve any allegation of fraud by the directors or any misappropriation of company assets by the majority. The claim was based on negligence alone and it was open to the company, by a vote of the majority, to decide if proceedings should be brought against the directors.

An asbestos mine in Cyprus

Acting in bad faith An act of the directors in bad faith is not ratifiable by the company, but where the directors use their powers in good faith but for an improper purpose, their conduct can be ratified by the company. In ***Hogg v Cramphorn Ltd (1967)***, the court held that, although the directors had used the power of issuing new shares for an improper purpose, this was something that was capable of being condoned by the company and, subsequently, the shareholders at a general meeting approved the directors' actions.

Misuse of voting power It is reasonably well settled in company law that shareholders can vote in their own interests, except where they are **voting** on an alteration of the company's articles of association, as we saw in Chapter 14. In such circumstances, the shareholders must act in good faith in the interests of the company as a whole and, where they unfairly discriminate against a minority shareholder, that can be a ground for the court to attack the alteration. It is rare, however, for such a restraint to operate in other circumstances, but in exceptional cases, the courts have been prepared to intervene in respect of how shareholders vote at a general meeting.

In ***Clemens v Clemens Bros Ltd (1976)***, a dispute arose between the defendant, one of five directors, who owned 55% of the issued share capital of the company, and her niece, who owned 45% of the shares. The defendant used her majority voting power to approve the directors' act of issuing further shares in the company to non-shareholding directors, and employees of the company. The niece objected to the resolution as its effect would be to dilute her shareholding to under 25% and deprive her of her right to veto special resolutions. The court held that the defendant was not entitled to exercise her majority votes as an ordinary shareholder in any way she pleased. That right was subject to equitable considerations that could make it unjust if exercised in a particular way, as was the case here, and the resolution was set aside.

Wrongdoer control Wrongdoer control can be established where the wrongdoer has a majority of the votes or the majority has approved a **fraud on the minority**. Usually, control will mean numerical control, i.e. the wrongdoers have a majority of the voting power at the general meeting, but in ***Prudential Assurance Co Ltd v Newman Industries Ltd (1980)***, an issue arose as to whether the wrongdoers, who were directors of the company but not the majority shareholders, could exert control over the general meeting through influence and apathy.

Other barriers to a derivative claim Where a minority shareholder does establish a fraud on the minority, he may be denied from proceeding with a claim where a majority of other minority shareholders, independent of the wrongdoers in control, decide in the interests of the company to vote against taking action or vote in favour of discontinuing such action. In ***Smith v Croft (No 2) (1987)***, the claimant and other minority shareholders held shares carrying 14% of the voting rights. The defendants and majority shareholders held 63.5% of the voting rights. The claimant brought an action, making various allegations against the defendant. It was held that, although some of the claims had been made out, the claimant was not the proper claimant to take action, as shareholders, independent of the majority and representing 2% of the voting rights, chose for genuine reasons not to take action against the defendants. The view of the larger of the two minority shareholders therefore was held to prevail.

FAQ

What reasons might exist for not involving the company in legal proceedings against alleged wrongdoers?

As we saw in Chapter 1, on the introduction to the English legal system, only a small percentage of legal disputes lead to court proceedings. This applies whether the parties in dispute involve individuals or companies. Resolving disputes before taking legal proceedings is one reason why legal proceedings may not be brought by a company against alleged wrongdoers. There are other reasons, however, and they may also explain why proceedings may not be brought. Win or lose, bringing a claim may generate unwanted publicity and the possibility of damage to a company's reputation. Taking legal proceedings may also use up resources, in terms of money and time, in particular management time. A further factor in not bringing proceedings is that internal disciplinary proceedings may resolve the matter and act as a suitable deterrent for others employed by the company.

Statutory protection

Given the difficulties posed by the rule in *Foss v Harbottle*, minority shareholders have turned increasingly to statutory measures of shareholder protection. There are two main forms of statutory protection for shareholders. First, a shareholder can petition for a winding-up order under s122(1)(g) Insolvency Act 1986 and, second, a shareholder can petition for relief on the ground of unfair prejudicial conduct under s459 Companies Act 1985. Prior to 1980 when s459 CA 1985 was introduced as s75 CA 1980, a petitioning shareholder had to rely on s210 CA 1948, which proved to be highly unsatisfactory – only two cases were ever successful under it.

Winding up on the just and equitable ground

Under s122(1)(g) Insolvency Act 1986 (IA), a shareholder, with 'a tangible interest' (i.e. a shareholder with an expectation of receiving a return of surplus assets on a winding up), may petition for a winding-up order on the just and equitable ground. Where the court considers that the conduct complained of warrants that it is just and equitable to wind up the company, it will grant an order to that effect. A winding-up order may, however, be considered as a drastic remedy as it will lead to the demise of a solvent company and a resultant loss of jobs.

Section 122 (1)(g) IA 1986 applies regardless of the size of the petitioning shareholder's shareholding, so long as the application is not seen as an abuse of process. Similarly, as the relief is essentially equitable, the petitioner's own misconduct may lead to the court refusing an order and a petition may also be unsuccessful where the shareholder has a viable, alternative remedy, such as bringing a petition under s459 CA 1985 (s125(2) IA 1986). The fact that there may be an alternative remedy available to the petitioner, e.g. relief under s459 CA 1985 or an offer to buy the petitioner's shares at a fair value fixed by an independent valuer, does not prevent the court from granting a winding-up order. However, it will do so where the petitioner acted unreasonably in not pursuing the alternative remedy. In ***Re a Company (No 002567 of 1982) (1983)***, the court held that the petitioner had refused wrongly an offer to buy out his shares at a fair price. In ***Re Wessex Computer Stationers Ltd (1992)***, however, it was held that, although the existence of an offer to purchase the petitioner's shares could amount to an alternative remedy, the petitioner was not disentitled from bringing a winding-up order, as no accounts had been made available on which an acceptable valuation could be made.

Instances where a winding-up order has been sought have involved companies referred to as '**quasi-partnerships**', i.e. a company that is run like a partnership but has incorporated status. As with a partnership, such a company will have been founded on mutual trust and confidence, with a small number of shareholders, most of whom are likely to be participating in the management of the company but whom are prevented by restrictions in the articles of association from transferring freely their shares. Where there followed a breakdown of the personal relationship on which the company is based, such as wrongful exclusion from management or a loss of confidence, a winding-up order may be granted. Examples of an application for a winding-up order can be seen in the following circumstances.

Exclusion from management

It is likely that a quasi-partnership involves most of, if not all, the shareholders participating in management of the company, and wrongful exclusion from management can be ground for a successful winding-up order. The House of Lords decision in ***Ebrahimi v Westbourne Galleries Ltd (1972)*** (see case study) represents a good example.

Deadlock

Deadlock among the directors or among the shareholders can be a ground for raising a winding-up petition on the just and equitable ground. Deadlock can be

Ebrahimi v Westbourne Galleries Ltd (1972)

E and N were partners in a business dealing in carpets with an equal share in management and profits. In 1958 they formed a private company to take the business over, E and N becoming the directors and each having an equal shareholding of 500 £1 shares. The articles provided that shares could not be transferred without the directors' consent. Subsequently, N's son, G, joined the board and became a shareholder of the company. The business was successful with directors' remuneration based on profits made. No dividends were paid to shareholders. The relationship between E and N slipped into decline when N began to sell carpets on his own behalf, but invoicing the company, and using company premises to run his own antiques business. In 1969, as the relationship worsened, E was removed from the office of director by N, supported by G, passing an ordinary resolution under s303 CA 1985, thus losing his right to participate in the management of the company and to claim a share of the profits. E petitioned for an order that the company be wound up on the ground that it was just and equitable. The House of Lords, acknowledging that directors cannot usually complain of their removal from office under s303 CA 1985, agreed that it was just and equitable that the company be wound up. After a long association in partnership, during which he had had an equal share in the management and profits, E had joined in the formation of the company on the basis that the character of the association would remain the same. E had established that N and his son were not entitled, on the basis of equitable considerations, to make use of their legal power of expulsion.

illustrated by reference to the facts of *Re Yenidje Tobacco Co Ltd (1916)*. In this case, W and R, tobacco manufacturers, formed a company in which they were the sole shareholders and directors with equal rights of management and voting power. After a time they became quarrelsome, disagreeing over several business matters and choosing to communicate to one another through the company secretary. Eventually, W petitioned for a winding-up order on the basis of deadlock and a winding-up order was granted. The court held that, had this been a partnership, the circumstances of refusing to meet on matters of business and quarrelling continually would have led to it being dissolved. The same principle could apply to a small private limited company, which was, in essence, a partnership in all but name.

Loss of confidence

Where a shareholder has lost confidence in the way in which the company's affairs are being conducted by the majority shareholders, this may be a ground for the court granting a winding-up order. Such conduct, however, must be based on a lack of probity or impropriety on the part of the majority, as opposed to mere dissatisfaction in the management of the company's affairs.

In *Loch v John Blackwood Ltd (1924)*, the minority shareholders of a small, family-run company had lost confidence in the majority shareholder, who had failed to hold general meetings, had failed to submit accounts, had never recommended a dividend and who wanted to give the impression that the company was run down, so as to encourage the minority shareholders to sell their shares to the majority shareholder. An order to wind up the company was granted.

Unfairly prejudicial conduct

Section 459 CA 1985 provides that a member of a company may apply for a court order on the ground that the company's affairs are being or have been conducted in a manner that demonstrates **unfair prejudice** to the interests of its members or of some part of its members. Since its introduction, as s75 CA 1980, there have been many cases brought under s459 CA 1985, suggesting that the section is proving to be an invaluable means of redress for aggrieved, minority shareholders who are concerned at the way the company has been run as affecting their interests. Section 459 proceedings, however, can be costly and lengthy or fail at an early stage on the basis of amounting to an abuse of process. In *Re Elgindata Ltd (1991)*, legal costs of £320,000 were incurred in respect of litigation involving shares worth £24,600 and in *Re a Company (No 00836 of 1985) (1986)*, the minority shareholder's petition was struck out because the petitioning shareholder refused to pursue a reasonable offer to buy his shares.

In order to succeed under s459 CA 1985, the minority shareholder will have to show that the majority shareholder in the conduct of the company has breached a legitimate expectation of the minority shareholder that went beyond his or her strict legal rights. Such an expectation might come from the articles of association, a separate shareholder agreement or the circumstances surrounding the relationship between the shareholders and can include expectations arising before and after incorporation. In the only House of Lords decision on s459 CA 1985, Lord Hoffman in *O'Neill v Phillips (1999)* (see the 'Reality check' textbox) said:

> A member of a company will not ordinarily be entitled to complain of unfairness unless there has been some breach of the terms on which he agreed that the affairs of the company should be conducted. But there will be cases in which equitable considerations make it unfair for those conducting the affairs of the company to rely upon their strict legal powers. Thus unfairness may consist in a breach of the rules or in using the rules in a manner which equity would regard as contrary to good faith.

Section 459 petitions are likely to arise in the case of small private companies, such as quasi-partnership companies, rather than public companies where it is envisaged that any interests or rights a shareholder of a public company might enjoy are confined to the company's constitution, unaffected by any extraneous equitable considerations. In *Re Astec (BSR) plc (1998)*, a group of shareholders in a public company brought a s459 claim on the basis that the company's dividend policy and its failure to comply with the Stock Exchange Listing Rules and the code on corporate governance amounted to unfair prejudicial conduct. The claim failed. The court held that no claim could be founded on the basis that, the shareholders of a public company had a legitimate expectation that the provisions of the Listing Rules, etc. would be complied with.

Examples of unfair prejudicial conduct

Some of the common examples of conduct amounting to unfair prejudice are as follows:

Reality check

Decision of the House of Lords in O'Neill v Phillips (1999) and its effect on s459 petitions

P controlled a company involved in the construction industry. He owned the company's entire share capital and acted as its sole director. In 1983 the company employed O as a manual worker. He was later rewarded by P with a gift of 25% of the company's shares and a directorship of the company. O was also paid 50% of the company's profits. In December 1985, P retired from the company's board of directors, leaving O as sole director. The company was profitable for the next 5 years and there were discussions between O and P, but no formal agreement, with a view to O's shareholding being increased to 50%. Thereafter the company's fortunes declined and P regained control of the business, informing P that he would no longer be paid 50% of the profits. After leaving the employment of the company, O petitioned under s459 CA 1985, claiming that he had a legitimate expectation of acquiring a 50% holding in the company and an expectation of continuing to receive 50% of the profits. The House of Lords held that P had not acted unfairly. There was no basis, consistent with established principles of equity, for a court to hold that P was behaving unfairly in withdrawing from the negotiation and to hold otherwise would be imposing on P an obligation to which he never agreed.

The effect of the decision in *O'Neill v Phillips (1999)* is that the ability of members of smaller companies to take action under s459 CA is restricted to cases where there has been a breach of the company's constitution or a breach of duty or an agreement that makes it inequitable for the majority to act in a particular way. This is designed to discourage the practice that has developed under which minority members have made all sorts of allegations that might possibly sustain a case of unfairness.

Exclusion from management In *Re London School of Electronics (1986)*, X, the petitioner, and CTC Ltd owned shares in LSE, a company that ran degree courses in electronics. Subsequently, CTC Ltd registered LSE students to its own courses and X was dismissed as a director and tutor. X decided to set up another college, taking several LSE students with him. X's petitioned for relief under s459 CA 1985 and this action was successful. Although a petitioner's own conduct could be relevant to a s459 petition the court held that, X was entitled to relief as the overriding cause of the breakdown in relations was the unjustified conduct of CTC Ltd.

> **QUESTION 3** What would be a likely outcome were the facts of *Ebrahimi v Westbourne Galleries Ltd (1972)* to occur today?

Misleading information In *Re a Company (No 008699 of 1985) (1986)*, the court held that directors' inaccurate statements to shareholders recommending acceptance of a bid from a company to which the directors were connected could amount to unfair prejudicial conduct, where another bid, at a higher price, was in existence.

Issuing new shares In *Re a Company (No. 00836 of 1985) (1986)*, the court held that a proposed rights issue might amount to unfairly prejudicial conduct, where, for example, it was known that the dissenting shareholder could not afford to take up the offer of shares under the rights issue and this was the reason for making it or the dissenting shareholder was engaged in litigation and the offer was designed to reduce his available funds.

Payment of dividends In *Re Sam Weller & Sons Ltd (1990)*, a petition was presented under s459 CA 1985 by a brother and sister who were shareholders in a family-run company. They alleged their interests as members were unfairly prejudiced by the payment by the company of 'the same derisory dividend' of 14 pence per share for the past 37 years, despite the company being profitable and the shareholders having no other source of income from the company. The petition was successful.

Excessive remuneration In *Re Cumana Ltd (1986)*, the Court of Appeal held that two shareholders, L and B, had entered into an agreement involving mutual trust and confidence that had been broken by B's actions, as majority shareholder, in awarding himself an excessive salary. B's remuneration of £265,000 over a 14-month period was considered to be excessive and unfairly prejudicial to the petitioner's interests.

Expropriation of corporate assets In *Re London School of Electronics (1986)*, the majority shareholder's conduct in taking students away from the company to its own courses amounted to a misappropriation of a company asset and in *Re Cumana Ltd (1986)*, B's action of unfair prejudice included diverting business from the company to another company.

Negligence There is some doubt whether negligence by those in control of the company can form the basis of a successful s459 petition. In *Re Macro (Ipswich) Ltd (1994)*, the petitioning shareholders claimed that as a result of the mismanagement of properties owned by the company, the value of the shareholding of the petitioners had depreciated. The court held that the majority shareholders' conduct amounted to unfairly prejudicial conduct, and that a s459 action was sustainable in circumstances where the mismanagement of a company was related to the administration of the company's affairs. In *Re Elgindata Ltd (1991)*, however, the court considered that a s459 petition based on allegations of poor management could not normally form the basis of a claim for unfair prejudice.

Remedies

Section 461 CA 1985 provides that where the court is satisfied that a petition under s459 CA 1985 is well founded, it may make such order as it thinks fit for the giving of relief in respect of the matters complained of. The most common remedy is a buy-out order, where the court compels the company or the majority shareholder to buy the shares of the petitioning shareholder at a fair price. A rare example of the court ordering majority shareholder to sell to a minority share-holder is to be found in *Re Nuneaton Borough Association FC Ltd (1989)*, where the court held that the management failings of the majority jeopardised the proper running of the company and directed the chairman and majority shareholder to sell his shares to the petitioner.

The courts attempt to ensure that the valuation of a successful petitioner's shares is a fair one, so the date for valuing the minority shareholder's shares is prima facie the date on which the buy-out order is made.

Profinance Trust SA v Gladstone (2001)

Under a petition brought under s459 CA 1985, the first instance court ordered that the respondent purchase the petitioner's 40% minority shareholding in A Ltd for £46,400, which included an element of compensation. The petition was presented in December 1997, when the company's shares were worth £80,000, and the hearing took place in March 2000, when the shares were worth £215,000. The Court of Appeal held that the judge had erred in opting for December 1997 as the appropriate valuation date. The starting point was the general proposition that an interest in a going concern is to be valued at the date on which it was ordered to be purchased (i.e. in this case, March 2000). As their value at this date was £215,000, the respondent was ordered to buy the petitioner's shares at £86,000, an amount representing 40% of £215,000.

Other examples of relief a court can grant under s461 CA 1985 are:

- Making an order regulating the conduct of the company's affairs in the future.
- Requiring the company to refrain from doing or continuing an act complained of by the petitioner or to do an act that the petitioner has complained that the company has omitted to do.
- Authorising civil proceedings to be brought in the name and on behalf of the company, thus overcoming the rule in *Foss v Harbottle (1843)*.

Petitioner's own conduct

It is possible for a court to refuse to grant relief to the petitioning shareholder where his own conduct can be called into question. In ***Re RA Noble & Sons (Clothing) Ltd (1983)***, where the minority shareholder complained of his exclusion from management of the company, the petitioner's own disinterest in the company's affairs was a bar to the granting of relief under s459 CA. However, although the s459 petition failed, a winding-up order under s122 IA 1986 was granted on the basis of a breakdown in mutual confidence between the two members. In ***Re Castleburn (1991)***, the court considered that ignoring alternative machinery to resolve disputes, as provided for by the articles of association, may be a bar to s459 CA relief, unless the majority shareholders are guilty of bad faith or plain impropriety or the articles provide for an arbitrary or artificial method of valuation.

Company investigations

As a matter of shareholder and creditor protection, the secretary of state has extensive powers to investigate the affairs of a company. Sections 431 and 432 CA 1985 provide that the secretary of state may appoint inspectors, usually a lawyer and an accountant working together, to investigate a company's affairs. Investigations arise in the following circumstances:

- where the company's affairs are being or have been conducted with intent to defraud creditors or otherwise for a fraudulent or unlawful purpose or in a manner that is unfairly prejudicial to some part of the members

- where persons connected with the company's formation or management have been guilty of fraud, misfeasance or other misconduct toward the company or its members
- where the company's members have not been given all the information with respect to the company's affairs that they might reasonably expect.

These provisions are only used in the most serious cases, such as the investigations into House of Fraser Holdings plc, Barlow Clowes Gilt Ltd, Mirror Group Newspapers plc and Queen Moat Hotels. Investigations tend to be lengthy and expensive. The investigation into Mirror Group Newspapers, for example, took 9 years and cost £9.5m, while the Barlow Clowes investigation cost £6.25m.

The secretary of state also has powers to compel a company to produce documents (s447 CA 1985), to investigate ownership or control of a company (s442 CA 1985), to investigate directors' share dealings (s446 CA 1980) and, in addition to the powers of the Financial Services Authority, to investigate suspected breaches of insider dealing legislation (s168 Financial Services and Markets Act 2000).

Recently, the secretary of state's powers of inspection have been strengthened by the Companies (Audit, Investigations and Community Enterprises Act 2004).

The consequences of an inspection are that it may lead to one of the following:

- a petition by the secretary of state under s124(4) IA 1986 to wind the company up on the just and equitable ground
- civil proceedings being brought by the secretary of state in the name of the company (s438 CA 1985)
- a petition being brought by the secretary of state on the basis of unfair prejudice to the members (s460 CA 1985)
- an application for a disqualification order against individual directors or shadow directors (s8 of the Company Directors Disqualification Act 1986)

Reform

The question of minority shareholder remedies was the subject of an intensive study by the Law Commission (*Shareholder Remedies*) (1997). The Law Commission recommended that a member should be able to bring a derivative claim if the cause of action arises as a result of an actual act or omission involving either negligence, default, breach of duty or breach of trust by a director of the company, or a director putting himself in a position where his personal interests conflict with his duties to the company. The first part of the proposal would have the effect of overturning the rule in ***Pavlides v Jensen (1956)***.

These proposals were welcomed by the Company Law Review (2001), which proposed that derivative claims should be put on a statutory basis and that the nature of the company's constitution should be clarified so that there should be more certainty about what rights can be pursued by members under the constitution. Changes to this effect have been made by the Company Law Reform Bill (2005), which also proposes, in relation to company investigations, that the secretary of state should have the power to revoke the appointment of an inspector or to terminate an inspection if he considers the inspection will take too long.

Answers to in-text questions

> **QUESTION 1** Noting what was said in Chapter 16 on the division of powers, would a decision by a company to instigate legal proceedings lie with the board of directors or the general meeting?

Whether the board of directors or the general meeting can exercise the power to sue depends on examining the company's articles of association. Where the articles are based on Table A, the board of directors would possess the power to sue as Art 70, Table A, provides for a wide power of management to vest with the board of directors and the power to instigate legal proceedings is seen as an example of the power to manage. However, it is possible under Art 70 for the general meeting to instruct the board of directors on whether to litigate, but that would require the passing of a special resolution and such resolution could not invalidate a prior act of the board.

> **QUESTION 2** Another example of a case involving a misappropriation of corporate assets is *Cook v Deeks (1916)*, a case we looked at in Chapter 17. In that case, how did the wrongdoers, who were directors and shareholders of the company, attempt to prevent action being taken against them and was it effective?

As the directors in *Cook v Deeks (1916)* held 75% of the shares in the company, they were able as shareholders to pass a resolution at a general meeting approving their actions. The court held the **ratification** to be ineffective as it amounted to a misappropriation of a corporate asset to the wrongdoers.

> **QUESTION 3** What would be a likely outcome were the facts of *Ebrahimi v Westbourne Galleries Ltd (1972)* to occur today?

Were the facts of *Ebrahimi v Westbourne Galleries Ltd (1972)* to arise today, E's removal as director would likely lead to a successful petition under s459 CA 1985 on the ground of unfair prejudical conduct (see *Re London School of Electronics (1986)*).

By the end of this chapter, you should be able to explain:

- **The nature and scope of different forms of corporate insolvency**
- **The changes to corporate insolvency law introduced by the Enterprise Act 2002**
- **The liability of directors for fraudulent and wrongful trading**

Introduction

In Chapter 13, we considered the means by which a company comes into existence and the protection afforded to individuals who choose to run a business through an incorporated company. A feature of incorporation is that where an individual director or shareholder dies, the company remains in existence and is free to continue to trade. However, it is possible for a company to 'die' and in this chapter, we examine the means by which a company's existence comes to an end, i.e. the **dissolution** of a company following, usually, a period of insolvency.

Insolvency occurs where a company is unable to pay its debts. Section 123 Insolvency Act (IA) 1986 states that a company is deemed to be unable to pay its debts where, within 3 weeks, the company fails to satisfy a written demand for payment of a sum exceeding £750 or where its assets are less than its liabilities.

Corporate insolvency should be contrasted with personal insolvency. A company becoming insolvent is likely to lead to its demise through the process of liquidation where its assets are distributed to meet the claims of its creditors. An individual who is insolvent becomes bankrupt and a trustee in bankruptcy is appointed to manage the affairs of the bankrupt. In business, such persons would include sole traders and partners of an ordinary partnership where the business had failed. Where a company or a limited liability partnership fails, the company or the limited liability partnership becomes insolvent and not the members of the entity.

Large and well-known companies becoming insolvent often attract media attention. Recent examples of companies becoming insolvent are

MG Rover (administration), Courts (administration), BCCI (liquidation), Polly Peck International (administration) and Leyland-Daf (receivership). Although insolvent, not all these companies went into liquidation. There are different forms of corporate insolvency and companies that go into **administration** or receivership may be able to 'trade out' of their difficulties and continue as a going concern.

Methods of dissolution

A company ceases to exist on becoming dissolved. There are four methods of dissolving a company, with **winding up** (or liquidation) the most common form.

Proceedings by the Attorney-General

The Attorney-General may apply to cancel the company's registration. In **Attorney-General v Lindi St Claire (Personal Services) Ltd (1981)**, the Attorney-General was successful in an application to have a company's registration cancelled because the company's objects, which referred to the business of prostitution, were immoral and contrary to public policy.

Dissolution under a scheme of reconstruction or amalgamation

Section 427 of the Companies Act (CA) 1985 provides for a court to order the dissolution of a company, without winding up, where the company is transferring its undertaking to another company under a scheme of reconstruction or amalgamation.

Defunct company may be struck off

Where the registrar of companies has reasonable cause to believe that a company is not carrying on business or is not in operation, he may proceed, subject to giving due notice, under s652 CA 1985, to have the company struck off from the register. Under s652A CA 1985, directors of a small company that becomes defunct can seek to have the company struck off by application to the registrar. Where a defunct company is dissolved under this method, the liability of every **director**, managing director and member of the company continues as if the company had not been dissolved and the court retains the power to wind up such a company.

Compulsory and voluntary winding up

A winding up (or liquidation) of a company is the formal process, where, following the appointment of a **liquidator**, who must be a qualified licensed practitioner, a company's affairs are brought to a close and its liabilities settled and any surplus assets distributed to its members. On completion of a winding up, the company becomes dissolved. Section 73 Insolvency Act (IA) 1986 provides for two types of winding up:

- winding up by the court, i.e. **compulsory winding up**
- a **voluntary winding up**, which is either a members' voluntary winding up or a creditors' winding up.

On completion of a winding up, the liquidator must make up an account of the winding up, showing how it had been conducted and how the property of the company had been disposed of. He must call a general meeting of the company in order to lay the account before it and, within 1 week following the meeting, the liquidator must send to the registrar a copy of the account and a return relating to the holding of the meeting. The registrar registers the account and return and, 3 months after registration, the company is deemed to be dissolved. The court has the power to defer dissolution on application by the liquidator or an interested person.

Compulsory winding up

Under s122 IA 1986, a petition for winding up may be presented by the company or a creditor. A petition for winding up by a creditor is the most common ground, on the basis that the company is unable to pay its debts. Another example is the granting of a winding-up order by the court on the **just and equitable ground** under s122(g) IA 1986, as we saw in Chapter 18.

Under s124A IA 1986, a petition for winding up can be presented by the secretary of state where, following an investigation of the company's affairs, it is expedient in the public interest that a company should be wound up and the court thinks it is just and equitable to do so. A number of companies promoting illegal pyramid selling schemes or illegal lotteries or conducting unauthorised investment advice have been the subject of public interest petitions.

Where the company's affairs are fully wound up, the court, subject to a power of deferral, will make an order dissolving the company and the registrar of companies makes an entry on the register dissolving the company from the date of the court order. The secretary of state has the power to defer dissolution on application by the official receiver or an interested person.

Voluntary winding up

A voluntary winding up is one commenced by a company and does not involve a petition to a court. The most common reason a company may choose voluntary winding up is on the basis that the members no longer wish to continue to run the business of a company and resolve that the company be wound up. The company may be solvent in such cases and the members are seeking a return of surplus assets after any outstanding creditor liability has been met. Section 84 IA 1986 provides for a voluntary winding up of a company on the passing of either a special resolution or an extraordinary resolution and in such cases the winding up is referred to as a members' winding up.

Where it is proposed to wind up a company voluntarily, the directors must make a statutory declaration that they have made a full enquiry into the affairs of the company and have formed the opinion that it will be able to pay its debts within a stated period of not more than 12 months from the beginning of the winding up. In the absence of such a declaration, the winding up becomes a creditors' voluntary winding up.

Alternatives to winding up

Insolvent companies may not necessarily be subject to a winding-up petition or a resolution of the company for a winding up. It is possible for a company in financial difficulty to be subject to a different insolvency procedure where the

must state th
affairs. Cred

The admi
ment of the
appointing o
company is
to a floating
property acq
fixed charge.

Reconstr

Although not
schemes of a
of a method
necessarily be
to be done is
methods invo

- reductions
- a proposal
  ss110–111
- **schemes**
- voluntary
  This is a pr
  its creditor:
  arrangemer
  qualified in

The proced
1985 and the
City Panel on
Takeover Bids
Reform Bill 20

As we saw
(CDDA) 1986,
or wrongful tr
15 years. Dire
breaches of the
are considered
sonal liability
fication order
directors where
misapplied or
Section 216
i.e. a situation
to purchase the
the old compa
shadow directo
liquidation is p

company can, following that procedure, remain intact. Two of the most common of these procedures are receivership and administration and, as shall be explained, it is the second of these that is more likely to lead to the company's survival as a going concern.

Receivership

An alternative to liquidation, where a company is in financial difficulty, is the right of a secured creditor to appoint a receiver or **administrative receiver** to manage the company's assets that are the subject mater of the creditor's security. Receivership involves appointing a person to either sell or collect any income arising from the assets subject to the charge in order to satisfy the outstanding debt owed to the creditor. A receiver is a person appointed to manage the assets that are subject to a fixed charge, while an administrative receiver acts as a manager of all or substantially all the assets that are subject to a floating charge. However, with effect from 15 September 2003, the changes introduced by the Enterprise Act 2002 diminish the right of floating charge holders, particularly those creditors providing finance to companies, such as banks, to appoint an administrative receiver. As soon as a receiver or administrative receiver is appointed, that person, and not the directors, has the power to deal with the property that is subject to the charge. The right to appoint a receiver or an administrative receiver will have been contained in the contract that created the charge. Appointment of a receiver or administrative receiver often leads to the company proceeding into liquidation, as the company is likely to have few assets left to trade with, but this is not always the case and it may be possible to sell the company as a going concern. In the late 1990s Leyland-Daf Trucks Ltd was able to come out of receivership and to continue to trade without going into liquidation. This meant that the company's business of manufacturing commercial vehicles remained intact along with the protection of hundreds of jobs in the Midlands where the company was based.

Care should be taken not to confuse the term receiver with the office of the official receiver who is a court appointed official with the function of protecting all the company's assets during the time between a petition for winding up and the granting of a winding-up order.

Administration

Prior to the IA 1985, a company becoming insolvent was likely to be wound up. There was no formal system in the UK for nursing back to health a company in financial difficulty and little protection afforded to unsecured creditors. By contrast, in the USA, companies in financial difficulty can file for Chapter 11 bankruptcy, which results in a moratorium on creditor claims against the company. A number of American airlines have filed for Chapter 11 protection in recent years.

To address this issue, the IA 1985, which later became the IA 1986, introduced a procedure where an administrator could be appointed to manage a company's affairs with the purpose of salvaging the company as a going concern or at least to consider whether a winding up could be done more efficiently by considering the needs of all

The collapse of MG Rover in 2005

© Steve Nichols/Alamy

concerned in the management of a company that uses a name the same as or suggesting an association with the company that has gone into liquidation. Infringing s216 IA 1986 constitutes a criminal offence and, under s217 IA 1986, a director is liable for the debts of the second company during the period for which the director managed it.

FAQ

Can action be taken against directors who have contributed to causing a company's insolvency?

Under the IA 1986, a director who is guilty of fraudulent trading (s213 IA 1986) or wrongful trading (s214 IA 1986) may find the court imposing an order to the effect that the director has to make a personal contribution to the assets of the liquidated company. The director, therefore, is being ordered to restore the company's wrongfully depleted assets in order to benefit the company's creditors.

Fraudulent trading occurs where, in the course of the winding up, it appears that any business of the company has been carried on with intent to defraud creditors of the company or for any fraudulent purpose. The liquidator can apply to the court for a declaration that any persons who were knowingly parties to the carrying on of the business in this way be liable to make such contributions to the company's assets as the court thinks proper. Successful actions under s213 IA 1986 are rare for what has to be proved is actual deceit, i.e. conduct that is deliberately and actually dishonest according to the notions of ordinary decent business people. The section is not limited to directors or officers of the company and any person knowingly involved may have action taken against them, e.g. a creditor or an accountant of the company. In *BCCI v Morris (2001)*, the court held that a company's financiers were found to have encouraged the carrying on of a business for a fraudulent purpose.

Section 458 CA 1985 makes it a criminal offence for those engaged in fraudulent trading, although the company does not have to be insolvent for proceedings under s458 CA 1985 to be brought.

Wrongful trading was introduced as a means of overcoming the difficulties of establishing fraudulent trading under s213 IA 1986. Under s214 IA 1986, where a company has gone into insolvent liquidation, a director or shadow director of the company who, at some time before the commencement of the winding up of the company, knew or ought reasonably to have known that the there was no reasonable prospect that the company would avoid going into insolvent liquidation can be held liable by the court to make such contribution to the company's assets as the court thinks proper. The court will not make a declaration where it is satisfied that the director concerned took every step that he ought to have taken with a view to minimising the loss to the creditors. The court is required to take into account the director's own knowledge, skill and experience and the skill and experience that can be expected from a reasonably diligent director. In *Re Produce Marketing Consortium Ltd (1989)*, two directors continued to run a fruit importing business where they ought to have known that there was no chance of the company remaining solvent. Although the directors did not know that the company was in a grave financial state, they were held liable under s214 IA 1986 as they should have obtained the necessary information to determine the company's financial position as would have been expected of any reasonable director with an appropriate level of general knowledge, skill and experience. They had not acted fraudulently or dishonestly, but continued to trade in the unrealistic hope that the company would be able to trade out of its difficulties. The directors were ordered to make a contribution of £75,000 plus interest, for which they were jointly and severally liable.

Fair dealing provisions

Certain transactions that are close to a company's onset of insolvency can be avoided under the IA 1986. These were dealt with in Chapter 15, in relation to debentures and charges.

Website summary

The book's website contains the following material in respect of Part 4:

- PowerPoint slides containing relevant information from each chapter to help with revision
- Four additional questions with answers per chapter
- Quiz containing 10 multiple-choice questions for each part
- Biannual update bulletins to the book, which will consist of brief details of any major common law, statutory and constitutional developments affecting the currency of the book

PART FIVE

Consumer, employment and agency law

This part deals with a number of more specialist areas of law, namely:

- *Consumer protection*: consumers, i.e. individuals acting in a non-business capacity, are given special legal protection against sharp practices by businesses. Failure to comply with consumer protection legislation can have serious consequences for businesses

- *Employment*: most businesses need to employ staff. Employees – like consumers – are given special legal protection. Failure to comply with employment legislation can have serious consequences for businesses

- *Agency*: businesses that are legal persons, such as companies, can only carry out their activities through human agents, such as directors and employees. They may also appoint other types of agent to act on their behalf, such as recruitment agents. These relationships are governed by special principles based on agency law

Although these topics are more specialised than say, contract law, they are still relevant to a wide range of businesses. They will broaden your understanding of topics such as contract, tort and company law. You may also find that knowledge of these topics is useful in your own dealings with businesses, for example, as a consumer or as an employee.

20 | Consumer protection

Learning objectives

By the end of this chapter, you should be able to explain:

- **What is normally meant by the term 'consumer'**

- **Why consumers need special protection from certain business practices**

- **The pros and cons of different approaches to consumer protection, ranging from criminal offences to voluntary schemes**

- **The protection offered by legislation on trade descriptions, consumer credit, product liability and unfair contract terms**

- **The role played by consumer regulators such as the Office of Fair Trading and consumer representative bodies, such as Which? (formerly the Consumers Association)**

Introduction

'Consumer protection' refers to legal measures that are intended to give special rights to consumers. For the purposes of this chapter, the term 'consumer' is generally used to mean an individual (i.e. a natural person, not a legal person such as a company) who is buying goods or services for his own private use, rather than for any business-related purpose. However, as explained later, there are several pieces of consumer protection legislation that, although intended primarily to help consumers, are capable of assisting businesses as well as individuals.

Any business that sells to consumers needs to ensure that it complies with relevant consumer protection law. Failure to do so could lead to any or all of the following:

- prosecution for criminal offences

- investigation or enforcement action by consumer regulators

- legal action from consumers seeking damages.

Why do consumers need protection?

Historically, English law treated consumers in the same way as businesses. The general rule was **'caveat emptor'**, which is Latin for 'let the buyer beware'; this meant that the buyer was expected to look out for himself and was given no special protection. However, unlike many businesses, consumers do not necessarily know much about what they are buying and are often in a poor position to negotiate a better deal from the seller. This imbalance provides an obvious opportunity for unscrupulous businesses to exploit the weakness and ignorance of many consumers for their own benefit. As a result, Parliament and the European Union have intervened with legislation designed to protect consumers from sharp practices. Businesses, by way of contrast, are still generally expected to look out for themselves.

Consumer protection: an overview

Although consumer protection is a relatively recent phenomenon, there is already enough UK and EU legislation on the subject to fill several volumes. As a result, this chapter does not attempt to cover all law relating to consumer protection. Instead, it concentrates on a selected range of measures that are used to illustrate the various different approaches to consumer protection:

- making certain types of conduct a *criminal offence*
- requiring businesses to obtain *licences* in order to carry out certain activities
- imposing additional *liability* on businesses so that it is easier for consumers to sue them for unacceptable performance
- preventing businesses from relying on *unfair contract terms*
- allowing *regulators and/or consumer representative bodies* to take action against businesses on behalf of consumers
- encouraging businesses to sign up to *voluntary schemes* designed to protect consumers.

Note: the sections of this chapter on the Consumer Credit Act 1974 assume that the legislation has been amended by the Consumer Credit Bill, which, at the time of writing (January 2006), was before Parliament.

Criminal conduct

One way of deterring businesses from engaging in practices that may be detrimental to consumers is to make the conduct in question a criminal offence; any business that fails to comply risks being prosecuted in the criminal courts. Prosecutions for offences relating to consumer protection are usually brought by local trading standards departments. The sanction is usually a fine, although in more serious cases, the individuals responsible (e.g. sole traders, partners or, in the case of a company, directors or employees) may be given prison sentences. If the business has a high profile, adverse publicity may also result – as illustrated by the Ryanair case highlighted in the 'Reality check' textbox.

Reality check

Ryanair prosecuted for misleading prices

Don't forget to add the tax

In March 2005 budget airline Ryanair was fined £24,000 for breaching section 20 of the Consumer Protection Act 1987, which makes it a criminal offence to give misleading price indications to consumers in the course of a business. The airline had failed to indicate that prices for various airfares featured on its website were exclusive of taxes such as airport tax and VAT; this made the prices misleading, because, in reality, customers would have to pay significantly more than the advertised sum. The case was reported in a number of newspapers at the time, demonstrating the adverse publicity that can result from this type of offence.

Examples of criminal offences

The Ryanair case provides an example of how it may be a criminal offence to give a misleading price indication. Other examples of criminal offences in the field of consumer protection include:

- *Misleading descriptions*: under the Trade Descriptions Act 1968, it is an offence for a business to apply a false description to goods (section 1), supply goods carrying a false description (also section 1) or make a false statement regarding the provision of services (section 14). In contrast to the position regarding misleading price indications under the Consumer Protection Act 1987, the false description or statement does not have to be made to a consumer. The Trade Descriptions Act therefore protects businesses as well as consumers. In practice, however, prosecutions tend to be brought where the products or services in question were aimed primarily at consumers.

- *Product safety*: under Regulation 20 of the General Product Safety Regulations 2005 (which implement an EU directive), it is an offence for a business to place a product on the market that is intended for consumers or likely to be used by consumers and that is not safe. The level of safety required is determined by various criteria set out in the regulations and varies according to the product in question. Section 10 of the Consumer Protection Act 1987 contains a similar offence relating to supply of unsafe products.

What the prosecution must prove

For some criminal offences, it is necessary to prove the defendant's state of mind at the time of the offence; in relation to murder, for example, the prosecution must show not only that the defendant killed someone, but that the killing was intentional. However, for less serious offences, liability may be strict. This means that the prosecution only needs to prove that the defendant committed the act prohibited by the offence; there is no need to prove the defendant's state of mind (sometimes referred to by its Latin name of **mens rea**).

The offences under section 1 of the Trade Descriptions Act 1968 are **strict liability** offences. This means that the prosecution only needs to prove that the defendant either applied a false description to the goods or supplied goods carrying a false description. Whether the defendant actually *intended* to mislead consumers is irrelevant. If the prosecution is able to establish that the offence has been committed, it is up to the defendant to show that – although there was a false description of goods – this was due to a mistake or factors beyond his control and he had taken all reasonable precautions to prevent the false description being applied.

The offence in section 14 of the Trade Descriptions Act 1968, however, is not a strict liability offence. The prosecution must therefore prove that:

- a false statement was made about services and
- the defendant either knew the statement was false or did not care whether it was true or false (this is known as the mens rea of the offence).

The requirement for the prosecution to show the defendant's state of mind can make this offence significantly more difficult to prove than the strict liability offences just described.

> **QUESTION 1** Why doesn't the law criminalise all practices that may be harmful to consumers? Can you think of any disadvantages of the criminal law approach to consumer protection?

Licensing

For certain activities involving the supply of services to consumers, it is necessary to obtain a licence from the government. That licence may be withdrawn if the business in question is found to have engaged in practices that are harmful to consumers.

For example, a furniture store run by a sole trader that wants to allow its customers to buy furniture on credit will need to obtain a licence under the Consumer Credit Act 1974 (CCA); if the sole trader offers credit without a licence he will be committing a criminal offence. In order to obtain the licence in the first place, the sole trader must prove to the **Office of Fair Trading** (OFT), which is responsible for enforcing the CCA, that he is a 'fit and proper person' to provide credit to consumers. For example, the licence may be refused if the OFT has evidence that, in the past, he has been involved in fraudulent, dishonest or violent conduct or has breached consumer protection law. Once granted, the licence may be withdrawn if the store owner fails to comply with the CCA or the terms of the licence. The effectiveness of this sanction is discussed in the FAQ textbox.

Scope of the CCA

The CCA applies to a wide range of credit facilities, including personal loans, credit cards, bank overdrafts, 'buy now pay later' deals and hire purchase (i.e. where the customer rents the goods but with an option to purchase them later).

FAQ

How effective is the threat of withdrawal of CCA licences in practice?

Where the main activity of the business is lending money to consumers, the business cannot carry on without a licence – so the threat of withdrawal is likely to be very effective. For a business such as the furniture store discussed earlier, withdrawal of a consumer credit licence may be less of a threat, because the business's main activity is the sale of furniture (for which no licence is required). However, if the store cannot offer credit, it will be likely to lose sales, because items of furniture are relatively expensive and a fair proportion of potential customers are likely to want to buy on credit. (The OFT also has the power to impose a range of other sanctions for failure to comply with CCA licences, including fines.)

These are known as **regulated consumer credit agreements**. However, loans secured against land, such as mortgages, are not covered by the CCA (they are regulated under separate arrangements enforced by the Financial Services Authority). The CCA also applies to agreements lasting for at least 3 months under which goods are hired or rented. An example would be an agreement for hire of a television set for 6 months (but an agreement to hire a car for a month would *not* be covered). These are known as **regulated consumer hire agreements**.

For many years the CCA only applied to agreements involving credit of up to £25,000 between a lender and either an individual or a partnership; this meant that as well as protecting consumers, it also protected some businesses such as sole traders and partnerships. The £25,000 limit has been removed but the class of persons protected by the CCA has been narrowed; it now applies only to agreements with individuals, a partnership of up to three partners or an unincorporated association. However, agreements involving credit of more than £25,000 provided to sole traders, partnerships of up to three partners and unincorporated associations are exempt from the CCA. This exemption is intended to preserve the protection of the CCA for smaller businesses taking out loans of £25,000 or less while excluding larger businesses. Limited companies do not enjoy any protection under the CCA (even limited companies that employ three people or fewer).

How the CCA protects consumers

In addition to the licensing system (which should mean that only businesses that are 'fit and proper persons' are able to offer credit to consumers), the CCA includes specific measures designed to protect consumers against the following potentially harmful practices:

- *Confusing 'small print'*: regulated agreements must be in writing and follow a special format. Among other things, this format is designed to make it clear to consumers how much they will have to pay and what may happen if they do not pay on time. If the credit provider fails to comply with these requirements, the agreement may be unenforceable; this may mean that the provider cannot reclaim the money lent to the consumer (see **Wilson v First County Trust (2003)**, highlighted in the 'Reality check' textbox).

Reality check

Wilson v First County Trust

Lender pays heavy price for non-compliant agreement

In *Wilson v First County Trust (2003)*, Mrs Wilson pawned her car in order to borrow £5000 from First County Trust. She repaid the loan and First County returned the car to her. However, Mrs Wilson then applied to court, arguing that the loan agreement had been unenforceable because it did not comply with the requirements of the CCA. This was because First County had included the £250 charge for arranging the loan in the total amount being borrowed, suggesting that she was borrowing £5250; in fact, the agreement should have said that Mrs Wilson was borrowing £5000 and would be charged £250 + interest in order to do so. The House of Lords agreed with this analysis and ruled that – even though the mistake was relatively minor – First County was obliged to repay the loan (together with interest payments and charges) to Mrs Wilson. Among other things, First County argued that its inability to enforce the agreement amounted to a breach of its rights under the European Convention on Human Rights (specifically, Article 1 of Protocol 1 on the right to property). The House of Lords rejected this, ruling that it was perfectly reasonable for Parliament to deprive lenders of the ability to enforce credit agreements in order to provide a strong incentive for them to comply with the CCA. However, the CCA has since been amended to allow the courts to use theiir discretion to decide whether lenders should be penalised in this way.

- *Pressure selling outside business premises*: some credit providers market their products by visiting consumers in their homes. While home visits can be advantageous for consumers who are not very mobile, such as the elderly or disabled, the danger is that the home environment lulls some consumers into a false sense of security; this may be exploited by some businesses. The CCA, therefore, provides that any agreement concluded away from business premises is subject to a 'cooling-off period' of 5 days; if the consumer has second thoughts about the agreement during this period, he is free to cancel it.

- *Very high rates of interest*: some credit providers seek to take advantage of consumers who are unable to obtain credit elsewhere by imposing very high rates of interest. The CCA allows consumers in this position to apply to court to have the interest rate reduced to a more reasonable level.

- *Misleading advertising*: the CCA also regulates the types of advertisement that credit providers may engage in. For example, interest rates must be calculated in accordance with detailed provisions (set out in delegated legislation) designed to enable consumers to make valid comparisons between the rates offered by different providers.

Reform

At the time of writing, the government was in the final stages of a major reform of the CCA, and this section states the law as amended by the reform programme. The European Commission had also proposed a directive on consumer credit, which is designed to ensure that consumers benefit from the same levels of protection throughout the EU. More material on these reforms and about consumer credit generally can be found on the companion website.

Imposing additional liability

Another way of protecting consumers is to make it easier for them to take legal action when they are the victims of harmful practices by businesses. One example of this approach is Part 1 of the Consumer Protection Act 1987 (CPA). It implements an EU directive that was mainly intended to make it easier for consumers to bring claims against businesses for personal injuries or damage to property caused by defective products.

How the CPA makes it easier to claim

Before the CPA, a person who had been injured by a defective product could normally only bring a claim where:

- There had been a breach of contract by the supplier of the product (in which case the claim would be based on contract law – probably a breach of the implied term of satisfactory quality, which requires products to be safe, as discussed in Chapter 6.

- Or the supplier of the product had breached a duty of care in negligence (in which case the claim would be based on tort – see Chapter 11).

If a consumer claims under the CPA, however, he only needs to prove that the product was defective and he was injured by it. Once these facts are established, it is up to the defendant to show that it is covered by a limited range of defences set out in the legislation (see later) – otherwise it will be liable to pay damages to the consumer (based on the tort of breach of statutory duty, rather than the tort of negligence). Liability under the CPA is referred to as strict liability, because there is no need to prove that the defendant was at fault. The concept of strict liability has already been explained in the discussion of criminal offences relevant to consumer protection, but note that Part 1 of the CPA is concerned with civil, not criminal, liability.

The CPA also makes it easier for consumers to obtain compensation because it allows them to sue a wider range of defendants. These include the producer of the product, any person who imports the product into the EU and 'own branders' who apply their brand name to a product they themselves did not actually produce.

Defences under the CPA

Although liability under the CPA is strict, there are a number of defences to such claims, including the following:

- The product was not supplied in the course of a business.

- The defect came into existence after the product had been put into circulation (i.e. it was not a defect inherent in the product but has arisen because of e.g. normal wear and tear).

Reality check

Abouzaid v Mothercare (UK) Ltd

Consumer wins on CPA, fails in negligence

In *Abouzaid v Mothercare (UK) Ltd (2000)*, a 12-year-old boy was injured by a metal buckle on the end of an elasticated strap attached to a sleeping bag intended for use on a use child's buggy. The strap sprang back when pulled and the impact of the metal buckle left him almost blind in one eye. Claims were brought against Mothercare based on both the tort of negligence and the CPA. The claim in negligence failed because it was not reasonably foreseeable that the product would have caused such an injury. The Court of Appeal reached this conclusion because of evidence given by a safety expert that no reasonable producer would have recognised the potential danger in 1990, when the product

was supplied. However, the claim under the CPA succeeded. Once it had been established that the injury was caused by the design of the product, it was up to Mothercare, as producer of the product, to show that it benefited from one of the defences in the legislation. Mothercare relied on the 'state of the art' defence, arguing that the evidence of the safety expert showed that the state of scientific and technical knowledge in 1990 was not sufficient to enable it to identify the danger. The Court of Appeal ruled that the 'state of the art' defence was irrelevant because detection of the defect did not require expert scientific and technical knowledge; it could have been discovered by performing simple practical tests, such as pulling the elasticated strap. The failure to do so meant that the producer had fallen below the standard of safety the public was entitled to expect under the CPA. This shows how the CPA allows consumers to make successful claims for defective products in circumstances where a negligence claim would fail.

- The state of scientific and technical knowledge at the time the product was supplied was not such that a producer of products of the same description could have been expected to discover the defect (this is sometimes known as the **development risks** or **state of the art defence**).

Some commentators have suggested that the state of the art defence makes it too easy for businesses to escape liability under the CPA. However, ***Abouzaid v Mothercare (UK) (2000)***, highlighted in the 'Reality check' textbox suggests that the scope for using the defence to avoid liability may be fairly limited in practice. It also underlines the difference between liability under the CPA and liability in negligence.

> **QUESTION 3** At the time of writing, the CPA had been in force for over 15 years but there had been very few cases where consumers had relied on it. Does this mean that the legislation has been a failure?

Sale of goods legislation

Another example of legislation that seeks to protect consumers by imposing additional liability on business (over and above normal obligations in contract and tort) is provided by amendments made to the Sale of Goods Act 1979 (SGA) and other similar legislation such as the Sale and Supply of Goods to Consumers Regulations 2002. The amendments were required in order to implement an EU directive on certain aspects of the sale of consumer goods and associated guarantees.

They make it easier for consumers to bring claims against businesses for defective goods in the following ways:

- *Manufacturers' guarantees*: historically, most manufacturers' guarantees were not legally binding because there was no privity of contract between the manufacturer and the final customer (who will normally have purchased from a retailer, rather than direct from the manufacturer). As a result of the 2002 regulations, however, manufacturers who choose to offer a guarantee can now be sued by consumers as if there had been a direct contractual relationship between the parties. This is particularly helpful to consumers in situations where the retailer from whom they originally bought the product has gone out of business and cannot therefore be sued for breach of contract; if the product is the subject of a manufacturer's guarantee and is still within the guarantee period, the consumer should be able to obtain redress from the manufacturer instead.

- *Reversing the burden of proof*: in the past, consumers wishing to sue a supplier for breach of the implied terms of satisfactory quality or fitness for purpose in the SGA had to prove that any problem with the goods was due to a defect present at the time of delivery. This was not always easy to establish. For example, if a pair of shoes falls apart a month after they were purchased, the supplier could easily argue that this was due to heavy wear and tear and it would be up to the consumer to show that this was not in fact the case. As a result of changes made by the 2002 regulations, the consumer may now rely on a presumption that, since the shoes have failed to live up to normal expectations of durability (based on the implied term of satisfactory quality), they must have been defective at the time they were bought; it will then be up to the supplier to prove that this is not the case. The presumption applies for 6 months from the date of delivery. Such a reversal of the normal burden of proof makes it easier for consumers to bring successful contractual claims for breach of the SGA.

Contract terms

In Chapters 6 and 7, we saw how the Unfair Contract Terms Act 1977 (UCTA), the Sale of Goods Act 1979 (SGA) and the Supply of Goods and Services Act 1982 (SOGASA) protect consumers by means of the following:

- SGA and SOGASA imply terms into most contracts for supply of goods and services setting minimum standards on issues such as the quality of goods supplied (see Chapter 6 for details).

- Sections 6 and 7 UCTA prevent liability for breach of those terms being excluded or limited in any contract between a business and a consumer. UCTA also prevents businesses imposing unreasonable limitations or exclusions of liability on consumers for other breaches of contract (section 3) or for breaches of their duty of care in negligence (section 2(2)). Finally, section 2(1) UCTA prevents businesses seeking to exclude or limit liability for personal injury or death (see Chapter 7 for more detail).

All these measures are examples of legislation that seeks to protect consumers by regulating the contract terms used by businesses. They work by preventing businesses from relying on such terms in order to defeat claims by consumers.

However, UCTA, SGA and SOGASA only regulate a limited range of terms. They do not, for example, allow a consumer to challenge a clause stating that a business can keep the whole of a £1000 deposit if the consumer cancels the contract 6 months in advance, even though the costs incurred by the business as a result of the cancellation are only £100; this is because the clause is not concerned with liability or the terms implied by SGA/SOGASA. However, such a clause (together with most other clauses commonly found in consumer contracts) could be challenged under the Unfair Terms in Consumer Contracts Regulations 1999 (UTCCR).

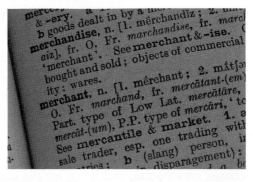

Unfair Terms in Consumer Contracts Regulations

The UTCCR apply to any term in a consumer contract that has not been individually negotiated. Any such term must be:

- fair (unless the term is a **core term**) and
- written in plain, intelligible language (even if the term is a core term).

These requirements, together with the concepts of core terms and 'individually negotiated terms', are now explained in more detail.

Terms that do not comply with the requirement of fairness and/or plain intelligible language cannot be enforced against consumers. Businesses including them in their contracts may also be investigated by the Office of Fair Trading (see later section, headed 'Regulators and consumer bodies').

Core terms and individually negotiated terms

The UTCCR do not apply to terms that are core terms or that have been individually negotiated. A core term is one that sets out the price of the goods or services or is concerned with describing the 'main subject matter of the contract', i.e. in most cases, terms that simply set out what is being provided by the supplier. In practice, most contracts only contain a relatively small number of core terms; the vast majority are therefore capable of being challenged under the UTCCR.

Similarly, it is rare for a term to be regarded as 'individually negotiated', because the vast majority of consumer transactions are based on standard terms. In order to be individually negotiated, the term would generally have to be based on suggestions from the consumer; merely allowing the consumer to choose between several different sets of terms written by the supplier would not normally be sufficient.

The UTCCR and UCTA: different definitions of consumer

The UTCCR define a 'consumer' as 'any natural person who ... is acting for purposes outside his trade or profession'. This means that companies cannot benefit from protection under the UTCCR because they are artificial, legal persons, *not* natural persons. It also means that a sole trader who buys goods or services for use in his business cannot benefit from the UTCCR (because he would not be acting 'outside his trade or profession').

UCTA, by contrast, says that a person 'deals as a consumer' if he did not make the contract in the course of a business or if he did not hold himself out as doing so. Unlike the UTCCR, there is no requirement for the consumer to be a natural person. This means that – perhaps somewhat surprisingly – companies may be consumers for the purposes of UCTA. Even more surprisingly, the definition of consumer in UCTA means that a business may be regarded as a consumer if, for example, it buys a product that is not integral to its business and that is only purchased on an occasional basis; see the case study textbox.

Finally, note that UCTA and the UTCCR only apply where one party (usually the buyer) is a consumer (as earlier defined) and the other party (usually the supplier) is acting in a business capacity. For example, if the agreement is between two individuals, both of whom are acting in a private, non-business capacity, neither UCTA nor the UTCCR will apply. This means that in principle, the parties are free to agree whatever terms they like.

> **QUESTION 4** Are the definitions of 'consumer' in UCTA and the UTCCR consistent with the approach in the Consumer Credit Act 1974 and the product liability provisions of Part 1 of the Consumer Protection Act 1987?

The UTCCR and fairness

In ***Director General of Fair Trading v First National Bank (2001)***, the House of Lords said that the test of fairness in the UTCCR required consideration of two criteria:

- Whether the term had been presented in a clear and straightforward manner (sometimes referred to as the requirement of **good faith**).
- Whether the term gave rise to a significant imbalance in favour of the supplier.

Businesses can sometimes be consumers under UCTA

In ***R&B Customs Brokers v United Dominions Trust Ltd (1988)***, a company had bought a car for one of its directors, partly for business use and partly for his own private use. The Court of Appeal ruled that the company was dealing as a consumer under UCTA. It said that the transaction was not integral to the company's business because buying cars did not form part of its core business activity and it did not purchase them on a regular basis. Although the Court of Appeal recently affirmed this approach in ***Feldaroll Foundry plc v Hermes Leasing (2004)***, it has been much criticised as giving businesses more protection than they require. The Law Commission has recommended that the definition of consumer in UCTA should be changed so that businesses do not benefit from legal protections that were intended primarily to help individuals buying in a private capacity.

In practice, it is the second of these criteria that most commonly leads to a finding that a term is unfair; the requirement of good faith is normally only relevant where the supplier has failed to draw sufficient attention to a particularly onerous term or has said something misleading about what it actually means.

[You can read more about the *First National Bank* case (which concerned a number of quite complex factual and legal issues) on the companion website, together with additional materials on the UTCCR generally such as links to guidance provided by the Office of Fair Trading (OFT). Further guidance on what may be an unfair term is provided by a number of examples set out in Schedule 2 of the UTCCR, which you can also access on the companion website.]

The practical application of the fairness test is best illustrated by the examples in the 'Reality check' textbox, which are taken from OFT guidance based on actual investigations of unfair terms. However, note that decisions of the OFT on unfair terms do not set binding precedents and may be challenged in the courts (which is what gave rise to the *First National Bank* case).

Reality check

Examples of unfair terms in consumer contracts

'In the event of a dispute over any of the terms of this contract, [the mobile phone company] reserves the right to disconnect [you].'

The OFT insisted on the deletion of this term because it would have allowed the mobile phone company to stop performing the service that it had promised to provide without paying any compensation to the consumer or refunding any charges paid in advance. It also allowed the mobile phone company to disconnect the consumer in circumstances where the consumer might have a perfectly justifiable complaint. It therefore resulted in a significant imbalance between the supplier and the consumer.

'You can terminate this contract ... if you give us one month's written notice. We can terminate this contract at any time by giving you a minimum 7 days' written notice.'

This term, which was in a contract for provision of a fixed-line telephone service, was found to be unfair because it gave the supplier much more favourable cancellation rights than the consumer.

The OFT insisted on its being redrafted to give the parties equal cancellation rights.

'This car wash is used entirely at owner's risk.'

The OFT insisted on deletion of this term because it attempted to exclude liability for death and personal injury and negligence by the car wash operator. It could also have been challenged under UCTA.

'The deposit shall be non-returnable.'

The OFT insisted on deletion of this term, which was in a contract for supply of double-glazing. It would have allowed the supplier to retain the deposit if the consumer decided to cancel the contract, whatever the surrounding circumstances. In the OFT's view, such a clause would only be fair if the amount of the deposit corresponded to the amount of the supplier's loss at the time of the cancellation. For example, if the supplier had already started to make the windows and could not sell them to another customer (because they were being tailor made to the original customer's specifications), then it would be fair for the supplier to retain the amount that it had spent on manufacture (but not necessarily the whole of the deposit). However, if it had not started manufacture, then it might have suffered no loss at all, in which case it would be unfair for the supplier to retain any of the deposit.

Plain intelligible language

The UTCCR also require terms (including core terms) to be expressed in plain, intelligible language. This means that even terms that meet the test for fairness may be unenforceable if they are difficult for someone who is not a lawyer to understand. For example, some of specialist legal terminology, such as many of the words and phrases you have had to learn in your study of business law, is unlikely to meet this requirement unless someone who had never studied law would know what you meant. In other cases, the clause may simply be written in a rather impenetrable, technical style, such as the example given in the following textbox (which is taken from the OFT's guidance).

Reality check

Plain intelligible language under the UTCCR

'This agreement ... shall, subject to Clauses 7 and 8, continue for a minimum term of 15 months inclusive of the 90-day notice period referred to in Clause 8(c).'

This is an example of the sort of clause one would expect to find in a business-to-business contract where both parties were being advised by lawyers, who are experienced at making sense of relatively technical drafting. The OFT required the clause to be redrafted so that it stated clearly how long the agreement was supposed to last, without the need for the consumer to refer to all the other clauses mentioned in the original version.

QUESTION 5 In what ways do the UTCCR give consumers greater protection than UCTA?

Regulators and consumer bodies

One of the problems with consumer protection legislation is that consumers themselves are not always in a good position to take advantage of it. For example, many disputes over consumer transactions do not involve sufficient amounts of money to justify the time, expense and stress involved in court action (even using a relatively simple, inexpensive procedure such as the small claims court). Even where the amounts at stake are substantial, consumers may feel that they are at serious risk of being 'outgunned' by lawyers acting for the business they are attempting to sue. This means that there is a real risk of consumer protection measures proving ineffective because businesses know that if they fail to comply, there is little that consumers can do in practice.

In order to correct this imbalance, Parliament and the EU have empowered regulators, such as the Office of Fair Trading (OFT) and local authority trading standards departments, to take action to ensure that consumers are protected. The most striking manifestation of this is the ability for the OFT and various other regulators to obtain **Stop Now Orders** to prevent breaches of consumer protection legislation. Parliament and the EU have also recognised the importance of groups such as Which? (formerly the Consumers' Association) in helping consumers 'stand up for their rights'.

Stop Now Orders

The OFT (together with trading standards departments and a number of other regulators concerned with particular sectors, such as the Financial Services Authority) has power to enforce a wide range of consumer protection legislation, including the UTCCR (see earlier). If it receives a complaint from a consumer about a breach of consumer protection legislation, it will usually seek voluntary undertakings from the business concerned not to repeat its behaviour. However, if the business in question refuses to comply, the OFT can apply to court under Part 8 of the Enterprise Act 2002 for a special type of injunction known as a 'Stop Now Order'.

If the business continues to break the law after such an order has been issued, it will be in contempt of court; this means it can be fined and any individuals involved could be sent to prison. The OFT obtained its first Stop Now Orders in April 2002, when injunctions were issued against four individuals in the Manchester area who had been involved in serious, repeated breaches of consumer protection legislation over the supply of fitted kitchens.

Consumer representative bodies

The Enterprise Act 2002 enables the Secretary of State for Trade and Industry to give special status to bodies such as Which? (formerly the Consumers' Association) to seek Stop Now Orders on behalf of consumers generally. This means that if the OFT or other regulators are not prepared to act, Which? and other so-called **designated consumer representative bodies** can apply to court instead. If it were felt that designated consumer representative bodies were not using their powers responsibly, the Secretary of State has the power to remove their special status.

Parliament has also tried to involve such bodies in the operation of consumer protection legislation by allowing them to make so-called '**super-complaints**' to the OFT. The Enterprise Act 2002 provides that, when the OFT receives a 'super-complaint', it has 90 days in which to consider what action to take. For example, in 2002, a super-complaint from the National Association of Consumer Advice Bureaux led to a detailed OFT investigation into doorstep selling, which resulted in various recommendations for changes to consumer protection legislation in this area. However, it is important to note that consumer representative bodies are not given the same status as regulators in either UK or EU legislation; their main role is seen as being to help the legal framework for protecting consumers work better.

QUESTION 6 What are the advantages of involving consumer bodies more closely in the operation of consumer protection legislation?

Voluntary schemes

So far we have been looking at how consumers may be protected by the law. In some sectors, however, voluntary schemes play a very important role. For example, consumer protection in relation to misleading advertising claims (other than broadcast advertising) is achieved largely by the British Code of Advertising, Sales Promotion and Direct Marketing (known as the CAP Code). The code is devised, administered and paid for by the advertising industry. Compliance with the code, which is administered by the Advertising Standards Authority (ASA), is achieved in two main ways:

- The ASA monitors a large number of advertisements on a regular basis to check that they are compliant. It also allows advertisers to send their advertisements for 'pre-vetting' – so if an advertiser is concerned about breaching the code, it can take action to make this less likely.
- The ASA also administers a complaints scheme that can result in advertisers being instructed to stop using a particular advertisement.

Most advertisers comply with the ASA's rulings but if they fail to do so, the ASA can:

- demand that future advertisements are submitted for 'pre-vetting'
- request publishers and media owners to refuse more space for an advertisement until it has been changed and ask trade bodies to stop giving financial discounts and other privileges to the advertiser
- refer the advertiser to the Office of Fair Trading (OFT), which can seek a Stop Now Order based on the Control of Misleading Advertisements Regulations 1988 to prevent the same claims being made in future advertisements.

[You can find out more about this scheme on the companion website.]

QUESTION 7 What are the main advantages of the voluntary approach to consumer protection in the advertising sector as compared with an approach based on legislation?

Answers to in-text questions

QUESTION 1 Why doesn't the law criminalise all practices that may be harmful to consumers? Can you think of any disadvantages of the criminal law approach to consumer protection?

Criminalising certain types of conduct can be highly effective, as it sends a strong message to businesses that the conduct in question is viewed by the state as a serious breach of the law. However, there are many practices that can be harmful to consumers and not all of them are equally serious. If they were all made criminal offences, it would be impossible for trading standards officers to prosecute all the potential offenders and it is possible that many businesses would become blasé about the risk of committing criminal offences. Making something a criminal offence is therefore only an effective approach to consumer protection if it is applied relatively sparingly to key issues such as the description, price and safety of goods and services. One important disadvantage of the criminal law approach to consumer protection is that it does nothing to compensate consumers who may have suffered loss as a result of the criminal conduct; this is because the purpose of the criminal law is to punish and deter, not to provide redress.

> **QUESTION 2** What is the main advantage of the licensing approach to consumer protection as compared with the criminal law approach? Why isn't the licensing approach used more widely?

The licensing approach allows the state to filter out at least some of the businesses that are considered unsuitable to offer particular services to consumers; it therefore helps to prevent such businesses ever being given the chance to harm consumers. The criminal law approach, in contrast, does not allow any controls to be exerted over who is offering particular services; it merely acts as a deterrent to businesses who might otherwise be tempted to engage in practices that are harmful to consumers.

Having said that, the licensing approach is not suitable for wide application because it is quite expensive to operate; taxpayers must pay for organisations such as the OFT to monitor and enforce the regime and businesses must pay for the costs of obtaining licences and complying with relevant legislative requirements. As a result, licensing tends to be reserved for fairly specific activities (such as consumer credit), where there is perceived to be a serious risk of harmful practices unless businesses are subject to quite strict controls.

> **QUESTION 3** At the time of writing, the CPA had been in force for over 15 years but there had been very few cases where consumers had relied on it. Does this mean that the legislation has been a failure?

Possibly – but not necessarily. When the European Commission reviewed the EU Product Liability Directive (on which the CPA is based) in 2000, it decided that there was not enough evidence of problems with claims to justify further changes designed to make it even easier for consumers to sue. While the small number of cases could be seen as a sign that the CPA does not make it easy enough for consumers to claim, there may be other explanations for this state of affairs, such as:

- *Consumers prefer to sue in contract*: where consumers have a contract with the seller, they may prefer to claim in contract rather than rely on the CPA. This is because – as you should be aware from your study of contract and tort – it may be possible to claim a higher level of damages for breach of contract than for torts such as breach of statutory duty under the CPA.

- *Businesses prefer to settle*: as a result of the CPA, businesses may be more inclined to settle claims for defective products (because they know that if the case comes to court, the CPA will make it more difficult for them to defeat the claim). If true, this suggests that the legislation has, in fact, been quite successful.

- *Business are more safety conscious*: businesses are increasingly sensitive to the potentially disastrous bad publicity that can result from defective products; as a result, they take greater care when designing products and prefer to recall products where there is any suggestion of a problem. A recent example of this is the recall of contaminated soft drinks by Britvic, outlined in Chapter 7; while the drinks were not thought to be sufficiently seriously contaminated to cause anyone lasting harm, the company was clearly not prepared to take the risk of leaving them in the market.

> **QUESTION 4** Are the definitions of 'consumer' in UCTA and the UTCCR consistent with the approach in the Consumer Credit Act 1974 and the product liability provisions of Part 1 of the Consumer Protection Act 1987?

Neither the Consumer Credit Act 1974 (CCA) nor Part 1 of the Consumer Protection Act 1987 contains any definition of the term 'consumer'. However, like UCTA, the CCA is capable of assisting businesses in certain limited circumstances; the UTCCR, by way of contrast, cannot be used by anyone acting in a business capacity. The trend in more recent legislation, particularly at EU level, has been to adopt the definition in the UTCCR, with the result that it is now increasingly rare for consumer protection measures to be capable of assisting businesses.

> **QUESTION 5** In what ways do the UTCCR give consumers greater protection than UCTA?

There are three main ways in which the UTCCR give consumers greater protection than UCTA:

- They protect consumers against a very wide range of potentially unfair clauses, not just attempts by businesses to limit or exclude their liability (as is the case with UCTA).
- They require clauses in consumer contracts to be drafted in plain English (UCTA does not require this).
- Consumers can complain to powerful regulators such as the OFT, who are under a duty to enforce the UTCCR (see under the heading 'Regulators and consumer bodies').

Having said that, the UTCCR only protect consumers against unfair terms in agreements; they do not protect consumers against other practices that may be harmful to consumers, such as high-pressure sales tactics. However, in 2005 the EU passed a directive intended to offer consumers similarly broad protection in relation to unfair commercial practices of this type. [You can find out more about this on the companion website.]

QUESTION 6 What are the advantages of involving consumer bodies more closely in the operation of consumer protection legislation?

Consumer bodies are often quicker to detect problems 'on the ground' than regulators, because they make it their business to know about practices that may be harmful to consumers. They also help to filter out the less deserving complaints from the ones that merit further investigation. Without input from consumer bodies, regulators would probably have to spend considerably more time and money analysing complaints and working out which ones to investigate in more detail.

QUESTION 7 What are the main advantages of the voluntary approach to consumer protection in the advertising sector as compared with an approach based on legislation?

The main advantages of the voluntary approach (as compared with legislation) are as follows:

- It is more flexible than legislation; this allows advertisers more creative freedom while enabling the rules to be changed more quickly in response to new developments.
- Unlike many other areas of consumer protection (where there is an increasing reliance on regulators), the cost of enforcement in a voluntary system is borne by industry itself rather than the taxpayer.
- As a general rule, it is easier to get advertisers to comply with a system over which they feel they have at least some control than with a set of rules laid down by Parliament.

However, although the voluntary approach has much to commend it, legislation – in the form of the Control of Misleading Advertisements Regulations 1988 – is still required as a last resort, should an advertiser refuse to comply. Advertisers also know that if they cannot make a success of self-regulation, Parliament will probably intervene with a system of regulation that relies far more on legislation (and may well be less to their liking).

Aspects of employment law

By the end of this chapter, you should be able to explain:

- **The nature and scope of the employer/employee relationship**

- **The criminal and civil liability of employers in accordance with health and safety law**

- **The statutory protection of employees in respect of equal opportunities and anti-discrimination legislation**

Introduction

In contract law, we were mainly concerned with how businesses contract with others, such as customers and suppliers. Businesses, however, can also enter into contracts with those they employ. This relationship is governed by the same contractual principles as apply to contracts generally. However, given the nature of the relationship between employer and employee, general contractual principles are unlikely to provide or maintain equality of bargaining power, job security or equal treatment. To this extent, in order to protect employees within the employment relationship, the **contract of employment** is subject to statutory regulation, so that employees receive greater protection than they would otherwise under the common law. Protection of employees interests is also provided by EU law, such as the Equal Treatment Directive (1977) and the Working Time Directive (1993), and UK employment law has also been influenced by decisions of the European Court of Justice and the European Court of Human Rights.

It is not the intention of this chapter to provide an extensive coverage of employment law but to provide an overview of how businesses are affected by key aspects of the employment relationship, such as pay, dismissal, redundancy, discrimination, and health and safety.

Employment disputes are heard mainly by an employment tribunal, although cases involving general contractual or tortious claims can also be heard in a first-instance court, e.g. claims involving **wrongful dismissal** or personal injuries. An appeal from an employment tribunal lies to the Employment Appeal Tribunal and from there to the Court of

Appeal and the House of Lords. There is further detail on employees bringing a claim in employment law at the end of the chapter.

Contract of employment

A business may be served by employees under a contract of service and by independent contractors under a contract for services. The distinction between an employee and an independent contractor is an important one, since it determines, for instance, the employer's liability in tort for harm caused to third parties. Similarly, an employer has greater legal obligations to an employee than to an independent contractor. These include liability for paying national insurance contributions and sick pay and the responsibility for deducting income tax. An employee may also be entitled to statutory protection against **unfair dismissal** and redundancy. Whether a person is an employee or an independent contractor is a question of fact for the courts to consider in all the circumstances, as we saw in Chapter 12 on the doctrine of vicarious liability.

A contract of employment is not required to be in writing, it can arise simply by word of mouth. However, the Employment Rights Act (ERA) 1996 obliges an employer to provide an employee with a written statement of the key terms of the employee's contract within 2 months of starting work. The statement does not represent all the terms of the contract of employment, but it must include the following:

- the parties' names
- the date of commencement of employment and the date of commencement of **continuous employment**
- a reference to any disciplinary and grievance procedures and the statutory scheme on disciplinary procedures set out in the Employment Act 2002
- particulars of pay, holiday entitlement, hours of work, pension rights and length of notice required to be given by either party
- the title of the employee's job and a brief description of what it involves and the place of work

FAQ

What is the source of the terms of a contract of employment?

The terms of a contract of employment may not be found in a single written document since there may be express and implied terms of a contract of employment. Express terms are those things agreed on by the parties. They are stated usually in a contract of employment as written terms, but the contract can include oral promises as well.

Implied terms, which are prevalent in employment law, arise from custom and practice, works rules, statute, EU law and collective agreements between employers and trade unions. They also arise from the common law, which is an important source of implied terms in a contract of employment, for it is the common law that imposes a number of duties on employers and employees and that forms an essential part of the relationship between the employer and the employee, such as pay, the duty to act in good faith and to provide a safe system of work.

- references to other documents that give detailed explanation and are made available to employees to consult.

Failure to provide **written particulars of employment** entitles the employee to make a reference to an employment tribunal, which can confirm or amend the statement. Any changes to matters specified in the written statement must be notified to the employee within 1 month of the change.

Pay

Employer's duty to pay the employee

It is likely that a contract of employment provides for an express obligation on the part of the employer to pay a salary or wages to the employee. However, in the absence of such an express term, employers are under a common law duty to pay their employees and to reimburse them for any expenses incurred during the course of employment, such as travel and accommodation.

The employer has no right to make deductions from an employee's pay, unless, as with income tax and national insurance contributions, these are authorised by statute or agreed in writing with the employee. In practice, the contract of employment provides for employers to make such deductions.

Apart from common law protection, statute provides that most employees are entitled to a minimum wage under the National Minimum Wage Act (NMWA) 1998. At the time of writing, the minimum rates of pay are £4.20 per hour for adults, £3.50 for young people between 18 and 21 and £3.00 for 16–17 year olds. With some limited exceptions, the NMWA 1998 protects all workers whether or not they work under a contract of employment. HM Revenue and Customs is able to enforce the NMWA 1998 and can serve penalty notices on employers not complying with its provisions. In addition, an employer breaching the NMWA 1998 commits a criminal offence and is liable to a maximum fine of £5000.

Equal pay

Legislation also provides a measure of protection for employees by promoting **equal pay** between men and women within employment. Businesses have to be aware of the need to ensure that women and men receive the same pay for the same work. The protection is provided by the Equal Pay Act (EPA) 1970 whose purpose is to eliminate discrimination between men and women in regard to pay and other terms of their employment contract, e.g. overtime, bonuses, holidays and sick leave.

The **Equal Opportunities Commission**, set up by the EPA 1970, plays an active role in promoting the legislation, offering guidance, assistance and legal support in pursuing cases. A similar role is intended to be provided by the Equality Commission when it comes into existence in 2006, being a merger of the Disability Rights Commission, the Commission for Racial Equality and the Equal Opportunities Commission.

As with anti-discrimination legislation, the EPA 1970 has immediate application to persons entering into any type of employment contract. There are no qualifying provisions, although there are some limited exceptions to its operation. A man or woman may make an application to an employment tribunal at any time while they are doing the job to which the claim relates or within 6 months after the termination of the job.

Equality clauses

The EPA 1970 works by way of placing an implied 'equality clause' into the individual woman's or man's contract requiring that the contract should be equalised in respect of all terms and conditions in any of the following three situations:

- where a woman or man is employed on the 'same work' or work of a 'similar nature' at the workplace
- where a woman or man is employed on work 'rated as equivalent' as determined by a job evaluation scheme
- where a woman or man is employed on work of 'equal value' (subject to determination by an employment tribunal).

Any woman or man who believes they satisfy any of these criteria may apply to an employment tribunal requesting an 'equality clause' be implied into their employment contract. For example, where a woman does like work, or work rated as equivalent to that of a male comparator, her contract should be deemed to include an 'equality clause'. An employee, however, will lose their claim where the employer can show that any inequality was due to a 'genuine material factor' that was not based on sex. Genuine material factors relied on by employers have included location, different responsibilities and economic necessity.

An example of how the provisions of the EPA 1970 work can be seen in the 'Reality check' textbox, which concerns a case involving a claim based on 'same work'.

Reality check

Like work – Shields v E Coomes (Holdings) Ltd (1978)

Miss Shields was employed as a counter hand by her employer's bookmakers in central London on an hourly rate of 92p. A male counter hand was also employed at the shop on the higher rate of £1.06 an hour. The shop was one of nine operated by the company that it considered to be vulnerable to trouble, from the risk of attack on the premises by robbers and from the risk of disturbance from customers in the shop. To guard against these potential dangers, the policy of the company was to employ male counter hands at the nine shops. The main work of the men was the same as that of the women counter hands, but, in addition, they were required to be around when the manager opened the shop as a reinforcement in case of trouble.

An employment tribunal rejected a claim by Miss Shields for equal pay with the male counter hand employed at the shop. The Employment Appeal Tribunal however reversed the tribunal's decision. It held that the tribunal had erred in refusing Miss Shields' claim for equal pay with a male counter hand employed in the same bookmakers' shop. As male counter hands received the same rate, being 14p an hour higher than the female rate, whether or not they exercised the protective and deterrent functions, the EAT held that it was impossible to escape the conclusion that the money differential was due only to the difference of sex and not to any differences of practical importance in relation to terms and conditions. The man was required to perform his duties as protector and deterrent simply because he was a man and not because he was in any way trained in security guard duties. A properly selected and trained woman could have done that part of the job just as well as a man.

Acting faithfully

Employees must act with complete honesty towards their employers in carrying out their contractual duties and employees must not compete with the employer's business. Where the employee's contract requires the employee to work for the employer exclusively, doing any paid work for another employer is a breach of duty. An employee must not disclose confidential information about an employer's business, such as profits, customers, work systems, products or services, neither must an employee make any unauthorised profit from the job, such as a secret commission.

Similarly, employers are under a duty not to undermine the trust and confidence of the employee, by, for example, indulging in unreasonable and abusive conduct towards the employee. In *Isle of Wight Tourist Board v Coombes (1976)* for example, a director within earshot of his personal secretary, said to another employee: 'She is always an intolerable bitch on Monday mornings.' He did not apologise and she later resigned. It was held that his behaviour breached a duty of trust and confidence.

FAQ

What type of conduct by an employee amounts to acting in bad faith?

The duty to act in good faith is based on the notion that an employee should act loyally and honestly in the course of his employment. A recent example can be found in *LC Services Ltd v Brown (2003)*. In this case, a director and employee of a company, who had, during the course of employment, provided an electronic database to a rival company for which he worked, was held to be in breach of duty. He had also removed company documents and copied maintenance procedures for the benefit of the rival company. Another example arose in *Hivac Ltd v Park Royal Scientific Instruments Ltd (1946)* where two employees of a valve manufacturer spent their Sundays working for a rival company. The court granted an injunction preventing the arrangement continuing as they had breached their duty of fidelity.

Health and safety

There are two important considerations in respect of health and safety law. There is the civil liability of employers in failing to provide a safe system of work and there is the possibility of an employer becoming liable under the criminal law for breaching health and safety legislation.

As with other parts of employment law the impact on businesses is a mix of the common law and legislation. Under the civil law, the courts have implied into the contract of employment a duty to ensure the employee's safety and breach of that duty gives rise to liability for breach of contract. Failure by the employer to take reasonable care for the safety of the employee may also render the employer liable in the tort of negligence (see Chapter 11) and breach of safety legislation can lead to a civil action for breach of statutory duty (see Chapter 12).

Health and safety at common law

At common law, there is an implied term of a contract of employment that employers must take reasonable care to provide safe working conditions for their employees. This duty includes employing competent staff, providing safe premises and machinery and providing a safe system of work. As we saw in Chapter 11, whether an employer exercised reasonable care depends on assessing the degree of risk involved, the cost of guarding against the risk and the seriousness of the harm. In ***Hudson v Ridge Manufacturing Co Ltd (1957)***, an employee, who had been reprimanded on previous occasions for horseplay, injured the claimant, a fellow employee in the course of playing a practical joke. The employer was held liable for failing to take proper care of the claimant's safety., The employer was aware that the employee was a potential danger and should have taken adequate steps to control him. In ***Pagono v HGS (1976)***, an employer who failed to maintain vehicles in a safe condition, despite having received complaints from employees, was held liable for failing to provide a safe system of work.

The duty to provide a safe system of work includes providing protective clothing with instructions about its use, setting up safe working procedures and the provision of adequate washing and first aid facilities. Under the Employers' Liability (Defective Equipment) Act 1969, where equipment is defective due to the fault of a third party, such as a manufacturer or repairer, the employer can be held liable, even though the employer was not at fault or could not have known of any defect.

More recently, a failure to provide a safe system of work has arisen in cases where employees have claimed damages for repetitive strain injury or stress-induced mental illness, although not all employees' claims have been successful and the law is continuing to develop in this area (see the FAQ textbox).

The impact on businesses apart from the costs of meeting stress-related awards is that the presence of stress can undermine the workplace and, therefore, affect staff morale and productivity. Businesses need to consider that faults in the management system have often been identified as the causes of stress, arising from poor leadership, inadequate supervision or inadequate training and education.

Health and Safety at Work Act 1974

Under the criminal law, an employer's health and safety duties are set out in health and safety legislation, principally the Health and Safety at Work Act 1974 and related regulations. The justification for imposing criminal liability on businesses for failing to provide for the health and safety of their employees is highlighted in the 'Reality check' textbox.

The Health and Safety at Work Act (HSAWA) 1974 is an enabling act and sets out general responsibilities of employers, subcontractors, the self-employed and employees, as well as suppliers and manufacturers of goods, with respect to health and safety. Health and safety regulations, including codes of practice and those that implement European directives, are made under the HSAWA 1974.

Under the HSAWA 1974, employers must ensure the health, safety and welfare of their employees by:

- providing and maintaining safe plant and systems of work
- making arrangements for the safe use, handling, storage and transport of articles and substances

FAQ

To what extent can employers be held liable for mental illness caused by an unsafe system of work?

The courts are prepared to rule that mental illness (or stress) is a recognised form of harm for which damages are recoverable. In **Walker v Northumberland County Council (1995)**, an employee suffered a nervous breakdown as a result of working under extremely stressful conditions. He sued for damages, claiming breach of duty of care owed by the employer to its employees, which resulted in psychiatric illness. In allowing his claim, the House of Lords stated that there could be recovery for the psychiatric damage caused by a breach of duty of care owed by the employer to its employees and psychiatric harm was to be treated in the same way as if the employer's failure to provide a safe system of work had caused physical harm. In **Johnstone v Bloomsbury Health Authority (1991)** a junior doctor was successful in his claim for damages for stress against his employer for requiring him to work an unrealistic number of hours. His contract of employment provided that he worked 40 hours a week and to be available for a further 48 hours.

Since *Walker v Northumberland County Council (1995)*, a number of cases have been brought on the basis of psychiatric harm. This has caused a considerable financial burden to be placed on businesses and their insurers. However, in 2002, in order to lessen this burden, the Court of Appeal in **Hatton v Sutherland (2002)** set out guidelines in relation to stress-related claims with the intention of reducing the likelihood of such claims being brought by employees. Among other things, the Court of Appeal said that:

- No occupation should be regarded as intrinsically dangerous to mental health.

- Injury to health must be reasonably foreseeable and emotional stress is not recoverable.

- It is reasonable for the employer to assume that the employee can cope with the level of stress normally associated with the job. Employees, therefore, need to bring the issue to the employer's attention and not to be suffering in silence.

- Stress-related illness can come from a number of sources apart from the working environment.

Falling Down: an extreme pursuit of damages by a stressed executive

- providing health and safety information, instruction, training and supervision
- maintaining the place of work, so that it is safe and without risks to health
- providing and maintaining a safe working environment and adequate welfare facilities.

Reality check

The justification for imposing criminal responsibility on employers for health and safety

In theory, resolution of health and safety problems at work should be a matter for shared objectives between management and employees. This is, unfortunately, not always the case. Increasingly, the law is setting minimum standards that must be applied in almost all workplaces and by almost all employers. Such legislation was passed because employers did not always give due attention to the well-being of their employees, without the backing of health and safety legislation and there may be a tendency for employers not to give attention to their responsibilities on health and safety unless these responsibilities are enshrined in law.

Some of the most common reasons why management must take a key responsibility for health and safety at work can be identified as follows:

1 The employing organisation decides what products are to be made and what services are to be delivered. It is management therefore who has the authority to decide how those processes are to be put into effect.

2 Employers have the knowledge and expertise to ensure that appropriate training, instruction and supervision are provided to employees on all matters, including health and safety.

3 Employers can suffer financial penalties through increased insurance premiums, through fines and through claims in the civil courts for compensation if they fail in their duties and neglect responsibilities under health and safety law.

4 Employers have a legal and a moral responsibility toward their employees. A lack of concern in this area may lead to resentment and dissatisfaction among the workforce and to poor employee relations.

Under the Act employers are also under a duty to provide for the safety of visitors and employees are under a duty to take care towards fellow employees. Employers with more than five employees must also prepare a written safety policy and, where appropriate, they must consult safety representatives appointed by recognised trade unions and, where requested by two or more safety representatives, they must set up a safety committee. A safety policy should include a general statement of policy concerning health and safety, the organisation and administration of the policy and safety rules and arrangements or a code of safe practice. Safety policies normally indicate who within the organisation is responsible for health and safety of the workplace and how the policy is to be implemented.

Remedies for breach of the HSAWA 1974

The HSAWA 1974 provided for the creation of the Health and Safety Commission, to administer health and safety law, and the Health and Safety Executive (HSE), to ensure compliance with the legislation through the appointment of inspectors. There are different types of inspector, dealing with factories, agriculture, mines, quarries, nuclear installations and explosives.

HSE inspectors can require improvements in work through the issue of improvement notices or prohibit the continuation of work through prohibition notices until specified improvements are made. Figures for 2001–2002 show that the HSE issued over 11,000 improvement and prohibition notices.

Breaching the HSAWA 1974 is a criminal offence and the HSE has the power to prosecute an employer. Prosecution can be initiated for failure to comply with an improvement notice or a prohibition notice, failure to carry out any of the general duties of the HSAWA 1974 or breaching any health and safety regulations. For the period 2001–2002, 1064 prosecutions were brought by the HSE, of which 84% resulted in a conviction.

Fines imposed on employers in the past have been low; until 1992, the maximum fine that could be imposed on conviction was £2000. This is an area that successive governments have addressed by imposing stiffer penalties on employers who breach health and safety requirements and who do not treat health and safety issues seriously. Currently, depending on the nature of the offence a Magistrates Court can impose a fine up to £20,000. A Magistrates Court also has the power to impose a sentence of up to 6 months' imprisonment for a breach of an improvement or prohibition notice. A Crown Court has the power to impose an unlimited fine or up to 2 years' imprisonment for breach of the HSAWA 1974. To date, the highest fine imposed on a company for breach of health and safety legislation was £15m in 2005 for an offence that occurred in 1999. The fine was imposed on Transco, which had failed to check the state of a gas main under a house in Scotland. The severely corrosive pipe fractured and the resultant explosion killed four members of a family living in the house.

[Further details on health and safety regulations, including the Working Time Regulations 1998, for which the HSE has responsibility, can be found on the companion website.]

Dismissal

The employment relationship can be brought to an end by either party acting in accordance with the terms providing for termination in the contract of employment. Usually, one party will terminate the contract of employment by giving notice. It is also possible for the relationship to come to an end on the basis that the contract has become frustrated. Frustration was discussed in Chapter 8, where we considered the doctrine of frustration as it applies to contracts generally.

Where, the common law determines the termination of an employment protection an employee is unlikely to be protected against an employer operating a 'hire and fire at will' policy, unless the employer failed to give notice in accordance with the contract of employment. At common law an employee dismissed without appropriate notice is able to sue for breach of contract at common law. This is known as wrongful dismissal. Beyond wrongful dismissal, however, in order to protect the employee as the weaker of the two parties to the employment relationship, statutory law provides for the protection of employees in the form of unfair dismissal. The effect of statutory intervention is that there is a legal mechanism allowing for an employer's decision to dismiss an employee to be challenged through an employment tribunal. This area of the law, which has been subject to constant change, is largely governed by the Employment Relations Act (ERA) 1996, as amended.

FAQ

What is wrongful dismissal?

Wrongful dismissal is an action for breach of contract that may be brought by either party where the contract of employment is terminated without the appropriate notice or, in the case of a fixed-term contract, where termination is enforced before the date of completion. Summary dismissal (i.e. dismissal without notice) may be justified, however, but only where the employer can prove that the employee was guilty of gross misconduct, such as theft, fraud, violence or wilful refusal to obey a reasonable order. The notice period for employees is determined by the ERA 1996 and depends on the length of service of the employee, unless a longer period of notice is specified in the contract of employment.

Unfair dismissal

The ERA 1996 provides that an employee has a statutory right not be unfairly dismissed. This means that an employee who believes that his dismissal was unfair can make an application to an employment tribunal for a hearing within 3 months of the termination of the contract.

Not every employee has the right to complain to an employment tribunal. In order to be eligible to claim unfair dismissal, the employee must have been in continuous employment (whether full time or part time) for at least 1 year and not to fall within one of the following categories:

- employees over retirement age
- employees whose contracts of employment require them to work primarily outside Great Britain
- employees on short-term contracts who have waived their rights to claim.

An employee must be able to show that they have been dismissed, but the burden of disproving unfairness lies with the employer. The employer must prove (i) the ground for dismissal and (ii) that in the circumstances the dismissal was fair.

Ground for dismissal

Section 98 ERA 1996 lays down five grounds, any of which may justify dismissal. These are:

- lack of appropriate qualifications or capability to do the job
- the employee's conduct
- the employee was made redundant as the job had ceased to exist
- continuance of employment would result in illegality
- any other substantial reason.

Lack of qualification or capability This ground must relate to the proper performance of the job. In ***Lister v Thom & Sons Ltd (1975)***, Lister was given a job on condition that he obtained an HGV licence. However, he failed the test and was transferred to a fitter's post. Later he was given notice of dismissal. It was held that he had been unfairly dismissed. The failure to obtain a licence had not prevented him from working for the employer in another capacity.

Negligence on the part of an employee may justify dismissal, but a single act of negligence is unlikely to be sufficient grounds for dismissal unless it amounts to gross negligence or endangers the safety of others. Long-term sickness may also make a dismissal fair where the absence of the employee places an unreasonable burden on the employer, but the employer must show that they made proper enquiries, including, where appropriate, seeking medical advice.

Misconduct Misconduct covers such things as lying, fighting, theft, dangerous or careless behaviour, swearing, drinking on duty and refusing to comply with management instructions. The misconduct must be incidental to the job that the employee was employed to do. In ***Thomson v Alloa Motor Co (1983)***, a petrol pump attendant was dismissed after she demolished a petrol pump as a result of careless driving. Her dismissal was held to be unfair, as her driving skill was not relevant to the performance of her job. In ***Moore v C & A Modes (1981)***, a shop assistant was dismissed following her arrest for theft in another shop. Her dismissal was held fair as it was reasonable for the employer to suspect that she might steal property belonging to the business.

Redundancy An employer may need to reduce the size of the workforce, but an employee consequently made redundant may have a statutory entitlement to compensation. This topic is dealt with later in the chapter.

Statutory restriction Under this ground, an employer is claiming that the employee can no longer be legally employed or can no longer legally perform the job. Disqualification from driving is an example, provided driving is part of the job. Dismissal, however, is not automatically fair in such circumstances, as the nature of the job, the length of disqualification, the type of criminal offence and the possibility of redeployment must all be considered. In ***Mathieson v Noble & Sons Ltd (1972)***, a travelling salesman who lost his driving licence arranged for a driver at his own expense to enable the salesman to carry out his duties. His employer, however, dismissed him. It was held that he should not have been dismissed until it could be shown that the arrangement was unworkable.

Some other substantial reason This category covers circumstances that do not fit into any of the other categories. In ***Farr v Hoveringham Gravels Ltd (1972)***, a term in an employee's contract required him to live within reasonable travelling distance of his workplace, as he was sometimes needed to deal with emergencies outside working hours. His employer was held to have fairly dismissed him after he had moved house to an address 44 miles away.

Economic reasons may also be treated as some other substantial reason, provided that the employer can show that such reasons are based on sound business practice.

Fairness of dismissal

Whether a dismissal is fair or unfair is a matter for a tribunal to consider in the circumstances, taking into account the size and administrative resources of the employer and the merits of each case. The tribunal must also consider whether the decision to dismiss the employee fell within the band of reasonable responses that a reasonable employer might have adopted (***Iceland Frozen Foods Ltd v Jones (1983); Post Office Ltd v Foley (2000)***). A tribunal is likely to consider the dismissal unfair if the employer cannot show that it went through the proper procedures and did not act as a reasonable employer would have acted. In fact, s98A(1) ERA 1996 provides that it is unfair automatically for an employer to dismiss an employee without going through one of the dismissal and disciplinary procedures set out in the Employment Act (EA) 2002.

Dismissal is automatically unfair in certain specified circumstances Certain classes of employees, who are vulnerable to victimisation, are automatically treated as unfairly dismissed in certain circumstances. The following employees are entitled to take their case to the tribunal without having to satisfy the requirement of a year's continuous employment:

- employees dismissed in connection with the exercise of **maternity or paternity rights**
- health and safety representatives
- trustees of occupational pension schemes
- representing the workforce in redundancy consultations
- employees dismissed for 'whistleblowing' and employees who have taken legal action against the employer to enforce statutory rights
- employees who have been made redundant
- trade union member or activity
- employees accompanying workers to a disciplinary hearing.

Remedies for unfair dismissal

Where an employment tribunal has determined that the dismissal of an employee was unfair, the tribunal has the power to grant one of the following remedies.

Reinstatement Reinstatement may be ordered at the request of the employee where it is a practicable option. Where such an order is granted, the employee resumes the job under the same pay and conditions as before.

Re-engagement Under this order, the employer may be ordered to find a job for the employee that is reasonably comparable to the post from which the employee was dismissed. This can include a new job with an associated employer.

Compensation An employer may be liable to compensate an employee who is unfairly dismissed. There are two types of award – a basic award and a compensation award. The basic award is intended to protect the employee against losses caused by a break in continuous employment and is calculated in the same way as a statutory redundancy award with reference to the employee's age, current gross weekly pay and years of service. The compensatory award is intended to cover losses arising from the dismissal to the extent that these may be seen as the fault of the employer. At present, the maximum amount of compensation that an employment tribunal can award is £56,800. A tribunal can reduce the award where there has been a failure on the part of the employee to mitigate his or her loss or on the ground of contributory conduct.

QUESTION 1   What would you consider to be the most likely remedy an employment tribunal would grant an employee who had been unfairly dismissed?

Redundancy

One of the purposes of the ERA 1996 is to compensate an employee for loss of his or her job so as to make employers aware of the need to retain the services of employees and to offer alternative employment where this is not possible. Redundancy may occur where the employer ceases to carry on business or ceases to carry on business at the location where the employee worked or the employer restructures the business or changes production methods so that fewer employees are needed.

A redundant employee may have the right to make a claim that, while it is legitimate to reduce the size of a workforce, thus rendering some employees surplus to requirements, those employees may have statutory entitlement to compensation for losing their jobs. Further, employees who can prove that the method by which they were selected for redundancy did not meet the standards of good employment practice, may additionally have a claim for unfair dismissal that might result in a compensatory award or an order for reinstatement (as already discussed).

Eligibility

In order to be able to claim compensation (i.e. redundancy pay) the claimant must be able to prove that he or she had a year's continuous service with the relevant employer. The categories of employees excluded from claiming unfair dismissal are also excluded from statutory redundancy protection and the statutory right to redundancy is not available to the self-employed.

Employees must be able to show that they have been dismissed within the meaning of the ERA 1996 and redundancy has caused the dismissal. An employee who leaves voluntarily having been warned of the threat of redundancy is not dismissed and where the employee's contract contains a term that the employee may be required to work at any place of business the employer directs, the employee is not made redundant by being moved.

Offer of suitable alternative employment

The ERA 1996 provides a defence to a redundancy claim where the employer offered the employee suitable alternative employment that the dismissed employee unreasonably refused. What is suitable and what is an unreasonable refusal will depend on the facts of each case. Factors like travelling distances, domestic problems and lack of appropriate educational facilities for the employee's children may all have to be taken into account. An employee who takes up an alternative post has at least 4 weeks to decide if it is workable. If the employee declines the job within the time limit, any rights to redundancy pay are not prejudiced.

Nature of claim

Employees must bring their claims within 6 months of the date when their notice period or short-term contract expired. The financial entitlement of the employee is calculated with reference to the age of the employee and the length of service (up to a maximum of 20 years), as follows:

- 18–21: half a week's pay per year of service
- 22–40: one week's pay per year of service
- 41–64: one-and-a-half weeks' pay per year of service.

What is the difference between voluntary redundancy and compulsory redundancy?

In both situations, an employer is contemplating a reduction of the workforce. The employer could choose to arrange for such a reduction by making employees redundant on a compulsory basis, but an employer may find that the reduction required can be achieved by asking for employees to be made redundant on a voluntary basis. The terms of both forms of redundancy may be the same. As long as the statutory minimum of redundancy pay is provided, an employer does not have to offer any more, although many contracts of employment do provide for additional payment in the event of voluntary or compulsory redundancy. The advantage to the employer in employees accepting voluntary redundancy is that it may be less harmful to employer/employee relations.

A week's pay is currently subject to an upper limit of £220, so the maximum statutory redundancy payment is £330. An employer, however, may choose contractually to offer more than the statutory minimum.

Discrimination

Some of the most important statutory provisions affecting employment contracts are in respect of avoiding discrimination in the workplace. An example is equal pay, which we looked at earlier, but anti-discrimination legislation also exists to ensure equal opportunity in respect of sex, sexual orientation, race, religion and disability. When in force, legislation will also prohibit discrimination in respect of age.

Job advertisements

Employers should take care not to select persons on criteria that may lead to discrimination. For instance, the type of activity the Sex Discrimination Act 1975 is designed to prohibit can be seen in respect of an advertisement that states 'wanted, dynamic man for management training', or an advertisement that uses the words 'salesgirl', 'barman', 'fireman' etc. Employers must use neutral terms that make it clear that the post is open to both sexes. So looking at the advertisements, they should read 'dynamic person wanted for management training' or 'sales person required', 'bar person needed', 'firefighter', etc.

Sex Discrimination Act 1975

The Sex Discrimination Act (SDA) 1975 prohibits employers from discriminating in a wide range of circumstances, although the SDA 1975 also applies to non-employment-related matters, such as education and housing. In employment, **sex discrimination** is outlawed in relation to recruitment and selection arrangements, terms of employment, facilities at work, provision of training, opportunities for promotion and transfers within employment and dismissal. The SDA 1975 also prohibits the subjecting of a person to any other detriment at the workplace, such as a differential dress code and sexual harassment.

Another example of sex discrimination is in relation to age bars, as unnecessary age bars may discriminate against suitable qualified women who often enter or re-enter the job market after having children. Refusing to interview married women or women with children in the belief that they may not be fully dedicated to the job, flexible in their working hours, or likely to be frequently absent from work are all examples of practices that employers should avoid. Employers should guard against asking questions at interviews that may suggest a discriminatory intention. For instance, women may be questioned about their intentions regarding having children or childcare arrangements, whereas male applicants are less likely to be asked such questions.

Meaning of sex discrimination

The SDA 1975 embodies three kinds of discrimination:

- direct discrimination
- indirect discrimination
- discrimination by victimisation.

Direct discrimination Direct discrimination occurs where a person is treated less favourably than another on the grounds of their sex or marital status. Examples of direct discrimination are:

- refusal to appoint women in a particular post
- refusing to employ married women with dependent children
- subjecting or permitting the sexual harassment of women at the workplace
- provision of facilities at the workplace for men only.

Direct discrimination does not occur as frequently in practice as indirect discrimination as generally employers have been more effective in eliminating direct discrimination. An example of a case involving a claim based on direct discrimination can be seen in the case study highlighting *Porcelli v Strathclyde Regional Council (1986)*.

Indirect discrimination The most common type of discrimination is indirect discrimination. This occurs where:

- the employer applies a condition or requirement to both sexes
- the proportion of one sex or married persons that can comply with the condition is considerably smaller than the other sex or single persons
- the requirement cannot be justified with reference to the job and therefore is detrimental in its effect on one sex or married persons.

Porcelli v Strathclyde Regional Council (1986)

Mrs Porcelli was employed as a science laboratory technician at a school. In 1982, two male laboratory technicians were appointed. According to Mrs Porcelli, the two employees sexually harassed her as part of a campaign to try to persuade her to leave the school. This led Mrs Porcelli to apply for a transfer to another school. Subsequent to her transfer, she complained to an employment tribunal that the employers had discriminated against her contrary to the SDA 1975. On appeal from the tribunal, it was held that the employee had been discriminated against on grounds of sex when she was subjected to a campaign of unpleasant treatment, including an element of sexual harassment, by two male colleagues. She had been less favourably treated on the ground of her sex because the employees would not have treated a man they disliked equally unfavourably.

An example of indirect discrimination is age bars. Where an age bar is not justified by the requirements of the job, it can be indirectly discriminatory against women. In *Price v Civil Service Commission (1977)*, there was an age bar of 28. Mrs Price, at 36, was suitably qualified for the post but the age requirement prevented her from applying. The Employment Appeal Tribunal felt that the requirement could be indirectly discriminatory to women. It was considered that many suitably qualified women have left the employment market at this age due to family commitments and are unable to comply with the requirement on re-entering the market. In comparison, more suitably qualified men could comply with the requirement, as they were not likely to be involved with childrearing at this age. The requirement could therefore in practice have an adverse impact on suitably qualified women and was found not to be justified with respect to the demands of the post in question.

Discrimination by victimisation The SDA 1975 declares it to be unlawful to treat less favourably any person who has brought proceedings under the Act, or who assisted, by the giving of evidence or information, in connection with any proceedings or alleged offences under the SDA 1975.

Other unlawful acts

As well as the three specific forms of discrimination outlined above the SDA 1975 also contains three other provisions:

- It is unlawful to instruct another to commit a discriminatory offence under the SDA 1975 (e.g. an employment agency or a personnel manager).

- It is an offence to knowingly aid another person to commit an unlawful act under the statute.

- Employers are vicariously liable for their employees 'discrimination unless they can show they have taken reasonable steps to prevent the employees contravening the statute.

Exclusions from the SDA 1975

There are some exclusions in the SDA 1975, i.e. circumstances in which discrimination is permitted. The most important is what is known as the 'genuine occupational qualification'. This exclusion allows for situations where it is thought that being a man or woman is a genuine occupational requirement of the job. Examples relate to the need for a female social worker dealing with unmarried women, a male warder at a male prison or for reasons of authenticity in connection with works of drama and entertainment.

Enforcement of the SDA 1975

A person wishing to bring a complaint before an employment tribunal under the SDA 1975 must do so within 3 months of the alleged discriminatory act. The burden of proof is on the employer to show that there was no discrimination. Where the tribunal finds the complaint well founded it can make a recommendation that any condition, requirement, action of the employer be altered or changed and order the payment of compensation to the applicant, which can include a sum representing injury to feelings. Unlike a claim for unfair dismissal, there is no maximum amount a tribunal can award on the basis of sex discrimination.

The SDA 1975 provided for the setting up of the Equal Opportunities Commission (EOC). Under its powers, the EOC conducts research and collects data on discriminatory practices. It also carries out formal investigations and, where the EOC is satisfied discrimination has occurred, it may institute proceedings under the SDA 1975 to prevent future discrimination arising. The EOC can also serve non-discrimination notices on an employer requiring them to improve their workplace practices and procedures. The EOC also gives advice, information, assistance and sometimes legal support to individuals seeking to bring an action under the SDA 1975. The EOC also publishes a Code of Practice that explains to employers and employees how the SDA 1975 operates in practice.

Sexual orientation

The Employment Equality (Sexual Orientation) Regulations 2003 prohibit discrimination on the grounds of *sexual orientation*. The regulations are based on the SDA 1975 in terms of direct discrimination, indirect discrimination and victimisation. The regulations extend also to harassment. Discrimination is permitted where there is a genuine occupational qualification or to avoid a conflict with the religious beliefs of a significant number of followers of that belief.

Race Relations Act 1976

The aim of the Race Relations Act (RRA) 1976 is to prohibit **race discrimination** and discrimination on the grounds of colour, nationality or ethnic or national origins. As with the SDA 1975, it covers areas outside of employment, such as housing and education. Under the RRA 1976, the Commission for Racial Equality (CRE) was established and it carries out similar functions to the EOC under the SDA 1975.

As with the SDA 1975, there are no qualifying provisions under the RRA 1976. The RRA 1976 applies immediately for the benefit of all prospective and actual employees, although there are some excluded areas.

Areas of employment covered

The areas covered by the RRA 1976 regarding employment are similar to those we looked at under the SDA 1975, namely, recruitment arrangements, choice of applicants, terms of employment offered, facilities at work, provision of training, opportunities for promotion and transfers, dismissal and the subjecting of a person to any other detriment at the workplace. This means that employers should

take care with their advertisements, recruitment arrangements, selection procedures and conduct of interviews to ensure that they do not lead to or perpetuate
discrimination in the workplace.

Discrimination defined

As with the SDA 1975, the RRA 1976 embodies three kinds of discrimination:

- direct discrimination
- indirect discrimination
- discrimination by victimisation.

Direct discrimination Direct discrimination occurs when someone is treated less
favourably than another on the grounds of race, colour, nationality, or ethnic or
national origins (see the 'Reality check' textbox). Examples of direct discrimination would be refusing to interview black people for posts, refusing to appoint a
black person to a particular post or subjecting or permitting racial abuse at the
workplace.

Indirect discrimination As with sex discrimination, this occurs when the employer
applies a condition or requirement such that the proportion of one racial group that
can comply with the condition or requirement is smaller than another and the condition or requirement cannot be justified and the complainant suffers a detriment.
In ***Bayoomi v British Railways Board (1981)***, applicants for the post of telex
operator were required to become competent in the use of a particular British
machine within 6 months and without training. An employment tribunal held this
to be indirectly discriminatory. The requirement, although administratively convenient, had an adverse impact on applicants not born and trained in England. In
Panesar v Nestlé Co Ltd (1980), however, a company's requirement that applicants should not have long hair or beards was found to be a justifiable requirement
even though it had the effect of indirectly discriminating against Sikhs. This was

---

Reality check

An example of direct discrimination – Owen & Briggs v James (1981)

Miss James, a black English woman, saw an
advertisement by a firm of solicitors in a local
newspaper for a young shorthand typist. She
applied for the job and was interviewed, but was
unsuccessful. Several months later she saw
another advertisement, which stated: 'Competent
shorthand typist required by litigation solicitor.
The applicant must be competent.' Miss James
phoned and found that it was the same firm. She
asked whether experience was necessary and
was told that it was not necessarily required. She
was given an appointment for an interview. When
Miss James arrived for her interview, she saw the
partner who had interviewed her on her previous
application. He said that there was no point in
interviewing her again and the discussion
became hostile. On the same afternoon, a white
woman was interviewed. She was offered the job,
although she had a shorthand speed of 35 words
per minute, compared with Miss James's speed
of 80 words per minute. Miss James complained
to an employment tribunal that she had been
unlawfully discriminated against on grounds of
race. The tribunal found that Miss James's colour
was one of the important factors in the
employer's decision to reject her application and
awarded her £75 for injury to feelings and loss of
opportunity.

because the employer was in the business of manufacturing chocolate products and the rule was reasonable on the grounds of safety and hygiene.

Discrimination by victimisation This arises where someone is treated less favourable because they have brought proceedings under the RRA 1976 or assisted by giving evidence or information in connection with any proceedings or alleged offences under the RRA 1976. In *Chief Constable of West Yorkshire v Khan (2000)*, a refusal of a reference for a person who had alleged discrimination was held to amount to victimisation.

Other unlawful acts

As well as the three specific forms of discrimination it is also unlawful to instruct another to commit a discriminatory offence under the RRA 1976 or knowingly aid another person to commit an unlawful act. Employers are vicariously liable for discrimination by their employees unless they can show they have taken reasonable steps to prevent the employee(s) contravening the statute.

Exclusions from the RRA 1976

As with the SDA 1975, there are a number of exclusions in the RRA 1976. The RRA 1976 identifies circumstances where membership of a particular racial group is a genuine occupational requirement. Examples relate to dramatic, entertainment, artistic or photographic work in order to achieve authenticity, or bar or restaurant work where the setting requires an employee from a particular race. Exemptions also apply to private households, rules in relation to immigration, certain posts within the civil service, such as defence, and where nationality qualifications have been set in connection with sport.

Enforcement of the RRA 1976

A person wishing to bring a complaint before an employment tribunal under the RRA 1976 must do so within 3 months of the alleged discriminatory act. The burden of proof is on the employer to show that there was no discrimination. Where the tribunal finds the complaint well founded it can make a recommendation that any condition, requirement, or action of the employer be altered or changed and order the payment of compensation to the applicant. This payment can include a sum of money for injury to feelings. As with the SDA 1975, unlike a claim for unfair dismissal, there is no maximum award a tribunal can make.

Harassment

The RRA 1976 also outlaws harassment. The RRA 1976 states that a person subjects another to harassment where on grounds of race or ethnic or national origins he engages in unwanted conduct that has the effect of violating that person's dignity or creating an intimidating, hostile, degrading, humiliating or offensive environment.

Other discrimination

Legislation prohibits other forms of discrimination in the workplace, namely discrimination on the grounds of disability, religion or religious belief or workers who are on fixed-term contracts. When in force, legislation in the form of the Employment Equality (Age) Regulations will also prohibit discrimination on the ground of age. In respect of disability discrimination, the work of the Disability Rights Commission (DRC) is similar to that of the EOC and the CRE.

How does an employee bring a claim against an employer?

In Chapter 1, we saw that claims for breach of contract commence in a court of first instance, either a County Court or the High Court. Similarly a claim by an employee that an employer breached a term of a contract of employment can be started in this way. However, the statutory protection of employees provides for employees to make an application to an employment tribunal where an employer has breached employment law in relation to such matters as unfair dismissal, discrimination and equal pay, and the time limits for an application to an employment tribunal are stricter than they are for bringing a claim for breach of contract.

It is possible for an employee to bring different proceedings based on the same conduct of the employer. For example, an employee unfairly dismissed by an employer may bring court proceedings for wrongful dismissal, as this is a common law form of action and, where qualified, make an application to an employment tribunal for unfair dismissal in accordance with the ERA 1996. However, in *Johnson v Unisys Ltd (2001)*, the House of Lords held that where a breach of contract claim is not separate from an application for unfair dismissal, only the latter can be brought. This case, however, was distinguished in *Eastwood v Magnox Electric plc (2004)* where the House of Lords ruled that although the employee had to use the statutory procedure for unfair dismissal, he could succeed in a separate common law claim for breach of a term of the contract of employment where the breach of contract occurred prior to the dismissal procedure. In this case, an employee suffering from mental illness was entitled to bring a High Court claim for damages for mental illness as well as proceedings before an employment tribunal for unfair dismissal, as the breach of contract arose before the dismissal procedure began.

An alternative to bringing court proceedings or making an application to an employment tribunal is for the employee and employer to pursue alternative forms of action as a means of resolving a dispute. Employees are expected usually to make use of grievance procedures while employers are expected to follow a proper disciplinary procedure. Alternatively, both parties can make use of mediation services, such as that provided by the Arbitration, Conciliation and Advisory Service (ACAS). Even where an application to an employment tribunal is made, the employment tribunal can attempt to resolve the matter before full hearing takes place. Further details of the services offered by ACAS can be found on www.acas.org.uk.

Answer to in-text question

> **QUESTION 1** What would you consider to be the most likely remedy an employment tribunal would grant an employee who had been unfairly dismissed?

The most common remedy is compensation, as it is likely that the relationship between the employer and employee has deteriorated to such an extent that there is an irretrievable breakdown between the parties.

22 | Agency

Learning objectives

By the end of this chapter, you should be able to explain:

- **The ways in which an agency relationship comes into existence**
- **The different types of authority an agent can possess**
- **The rights and duties of an agent**
- **The relationship between principal and third party and third party and agent**

Introduction

It is often assumed that parties contracting with each other are contracting in their personal capacity. In business, however, this is rarely the case. For example, a company is a legal person but it must depend on individuals to enter into contracts on its behalf. This power is delegated to directors, who, in turn, may delegate that power to managers and other employees. Similarly, while partnerships and sole traders are not legal entities, the owners of those businesses may not have the time to enter into every contract and may wish to use employees or independent contractors to contract on their behalf.

The law of agency enables this power of delegation to occur without affecting the state of contractual liability between the parties. Agency is the relationship that exists between a legal person (the **agent**) and another person (the **principal**) in which the agent is given **authority** to enter into a contractual relationship with a third party, so that a contract exists between the principal and the third party. The relationship may, and often is, a contractual one, for example, employer and employee and manufacturer and factor, but an agency relationship can also be gratuitous, as in ***Chaudhry v Prabhakar (1988)*** where an agency relationship arose between two friends. This case is featured later in the chapter.

FAQ

Apart from directors and employees, how important is the role played by agents in the world of business?

Many businesses rely on agency in order to conduct business. Manufacturers may wish to use commercial agents to sell their goods or to supply their services. In other cases, a business may be carrying on the business of an agent, such as an auction house, an insurance broker or an estate agency. However, the use of the term 'agent' does not necessarily mean that an agency relationship exists. A car dealership, for example, is not an agent of a car manufacturer but a distributor dealing at arm's length from the manufacturer.

In this chapter we shall be looking as various aspects of the law of agency but it should be noted that two of the most important aspects of agency are how an agency relationship arises and the nature of an agent's authority in respect of entering into contracts.

Types of agent

In the law of agency there are a number of types of agent that exist. Some of the more common ones as applying to businesses are as follows.

Commercial agent

A **commercial agent** is defined by the Commercial Agents (Council Directive) Regulations 1993 as a self-employed intermediary who has continuing authority to negotiate, or to negotiate and conclude, the sale and purchase of goods on behalf of another. The regulations set out particular rights and duties of commercial agents and their principals, such as rights to remuneration and commission and to compensation should a commercial agency agreement be terminated prematurely. The right to compensation has served to protect a number of agents since the regulations came into force. In *Ingmar GB Ltd v Eaton Leonard Technologies Inc (2001)*, in order to avoid making a termination payment to an agent, the principal argued that the agency relationship was subject to US law as stated in the agreement between the parties. The ECJ held that, despite the term in the contract, the agent's territory was within the EU and he was entitled to compensation in accordance with the directive.

Factor or mercantile agent

A factor is an agent who has authority, with full knowledge of his principal, to take possession of the principal's property for the purpose of sale. The sale will normally be in the agent's own name. A factor is a type of mercantile agent, as defined by the Factors Act 1889, which states that a mercantile agent is an agent who has in the customary course of his business the authority to sell goods, to consign goods for the purpose of sale, to buy goods or to raise money on the security of goods. Such agents will include factors (who have possession of the property in question) and brokers (who do not). Examples of such agents can be seen in the jewellery and motor trades.

General agent

Often contrasted with a special agent, a *general agent* has authority to act in the ordinary course of a particular trade, business or profession. For example, a director of a company will be considered a general agent of the company.

Special agent

Unlike a general agent, a special agent's authority is limited to doing a particular act or to representing the principal in respect of a particular transaction. The act or transaction does not have to be in the ordinary course of his trade, business or profession.

Creation of agency

There are a number of methods by which an agency relationship may be created.

Express appointment

Generally, an express agreement appointing someone as an agent need not be in any particular form. An agreement can be made orally or in writing and is subject to the ordinary rules of contract law. An exception is where a person confers a power of attorney on someone whom he wishes to act on his behalf in order to look after their business or personal affairs. The Powers of Attorney Act 1971 requires that the document appointing the agent must be in the form of a deed, i.e. signed and sealed.

Once appointed, the agent must not exceed the powers given to him by the agreement. Where he acts within his authority, the principal will be bound by the contracts made on the principal's behalf. Where he exceeds his authority, the principal will not be bound by the contract, unless the principal chooses to ratify the agent's unauthorised act (see 'Ratification').

Implied appointment

Many agency relationships are implied. Such an agency can arise in several ways, for example, from the conduct of the parties or in relation to the surrounding circumstances.

Agency by estoppel

In this case, the principal by his conduct allows a third party to believe that a particular person is acting as his agent. Where this is the case, the principal will be prevented from denying the existence of the agency relationship and will be liable on any contract entered into on his behalf by such a person.

Agency of necessity

Agency of necessity arises where a person is faced with an emergency in which the property or interests of another person are in imminent jeopardy and it becomes necessary, in order to preserve the property or interests, to act for that person without his authority. Certain conditions need to be satisfied before an agency of necessity can arise:

- The agent was unable to obtain instructions from the principal.
- The agent acted in the interests of the principal and in good faith.
- The action taken by the agent must have been reasonable and prudent in the circumstances.

In ***Great Northern Railway Co v Swaffield (1874)***, Swaffield sent a horse by train from King's Cross to Sandy in Bedfordshire. As it was not collected by anyone and Swaffields's address was not known to the station staff, the horse was put in a stable. When Swaffield later came to collect the horse, he had to pay the costs of having the horse stabled. It was held that the claimants were agents of necessity. They had not been able to contact Swaffield as a matter of urgency and had acted in good faith.

The concept of agency of necessity is less important in today's commercial world owing to modern telecommunications and it is less likely that a person would be unable to contact the owner of merchandise for instructions in the event of an emergency.

Ratification

Where an agent has no authority or goes beyond the authority given to him by the principal and the agent purports to act as an agent, the principal may ratify (i.e. adopt) the contract and become liable on it. Such adoption may be expressed or by implication. The effect of **ratification** is that the principal's adoption, where validly given, dates back to the time when the contract was made.

Certain conditions must be present before ratification can take place:

- The agent must have purported to act as such and to have named or identified the principal. Otherwise, the other contracting party is likely to think that it is contracting with the agent.
- The principal must have had full capacity when the agent made the contract and at the time of ratification.
- The principal must at the time of ratification have full knowledge of all the material facts or intend to ratify the contract whatever the facts might be.
- A void contract cannot be ratified.

In ***Bolton Partners v Lambert (1889)***, L made an offer to the managing director of a company to purchase the lease of a factory. The managing director without authority accepted the offer but L later withdrew the offer. The board of directors of the company ratified the managing director's acceptance of the offer. The court held that, by virtue of ratification, there was a binding contract between L and the company and L's withdrawal from the contract was of no effect. By contrast, in *Keighley Maxsted & Co v Durant (1901)*, an agent purchased grain on behalf of a partnership at a price beyond his express authority, but failed to disclose to the sellers that he was contracting as an agent. The partnership ratified the contract the following day but later refused to pay for the goods. The court held that there was no contract with the partnership since the partnership was incapable of ratifying a contract made by an agent who had failed to declare that he was acting as an agent.

Rights of an agent

The rights of an agent depend on the contract, if any, between an agent and a principal or, in the case of commercial agents, on the Commercial Agents (Council Directive) Regulations 1993.

Right to receive remuneration

A contract of agency contains usually an express term providing for commission to be paid to an agent. In commercial agency matters, remuneration will be readily implied, either at a reasonable rate or at that rate which is usual in the trade or profession concerned. In the case of a commercial agent, there is provision under the Commercial Agents (Council Directive) Regulations 1993 to ensure remuneration is paid.

Where an agent is also an employee, commission will be paid in addition to any wage or salary. In *Rolfe & Co v George (1968)*, R was employed to sell G's grocery business. A purchaser was introduced to G by someone else but R was actively involved in subsequent negotiations and sale. It was held that the agent had caused the sale to take place and was therefore entitled to commission.

Where an agent tries to bring about a sale but does not succeed, no commission is payable. In *Luxor (Eastbourne) Ltd v Cooper (1941)*, an agent was engaged to sell two leasehold cinemas for the owner and introduced someone willing to purchase them. However, the owner refused to sell. It was held that the agent was not entitled to commission.

Some agents (e.g. estate agents) make themselves sole agents with the sole and exclusive right to sell. This entitles them to commission where the sale is effected by another agent or by the principal. In *Gross, Fine & Krieger Chalfen v Gaynor (1974)*, the claimants were appointed sole agents to sell land by auction. The land was sold by another agent before the auction took place. It was held that the sole agents could claim their commission.

A principal must not wrongfully prevent his agent from earning contractual commission and an agent is not usually entitled to remuneration where he exceeds his authority and the principal does not ratify the transaction.

Right of indemnification

An agent has a right to be reimbursed for any expenses incurred on behalf of the principal and to be indemnified for any loss or liabilities incurred in carrying out his duties as agent. The agent cannot claim to be reimbursed or indemnified in respect of unlawful or unauthorised acts. Agents have a lien on the goods of their principals in respect of any lawful claims they may have against their principals for remuneration, expenses or liabilities incurred.

Duties of an agent

Where people employ agents to sell or buy their goods or property, they expect them to be trustworthy and competent. These duties are often set out as express terms in the contract between the principal and the agent, but due to the nature of the relationship, the law will imply such duties where they are not expressly stated in the contract. For example, an agent who became incompetent would be regarded as in breach of contract with the principal even where the contract had made no reference to the agent having to do a competent job. Other duties are based on the notion of trust or on the existence of a fiduciary relationship. Similar duties are imposed on commercial agents under the Commercial Agents (Council Directive) Regulations 1993.

Reasonable skill and care

A principal is entitled to expect an agent to exercise such skill and care as is reasonable in the circumstances (also known as a **duty of care**). The standard of skill and care expected of an agent will vary depending on the nature of the agency and, where the agent is an expert or professional, the law will expect compliance with the standards of that profession or business. In *Keppel v Wheeler (1927)*, an estate agent carelessly accepted on behalf of his principal a lower purchase price for a block of flats than he could otherwise have obtained. It was held that, in an action against the agent, the principal could recover the difference between the price he could have obtained and the price he received. (See also *Chaudhry v Prabhakar (1988)*, highlighted in the 'Reality check' textbox.)

Fiduciary duties

An agent is under a fiduciary duty not to put himself into a position where his personal interest and that of his principal conflict, such as making a secret profit or receiving a bribe. An agent who accepts a bribe or makes a secret commission is liable to account for it to his principal. He is also usually liable to forfeit any commission. An agent may also be liable in damages for any loss suffered by the principal. In *Mahesan v Malaysian Govt Officers' Cooperative Housing Society*

Reality check

Chaudhry v Prabhakar (1988) – a failure of a friend to exercise reasonable care and skill

In this case, the claimant was a newly qualified driver who asked a friend to find a suitable car for her to drive. She stipulated that she did not want a car that had been involved in an accident. Her friend claimed to be knowledgeable about cars and found a car that seemed to suit her needs.

He noticed some damage to the bonnet of the car, but recommended that she purchase the car from the seller, which he knew to be a garage of crash repairers. On discovering that the car had been damaged seriously in an accident and was unroadworthy, the claimant sued her friend in negligence. The Court of Appeal held the friend was in breach of an agent's duty to exercise reasonable skill and care in the performance of their duties. He had failed to exercise the level of care and skill expected from somebody with the level of expertise he claimed to possess and on which the claimant had reasonably relied.

Ltd (1979), a manager and agent of a housing society agreed with a third party for the society to purchase a piece of land for £900,000, £500,000 more than its market value. For this, the third party gave the manager a commission of £120,000. On discovering these events, the society claimed from the manager the secret profit and damages covering the loss it made, the loss being the difference between the price paid for the land and its true value. The court held that the society was entitled to either damages or account of profit.

> **QUESTION 1** What do you think the society would claim?

An agent is also under a fiduciary duty not to take advantage of information or knowledge obtained on his principal's behalf or abuse any position of authority to which the principal has appointed him. In ***Boardman v Phipps (1967)***, a solicitor, who had in the course of his agency discovered information about the profitability of a company, was held not to be entitled to keep the profits from the sale of shares he held in the company as this was based on the use of confidential information. He was, however, entitled to remuneration he had earned as an agent in making a profit for the principal on selling the principal's shares in the company.

To perform duties personally

Generally, an agent must not delegate his duties to another. The principal may, however, authorise delegation and in certain cases delegation is accepted by custom. A contractually appointed agent must perform his duties in accordance with the terms of the contract and must not exceed his authority.

Duty of obedience

A principal will often give instructions to an agent, for example, when or whether to sell the principal's property and/or at what price. The agent is under a duty to comply with all lawful instructions given to him by the principal, although some agents are given discretion to use their judgement in some matters or to exercise any discretion in accordance with commercial custom. In ***Bertram Armstrong & Co v Godfray (1830)***, B instructed G, a broker, to sell stock when the market price reached £85 per unit. G did not do so but held on to the stock and later sold it at less than £85. It was held that G was liable for not having acted in accordance with B's instructions.

Authority of an agent

An agent binds a principal to a contract with a third party where his act is authorised. An agent's authority is not limited to his express authority, for there are other types of authority an agent can possess, such as implied authority and apparent authority. A principal is not bound by an unauthorised act unless he chooses to adopt the contract by ratification (as discussed earlier).

It is a common misconception that an act of an agent beyond his express authority cannot bind the principal. However, a principal is bound to a contract where the act is impliedly authorised or comes within the scope of the agent's usual or apparent authority. In business, it is unlikely that third parties would necessarily know that an agent they were dealing with had express authority to perform the particular task. It is more likely that a third party will be relying on a representation by the principal that the agent has authority to act on his behalf.

In business, it is not uncommon for employees to exceed their express instructions of work in ordering goods on the business's behalf, perhaps by not obtaining an order number or exceeding a limit on price. It is possible for the employer to choose not to pay for the goods in such instances, but often the employer will adopt the contract and be content to reprimand the employee and to tighten its procedures. Alternatively, contesting the case might lead to protracted litigation and the possibility that, although not expressly authorised, the transaction is binding as coming with the employee's implied, usual or apparent authority. In each of the following cases, a principal contested an agent's authority to act, but the courts, held that the particular contract in dispute was authorised and binding on the principal.

Actual express authority

Express authority is that authority conferred specifically on an agent and any act performed by the agent within the scope of his express authority will be binding on both the principal and the third party. (See the case study highlighting **SMC Electronics Ltd v Akhter Computers Ltd (2001)**.

Actual implied authority

It may be possible to imply from the authority given to the agent that he has power to do whatever is necessarily or reasonably incidental to the purpose for which he was appointed agent. In *SMC Electronics Ltd v Akhter Computers Ltd* the

SMC Electronics Ltd v Akhter Computers Ltd (2001)

The defendant company sold printed circuit boards known as power supply units (PSUs). The employee in charge of promoting sales of PSUs was not a director of the company but had the job title of 'Director PSU Sales' and his terms of employment required him to 'perform such duties as may be reasonably associated with his job title'. In 1993 the employee agreed with the claimant to split equally commission earned on sales made by the defendant to customers introduced by the claimant. The defendant sold a large quantity of PSUs to a customer, but refused to account to the claimant for any commission on the sales. The claimant brought an action claiming 50% of the profits that the defendant had made on the sale. The defendant contended that they were not required to pay any commission to the claimant as the employee had no authority to make the contract to share commission. The Court of Appeal held that the defendant was bound by the agreement. The employee had actual express authority to enter into the agreement with the claimant as entering into a commission arrangement was reasonably associated with his job as 'Director of PSU Sales'.

Hely-Hutchinson v Brayhead Ltd (1968)

R was a director and chairman of B Ltd, whose articles of association provided for the appointment of a managing director. Although none was appointed, R, to the knowledge and acquiescence of the board, acted as the company's managing director. In the past he had entered into transactions of a financial nature on the company's behalf, transactions that had gone unchallenged by the company. H was the managing director of P Ltd, which was in need of financial assistance and in connection with which he had agreed with a bank to guarantee a loan made to P Ltd of £50,000. R, on B Ltd's behalf, agreed with H that B Ltd would indemnify H against any loss on his guarantee of P Ltd's bank loan and against any loss in connection with a separate loan of £45,000 made by H to P Ltd. The assistance failed and P Ltd went into liquidation. H sought to make B Ltd liable for his loss of £95,000. B Ltd claimed that R did not have authority to enter into the contract with H. The Court of Appeal held that B Ltd was bound to the contract on the basis that R had actual authority implied from the conduct of the parties and the surrounding circumstances. He had entered into contracts of a financial nature in the past that had gone unchallenged by the board and therefore had acquired additional, implied authority to act in the instant matter.

Court of Appeal held that the employee had implied authority to enter into commission agreements generally because that was something that was ordinarily incidental to his duties.

An agent's authority can also be implied, for instance, from the conduct of the parties and the circumstances of the case. An agent who on previous occasions had been allowed by his principal to act in excess of his express authority may have acquired implied authority to continue to so act (see the case study highlighting **Hely-Hutchinson v Brayhead Ltd (1968)**).

Apparent or ostensible authority

This is authority as it appears to others, as was so described by Lord Denning in **Panorama Developments (Guildford) Ltd v Fidelis Furnishing Fabrics Ltd (1971)**. In order for apparent authority to be established, there needs to be a representation by the principal (by words or conduct) to a third party, which the third party relies on, that the agent has authority that he does not possess. Apparent authority consists of either that authority that a person in the position and in that type of business can reasonably be assumed to have or that authority that the particular agent has been held out by his principal as possessing. In **Freeman & Lockyer v Buckhurst Park Properties (Mangal) Ltd (1964)**, K and H were the directors of the defendant company. The company's articles provided for the appointment of a managing director but none was appointed. K instructed a firm of architects to undertake some work in connection with property the company had acquired. The firm submitted an invoice for the work done, but the company refused to pay, claiming that K had no authority to make the contract. The Court of Appeal held that the company was bound to the contract as K had acted within the scope of his apparent authority. He had been allowed to act as if he were a managing director to the knowledge of the board, by seeking potential purchasers for the

Racing UK Ltd v Doncaster Racecourse Ltd (2005)

Racing UK Ltd entered into an agreement with Doncaster Racecourse Ltd, acting on behalf of Doncaster Council, for the media rights in connection with horse racing at Doncaster Racecourse. Doncaster Council owned the course while Doncaster Racecourse was engaged to manage it. The agreement with Racing UK was signed by S, chief executive of Doncaster Racecourse. Another company was negotiating with Doncaster Council for the same media rights as part of a major development of the racecourse. When Doncaster Council informed Racing UK that it did not intend to proceed with the media rights deal, Racing UK brought proceedings against the council claiming that, as S was acting on the council's behalf, the council was bound by the agreement. The Court of Appeal held that the agreement was binding on the council as principal. Although S had no actual authority to enter into the agreement, he did have apparent authority in respect of the media rights. This was because the council had put him in charge of most aspects of the business at the racecourse and there was no reason why a third party would think that S and Doncaster Racecourse did not have authority to deal with media rights.

property and employing other agents to carry out work. The board, by such conduct, had represented that he had authority to enter into contracts of a kind that a managing director responsible for finding a purchaser would in the normal course be authorised to enter into on behalf of the company.

A more recent example of apparent authority is featured in the 'Reality check' textbox highlighting **Racing UK Ltd v Doncaster Racecourse Ltd (2005)**, where the court held that all the requirements of apparent authority had been set out, in particular that the council (the principal) had led the third party to believe that the chief executive (the agent) had the authority to act on behalf of the council.

Usual authority

A difficulty that lies with this form of agency is the inconsistent way the words 'usual authority' have been treated by the courts. Sometimes, the courts have treated usual authority in the context of actual implied authority as being the authority conferred on the agent as a result of the circumstances of the case, i.e. the usual authority of an agent from a particular trade or custom. In other cases, usual authority has been considered to be an aspect of apparent authority in that once a representation has been made in respect of an agent, the agent is conferred with all the usual authority associated with that type of agent. In either case, usual authority is seen as an aspect of actual or apparent authority. However, there is another view, which is to regard usual authority as a distinct ground for creating an agency relationship, outside that of implied or apparent authority. The case often cited to explain this type of usual authority is **Watteau v Fenwick (1893)** (highlighted in the case study).

Watteau v Fenwick (1893)

Humble was the manager of a public house, owned by Fenwick. As part of his instructions, he was expressly forbidden from ordering cigars, although this type of activity was usual to the business of a pub manager. Humble ordered cigars from Watteau, who believed he was contracting with Humble, not Fenwick, since it was Humble's name that appeared above the entrance to the pub. The cigars were not paid for and Watteau sued Fenwick for the purchase price. The court held that the contract was binding on Fenwick since the order-ing of cigars was an activity that was within the usual authority of a pub manager. Although Fenwick did not make any representation to Watteau (i.e. there was no apparent authority) and he instructed Humble not to enter into a certain type of contract (and therefore Humble had no actual authority), he was bound by the contract.

Effect of agency on contractual relations

The effect of agency on the contractual relationship depends on whether the agent contracted as an agent (and disclosed that fact) and/or whether the agent exceeded his authority.

Relationship between agent and third party

As a contract made by an agent is a contract of the principal, the agent can nei-ther sue nor be sued in respect of it. However, where in making the contract the agent assumes liability to the third party, he will be liable in accordance with and to the extent to which he undertook personal responsibility. For example, where the contract is signed by the agent in his own name and with no reference to the fact that he signs as agent, he is deemed to have contracted personally, unless a contrary intention appears elsewhere in the contract. However, where he signs 'as agent', or 'for or on behalf' of a principal, he is deemed to have contracted as an agent and he is not therefore liable.

Similarly, where a person purports to contract as agent, but the principal is fic-titious or non-existent, or the agent is shown to be the principal, the agent is liable.

Where an agent has no authority to bind a principal to a contract with a third party, the third party can sue the agent for breach of warranty of authority, unless the principal ratifies the agent's unauthorised act. In such circumstances, the third party may sue the agent for any loss suffered using the rules on damages set out in **Hadley v Baxendale (1854)** (see Chapter 8). The action is based on the agent having made a representation to the third party that the agent had the requisite authority to enter into the contract on the agreed terms, i.e. he warranted his authority to contract.

Where a third party knows of an agent's lack of authority, he cannot hold the principal liable, as the contract is with the agent. In ***Watteau v Fenwick (1893)***, for example, the manager and not the owner, would have been liable to pay for the cigars if the third party knew that the manager had no authority to order cigars on the owner's behalf.

Relationship between principal and third party

As we discussed earlier, a contract made by an agent within the scope of his actual authority (express or implied) binds the principal to the same extent as if the principal had made it. We also noted that where an agent has not been given express or implied authority, the agent can bind the principal to a contract where the agent has acted within the scope of his apparent authority or where the principal ratifies the agent's contract or where an agency of necessity arises.

A principal is also bound where an agent is acting fraudulently or furthering a personal interest. In ***Lloyd v Grace, Smith & Co Ltd (1912)***, a firm of solicitors was held liable to the claimant in the tort of deceit in connection with a fraudulent transaction carried out by a clerk of the firm. The clerk worked unsupervised and he had persuaded the claimant, an elderly widow and client of the firm, to execute two documents, which, unknown to her, transferred the property into his name. It was held that the act, although fraudulent, came within his authority of handling conveyancing transactions. Although he was not expected to carry out such transactions in a fraudulent manner, he was nonetheless doing the job he was employed to do.

An agent, being outside the contract between principal and agent is not normally liable on the contract. However, an agent can be held liable where he executes a deed in his name or where the agent signs a cheque, promissory note or bill of exchange. In addition, under the doctrine of the **undisclosed principal**, where an agent contracts with a third party without revealing that he is acting on behalf of a principal, the principal can enforce the contract against the third party and the third party can enforce the contract against either the agent or the principal. The third party is entitled to treat the agent as though he were a principal.

The doctrine of the undisclosed principal, although well established in law, appears to contradict the rule of privity of contract, which we looked at in Chapter 5. The reason for the doctrine is based on commercial convenience. Agents are used frequently in business transactions and in most contracts neither party may care whether there is an undisclosed principal or not. Where there is one, however, it is very convenient that he should be able to sue and be sued.

Termination of agency

Having examined the nature of an agency relationship, in the final part of this chapter we consider how an agency relationship can come to an end. The authority of an agent may be terminated in the following ways.

By express revocation

A principal can revoke the authority of an agent to act on his behalf unless he has expressed that authority to be irrevocable. Any revocation of authority is, however, without prejudice to the rights of third parties, until the principal has communicated the fact to the third parties. The fact that revocation may be a breach of contract as between principal and agent does not prevent it from being effective.

By death or bankruptcy

The death or bankruptcy of either principal or agent usually terminates an agency relationship.

By execution of the contract

Where the agency is for a specific contract or purpose, the execution of that contract or purpose serves to determine the agency.

By other events

This refers to the destruction of the subject matter of the agency or the happening of an event that renders the agency or its objects unlawful or impossible. These concepts were explored more fully in Chapter 9, on mistake and illegality, where they can be seen as applying to contracts more generally.

Irrevocable agencies

In a few limited circumstances agency is irrevocable, such as provided for by the Powers of Attorney Act 1971 and Enduring Powers of Attorney Act 1985. Furthermore, in cases where the principal is attempting to revoke the agent's authority, the authority is regarded as being irrevocable where there remains an outstanding liability by the principal to the agent, unless the agent agrees to termination.

Answer to in-text question

QUESTION 1 What do you think the society would claim?

The housing society would likely choose to sue for damages as this would represent a greater amount to claim from the agent than an account of profit. You may recall that the case was featured in Chapter 17 and the reason for this is that fiduciary duties are common to company law and agency law. The remedies for breach of a fiduciary duty by a company director who is an agent of a company would be the same as where the breach of duty was caused by an agent who was not a company director, such as the housing society manager in the *Mahesan* case.

Website summary

The book's website contains the following material in respect of Part 5:

- PowerPoint slides containing relevant information from each chapter to help with revision
- Four additional questions with answers per chapter
- Quiz containing 10 multiple-choice questions for each part
- Biannual update bulletins to the book, which will consist of brief details of any major common law, statutory and constitutional developments affecting the currency of the book

PART SIX

Test your knowledge

This part is intended to help you test your understanding of all the topics covered in this book. For students facing exams in the subject, it also provides useful material for revision. Each section corresponds to one of the chapters. For each chapter there is:

- **A bullet point summary of the main issues covered in the chapter, including references to key cases and legislation**
- **A list of key terms setting out definitions of legal terms introduced in that chapter**
- **A 'quick quiz' section consisting of self-test questions with answers, which you can use to test your understanding of the subject**

English legal system

What is law?

Summary

Law: basic concepts

- Law can be defined as a body of rules created by the state that governs the conduct of its citizens and the state itself. Those rules are enforced by the courts.

- A distinction is made between criminal law, whose main aim is to punish and deter wrongdoers, and civil law, which is generally more concerned with providing the injured party with a means of rectifying the damage caused to it.

- Under English law, the standard of proof in criminal cases is 'beyond reasonable doubt'. This is a higher threshold than in civil cases, where the standard of proof is 'on the balance of probabilities'.

English law: basic concepts

- English law applies within the territory or jurisdiction of England and Wales. England and Wales is a common law jurisdiction and may be contrasted with civil law jurisdictions such as France or Germany.

- Another usage of the term common law is to distinguish between judge-made rules, which are based on a concept known as equity (known as 'equitable rules') and those that are not (known as 'common law rules'). Equitable rules are capable of overriding inflexible common law rules, particularly where the latter would give rise to unfairness, but they may only be applied at the court's discretion.

- The rules of English law are contained in a mixture of legislation, which is made by Parliament (or with Parliament's authority) and precedents set out in case law, which are made by judges.

The doctrine of binding precedents

- There are two types of precedent:
  - *binding precedents* – a decision on a point of law that the court is obliged to follow, even if the court itself disagrees with it
  - *persuasive precedents* – a decision on a point of law that the court is not obliged to follow, but it may *choose* to use the case as a guide.
- Precedents made by higher courts must be followed by lower courts, e.g. the Court of Appeal must normally follow decisions of the House of Lords.
- A distinction is made between what a court says when applying the law to the facts of a case (the ratio decidendi) – which is binding on lower courts – and other comments made by the court about what the law is (obiter dicta) – which are not binding.

Legislation

- There are two main types of UK legislation:
  - *Acts of Parliament*, sometimes also referred to as primary legislation or statutes and
  - *delegated legislation*, sometimes also referred to as secondary legislation.
- EU legislation consists of:
  - rules set out in the various EU treaties, which may be directly applicable
  - EU regulations
  - EU directives
  - EU decisions.
- *International treaties* are another important source of English law, e.g. the Human Rights Act 1998 empowers the English courts to apply the European Convention on Human Rights.

Key terms

Case law — law set out in a judgment concerning a dispute before the courts (may be contrasted with *legislation*). Sometimes also referred to as 'judge-made law'.

Civil law — rules of English law (whether derived from *legislation* or *case law*) that are not concerned with the *criminal law* and where the primary aim is normally to provide rights that persons can enforce (as opposed to punishing or deterring criminal activity). Can also be used to describe a type of legal system based on *Roman law*, which is usually contrasted with *common law* legal systems.

Codified rules — rules of law such as *legislation* where an attempt has been made to set out the law in a systematic way (as opposed to laws derived from *case law* where points of law may have to be extracted from a judgment).

Common law — generally refers to judgments or *case law* developed by English judges, but does not include case law relating to principles of *equity*, nor does it include laws based on *legislation* or *statutes*. May also be referred to when seeking to make a distinction between *common law* systems and those based on *civil law* or *Roman law*.

Council of Europe — an international organisation consisting (at the time of writing) of 46 members, which has responsibility (among other things) for the *European Convention on Human Rights*. Not to be confused with the European Union or *EU*.

Court of Appeal — hears all appeals from the *High Court*, the *County Court* and certain appeals from the *Crown Court*. Appeals from the Court of Appeal are made to the *House of Lords*.

Criminal law — rules of English law that are enforced by the state and where the primary aim is to punish and deter law breakers (may be contrasted with *civil law*).

Decision — a form of *EU legislation* containing measures addressed to particular member states, businesses or individuals.

Delegated legislation — *legislation* made by bodies outside Parliament, such as government departments, usually under powers delegated to them by *primary legislation*. Another term for delegated legislation is *secondary legislation*.

Directive — a form of *EU legislation* setting out measures that member states are required to implement using their own national legislation by a particular deadline.

Distinguish — if a court 'distinguishes' Case A from Case B, it is indicating that, although the two cases may appear to be similar, there are important differences between the two. These differences are sufficient to justify a conclusion that Case A should not be used as a *precedent* to decide the outcome of Case B.

Directly applicable — refers to provisions of EU law that can be relied upon directly, without the need for national implementing legislation.

ECHR — abbreviation for *European Convention on Human Rights*.

ECtHR — abbreviation for *European Court of Human Rights*.

Equity or equitable principles/rules — a body of rules distinct from *common law* rules whose main characteristic is fairness.

EU — abbreviation for the European Union.

European Convention on Human Rights — an international treaty concerning human rights that is binding on member states of the *Council of Europe*.

European Court of Human Rights — acts as a final court of appeal on matters concerning the *European Convention on Human Rights*. Not to be confused with the European Court of Justice.

House of Commons — the elected chamber of the Houses of Parliament.

House of Lords — the second chamber of the Houses of Parliament or the highest court in the English legal system. See also *Supreme Court*.

Jurisdiction — the territory in which a particular law and legal system apply. May also be used in a slightly different sense, e.g. if the people involved in the dispute are asking the court to do something it does not have power to do, the court may say that it has 'no jurisdiction' to make a ruling.

Legal person — an 'artificial' person such as a company, which is regarded in law as having its own 'legal personality' (may be contrasted with *natural person*).

Legislation — laws passed by a law-making body (such as the Houses of Parliament in the UK); legislation may be contrasted with *case law*.

Natural person — a human being (as opposed to a *legal person* such as a company).

Obiter dicta — observations made by a judge on how the law might apply to a hypothetical situation (as opposed to a ruling on the situation in the dispute under consideration, known as the *ratio decidendi*).

Precedent — decision on points of law contained in judgments on earlier cases used by courts to assist them when making decisions on new cases raising similar issues. If the precedent is binding, the court must follow it. If it is merely persuasive, the court does not have to follow it.

Primary legislation — generally used to refer to acts of parliament (as opposed to *secondary* or *delegated legislation*).

Ratio decidendi — the decision of the court on a point of law arising from the facts of the dispute under consideration (may be contrasted with *obiter dicta*).

Regulation — a form of *EU* legislation which (unlike *directives*) does not require national implementing legislation.

Roman law — normally used as an alternative way of referring to legal systems based on *civil law* (and which may be contrasted with *common law* systems such as the English legal system).

Secondary legislation — see *delegated legislation*.

Statutes or statute law — refers to English *primary legislation* such as Acts of Parliament. Should not be used to refer to *EU* legislation.

Supreme Court — legislation has been passed to create a Supreme Court to take over the judicial functions of the *House of Lords*, but at the time of writing the Supreme Court had not been set up.

Quick quiz

1 A disgruntled customer has deliberately crashed his car into your shop. No one is hurt but it will cost you a lot of money to repair your shop and you believe the customer should be punished for his actions. Is this a matter for criminal law, civil law or, possibly, both?

2 True or false: if a motorcyclist is being sued by another driver for causing damage to the latter's car as a result of a collision, the standard of proof is beyond reasonable doubt.

3 To what does the concept of 'common law' refer?

4 A court is asked to rule on the legality of a TV rental contract between A and B. The judge rules that the contract is legal. To explain his reasoning, he also makes a number of general remarks about various other types of contract that he compares and contrasts with rental contracts. Which parts of the ruling are binding on lower courts?

5 You are a journalist researching a story involving EU legislation. The legislation requires member states to harmonise their rules on unfair contract terms. Is this legislation likely to be an EU regulation, an EU directive or an EU decision?

6 True or false: the Human Rights Act 1998 implements an EU treaty.

7 What is the leapfrog procedure?

Quick quiz answers

1 Potentially both. The customer could be prosecuted under the criminal law for causing criminal damage to your shop. You could also sue the customer under the civil law to obtain compensation for the damage that he has caused.

2 False. If the motorcyclist is being sued by the car driver for compensation, that means this is a civil action in which the standard of proof will be the balance of probabilities.

3 'Common law' may have two different meanings, depending on the context. It may refer to a system of law where many fundamental rules continue to be based on judge-made rules, as in: 'England and Wales is a common law jurisdiction, as opposed to France, which is a civil law jurisdiction.' It may also refer to judge-made rules that are *not* based on equity, as in: 'Damages are a common law remedy but an injunction is based on equitable principles.'

4 Only the ruling concerning the contract between A and B is binding (this is the ratio decidendi). The remarks about car rental contracts in general are not binding because they do not directly concern the matter the court was asked to rule on. They would probably be regarded as obiter dicta and would only be persuasive precedents.

5 A directive, because it requires member states to implement it via their own national legislation.

6 False. The Human Rights Act 1998 has nothing to do with EU law. It effectively incorporates the provisions of the European Convention on Human Rights into English law. That treaty was drawn up by the Council of Europe, which is entirely separate from the EU (although the UK is a member of both).

7 The leapfrog procedure refers to a situation where an appeal may 'leapfrog' the Court of Appeal and go straight to the House of Lords. It applies where the Court of Appeal has already ruled on the issue of law that is the subject of the appeal (so a further Court of Appeal ruling would be pointless, because the Court of Appeal is bound by its previous decisions and such a precedent can only be overruled by the House of Lords).

How the law is enforced

Summary

The English court system

- The English legal system has different court systems for criminal and civil law cases. Civil law cases normally start in the County Court or the High Court. Criminal cases normally start in either the Magistrates Court or the Crown Court.

- A civil case must start in the County Court unless the claim is worth more than £15,000 (£50,000 if the claim relates to personal injuries). If the claim is worth less than this, it is possible to have the case transferred to the High Court if the court is persuaded that:
  – the case is complex
  – the case involves an important point of law or
  – the County Court's procedures or remedies are not appropriate to deal with the case.

- Appeals from decisions of either the County Court or the High Court in civil cases are made to the Court of Appeal, with a further right of appeal from the Court of Appeal to the House of Lords.

- Some civil cases, such as those concerned with employment matters, may be dealt with in specialist tribunals (e.g. an employment tribunal), which generally have a more informal procedure.

European courts

- Cases concerning human rights issues may be appealed to the European Court of Human Rights (ECtHR), but only after all rights of appeal in the English court system have been exhausted.

- Courts dealing with cases concerning points of EU law may refer questions to the European Court of Justice (ECJ). Such a referral may be made at any stage; there is no need to 'appeal' to the ECJ as such. Once the ECJ has answered the questions referred to it, the matter will return to the referring court, which *must* apply the ECJ's judgment to the particular facts of the dispute – see *Arsenal v Reed (2003)*.

- The ECJ also has power to rule on whether the actions of EU institutions such as the European Commission are lawful and whether EU member states have infringed EU law (e.g by failing to implement a directive on time).

Civil procedure in the English courts

- To initiate legal action, the claimant must fill out a claim form setting out details of its claim and send it to the court, together with the relevant fee. The court will send the form to the defendant, who must respond within certain time limits.

- The defendant's response will set out reasons (known as the defence) why the claim should be rejected. It may also include a counterclaim against the claimant.

- Once the defence has been received, the court will allocate the case to one of the following 'tracks':
  – the small claims track – for straightforward claims of up to £5000
  – the fast track – for straightforward claims that are more than £5000 but not exceeding £15,000
  – the multi-track – for claims of over £15,000 (or less than this where the court concludes that the fast track or small claims track procedures would not be appropriate, e.g. because the case is complex).

- The judge will then order the parties to prepare for trial, e.g. by exchange of written evidence (disclosure).

- At any time before the end of the trial, the parties may reach an agreement (known as a settlement) not to pursue legal action.

- The trial will normally consist of the presentation of written and oral evidence to the judge, who will listen to arguments from lawyers for the claimant and the defendant and then give his judgment, explaining the reasons for his decision.

- If the claimant is awarded damages, payment may be enforced in the following ways:
  – a charging order
  – a garnishee order
  – a writ of fieri facias
  – attachment of earnings
  – insolvency proceedings against the defendant.

Other ways of dealing with disputes/enforcing the law

- Disputes between individuals or businesses may be resolved out of court by arbitration or alternative dispute resolution (ADR).

- In certain specialist areas, such as competition and consumer law or financial services, state-funded regulators such as the Office of Fair Trading or the Financial Services Authority play a key role in enforcing the law by issuing decisions (including fines) against businesses that have acted unlawfully. There is no need for regulators to apply to court before they issue such decisions, although their decisions can normally be challenged before a court.

- Individuals and businesses may challenge actions of the state in the courts on the grounds that the state has acted unlawfully by seeking judicial review.

Key terms

Alternative dispute resolution (ADR) — a broad term that may be used to refer to any method of resolving disputes not involving arbitration or court proceedings.

Arbitration — an out-of-court procedure where the parties to a dispute agree to appoint someone (an arbitrator) to resolve it and to be legally bound by the arbitrator's decision.

Attachment of earnings — if the *defendant* is an individual, his or her employer can be required to pay some of the defendant's salary direct to the *claimant* in order to pay off the amount owed.

Barristers — a lawyer who tends to specialise in work that involves appearing before a judge. See also *solicitor*.

Charging order — this means that the *defendant* may not sell any of its property until it has paid the amount owed to the *claimant*.

Claimant — a person bringing a claim in the civil courts.

Counterclaim — where, as part of his *defence* to a claim, a defendant makes a claim of his own against the *claimant*, this is known as a counterclaim.

County Court — one of the two main courts of the English legal system where civil claims may be started (the other is the High Court).

Cross-examination — a person who has given evidence for one party to a court action may then be cross-examined (or questioned) about that evidence by lawyers representing the other party, usually with a view to discrediting their evidence.

Crown Court — one of the two main courts of the English legal system where prosecutions under criminal law are first heard (the other is the *Magistrates Court*).

Damages — financial compensation that may be claimed in court by a person who has suffered loss as a result of another person's unlawful act.

Defence — a defence to a civil claim is a document setting out how the *defendant* proposes to argue against the claim. 'The defence' can also refer to the lawyers representing the defendant.

Defendant — a person defending themselves against either a claim based on civil law or a prosecution under criminal law.

Disclosure — the process of exchanging written evidence between the parties to a court action.

European Court of Justice (ECJ) — deals with questions on the interpretation of EU law referred from national courts and rules on whether member states have failed to comply with EU law. Not to be confused with the European Court of Human Rights (ECtHR).

Garnishee order — this is an order against the *defendant's* bank or some other person holding money belonging to the defendant which prevents payment of that money to anyone other than the *claimant*.

High Court — one of the two main courts of the English legal system where civil claims may be started (the other is the *County Court*).

Judicial review — a procedure allowing individuals or businesses to challenge actions of the state in the courts on the grounds that the state has acted unlawfully.

Magistrates Court — one of the two main courts of the English legal system dealing with prosecutions under criminal law (the other is the *Crown Court*).

Parties (to a case) — the persons involved in a dispute.

Plaintiff — term used historically to refer to the *claimant*.

Solicitor — a lawyer who (unlike a *barrister*) tends to specialise in work that does not involve appearing before a judge (although some solicitors do appear before judges on a regular basis).

Tribunal — a specialist court, normally dealing with a particular aspect of civil law. An example is the Employment Tribunal, which deals with claims for unfair dismissal.

Writ of fieri facias — this allows the *claimant* (or bailiffs acting on its behalf) to seize the *defendant's* property and sell it (but only up to the value of the amount claimed).

Quick quiz

1 In which court would a shoplifter be prosecuted for theft from a business?

2 In which court would a claim for damages resulting from defective machinery worth £14,000 be dealt with?

3 Which procedural 'track' would the claim for damages in question 2 most probably be assigned to?

4 What is disclosure?

5 What is a writ of fieri facias and when would it be used?

6 The High Court has given a ruling in a dispute involving issues under the European Convention on Human Rights. What would have to happen before these issues could be considered by a European court and which European court would be involved?

7 A tribunal is hearing a case involving issues of EU law. What would have to happen before these issues could be considered by a European court and which European court would be involved?

8 Alpha Business Machines believes that the government has acted unlawfully by imposing a new tax on computers. Can it challenge the tax and, if so, how?

Quick quiz answers

1 Either the Magistrates Court or the Crown Court, because theft is a criminal offence.

2 It would have to start in the County Court, although it could be transferred to the High Court if it proved to be a complex case.

3 Probably the fast track, but only if the claim is relatively straightforward. More complex claims would be dealt with under the multi-track.

4 The pre-trial exchange of written evidence by the defendant and the claimant.

5 If the claimant has been awarded damages but the defendant refuses to pay, the claimant may apply to court for a writ of fieri facias, which allows the claimant (or bailiffs acting on its behalf) to seize the defendant's property and sell it (but only up to the value of the amount claimed).

6 The relevant court here is the European Court of Human Rights (ECtHR). However, the ECtHR could only consider the matter once the parties had exhausted their rights of appeal in the English legal system, e.g. first of all, it would be necessary to appeal to the Court of Appeal against the High Court ruling and then to the House of Lords.

7 The relevant court here is the European Court of Justice (ECJ). A reference to the ECJ could be made by the tribunal – there is no need for an appeal to a higher court.

8 In theory, yes – by applying to court for judicial review of the government's decision to introduce the tax.

Contract

Contract law: an introduction

Summary

- A contract is a legally binding agreement between two or more individuals or businesses.
- The 'basic ingredients' of a legally binding agreement are:
  - intention to create legal relations
  - agreement (offer and acceptance)
  - certainty of terms
  - consideration
  - formalities (if any)
  - capacity.
- Most contracts do not have to be written down and can be oral. However, certain types of contract have to comply with certain 'formalities' if they are to be valid, e.g. the following have to be made in writing:
  - agreements for the sale or transfer of an interest in land such as a contract to buy a house or a lease (Law of Property (Miscellaneous Provisions) Act 1989)
  - agreements governed by the Consumer Credit Act 1974
  - agreements for the transfer of shares in a limited company (Companies Act 1985)
  - cheques (Bills of Exchange Act 1882).
- A guarantee will only be valid if it is written evidence of it signed by the person giving the guarantee (Statute of Frauds 1677).
- 'Capacity' refers to the ability of a person to make a contract.
- The contents of a contract are known as the 'terms'. 'Express terms' are those that have actually been agreed between the parties.
- Sometimes contracts contain very little by way of express terms – in which case the courts will sometimes 'read in' terms in order to fill in any gaps in what the parties have agreed. Alternatively, terms may be 'read into' the contract as a result of legislation. These are known as 'implied terms'.

- Freedom of contract is the idea that individuals and businesses should generally be free to make agreements on whatever terms they choose, with a minimum of interference from the law.
- The courts can take the following actions to enforce contracts:
  - order a party to pay compensation to the other party for the loss that it has suffered – this is known as damages
  - order a party to carry out its promises – this is known as specific performance
  - order a party *not* to do something – this is known as an injunction
  - issue a statement clarifying the status of a contract or what the parties' obligations are – this is known as a declaration and both parties are obliged to comply with it.

Key terms

Acceptance — an unconditional expression of willingness to be legally bound by all the terms of an *offer*, which has been properly communicated to the offeror (and gives rise to a legally binding agreement).

Capacity — a person's ability to make contracts.

Certainty of terms — the requirement for an agreement to be sufficiently clear and detailed for the courts to be able to work out what the parties intended.

Consideration — the requirement for one person's promise to do something in an agreement to be made in exchange for a promise by the beneficiary of the first person's promise (e.g. in an agreement for building a wall, the builder's promise to build the wall needs to be made in return for a promise by the customer to pay the builder – otherwise the agreement is said to be made 'without consideration' and will not be enforced by the courts).

Declaration — a statement from a court clarifying the legal position on a particular issue and which the parties to the dispute must comply with (e.g. in the context of a contract, a declaration might clarify exactly what one of the parties has promised to do, where the parties are in dispute over this issue).

Exemption clause — contractual terms or notices attempting to exclude or limit a person's liability to others.

Express terms — the terms that have been discussed and agreed between the parties to a contract (including the terms set out in any written agreement).

Formalities — the requirement for certain types of agreement to be made in a particular way, e.g. agreements for the sale or transfer of an interest in land are said to be 'subject to formalities' because they must be made in writing.

Freedom of contract — the idea that individuals and businesses should generally be free to make agreements on whatever terms they choose, with a minimum of interference from the law.

Implied terms — terms that have not been discussed and agreed between the parties (and which do not form part of any written agreement), but which a court would regard as forming part of the contract (e.g. because they are so obvious that they did not need to be discussed or because legislation provides that such terms must be 'read into' the contract, even though they have not actually been agreed by the parties).

Injunction — a court order requiring a person not to carry out certain actions (e.g. an order requiring a business not to use or disclose certain confidential information that it had received).

Intention to create legal relations — the requirement for the parties to an agreement to actually intend to be legally bound in order for that agreement to be regarded as a contract enforceable by the courts.

Offer — a statement of the terms on which a person (known as the 'offeror') is prepared to enter into a contract, which will become legally binding if accepted by the person to whom it is addressed (known as the 'offeree').

Specific performance — a court order requiring a person to carry out certain actions (e.g. in the context of a contract, a person could be ordered to carry out a promise he has made).

Terms (of a contract) — the contents of a contract, i.e. what the agreement says.

Quick quiz

1 Name the six 'key ingredients' of a legally binding agreement.

2 Your car has broken down. A friend agrees to fix it for you but there is no discussion of payment. Later on you fall out and he argues that you are legally obliged to pay him. What key ingredients of a contract would you suggest are missing in order to defeat his claim that there is a legally binding agreement here?

3 Name three types of agreement where special formalities are required.

4 You buy a second-hand car from a dealer. There is no discussion of the terms of the sale except for the price. It later turns out that the car belonged to someone else and the dealer had no right to sell it to you. You give the car back to its rightful owner and decide to sue the dealer for the return of your money. You claim that he made a promise to you that he had the right to sell you the car and that he has broken this promise. Was this an express or implied term of your contract with the dealer?

5 True or false: 'freedom of contract' refers to the ability of a person to make contracts.

6 What powers do the courts have to enforce contracts?

7 You are managing director of a business that makes pies according to a secret recipe. One of your employees has left to set up her own business making pies using your secret recipe. In her contract of employment with your business, she agreed not to do this. You want to enforce her promise. Should you ask the court for damages or some other remedy?

Quick quiz answers

1 Intention to create legal relations, agreement (offer and acceptance), certainty of terms, consideration, formalities, capacity.

2 Intention to create legal relations (because it appears that this was originally an agreement between friends, which was not intended to have legal consequences) and consideration (because it seems you never agreed to do anything in return for your friend's promise).

3 Any of the following: agreements for the sale or transfer of an interest in land, agreements governed by the Consumer Credit Act 1974, agreements for the transfer of shares in a limited company, cheques, guarantees.

4 It would normally be an implied term of your contract with the dealer that he had the right to sell you the car. Express terms are those that have

actually been agreed between the parties, either in discussion or in any written agreement.

5 False. The legal power of a person or a business to make contracts is known as capacity. Freedom of contract is the idea that as far as possible, businesses and individuals should be free to make agreements on whatever terms they choose without interference from the law.

6 They can award damages, give declarations and make orders for specific performance or injunctions.

7 You would probably be better off asking the court for an injunction, i.e. an order addressed to the employee telling her to stop using the secret recipe.

Contract formation: getting agreement

Summary

Intention to create legal relations

- The courts will not enforce an agreement unless they are satisfied that the parties intended to create legal relations. When considering intention, two presumptions are applied (but may be rebutted by evidence to the contrary):
  - businesses are normally regarded as having intention to create legal relations – *Rose & Frank v J R Crompton (1925)*
  - friends or family members are not normally regarded as having intention to create legal relations – *Balfour v Balfour (1919)*.

- The presumption relating to businesses may be rebutted by clear wording indicating that the agreement is not intended to be legally binding – *Rose & Frank v J R Crompton (1925)*; *Jones v Vernons Pools (1938)*.

- The presumption relating to family or friends may be rebutted where:
  - the relationship of trust has broken down – *Merrit v Merrit (1970)*
  - the agreement has a commercial character – *Albert v MIB (1971)*; *Coward v MIB (1962)*.

Offer and acceptance

- An agreement is made where there is a valid offer followed by a valid acceptance.

- An offer is a statement of the terms on which a person (the 'offeror') is prepared to enter into a contract, which will become legally binding if accepted by the person to whom it is addressed (the 'offeree'). It must be distinguished from an invitation to treat.

- An invitation to treat is a statement or action designed to draw a person into negotiations with a view to making a contract. It may usually be distinguished from an offer due to the lack of intention to create legal relations should the person to whom the invitation is addressed try to accept it. The following are usually invitations to treat:
  - advertisements – *Partridge v Crittenden (1968)*
  - goods on display in a shop – *Pharmaceutical Society of Great Britain v Boots Cash Chemists (1953)*
  - answers to requests for information – *Harvey v Facey (1893)*.

- Advertisements are capable of amounting to offers where there is evidence of intention to create legal relations – *Carlill v Carbolic Smoke Ball Co (1893)*.
- An offer must be communicated to the offeree (if the offeree is not aware of certain terms of the offer, he cannot accept them).
- An offer can usually be withdrawn (or revoked) at any time before acceptance but any such withdrawal must be communicated to the offeree – *Routledge v Grant (1828)*; *Byrne v Van Tienhoven (1880)*.
- An offer will not usually last indefinitely and will normally expire after a reasonable time has elapsed for acceptance – *Ramsgate Victoria Hotel v Montefiore (1866)*.
- An acceptance is an unconditional expression of willingness to be legally bound by all the terms of an offer, which has been properly communicated to the offeror (and gives rise to a legally binding agreement).
- If the offeree seeks to add new terms or does not accept all the terms of the offer, this will amount to a counteroffer (rather than an acceptance) and will destroy the previous offer – *Hyde v Wrench (1840)*; *Pickfords v Celestica (2003)*. Note also the 'battle of the forms' – *Butler Machine Tool v Ex Cell-O Corporation (1979)*.
- Acceptance will not normally occur until it has been communicated to the offeror by an authorised person – *Felthouse v Bindley (1862)*, *Powell v Lee (1908)*. It may take place by conduct or some other positive act – *Brogden v Metropolitan Railway Co (1877)*; *Pickfords v Celestica (2003)*.
- The following are exceptions to the rule that that acceptance must normally be communicated:
  – where the offeror indicates that he is prepared to dispense with communication (in which case, no communication is required) – *Carlill v Carbolic Smoke Ball Co (1893)*
  – where the postal rule applies (in which case the acceptance is deemed to be communicated when posted) – *Adams v Lindsell (1818)*.
- The postal rule does not apply:
  – where the offeror has made it clear that post is not a suitable means of acceptance or that acceptance will take place when actually communicated (rather than when sent) – *Holwell Securities v Hughes (1974)*
  – to electronic communications such as fax or telex – *Entores v Miles Far East Corporation (1955)*; *Brinkibon v Stahag Stahl (1983)*.

Key terms

Battle of the forms — refers to the exchange of correspondence between businesses where each attempts to incorporate its own *standard terms* as the basis of the contract between them.

Counteroffer — where B responds to an offer made by A by suggesting the addition of new terms, the amendment of certain terms or an entirely new offer, this will normally be regarded as a counteroffer, which the person who made the original offer (A) can either accept or reject.

Invitation to treat — refers to statements or actions that are not sufficient to amount to an offer as they are not made with the *intention to create legal relations* and are merely intended to draw the customer into negotiations, as a prelude to the process of offer and acceptance.

Objective approach (to contract formation) — an approach to contract formation that involves considering the overall context in which the agreement was made and how the parties have behaved, based on outward appearances rather than the parties' actual state of mind. This is the approach normally followed by the courts (see *Storer v Manchester City Council (1974)*).

Offeree — a person to whom an offer has been made.

Offeror — a person who has made an offer.

Postal rule — the rule that an acceptance, if sent by post (and properly addressed and posted), is deemed to be accepted when posted, rather than when it is received (but note that the rule only applies if post is an appropriate method of communicating acceptance).

Presumption — an assumption made by the court when considering certain situations. For example, where two businesses make an agreement, the court presumes that the two businesses have the intention to create legal relations. To *rebut* the presumption, one of the businesses must produce evidence that it did not intend the agreement to be legally binding.

Rebut — to 'rebut a presumption' means to produce evidence sufficient to satisfy a court that a particular *presumption* should not be applied to the set of facts under consideration.

Revoke — to 'revoke an offer' means to withdraw that offer so that it is no longer open for acceptance. To 'revoke a licence' means to cancel or withdraw a permit (often used in connection with licences awarded by the state to carry out certain activities, such as provision of consumer credit).

Standard terms — the terms on which a business is normally prepared to contract. They are normally designed to save businesses the trouble of negotiating a detailed formal agreement covering all aspects of the transaction (this means that only a small number of variables, such as price, quantity, and delivery date have to be agreed and there is no need for discussion of other issues, such as what happens if the goods are not delivered on time etc.).

Subjective approach (to contract formation) — an approach to contract formation that involves considering the parties' state of mind when they entered the contract (the courts follow an *objective approach*, not a subjective approach when it comes to contract formation).

Quick quiz

1 If a person can show that they never intended to make a legally binding agreement, will that be sufficient to satisfy a court that the agreement should not be enforced?

2 What cases would you refer to in support of (a) the presumption that businesses intend to be legally bound; and (b) the presumption that friends or family members do not usually intend to be legally bound?

3 Lonesome Pine Shelves Ltd sends Cowboy DIY Stores a letter offering to appoint Cowboy DIY as its exclusive UK distributor. The letter is headed 'Subject to contract'. Cowboy DIY posts a letter accepting the appointment. Is there a contract?

4 Does the postal rule apply to electronic communications and what case would you cite to support your answer?

5 Following an interview, Cowboy DIY sends Bob a letter offering him a job in one of its stores. The letter says that the offer remains open for the next 14 days. Is there a contract if (a) Bob posts a reply in the last post on day 14; or (b) Bob replies by fax at 8.00 pm on day 14?

6 If Cowboy DIY sends Bob a letter on day 12 telling him that the offer is withdrawn, can Bob still accept on day 14?

7 True or false: advertisements are always invitations to treat.

Quick quiz answers

1 No. The courts cannot be expected to see inside people's minds. They are concerned with their outward behaviour and the impression this will have made on others. So if a person has acted in a way that led others to conclude that a legally binding agreement would result, the courts are likely to conclude that there was intention to create legal relations (even if, in their own mind, that person never actually intended to make a contract).

2 (a) *Rose & Frank v J R Crompton (1925)*; (b) *Balfour v Balfour (1919)*.

3 Probably not, because the letter offering to appoint Cowboy DIY is headed 'subject to contract' – the courts usually regard this as indicating that the offeror, Lonesome Pine, does not intend to be legally bound unless and until a detailed formal contract is drawn up. However, if Lonesome Pine started to act as if Cowboy DIY had been appointed as its exclusive distributor, the courts might conclude that this was sufficient evidence of its intention to be legally bound for a contract to come into existence at that stage (based on the conduct of the parties rather than any exchange of documents).

4 No – *Entores v Miles Far East Corporation (1955)*; *Brinkibon v Stahag Stahl (1983)*.

5 (a) Yes, because owing to the postal rule the letter of acceptance is deemed to be communicated when posted; (b) probably not, because electronic communications are regarded as being similar to face-to-face communication; since 8.00 pm is outside office hours, there is unlikely to be anyone in the office to read the fax, so it will not be regarded as communicated until first thing the next day.

6 Cowboy DIY is entitled to withdraw its offer at any time, unless it has made a legally binding promise (supported by consideration from Bob) to keep it open for a particular period (it appears that no consideration has been provided by Bob here). However, Bob can still accept at any time up until he has been notified that the offer is withdrawn – so if the letter of withdrawal has not reached him by day 14, he can still accept – see *Byrne v Van Tienhoven (1880)*.

7 False. Although the vast majority of advertisements are likely to be regarded as invitations to treat, it is possible for an advertisement to constitute an offer – *see Carlill v Carbolic Smoke Ball Co (1893)*.

Contract formation: certainty of terms and consideration

Summary

Certainty of terms

- The courts will not enforce an agreement if its terms are unclear or do not contain enough detail – *Scammell v Ouston (1941)*; *Baird Textiles v Marks & Spencer (2001)*.
- However, the courts apply this rule with a degree of flexibility and there are situations in which they may be prepared to 'read in' or 'imply' the missing terms:
  - where the agreement is being performed, by reference to the parties' conduct – *Foley v Classique Coaches (1943)*
  - by reference to a previous course of dealing or custom and practice in the relevant industry – *Hillas v Arcos (1932)*
  - where there is a dispute resolution clause – *iSoft v Misys (2003)*; *Foley v Classique Coaches (1934)*; *Cable & Wireless v IBM (2002)*.

Consideration

- The courts will not normally enforce agreements where one party promises to do something but the other party has not promised anything in return. Such agreements lack consideration.
- Consideration is closely related to the principle of privity of contract. Subject to certain exceptions, a person will only be regarded as a party to the contract if he has provided some consideration.
- Lawyers divide consideration into two types:
  - executory consideration: a promise that will be carried out in the future
  - executed consideration: an act that has already been done.
- When deciding whether an agreement is supported by consideration, the courts apply three main rules:
  - consideration must move from the promisee – this rule concerns the *person providing consideration*
  - consideration must not be in the past – this rule concerns the *timing of consideration*
  - consideration must be sufficient – this rule concerns the *types of promise that may qualify as consideration*.
- Consideration must move from the promisee: the person wishing to enforce the promise must have provided some consideration themselves (sometimes referred to as the principle of privity of contract) – *Tweddle v Atkinson (1861)*.
- An exception to this rule is the Contracts (Rights of Third Parties) Act 1999, which allows the parties to a contract to agree that third parties (who have not provided consideration) can enforce certain rights under that contract.
- The Act may apply where the court is satisfied that (i) the parties intended to confer a benefit on the third party; and (ii) the third party can be clearly identified by name, class or description.
- Consideration must *not* be in the past: if a person makes a promise after the contract has been made, that promise cannot be consideration for the earlier promise – *Roscorla v Thomas (1842)*. This rule is not always applied rigidly – *Re Casey's Patents (1892)*.

- Consideration must be sufficient (it must have some material value) – *White v Bluett (1853)*. However, consideration need not be adequate (it need not be worth as much as the other side's promise) – *Chappell & Co v Nestlé Co Ltd (1959)*. It can take the form of a positive (e.g. a promise to do something) or a negative (e.g. a promise not to sue).

- Performance of an existing obligation (something a person is already obliged to do) cannot normally be sufficient consideration – *Collins v Godefroy (1831)*, *Stilk v Myrick (1809)*. However, there are exceptions to this rule – *Hartley v Ponsonby (1857)*; *Williams v Roffey Brothers (1990)*.

- Part-payment of a debt is not good consideration for a promise by the creditor to accept a lesser amount, unless the debtor has agreed to do something different from what was originally agreed – *Pinnel's Case (1602)*; *Foakes v Beer (1884)*.

- *Williams v Roffey (1990)* does not apply to cases involving part-payment of debts – *Re Selectmove (1995)*. However, where a promise to accept part-payment has been made, the courts may use their equitable powers to stop a creditor from recovering the whole of the debt (promissory estoppel) – *Central London Property Trust v High Trees House (1947)*.

- Promissory estoppel may only be used as a defence to an action for payment of the whole debt. It will only be permitted where the debtor has acted fairly – *D&C Builders v Rees (1965)*.

Key terms

Custom and practice — used to describe contractual terms that are common in the relevant industry and that may be used by the courts to imply terms into the parties' express agreement.

Debtor — a person who owes money to another person.

Deed — a special form of contract requiring particular formalities. Promises made in a deed do not need to be supported by consideration.

Executed consideration — consideration consisting of an act that has already been done.

Executory consideration — consideration consisting of a promise that will be carried out in the future.

Previous course of dealing — refers to a past contract or series of contracts between the parties, which may be used by the courts to imply terms into a subsequent agreement that would otherwise be uncertain or lacking in detail.

Privity of contract — the rule that a person may only enforce a contract if he is a party to that contract (related to the principle that consideration must move from the *promisee*).

Promisee — the person to whom a particular promise has been made by one of the other parties to the contract.

Promisor — in the context of a contract, the person who has made a particular promise to one of the other parties to the contract.

Promissory estoppel – an equitable principle developed in *Central London Property Trust v High Trees House (1947)*, which allows the court to prevent enforcement of a claim for payment of the full amount where the creditor has promised to accept a lesser amount. The debtor must have relied on the promise and it must have acted fairly.

Third party – in relation to a contract, a person who is not a party to that contract.

Void — a contract that is invalid and cannot be enforced by either party.

Quick quiz

1 A shop called 'Top Beds' agrees to buy mattresses exclusively from Comfort Co for a 3-year period. After 1 year, the shop decides that it wants to buy mattresses from other firms instead, as they are cheaper. It argues that the contract with Comfort Co is too uncertain to enforce because it contains no provisions concerning price. Is this argument likely to succeed and what case would you cite in support of your answer?

2 If you pay for some goods in advance, is the consideration provided by you executed or executory?

3 You fix a friend's car. Afterwards, she promises to pay you £50 for the work. Is there a problem with consideration here? Give a reason for your answer and a case to support it.

4 Would it make any difference if she had always paid you for similar work in the past? Give a reason for your answer and a case to support it.

5 You receive a bill for £100 from the shop that sold you your computer for carrying out repairs on it. However, you have an annual maintenance contract with the shop which covers 'all repairs'. The shop is threatening to take you to court over your refusal to pay. What arguments based on consideration could you put forward in your defence and what cases would you refer to?

6 Assume that the shop is entitled to charge you £100 for the repairs. You pay £25 and offer to help out in the shop for an afternoon. Can the shop enforce the remaining £75? What cases would you cite to support your answer?

7 In what circumstances would either you or the shop be able to rely on promissory estoppel? Give a reason for your answer.

Quick quiz answers

1 No, because the courts will be able to imply provisions dealing with price based on the prices that have been paid during the first year of the contract – *Foley v Classique Coaches*.

2 Executed.

3 Yes, because consideration must not be in the past (to be enforceable, her promise would have to be given in return for a promise by you to fix the car, but in fact it was made *after* you had done the work) – *see Roscorla v Thomas*.

4 Yes, probably – as in *Re Casey's Patents*, a court might well see this as a situation where there was an implied promise to pay you, even though the exact amount of the payment had not been agreed.

5 Since the shop is already obliged to carry out the repairs, it cannot charge you for them as it has provided no new consideration to support any promise to pay from you (performance of an existing obligation is not good consideration – see *Collins v Godefroy*; *Stilk v Myrick*).

6 Probably not. Although the general rule is that part-payment of a debt is not good consideration for a promise by the creditor to accept a lesser amount, the debt may be extinguished if the debtor offers something else in addition to the part-payment – see *Pinnel's Case; Foakes v Beer*.

7 The shop would not be able to rely on promissory estoppel at all because it only acts as a defence – so in this scenario it would only be relevant to you. You might be able to rely on it if, for example, the shop had promised to allow you to pay later than normally required and you had relied on that promise to your detriment.

Terms of the contract

Summary

- Contracts contain legally binding promises that are set out in the terms of the contract.

- A condition is a term of the contract that is so important that breach of it will enable the innocent party to repudiate the contract and claim damages.

- A warranty is a term of the contract that is not sufficiently important to be a condition (so the innocent party can only claim damages and cannot repudiate the contract – unless the contract itself expressly states that breach of warranty will entitle the innocent party to terminate the agreement).

- An innominate term is one that may be classified as either a condition or a warranty depending on the nature and seriousness of the breach – *Hong Kong Fir Shipping Co v Kawasaki Kisen Kaisha (1962)*.

- An express term is a term specifically agreed by the parties. However, terms may also be implied, i.e. 'read into' the contract by the courts in the following ways:
  - on the basis of a previous course of dealing or custom and practice (see Chapter 5 on certainty of terms)
  - where the term is (i) obvious to a reasonable person – *Shirlaw v Southern Foundries Ltd (1939)*; and (ii) necessary for 'business efficacy' – *The Moorcock (1889)*
  - where the term is required as a matter of law, e.g. either by legislation such as the Sale of Goods Act 1979 (see following) or based on the common law – *Liverpool City Council v Irwin (1976)*.

Implied terms: Sale of Goods Act 1979

- The following terms are implied into contracts for the supply of goods by the Sale of Goods Act 1979 (SGA):
  - the seller must have the right to sell the goods (section 12)
  - goods sold by description must correspond to their description (section 13)
  - the goods must be of satisfactory quality (section 14(2))*
  - the goods must be fit for their purpose (section 14(3))*
  - if goods are sold by sample, the quality of the sample provided must correspond to the quality of the bulk (section 15)*

- **NB***: = only implied into contracts for sale of goods by a person acting in the course of a business (see *Stevenson v Rogers (1999)*), not private sales.

- To meet the requirement of satisfactory quality under section 14(2) SGA, goods must generally:
  - be fit for the purpose for which they are normally supplied
  - be safe
  - be free from defects, including minor ones
  - function properly for a reasonable period of time
  - have a reasonably satisfactory finish and appearance.

- In relation to section 14(2) SGA, the courts are required to consider the 'description of the goods … and all other relevant circumstances', including any public statements made about the goods by the supplier or the manufacturer.

- In relation to section 14(2) SGA, safety and fitness for normal purposes are usually requirements whatever price the products are sold at – *SW Tubes Ltd v Owen Stuart Ltd (2002)*.

- With brand-new goods, even minor defects are likely to constitute a breach of section 14(2) SGA. However, if the goods are second hand or low price, a lower standard is generally applied, particularly where the seller has drawn the buyer's attention to any defects before the sale – *Bartlett v Sidney Marcus Ltd (1965)*.

- Section 14(3) SGA gives the buyer additional protection in situations where he has indicated to the seller that the product is needed for a specific purpose – *Jewson v Kelly (2003)*.

Implied terms: Supply of Goods and Services Act 1982

- The Supply of Goods and Services Act 1982 (SOGASA) applies to contracts for:
  - supply of services only, e.g. a taxi service
  - supply of a mixture of goods and services e.g. where a builder/decorator provides materials (goods) and carries out building work (services)
  - rental (as opposed to sale) of goods.

- Where the contract includes supply of goods (i.e. mixed goods and services contracts and rental contracts), SOGASA implies terms which are essentially the same as those as in sections 12–15 SGA (see earlier):
  - title: section 2 (note that for rental contracts, no transfer of ownership is implied)
  - description: section 3
  - satisfactory quality: section 4(2)
  - fitness for purpose: section 4(3)
  - sale by sample: section 5.

- In relation to services, the terms implied by SOGASA include:
  - section 13: the supplier will carry out those services with reasonable care and skill, i.e. the standard which a reasonably competent provider of the relevant services could have been expected to meet – *The Simkins Partnership v Reeves Lund & Co Ltd (2003)*

  - section 14: the supplier must carry out the services within a reasonable time (unless the time for performance has been fixed in the contract itself).

Effect of breaching SGA/SOGASA implied terms

- The terms implied by SGA and SOGASA are generally regarded as conditions of the contract. This means that:
  - in the case of a sale of goods contract, breach means that the customer can repudiate, i.e. reject the goods and demand his money back
  - however, the right to reject may be lost if the buyer is deemed to have accepted the goods (because of delay, affirmation, etc.) – *Clegg v Andersson (2003); Jones v Gallagher (2004)*
  - where the breach is of section 13, 14 or 15 SGA (or their equivalents in SOGASA) and the breach is so slight that it would be unreasonable to reject the goods, it is regarded as a breach of warranty and the customer can only claim damages. This only applies to business purchasers, not consumers.

- Consumers who do not wish to reject goods or claim damages can choose between the following additional remedies under the Sale and Supply of Goods to Consumers Regulations 2002:
  - requiring the supplier to replace the goods within a reasonable time
  - requiring the supplier to repair the goods within a reasonable time
  - accepting a reduction in the price
  - **NB**: (1) a person 'deals as a consumer' if he did not make the contract in the course of a business or did not hold himself out as doing so (see Chapter 20, on consumer protection); (2) the rights to repair or replacement are not available where it would be disproportionately expensive to carry them out.

Incorporation of terms

- The courts will not regard a term as having been incorporated into a contract unless the term was brought to the attention of the other party *before* acceptance – *Olley v Marlborough Court (1949)*.

- Where a party has signed a document, the courts will assume that he has read and understood its contents and any terms will therefore be incorporated into the contract – *L'Estrange v Graucob (1934)*.

- Where the agreement consists of several unsigned documents or notices, the courts will need to be satisfied that enough was done to draw attention to the relevant term before the contract was made. Where the term may have harsh or unexpected effects on one party's normal rights, more effort needs to be made to draw attention to it before acceptance – *Thornton v Shoe Lane Parking (1971); Interfoto Picture Library Ltd v Stiletto Visual Programmes Ltd (1988); O'Brien v Mirror Group Newspapers Ltd (2001); Spurling v Bradshaw (1956)*.

- Statements made by the parties in negotiations (either in writing or orally) are not normally regarded as terms of the contract and are known as pre-contractual representations. However, such statements can sometimes be regarded as terms, depending on the following factors:
  - the importance of the statement
  - whether the maker of the statement had special knowledge or skill
  - whether the parties had put their agreement in writing (and whether the written document contained any reference to the statement)
  - the timing of the statement.

- See *Bannerman v White (1861); Routledge v McKay (1954)*.

Key terms

Condition — a term of the contract that is sufficiently important that, if breached, it will entitle the innocent party to *repudiate* the contract. (See also *warranty* and *innominate terms*.)

Exemption clause — contractual terms or notices that attempt to exclude or limit a person's liability to others.

Incorporation of terms — a term is said to be incorporated into a contract if it forms part of the agreement reached between the parties.

Innominate term — a term that may be classified as either a *condition* or a *warranty* depending on the nature and seriousness of the breach.

Pre-contractual representation — usually a statement made in the course of negotiations prior to conclusion of a contract, but can take the form of non-verbal conduct likely to be interpreted as a statement.

Repudiate — to repudiate a contract means to regard the contract as being at an end (an innocent party may be justified in doing this if the other party has breached a *condition* of the contract, but not if there has only been a breach of *warranty*).

Warranty — a term of the contract that is not sufficiently important to be a *condition* and therefore will not normally entitle the innocent party to *repudiate* the contract (unless the contract itself expressly states that breach of warranty will entitle the innocent party to terminate the agreement).

Quick quiz

1 Classify the following terms according to whether they are conditions, warranties or innominate terms (assume the terms are in contracts between two businesses): (i) 'the seller has the right to sell the goods'; (ii) 'the goods must be delivered by 9.00 am on 6 June and time is of the essence (any delay will entitle the buyer to terminate the contract)'; and (iii) 'the paintwork on any second-hand cars must be in satisfactory condition'.

2 True or false: if a term has not been expressly agreed by the parties, it may be implied if it would have been obvious to a reasonable person.

3 You buy some shoes from a shop in an end of season stock clearance sale. After a couple of weeks, the right shoe falls apart. The shoe shop tells you that the goods were in a sale, so you have no cause for complaint. Legally, are they right?

4 Would it have made any difference if the shoe shop had put up a notice pointing out that some of the shoes were reduced because they were 'seconds', i.e. they did not conform to the manufacturer's normal standards?

5 Assuming there has been a breach of contract by the shoe shop, what would this breach entitle you to do? Would there be a problem if you delayed going back to the shoe shop with your complaint for 2 months?

6 True or false: in a contract for the supply and installation of a computer system, the supply of hardware would be governed by the Sale of Goods Act 1979 and the supply of installation services by the Supply of Goods and Services Act 1982.

7 Adrian has bought a vintage car from Brian. One of the main reasons why Adrian bought it was that Brian told him the car was a rare model (although he didn't tell Brian this and no mention of it was made in their written contract). Brian also said that he wasn't much of an expert and had only bought the car himself because he 'liked the look of it'. In fact, the car proves to be much less rare than Brian suggested. Is Brian's statement likely to be regarded as a term of the contract? Cite a case to support your answer.

Quick quiz answers

1 (i) Condition (this is one of the terms implied by the Sale of Goods Act 1979); (ii) also probably a condition because the term makes it clear that the delivery deadline is very important and expressly states that the buyer may terminate if the goods are delivered late; and (iii) almost certainly a warranty, as problems with the paintwork are unlikely to be regarded as serious enough to amount to breach of a condition.

2 False – the term must not only be obvious to a reasonable person, but must also be necessary for business efficacy – see *Shirlaw v Southern Foundries (1939)* and *The Moorcock (1889)*.

3 Probably not. A term that the shoes are of satisfactory quality and fit for their purpose will have been implied into your contract with the shoe shop for the sale of the shoes. Even cheap shoes would generally be expected to last more than a couple of weeks. In addition, although the courts take account of price when deciding whether something is of satisfactory quality, it is unlikely that the price would make any difference here. This is because the shoes appear to have been reduced in order to achieve a quick sale, not because there was any problem with their quality. If there had been a problem with their quality, which *was* the reason for the lower price, the shoe shop should have brought it to your attention.

4 Possibly – but much would depend on whether the notice had been displayed sufficiently prominently for customers to be aware of it before they bought the goods (in which case the notice would probably have been incorporated as a term of the contract). If the shop failed to do this, it cannot rely on the notice – see *Olley v Marlborough Court (1949)*.

5 The requirement of satisfactory quality is a condition, so breach would enable you to repudiate the contract and claim damages, i.e. reject the shoes and demand a refund. Alternatively, as you were acting as a consumer, you could choose between the additional remedies available under the Sale and Supply of Goods to Consumers Regulations 2002, e.g. choose to accept a repair. If you delayed acting for 2 months, a court might say that you have lost the right to reject because you delayed too long before informing the shop that you wished to do so – see *Jones v Gallagher (2004)*.

6 False – the contract is for a combination of goods and services, so it will be covered by the Supply of Goods and Services Act 1982 only.

7 Probably not. The term has not been included in the written contract. Brian does not appear to have much special knowledge or expertise and Adrian did not make it clear that the rarity of the car was particularly important to him – see *Routledge v McKay 1954)*.

Exemption clauses

Summary

- Exemption clauses are terms of the contract that attempt to limit or exclude the liability of one party to the other. The law seeks to control their use in three main ways: incorporation, construction and legislation.

- Incorporation: if an exemption clause has not been properly incorporated it will not be legally binding. See Chapter 6.

- Construction: if an exemption clause has been properly incorporated, the courts examine the wording in detail, applying the following rules:
  - the need for clear wording – *Casson v Ostley (2001)*
  - the contra-proferentem rule, i.e. that exemption clauses should be interpreted narrowly, against the interest of the party seeking to rely on them.

- Legislation: the Unfair Contract Terms Act 1977 (UCTA) allows parties to challenge certain types of exemption clause on the grounds that they are too harsh. A consumer who wishes to challenge an exemption clause can also do so under the Unfair Terms in Consumer Contracts Regulations 1999 (UTCCR) (see Chapter 20 for detail on the concept of 'consumer' and the UTCCR).

UCTA

- UCTA only applies to contracts where a business is seeking to limit or exclude its liability. It does not apply to sales by individuals in a private capacity.

- Under UCTA, certain exemption clauses are automatically void and unenforceable, while others may be enforceable, but only if they meet the reasonableness test (see later).

- The effect of UCTA varies depending on whether the contract is between (i) a business and a consumer; or (ii) a business and another business. A consumer under UTCA is any person who is not dealing as a business (see Chapter 20 for more detail on the concept of 'consumer' under UCTA).

UCTA and contracts with consumers

Type of liability excluded or limited	UCTA reference	Always void?	Other remarks
Death or personal injury due to negligence	Section 2(1)	Yes	—
Loss due to negligence other than personal injury or death	Section 2(2)	No	Subject to reasonableness test*
Loss due to breach of contract	Section 3	No	Subject to reasonableness test*
Loss due to breach of implied terms relating to goods under SGA or SOGASA (see Chapter 6 for details)	Sections 6–7	Yes	—

*Note that, because of consumers' weakness vis-à-vis suppliers, the reasonableness test is generally applied more strictly than is the case with business-to-business contracts.

UCTA and contracts between businesses

Type of liability excluded or limited	UCTA reference	Always void?	Other remarks
Death or personal injury due to negligence	Section 2(1)	Yes	—
Loss due to negligence other than personal injury or death	Section 2(2)	No	Subject to reasonableness test
Loss due to breach of contract	Section 3	No	Only applies if contract is on standard written terms. *Subject to reasonableness test
Loss due to breach of implied terms relating to goods under SGA or SOGASA	Sections 6–7	Only as regards attempts to limit/ exclude implied terms relating to title	Attempts to limit/ exclude implied terms other than those relating to title subject to reasonableness test

*Note that 'standard written terms' has generally been widely interpreted as covering not only pre-printed forms but also any exemption clause regularly put forward by a business as its starting point for negotiations.

The reasonableness test

- Section 11 UCTA says that the court must decide whether the clause was fair and reasonable having regard to 'the circumstances which were, or ought reasonably to have been known to or in the contemplation of the parties when the contract was made'. These include the following factors (see Schedule 2 and section 11(4) UCTA):
  - the bargaining strength of the parties – see *Watford v Sanderson (2001)*; *St Albans v ICL (1996)*
  - whether the party seeking to challenge the term was given any inducement to accept the term – see *Watford v Sanderson (2001)*
  - knowledge of the existence and extent of the term by the party seeking to challenge it under UCTA
  - whether liability is accepted only if certain conditions are complied with – see *Messer UK Ltd v Britvic (2002)*
  - whether the goods were made to special order
  - the resources of the parties and the availability of insurance – see *St Albans v ICL (1996)*; *George Mitchell v Finney Lock Seeds (1983)*; *Photo Production v Securicor (1980)*.
- As a general rule, the courts prefer not to intervene with the bargain struck by the parties where there is equality of bargaining power – *Watford v Sanderson (2001)*; *Photo Production v Securicor (1980)*. However, if there is either (i) inequality of bargaining power in favour of the party relying on the exemption clause or (ii) the clause is particularly destructive of the other party's rights, the courts will be more likely to

intervene – *St Albans v ICL (1996); George Mitchell v Finney Lock Seeds (1983); Messer UK Ltd v Britvic (2002)*.

Key terms

Construction — (of contracts) the process of interpretation that the courts use to decide what a contractual term means in practice.

Contra-proferentem rule – the rule that a clause such as an exemption clause should be interpreted narrowly, against the interest of the party seeking to rely on it.

Incorporation of terms – a term is said to be incorporated into a contract if it forms part of the agreement reached between the parties.

Liability – the extent of a person's legal responsibility to another person.

Reasonableness test – refers to the test applied to exemption clauses in the Unfair Contract Terms Act 1977 to determine whether they are enforceable.

Quick quiz

1 You are injured by a faulty piece of machinery as your car is going through a carwash. The carwash operators say that they are not liable on the basis of a notice stating: 'This carwash is used at your own risk.' The notice can only be seen as you drive out of the carwash, having already paid to use it and is quite easy to miss. Is the notice likely to be effective as an exemption clause? You should have *three* reasons for your answer.

2 How is section 3 UCTA different from section 2(2) UCTA?

3 True or false: sections 6–7 UCTA apply to contracts between businesses regardless of whether the agreement was based on standard written terms.

4 True or false: the reasonableness test requires the court to consider whether the clause was fair and reasonable at the time the breach of contract took place.

5 Alpha Business Machines has agreed to supply and install a computer system to SuperFast Mail Order for £500,000. The contract was largely negotiated but the exemption clauses were based on standard wording supplied by Alpha. Does section 3 UCTA apply here?

6 SuperFast alleges that the computer system is unusable and is claiming damages of £1,000,000. The contract contains a clause limiting Alpha's liability to 10% of the contract price, i.e. £100,000. Assume that section 3 UCTA applies to this clause. What other sections of UCTA could be relevant here?

7 What additional information would a court require to assess whether Alpha's limitation of liability is reasonable?

Quick quiz answers

1 The notice is almost certainly ineffective as an exemption clause. First, it is only visible after you have made your agreement to use the carwash, so it is unlikely to be incorporated into the contract (see *Olley v Marlborough Court (1949)*). Second, it is possible that it could be ineffective because it is not sufficiently clearly worded and/or the operators have failed to draw

enough attention to it. For example, it seems to be saying that the carwash operators have no liability for loss due to their own negligence; the courts have repeatedly said that businesses need to make it crystal clear to customers when they are seeking to impose such wide-ranging exemption clauses. Third, s2(1) UCTA provides that exemption clauses that attempt to exclude liability for personal injury or death caused by negligence are always void and unenforceable.

2 Section 3 UCTA deals with exemption clauses that attempt to limit or exclude liability for any breach of contract (regardless of whether it has been caused by negligence or the claim is based on the tort of negligence). In that sense it is capable of covering a wider range of exemption clauses than section 2(2). However, whereas section 2(2) applies to all contracts covered by UCTA, section 3 only applies where (i) the contract is with a consumer; or (ii) the contract is on the standard written terms of the party seeking to rely on the exemption clause.

3 True; the requirement for standard written terms in relation to business to business contracts is only relevant to section 3 UCTA.

4 False. The reasonableness test requires consideration of the circumstances *at the time the contract was made.*

5 Probably, because the courts have interpreted 'standard written terms' relatively widely to include situations where much of the contract was negotiated but the exemption clause was based on standard wording used by the party seeking to rely on it.

6 Section 7 UCTA would be relevant here because the clause attempts to limit liability for implied terms relating to goods under the Supply of Goods and Services Act 1982. Section 6 would not be relevant because the contract is for supply of a mixture of goods and services. Section 2(2) UCTA could be relevant if the failure of the system to work properly is due to negligence by Alpha.

7 A court would need to consider whether the reasonableness test was met. This involves considering all the circumstances at the time the contract was made, in particular: (i) whether the parties were of equal bargaining strength; (ii) whether SuperFast was given any inducement to accept the term; (iii) the extent to which SuperFast was aware of the term; (iv) whether Alpha is liable only if certain conditions are complied with; (v) whether the system was designed to meet SuperFast's special requirements; and (vi) the resources of the parties and the availability of insurance.

Discharge of contracts, performance and remedies for breach

Summary

Discharge of contracts

- When the parties are no longer under any contractual obligations to one another, the contract is said to be discharged. This may occur in the following ways:

– carrying out the obligations under the contract (discharge by performance)

– the parties agreeing to release one another from their obligations (discharge by agreement). Note that if one party has already performed its obligations, the discharge will be unilateral and will require consideration from the other party (accord and satisfaction)

– one party commits such a serious breach of the contract that the innocent party is entitled to repudiate it (discharge by breach)

– discharge by frustration – see next section.

Frustration

- If a contract is frustrated, both parties are relieved of their obligations from the time of the frustrating event onwards and the contract is discharged.

- Frustration may be relevant where, after the contract has been entered into, an event occurs that is (i) outside the control of the parties and (ii) not dealt with in the contract itself. The event must either make performance of the contract illegal, impossible or radically different from what was originally envisaged by the parties.

- Frustration may occur in the following circumstances:
  - *supervening illegality*: i.e. where the contract was legal when made but becomes illegal as a result of a change in the law
  - *government intervention*: e.g. requisitioning equipment in time of war
  - *death, illness or imprisonment*: where the contract can only be performed by a particular individual – *Robinson v Davison (1871)*
  - *destruction or unavailability of the subject matter*: – *Taylor v Caldwell (1863)*
  - *non-occurrence of event*: – *Krell v Henry (1903)*; *Herne Bay Steamboat v Hutton (1903)*
  - *radical change*: where it is possible to carry out the contract in theory but 'the circumstances in which performance is called for would render it a thing radically different from that which was undertaken by the contract' – *Davis Contractors v Fareham UDC (1956)*.

- Under the Law Reform (Frustrated Contracts) Act 1943 the courts can order the other party to make a payment corresponding to the benefit it has received – *BP Exploration v Hunt (1982)*.

Performance

- Contracts must generally be performed strictly in accordance with their terms, although this can sometimes have harsh effects where the contract is entire (i.e payment is due only on completion of all obligations), rather than divisible (i.e. payment is due in instalments) – see *Cutter v Powell (1756)*; *Morse v Cognesis (2003)*.

- The doctrine of substantial performance prevents a party from refusing to make any payment at all where the other party has carried out the majority of its obligations satisfactorily – *Hoenig v Isaacs (1952)*.

- A contractual obligation may also be discharged if one party agrees to accept part-performance by the other party. However, the innocent party must be in a position to choose whether to accept the part-performance – *Sumpter v Hedges (1898)*.

Time limits for legal action

- Under the Limitation Act 1980, legal action cannot normally be brought in relation to a contract if it is more than 6 years since the date of the breach.

Remedies for breach of contract

- Where one party is in breach of a contract, the following remedies may be available to the innocent party:
  - *repudiation*: allows the innocent party to terminate the contract immediately, but only if there has been a breach of condition (see Chapter 6)
  - *damages*: allows the innocent party to seek financial compensation for loss arising from breach of contract
  - *equitable remedies*: includes court orders such as injunctions. Generally only available in quite limited circumstances, where damages would not be an adequate remedy
  - **NB**: repudiation and damages are common law remedies.

Repudiation

- A party wishing to repudiate a contract must act promptly and avoid acting in a way that is inconsistent with an intention to terminate the contract, otherwise it may be regarded as having affirmed the contract (and the right to repudiate will be lost) – e.g. see *Jones v Gallagher (2004)*.

- In the case of an *anticipatory breach*, i.e. where one party decides that it does not want to proceed with the contract before the other party has begun to carry out its obligations, the innocent party is usually only allowed to proceed with performance if it has a legitimate interest in doing so – *Clea Shipping v Bulk Oil International (1984)* (but note also *White & Carter v McGregor (1961)*).

Damages

- Damages for breach of contract take the form of a financial award intended to put the innocent party in the position it would have been in if the contract had been performed properly. The amount of any award is limited by the following principles:
  - *remoteness of damage*: damages may only be claimed for loss that the party in breach either knew about or could reasonably have foreseen at the time the contract was made; all other loss is said to be too remote – *Hadley v Baxendale (1854)*; *Victoria Laundry v Newman Industries (1949)*
  - *duty of injured party to mitigate its loss*: the injured party must take reasonable steps to minimise its loss – *British Westinghouse Electric and Manufacturing Co v Underground Electric Railways Co of London Ltd (1912)*; *Messer v Britvic (2002)*
  - *causation*: the injured party loss must be able to show that the loss was caused by the breach – *Messer v Britvic (2002)*
  - *quantum*: the loss must be capable of being quantified by a court in financial terms. Generally, damages cannot be claimed for emotional distress or disappointment because these are impossible to quantify in financial terms. Exceptionally, damages for distress or disappointment may be claimed where one of the main aims of the agreement was to provide pleasure, relaxation or peace of mind – *Jarvis v Swan Tours (1973)*; *Farley v Skinner (2001)*

– *loss of amenity*: where damages are claimed for loss of amenity, the size of the award must bear some relation to the benefit that it will bring to the claimant – *Ruxley Electronics v Forsyth (1995)*.

- The amount of damages payable may be limited by exemption clauses in the contract.

- It is also possible to include contractual terms requiring a party in breach to pay *liquidated damages* (thus potentially avoiding having to go to court to have the level of damages assessed), but such clauses are only enforceable if the sum claimed is a 'genuine pre-estimate' of the loss likely to be suffered by the injured party – *Dunlop Pneumatic Tyre Co v New Garage & Motor Co (1915)*; *Jeancharm v Barnet FC (2003)*.

Equitable remedies

- Equitable remedies for breach of contract include:
  - *specific performance*: a court order compelling the party in breach to do something, such as transfer the shares in a limited company
  - *injunction*: a court order that prohibits the party in breach from doing something, such as not taking any steps to sell the shares in a limited company to anyone else.

- Equitable remedies are only available at the discretion of the court, where the court believes that it would be just and equitable to do so. In particular, the following conditions must normally be met:
  - damages would not be an adequate remedy
  - the innocent party has acted without delay and has 'clean hands', i.e. he or she has acted reasonably and honestly
  - the equitable remedy will not cause undue hardship or be especially difficult to supervise or enforce.

Key terms

Accord and satisfaction — in relation to a *unilateral discharge*, accord refers to one party's agreement to release the other from its contractual obligations and satisfaction refers to the consideration provided in return for that release.

Affirmation — in relation to contracts, refers to a situation where one party might have been entitled to *repudiate* the contract but has failed to do so and has acted in such a way that he will be regarded as having chosen to continue with it or 'affirm' it.

Anticipatory breach (of contract) — where one party decides (in breach of contract) that it does not want to proceed with a contract after agreement has been reached but before the innocent party has begun to carry out its obligations.

Bilateral discharge — where both parties to a contract agree that they are no longer subject to certain obligations (e.g. in return for a supplier of goods agreeing not to enforce payment, the customer agrees that it will not require the supplier to deliver the goods).

Discharge by agreement — a contractual obligation may be *discharged* by agreement, i.e. the parties may agree that it does not have to be performed.

Discharge by performance — a contractual obligation is *discharged* by *performance* where it has been properly carried out (in which case the party responsible for carrying it out is no longer under any obligation to the other party).

Discharged — a contractual obligation is said to be discharged when the party responsible for carrying it out is no longer obliged to do so (e.g. because the obligation has been properly carried out).

Divisible contract — one where payment is made in a series of instalments, following performance of particular obligations, rather than in a single lump sum on successful *performance* of all the promisor's obligations.

Entire contract — one where payment only becomes due on completion of all obligations.

Frustration — a contract may be frustrated where it has become either illegal or virtually impossible to perform it as originally envisaged (in which case both parties are released from their obligations and the contract is *discharged*).

Liquidated damages clause — contractual term requiring the party in breach to pay a specified sum to the other party if there is a breach of contract, so there is no need for the injured party to go to court to claim damages.

Loss of amenity — the loss of a facility that the claimant expected to have as a result of the *performance* of a legal obligation.

Mitigation — (of loss) refers to the principle requiring a party who has suffered loss as a result of another party's breach of contract or other unlawful act to take reasonable steps to minimise the loss they are likely to suffer.

Part-performance — in relation to a contract, refers to the carrying out of some but not the whole of a contractual obligation.

Performance — in relation to a contract, refers to the carrying out of a contractual obligation.

Remoteness (of damage) — refers to loss that is too far removed from the unlawful act to allow damages to be claimed (note that the tests for this in contract and tort are different).

Repudiate — to repudiate a contract means to regard the contract as being at an end (an innocent party may be justified in doing this if the other party has breached a condition of the contract, but not if there has only been a breach of warranty).

Rescission — an equitable remedy allowing the court to make an order setting a contract aside.

Substantial performance (doctrine of) — a rule of law that allows a party to claim payment in return for *performance* of obligations that have largely been performed properly (although they have not been completed).

Supervening event — in the context of *frustration* refers to an event that happened after the contract was entered into but before it could be fully performed.

Unilateral discharge — may occur where one party has already performed all its contractual obligations but agrees to release the other party from its remaining obligations.

Quick quiz

1 In which of the following situations would a contract for sale of a vintage car be frustrated: (i) unknown to the parties, the car is stolen before the contract is made; (ii) cars of this type are made illegal after the contract is made but before the car is delivered; (iii) after the contract is made, a sudden increase in diesel prices makes it three times as expensive to hire a lorry to deliver the car (which is not drivable), thus completely wiping out any profit the seller would have made on the deal.

2 Gerry the builder has agreed to construct a garden wall with payment in two instalments, the first after 1 week and the second when the work is complete. He has built most of the wall but failed to add decorative tiles along the top, as agreed. His customer is refusing to pay him anything. Is the customer within his rights to do this?

3 Choose the correct option to complete this sentence: 'The time limit for contractual claims is generally 6 years from' (a) the date of the contract; (b) the date of the breach; or (c) the date that the injured party became aware of the breach.

4 Jemima's Catering has made an agreement with Juicebuster Drinks for supply of a large quantity of soft drinks for a wedding. Jemima has paid a £500 deposit. The contract states that the drinks must be delivered the day before the wedding at the latest. Juicebuster fails to deliver but tells Jemima it will be able to deliver them just before the wedding starts. Jemima has found another supplier who can deliver immediately. She would like to terminate the contract with Juicebuster, but is worried about losing her deposit. What remedies does she have?

5 At the wedding, Jemima serves salmon purchased from her usual supplier, Something Fishy Ltd. Unfortunately, 80% of the guests develop food poisoning within an hour of eating the salmon and the wedding is ruined. The wedding was paid for by the parents of the happy couple. Can they claim damages from Jemima for emotional distress?

6 Faced with numerous damages claims from the wedding guests, Jemima has decided to sue Something Fishy Ltd for supplying salmon unfit for human consumption. Something Fishy argues that even if it was at fault, it cannot be liable to pay damages because it knew nothing about the wedding. Is this argument likely to succeed?

7 Fred is an inventor. He has been discussing commercial exploitation of one of his inventions with a number of firms. Before entering discussions, he always gets the firms to sign a confidentiality agreement so they cannot use any information he gives them in order to copy or develop something similar to his invention. He has discovered that one of the firms is developing a product similar to his invention using drawings supplied by him. What remedies are available to Fred?

Quick quiz answers

1 Only (ii). (i) is a case of mistake, not frustration, as the event occurred before the contract was made. (iii) is simply a case of the obligations becoming more expensive to perform, which is unlikely to result in frustration.

2 No. This contract is divisible (as payment is in instalments), so at the very least, Gerry is entitled to the first instalment. He might also be entitled to the final instalment, less what it would reasonably cost the customer to finish the job, based on the doctrine of substantial performance.

3 (b).

4 If the requirement to deliver by a particular time is a condition (as seems likely in this scenario), Jemima can repudiate the contract and claim damages (which would include recovery of the deposit and any additional

money she has had to pay to another supplier over and above what she would have paid to Juicebuster). If the delivery time is only a warranty, then Jemima can only claim damages. It is unlikely that any equitable remedies would be available in this scenario because a financial award will be sufficient to compensate Jemima for any loss suffered.

5 Yes. Although the courts do not usually award damages for loss of enjoyment and distress, they are prepared to do so where the main purpose of the contract was to provide enjoyment/peace of mind. A wedding would almost certainly fall into that category. However, the damages awarded are unlikely to be very high.

6 No; it would not be necessary for Something Fishy to know about the wedding in order to be liable to pay damages because it was reasonably foreseeable that a catering firm like Jemima's would be buying the salmon to provide a meal at an event of some description.

7 The most appropriate remedy here would be an injunction to stop the firm using Fred's drawings. Fred could also sue for damages based on breach of the confidentiality agreement but it would be difficult for him to show that he had suffered loss; he would only start to suffer loss when the firm began selling the product that it is in the process of developing. What Fred really wants to do is stop the firm using his drawings to develop that product in the first place; in the circumstances, therefore, damages would be unlikely to be an adequate remedy and the court might well be prepared to use its equitable powers.

Validity of contracts (1)

Summary

Misrepresentation

- Misrepresentation may be relevant where a false representation has been made that induced a person to enter into a contract.

- The misrepresentation may take the form of words or conduct. Mere silence is not usually sufficient, although continuing to act as if nothing has changed following a material change of circumstances may amount to a misrepresentation: *Spice Girls v Aprilia World Service (2002)*; *With v O'Flanagan (1936)*.

- In order to be actionable, the misrepresentation must meet the following conditions:
  - a reasonable person in the position of the injured party would have regarded the representation as one that was based on facts, rather than a mere expression of opinion (with no basis in fact): *Nelson Group Services v BG plc (2002)*; *Bisset v Wilkinson (1927)*
  - the representation was false: *Sykes v Taylor-Rose (2004)*
  - the injured party believed it to be true (it makes no difference if the injured party was given the opportunity to check the truth of the statement): *Redgrave v Hurd (1881)*

 – the representation was one of the reasons why the injured party entered into the agreement (but not necessarily the only reason): *Edgington v Fitzmaurice (1885)*; *Infiniteland v Artisan Contracting Limited (2005)*.

- The remedies for misrepresentation are:
  – rescission, i.e. an equitable order setting the contract aside and, depending on the circumstances, ordering the return of money, property etc.
  – damages based on the tort of deceit.
- Damages and rescission are available for both fraudulent and negligent misrepresentation.
- A representation is fraudulent if the person responsible knows that it is untrue or made it with a reckless disregard for the truth: *Derry v Peek (1889)*.
- A representation is negligent if the person responsible is unable to show that he believed it to be true and had reasonable grounds for that belief: section 2(1), Misrepresentation Act 1967. The burden of proving reasonable grounds for belief can be significant: *Howard Marine v A Ogden & Sons (1978)*.
- If the misrepresentation does not fall into these categories (i.e. the person responsible for it is not at fault), it will be regarded as innocent: section 2(2), Misrepresentation Act 1967.

Mistake

- Where one or more of the parties entered into a contract based on a misunderstanding of some factual issue (and the party in question is not to blame for that misunderstanding), the courts may decide that the contract is void for mistake.
- If the court concludes that there has been a mistake of fact, the entire contract as void, i.e. it is treated as if it never existed and neither party was ever under any contractual obligations. Equitable remedies are not available where there has been a mistake of fact: *Great Peace Shipping v Tsavliris (2002)*.
- A common mistake is where both parties are mistaken in the same way about the same issue. Where only one party is mistaken, this is known as unilateral mistake.
- Mistakes of fact may also be classified according to type:
  – mistake as to existence of subject matter: *Couturier v Hastie (1856)*
  – mistake as to quality of subject matter: *Great Peace Shipping v Tsavliris (2002)*; *Bell v Lever Brothers (1932)*
  – mistake as to identity: *Cundy v Lindsay (1878)*; *Kings Norton Metal Co Ltd v Edridge, Merrett & Co Ltd (1897)*, *Phillips v Brooks (1919)*
  – mistake as to terms: *Hartog v Colin & Shields (1939)*
  – non est factum: *Saunders v Anglia Building Society (1970)*.
- For certain types of mistake (but not mistakes of fact), equitable remedies may be available. These include:
  – *rectification* – a procedure that may allow genuine mistakes in a contract to be corrected: *Hurst Stores v ML Europe (2004)*
  – *mistakes of law*: *Kleinwort Benson v Lincoln City Council (1998)*.

Key terms

Common mistake — where both parties are mistaken in the same way about the same issue relating to a contract. See also *mistake*.

Fraudulent misrepresentation — a *misrepresentation* made knowingly or without regard to its truth.

Misrepresentation — a false statement of fact that induced a contract, giving rise to a cause of action that may allow the contract to be rescinded and/or damages to be awarded.

Mistake — a fundamental misapprehension regarding a contract that, if certain conditions are met, may affect the validity of the contract. See also *mistake of fact* and *mistake of law*.

Mistake as to identity — a *mistake* relating to the identity of one of the parties to a contract.

Mistake as to subject matter — a *mistake* relating to the main 'subject matter' of an agreement, e.g. in a contract for sale of goods, the goods would be the subject matter of the contract. Mistakes as to subject matter fall into two categories: mistakes as to existence of subject matter, e.g. whether the goods exist and mistakes as to quality of subject matter, e.g whether the goods have the attributes they were believed to have at the time of the agreement.

Mistake of fact — a fundamental misapprehension regarding the facts relating to a contract that, if certain conditions are met, may result in the contract being void at common law.

Mistake of law — a fundamental misapprehension regarding the law that, if certain conditions are met, may allow one or more of the parties to seek equitable remedies in respect of a contract that is affected by the *mistake*.

Negligent misrepresentation — a *misrepresentation* that is not fraudulent, but was made without reasonable grounds for belief in its truth.

Non est factum — a form of *mistake* where a person has signed a document believing it to be something fundamentally different from what it really is, which may result in the contract being void.

Pre-contractual representation — usually a statement made in the course of negotiations prior to conclusion of a contract, but can take the form of non-verbal conduct likely to be interpreted as a statement.

Rectification — an equitable procedure that allows a party to apply to court for an order correcting a genuine error in an agreement.

Unilateral mistake — where only one party is mistaken about an issue relating to a contract.

Quick quiz

1 True or false: if you keep silent about something you can never be sued for misrepresentation.

2 You have agreed to buy a second-hand car. The seller told you that he thought it was a very rare model, which proves to be false, although earlier he told you that he did not know much about it. You could have discovered this if you had looked at its logbook, which you were offered the chance to read. You asked a friend who is a mechanic to look the car over and he said that he thought it was a good buy. You paid a deposit but you have now decided that you do not want to proceed with the purchase. Can the contract be rescinded for misrepresentation?

3 Why is it so much easier to prove that a misrepresentation was negligent rather than fraudulent?

4 Which of the following types of mistake may result in equitable remedies being granted:
a mistake as to quality of subject matter
b mistake as to identity
c mistake of law
d non est factum
e mistake as to terms
f rectification?

5 You want to buy an antique vase from a website. The price is stated as £20. In response to your email offering to buy the vase, the sellers send you an email saying that your offer has been accepted. You then receive a further email denying that any contract was made and saying that the price of the vase is a mistake – it should have been £2000 and the sellers are only willing to sell at that price. A week later the vase is destroyed in a warehouse fire. Do any of these events mean that the contract is void for mistake and, if so, what sort of mistake?

6 You have ordered some CDs from what you believed was the website of a well-known retailer. Payment was made by direct debit card and the money has left your bank account. In fact, the website turns out to be a fake, deliberately designed to fool users into thinking that it was the website of the reputable retailer in question. Is the contract void for mistake and, if so, would this help you get your money back?

Quick quiz answers

1 False. Silence is not normally sufficient to amount to a misrepresentation. However, a person may be sued for misrepresentation if he makes a material representation that later becomes false owing to a change of circumstances and stays silent about it.

2 In order to establish misrepresentation, you must first establish that there was a false statement of fact, not opinion. It might be difficult to prove this given that the seller has told you that he did not know much about cars; this suggests that his statement about the car's rarity is not based on any particular expertise or factual knowledge (see *Bisset v Wilkinson*). Even if you can prove this, you would also need to show that you relied on his statement. Although you do not have to show that it was the only or main reason why you entered into the contract (see *Edgington v Fitzmaurice*), you are likely to have difficulty here if you relied primarily on the assessment of your friend, the mechanic, when deciding to buy the car (see *Attwood v Small*).

3 For fraudulent misrepresentation, you need to show that the representation was made in the *knowledge* that it was untrue or with a reckless disregard for its truth. For negligent misrepresentation, you merely need to show that the misrepresentation was false; it is then up to the defendant to show that it had reasonable grounds for belief in the truth of the statement (which is not always easy – see *Howard Marine v Ogden*).

4 c and f only. The others are all different types of mistake of fact, for which no equitable remedies are available (see *Great Peace Shipping v Tsavliris*).

5 The pricing error could be a mistake as to terms (see *Hartog v Colin & Shields*). However, it appears that the error would have to be obvious to the customer – so unless you were an expert yourself and knew that the £20 was probably an error, the sellers are likely to have difficulty arguing that the contract is void for mistake. The sellers are probably wrong to argue that no contract was made to sell you the vase – the exchange of emails would satisfy normal offer and acceptance criteria (see Chapter 4). Assuming this is correct, the destruction of the vase in the warehouse fire is an example of a frustrating event – not a mistake as to the existence of subject matter (the latter would only be relevant if the fire had occurred before the sellers sent their email accepting your order, i.e. before the contract was made).

6 The contract probably would be void for mistake as to identity (see *Cundy v Lindsay*) because you thought you were dealing with a particular person – the well-known retailer – but you were in fact dealing with a fraudster. However, if the retailer had not been well known and you were influenced mainly by its *apparent* respectability, a court would probably say that you were mistaken as to the attributes of the website, rather than its actual identity (in which case mistake would not have applied – see *Kings Norton Metal Co Ltd v Edridge, Merrett & Co Ltd*). In any event, mistake would not help you recover your money because it merely results in the contract being void at common law (and no equitable remedies are available). You would do better to sue the rogue for fraudulent misrepresentation, which would enable you to claim damages equal to your loss.

Validity of contracts (2)

Summary

Duress

- If a contract has been entered into as a result of threats of some kind (duress), it may be voidable at common law.
- Duress may consist of physical violence or threats to use physical violence: *Barton v Armstrong (1975)*. This is known as physical duress.
- Duress may also consist of economic pressure (economic duress), although only if stringent conditions are met: *Pao On v Lau Yiu Long (1979)*. In particular:
  – some form of illegitimate pressure must be applied and
  – the victim had no practical alternative but to give in to the pressure.
- The illegitimate pressure need not amount to an illegal act: *CTN Cash & Carry Ltd v Gallaher Ltd (1994)*. However, it must normally amount to more than hard-headed commercial tactics and be a threat that will have a significant adverse effect on the victim: *Atlas Express v Kafco (1989)*.

Undue influence

- If a contract has been entered into because one of the parties has unfairly exploited its relationship with the other party (undue influence), equitable remedies may be available, including rescission. There are two types of undue influence – actual and presumed.

- To establish actual undue influence, the party wishing to set the contract aside must prove that:
  - there is a 'relationship of dominance' that puts the other party in a position of power or authority, allowing them to influence the victim
  - the victim would not have entered into the contract without the influence exercised by the other party – *Williams v Bayley (1866)*.

- Presumed undue influence arises where there is a relationship of trust and confidence between the parties. A victim of presumed undue influence only needs to prove that:
  - there was a relationship of trust and confidence (note that there are some relationships where the courts accept that a relationship of trust and confidence *must* exist, e.g. solicitor–client, parent–child, doctor–patient etc.)
  - the relevant contract was manifestly disadvantageous to him.

- The alleged wrongdoer may defeat the presumption of undue influence if it can show that the victim was told to seek independent advice: *Lloyds Bank v Bundy (1975)*.

Illegality

- Where the *purpose* of a contract is illegal, the courts will not uphold it and neither party can enforce it. The purpose of a contract may be illegal as a result of:
  - statute, e.g. the Competition Act 1998, which prohibits agreements between businesses which significantly restrict competition within the UK (or a substantial part of the UK)
  - the common law, such as agreements that are contrary to public policy, e.g. *Parkinson v College of Ambulance Ltd and Harrison (1925)* and the doctrine of restraint of trade (see below).

- Where only part of a contract is for an illegal purpose, the courts may rule that the illegal portion can be 'severed' and the remainder of the contract can be upheld. However, the courts must be satisfied that the remainder of the agreement continues to make sense (both grammatically and in terms of continuing to reflect the parties' original intentions) if the illegal portions are removed: *Attwood v Lamont (1920)*.

- Where the contract itself is legal, but it has been carried out in a *manner* that is illegal (illegal performance), the courts will not allow the party responsible for the illegal performance to enforce the contract, but the innocent party can enforce it: *Birkett v Acorn Business Machines Ltd (1999)*.

Restraint of trade

- Employment agreements often contain restrictive covenants that may fall foul of the law on restraint of trade. Contracts in restraint of trade are illegal and cannot be enforced.

- The courts will only enforce restrictive covenants if:
  - the clause protects a legitimate interest of the employer
  - the clause goes no further than is reasonably necessary to protect that legitimate interest
  - it is in the public interest to enforce the clause.

- See *Herbert Morris v Saxelby (1916)*; *Anstalt v Hayek (2002)*.

Capacity

- A contract will not normally be enforceable if one of the parties did not have the legal power or capacity to make it.

- The general rule is that if it should have been obvious to one party that the other party did not have capacity (e.g. as a result of drunkenness, madness or mental illness), the contract will not be enforceable. However, contracts made while acting without capacity may become binding if ratified.

- Where someone has been 'sectioned', no contract they make will be binding.

- If a minor wants to enforce his contractual rights against a business, he will normally be allowed to do so and the courts will treat the contract as valid. But if a minor decides that he does not want to be bound by a contract, the general rule is that a business will not be able to enforce it, subject to the following exceptions:
  - contracts for 'necessaries' (i.e. goods or services that are suitable 'to the condition in life of the minor' and 'to his actual requirements at the time of sale and delivery') can be enforced against minors – *Nash v Inman (1908)*, section 3 of the Sale of Goods Act 1979
  - section 3 of the Minors Contracts Act 1987 allows the courts to make an order for the return of property if a minor refuses to pay (whether or not the property amounts to 'necessaries'), provided it is 'just and equitable' to do so
  - contracts of employment, education of apprenticeship can be enforced – but only where the contract as a whole is beneficial to the minor – *De Francesco v Barnum (1890)*, *Doyle v White City Stadium Ltd (1935)*.

Key terms

Actual undue influence — refers to a situation where one party has unfairly exploited its relationship of dominance to induce the other party to enter into a contract, which may allow the latter to seek equitable remedies in respect of the contract.

Capacity — a person's ability to make contacts.

Duress — refers to threats of a physical nature (physical duress) or economic nature (economic duress) that may render a contract *voidable*.

Minor — a person under 18 years old.

Necessaries — in the context of contracts with *minors*, refers to goods that are necessary to the condition in life of the minor and to his actual requirements at the time of sale and delivery.

Presumed undue influence — refers to a situation where one party is presumed to have unfairly exploited its relationship of trust and confidence with the other party resulting in a contract that is manifestly disadvantageous to the latter. May allow the innocent party to seek equitable remedies in respect of the contract.

Public policy — refers to factors that the courts take into account when justifying decisions on the grounds that they are necessary for the good of society as a whole and/or the effective functioning of the legal system.

Ratify — if a person ratifies an agreement that would otherwise be invalid (owing to lack of capacity, for example), they are confirming that they wish to be legally bound by it (despite the potential invalidity).

Restraint of trade (doctrine of) — refers to case law concerning the rule that the courts will not enforce certain contractual restrictions on the grounds that they are contrary to *public policy*.

Restrictive covenant — an agreement imposing certain restrictions on a person, typically used to refer to clauses in agreements restricting employees or businesses from competing with the other party to the agreement.

Severance — refers to the possibility of the courts deciding (usually in relation to cases involving illegality) that a void portion of a contract may be 'severed' or separated from the other provisions, thus allowing those remaining provisions to be upheld.

Undue influence — refers to a situation where a contract has been entered into because someone has unfairly exploited their relationship with one of the parties. (See also *actual undue influence* and *presumed undue influence*.)

Voidable — a contract is said to be voidable if it can be set aside at the option of the innocent party (to be contrasted with the position if a contract is void, where neither party can enforce the contract).

Quick quiz

1 True or false: if a contract has been obtained by duress, equitable remedies are available.

2 A solicitor persuades one of his elderly clients to transfer her house into his name. She says that she did not realise what she was agreeing to. Can she get out of the contract?

3 A manufacturer makes an agreement to supply a retailer with computers. The agreement requires the retailer not to sell the products below the manufacturer's recommended retail price. It also requires the manufacturer to submit accounting documents to the retailer for tax purposes. At the retailer's request, the manufacturer submits false documentation in order to allow the retailer to obtain better tax treatment. What types of illegality are involved here and what would be the effect on the contract?

4 Big Corp's managing director has resigned and intends to work for a competitor. His employment contract with Big Corp states that he cannot work for competing companies anywhere in the world for 5 years after he stops working for Big Corp. Is Big Corp likely to be able to enforce this clause?

5 Angela is 17 but looks older. Bob sells her his car for £200. She pays him £50 up front and promises to pay the rest tomorrow. If she fails to pay up, can Bob force her to pay?

6 Bob, who owns a taxi firm, decides to employ Angela as a driver. He has also offered to pay for her to learn to drive. Is the contract of employment enforceable? What case would you cite to support your answer?

Quick quiz answers

1 False. Duress is a common law doctrine, like mistake. However, unlike mistake, it does allow the contract to be set aside at the option of the innocent party.

2   The elderly client could argue that the contract is void for mistake based on non est factum (see Chapter 9). However, this is not easy to establish and it would probably be easier to show that it is voidable on the basis of presumed undue influence. The solicitor–client relationship is a relationship of trust and confidence that gives rise to an automatic presumption of undue influence. This can normally only be rebutted if the solicitor shows that he advised the client to obtain independent advice. The client then needs only to show that the contract was manifestly disadvantageous to her (as seems likely).

3   The term imposing minimum resale prices on the retailer would be a breach of the Competition Act 1998 and an example of a contract for an illegal purpose. That term would be void but could probably be severed from the remainder of the contract, allowing the other terms to be upheld. The provision requiring provision of accounting documents is not illegal in itself; however, the manner of its performance is illegal as it would amount to a fraud on the Inland Revenue. Since neither party is innocent in this case (both have been involved in the fraud), they might not be permitted to enforce the other terms of the contract.

4   This clause may be in restraint of trade, in which case it will be illegal and Big Corp cannot enforce it. While Big Corp may have a legitimate interest in preventing its managing director working for a competitor (e.g. to protect sensitive information, relations with customers, etc.), the scope of the clause is very wide, both in terms of time and geographical area. It is likely to be unreasonable by reference to the interest that Big Corp seeks to protect. The courts may also find that it is not in the public interest to prevent the executive working in his field of expertise.

5   Angela is a minor and the general rule is that contracts with minors are only enforceable at the option of the minor i.e. the non-minor party cannot enforce the agreement. However, Bob may be able to argue that a car is a 'necessary' item (see *Nash v Inman*), in which case the contract will be enforceable. Alternatively or in addition, he may be able to seek a court order under the Minors Contracts Act 1987 requiring Angela to pay the remaining £150, provided it is just and equitable to do so.

6   Yes, provided it can be said to be for Angela's benefit (as is probably the case here) – see *Doyle v White City Stadium Ltd*.

Tort

General principles of liability in tort and the tort of negligence

Summary

- Under the civil law, the wrongful actions of an individual or a business can result in tortious as well as contractual liability.
- The most important tort affecting the activities of a business is the tort of negligence.
- In order for a claimant to succeed in negligence, the claimant must establish that (i) the defendant owed the claimant a legal duty of care; (ii) that the defendant failed to take reasonable care and skill, (iii) that the breach of duty caused the claimant's loss, and (iv) that the claimant's damage was not 'too remote'.

Duty of care

- Whether a duty of care arises depends on whether the harm suffered was (i) reasonably foreseeable (*Donoghue v Stevenson (1932)*); (ii) that there was a close and proximate relationship between the claimant and the defendant (*Caparo Industries plc v Dickman (1990)*); and (iii) that it is fair and reasonable to impose a duty on the defendant (*Hill v Chief Constable of West Yorkshire Police (1987)*).

- Most cases of loss relate to physical harm or damage to property. However, the law does allow recovery in other cases of loss such as nervous shock, consequential economic loss (*Spartan Steel & Alloys Ltd v Martin & Co (1972)*) and pure economic loss in the case of negligent advice (*Hedley Byrne & Co v Heller & Partners (1963)*).

- For negligent advice, a special relationship needs to be established between the advisor and the advisee.

- For cases of nervous shock (e.g. post-traumatic distress syndrome and not mere grief or sorrow) recovery depends on whether the claimant is a primary victim, i.e. he fears for his own safety (*Dulieu v White (1901)*) or a secondary victim, where he fears for the safety of someone else (*Hambrook v Stokes (1925)*; *McCloughlin v O'Brien (1983)*; *Alcock v Chief Constable of South Yorkshire Police (1991)*).

Breach of duty

- Whether a duty of care has been breached depends on whether the defendant exercised the requisite degree of care and skill in all the circumstances.

- The standard expected is an objective one *(Nettleship v Weston (1971))* and the courts weigh up a number of factors in determining whether the defendant breached a duty of care.

- Such factors include the degree of risk to the claimant created by the defendant's conduct *(Bolton v Stone (1951))*, the seriousness of the harm that the claimant may suffer *(Paris v Stepney Borough Council (1951))*, the social utility of the defendant's action *(Watt v Hertfordshire County Council (1954))* and the expense and practicability of taking precautions against the risk *(Latimer v AEC Ltd (1953))*.

- With skilled persons, the standard expected is to be judged by what the ordinary person in the particular job, trade or profession would have done *(Bolam v Friern Hospital Management Committee (1957))*.

- As with the other elements of an action in negligence, the burden of proof is on the claimant. However, in relation to the breach of duty, where the facts speak for themselves, the defendant has to disprove negligence *(Scott v London & St Katherine's Docks (1865))*.

Causation

- The rule applied in relation to causation is the 'but for' test, i.e. *but for* the defendant's conduct, the claimant would not have suffered the harm or damage *(Barnett v Chelsea and Kensington Hospital Management Committee (1969))*. The defendant, however, will not be liable for any intervening act (called a novus actus interveniens) that breaks the chain of causation *(Lamb v Camden London Borough Council (1981))*, unless the intervening act was reasonably foreseeable as a result of the defendant's breach of duty.

- In some cases, in order to avoid an injustice, the courts are prepared to allow recovery even though the 'but for' test cannot be satisfied *(McGhee v National Coal Board (1972); Fairchild v Glenhaven Funeral Services Ltd (2002))*.

Remoteness of damage

- As well as establishing a causal connection between the breach of duty and the damage suffered, the claimant must also show that the damage was not too remote a consequence of the defendant's careless act and that the damage resulted from the type of risk that the defendant created.

- The test is one of *reasonable foreseeability (Overseas Tankships (UK) Ltd v Morts Dock & Engineering Co Ltd, The Wagonmound (1961))*.

- Although the damage must be of a type that is within the class of risk created, neither the precise extent of the damage nor the precise manner of its infliction need be foreseeable *(Hughes v Lord Advocate (1963))*.

- It does not matter if the claimant's damage is aggravated by some physical peculiarity he has, provided that the injury is within the class of risk created (the tortfeasor takes his victim as he finds him). This is known as the eggshell skull rule *(Smith v Leech Brain & Co (1962))*.

Defences to an action

- Defences to an action in tort include, where appropriate, contributory negligence and consent (*volenti*).
- Contributory negligence is a partial defence available under the Law Reform (Contributory Negligence) Act 1945 and, where relied on, will result in a reduction of the award of damages for the claimant on the basis that as a result of the claimant's conduct, the claimant was responsible for the damage or harm suffered (*Capps v Miller (1989)*).
- Consent is a complete defence and operates where it can be shown that the claimant consented voluntarily to running a risk (*ICI v Shatwell (1965)*; *Wooldridge v Sumner (1963)*).

Key terms

Breach of duty — a failure to exercise reasonable care and skill where a duty of care is imposed. The standard of care in an action for negligence is based on what a reasonable person might be expected to do considering all the circumstances.

Causation — the relationship between an act of the defendant and the consequences it produces.

Contributory negligence — a claimant's conduct that contributes to his injury and that the courts considers just and equitable that the claimant's award of damages should be reduced.

Duty of care — a legal obligation to take reasonable care to avoid causing damage or harm.

Economic loss — financial loss suffered by a claimant following a negligent act or negligent words.

Eggshell skull rule — a person committing a tort cannot complain if the harm he caused to the claimant was more serious than expected because the claimant suffered from a pre-existing condition, illness or weakness ('he takes his victim as he finds him').

Negligent misstatement — a false statement of fact made honestly but carelessly that is actionable in tort where a special relationship exists between the maker of the statement and the receiver of the statement.

Nervous shock — a psychological illness or injury such as post-traumatic distress syndrome.

Novus actus interveniens — a new act that breaks the chain of causation between the act of a defendant and the harm or damage suffered by a claimant.

Reasonable man — an ordinary person, sometimes referred to as the 'person on the Clapham omnibus'.

Remoteness of damage — the extent to which a defendant is liable for the consequences of a wrongful act or omission.

Volenti non fit injuria — a defence available to a defendant that the claimant consented to the injury suffered or the risk of being injured.

Quick quiz

1 Outline the ingredients of an action in the tort of negligence.

2 In what circumstances can a defendant be liable in the tort of negligence for a negligent statement?

3   What is meant by the defences of contributory negligence and consent?

4   Jake's cafe has been flooded by heavy rain and the floor is slippery. He sprinkles sawdust on the floor and puts up a warning notice for customers. Kim enters the shop using crutches after a skiing accident in which she broke her right leg. She slips and breaks the leg again. Can she sue Jake?

5   Asha is sitting in a hired car at the brow of a hill when suddenly the car begins to roll down the hill. She tries the handbrake, but it fails to work. As it gathers speed, she jumps from the car and breaks an ankle. The car stops at the foot of the hill. Had she stayed in the car, she would have suffered no harm. Could her conduct amount to contributory negligence?

Quick quiz answers

1   In order to succeed with an action in negligence, a claimant must show that the defendant owed the claimant a duty of care, that the defendant breached that duty and that a foreseeable type of injury or loss suffered by the claimant was caused by the defendant.

2   Liability for negligent words or advice arises where there is a special relationship between the claimant and the defendant. Such a relationship exists where the defendant gives advice in response to a request by the claimant in circumstances where it can be shown that (i) the defendant knew or ought to have known that the claimant would rely on the advice and (ii) the claimant did so rely. A defendant can exclude or limit liability for negligent advice subject to the provisions of the Unfair Contract Terms Act 1977.

3   Contributory negligence is a partial defence found in the Law Reform (Contributory Negligence) Act 1945 and allows a court to reduce a claimant's award of damages to the extent of the claimant's responsibility for the injury or loss the claimant suffered. Consent is a complete defence and allows a defendant to avoid liability where it can be shown that the claimant consented voluntarily, either expressly or impliedly, to running the risk which injured the claimant.

4   Jake owes a duty of care to his customers but an issue arises as to whether his conduct amounted to a breach of this duty. The risk of an accident must be weighed against the cost of avoiding it. On balance, in the light of the warning and the sawdust, a court may find that he did not breach his duty of care.

5   Ordinarily, if a person makes his injuries worse he is contributory negligent and any damages may be reduced. However, the claimant is only expected to do what a reasonable person would have done (and this can include things done in the 'heat of the moment'). On the facts, Asha should be able to recover damages in full.

Other business-related torts and vicarious liability

Summary

Nuisance

- A private nuisance is an indirect interference with another person's use and enjoyment of their land. Damages awarded to a claimant are designed to compensate the claimant for the reduction in the value of the land or the dimunition of the benefits of using and enjoying the land (*Leakey v National Trust (1980); Canary Wharf Ltd v Hunter (1997)*).

- A public nuisance is a nuisance that affects to a material degree the comfort and convenience of the public generally.

- Under the rule in *Rylands v Fletcher (1868)*, a person who brings onto his land, or allows to accumulate on his land, something that is likely to do harm if it escapes is strictly liable if the 'thing' escapes and causes harm. Damages, however, can only be claimed in respect of a type of loss that is reasonably foreseeable. There is no liability where the thing that has escaped is the result of a natural use of the land (*Transco plc v Stockport Metropolitan Borough Council (2004)*).

- Defences to an action in nuisance are an 'Act of God' (*Goldman v Hargrave (1967)*), act of a stranger, consent, statutory authority (*Allen v Gulf Oil Refining Ltd (1981)*) and prescription (*Miller v Jackson (1977)*).

- The usual remedy is an injunction, i.e. an order of the court instructing the defendant from continuing with the nuisance.

Occupiers' liability

- Under the Occupiers' Liability Act 1957, an occupier of premises owes a common law duty of care to visitors to take such care as required in the circumstances to ensure that they are reasonably safe in using the premises for the purpose for which they are invited or permitted by the occupier to be there.

- Under the Occupiers' Liability Act 1984, an occupier of premises owes a duty to take reasonable care in all the circumstances to non-lawful visitors (i.e. trespassers) where they are aware of a danger or have reasonable grounds to believe it exists and know or have reasonable grounds to believe that a non-lawful visitor is or might come into the vicinity of the danger.

Other torts

- Where a statute has been breached, it is possible for a claimant to bring a civil claim if the statute provides for such a duty to be owed or where the intention of Parliament can be ascertained from the statute (e.g. s41 CPA 1987).

- The most common economic torts affecting businesses are passing off, inducing a breach of contract, conspiracy and interference with a trade by unlawful means.

Vicarious liability

- The doctrine of vicarious liability provides the basis on which a business can be held liable for the torts of its employees.

- Whether an employer is vicariously liable depends on whether the employee was a worker and not an independent contractor (*Ready Mixed Concrete (South East) Ltd v Ministry of Pensions and National Insurance (1968)*) and on whether the employee acted in the course of employment as opposed to committing an independent act.

- The employee's course of employment is determined by defining the employee's *sphere* of employment, so that unauthorised acts (as well as authorised acts) of an employee may come within the course of employment where it can be shown that the act was connected so closely to the employee's work that it became an improper mode of doing an authorised act (*Century Insurance Co Ltd v Northern Ireland Road Transport Board (1942)*; *Kay v ITW Ltd (1967)*; *Limpus v London General Omnibus Co (1862)*; *Rose v Plenty (1976)*) and not an independent act falling outside the course of employment (*Twine v Bean's Express (1946)*; *Hilton Thomas Burton (Rhodes) Ltd (1961)*; *Beard v London General Omnibus Company (1900)*).

- Liability under the doctrine can relate to criminal acts of employees (*Lloyd v Grace Smith (1912)*; *Morris v CW Martin (1965)*; *Poland v John Parr and Sons (1926)*; *Lister v Hesley Hall Ltd (2001)*).

- Under the doctrine, the employer as well as the employee is liable, but it is the employer and not the employee that is likely to have the resources or insurance to meet the claim of the claimant.

- An employer may owe a direct duty of care to a claimant where the employer failed to exercise reasonable care in engaging, training or supervising an employee or in failing to provide a safe system of work. Acts of independent contractors do not result in an employer being held liable unless either the independent contractor performed a non-delegable duty of the employer or the employer was negligent in engaging the independent contractor.

Key terms

Breach of duty — a failure to exercise reasonable care and skill where a *duty of care* is imposed. The standard of care in an action for negligence is based on what a reasonable person might be expected to do considering all the circumstances.

Cartel — an agreement between, or association of, businesses in order to form a monopoly in a given trade or industry.

Contract of employment — a contract by which a person, an employee, agrees to undertake certain duties under the direction and control of an employer in return for a wage or salary.

Course of employment — the scope of work a person is employed to do.

Duty of care — a legal obligation to take reasonable care to avoid causing damage or harm.

Fiduciary — a person such as a trustee or director of a company who holds a position of trust or confidence with respect to someone else and who is obliged to act for that person's benefit.

Independent contractor — a person or a business engaged to do a particular job of work on behalf of another.

Restrictive (trade) practice — agreements by businesses designed to maintain high prices or earnings or in order to exclude outsiders from a particular trade or profession.

Quick quiz

1 To what extent can an occupier of land be liable in tort to those who visit his premises or for activities he conducts on his land?

2 What is the tort of nuisance?

3 What are the requirements for enabling an employer to be held vicariously liable for the acts of its employees?

Quick quiz answers

1 Under the Occupiers' Liability Act 1954, an occupier of premises owes a duty to take reasonable care to visitors so as to ensure they are reasonably safe when using the premises for the purpose for which the visitor is invited or permitted by the occupier to be there. Under the Occupiers' Liability Act 1984, an occupier of premises has a duty to take such care as is reasonable in all the circumstances to see that a trespasser does not suffer injury on the premises by reason of a danger of which the occupier is aware. The duty arises where the occupier knows or has reasonable grounds to believe that the trespasser is in the area of the danger concerned and the risk is one that the occupier might reasonably be expected to offer some protection.

2 There are two types of nuisance – private nuisance and public nuisance. A private nuisance is an indirect interference with another person's land or their use and enjoyment of that land. A public nuisance is taken to be any nuisance that affects the reasonable comfort and convenience of the public generally. It is not concerned with an individual's enjoyment of their land.

3 In order for an employer to be held liable vicariously for the acts of its employees, it must be shown that the employee is a worker and not an independent contractor, that the employee committed a tort (e.g. negligence) and that the employee's act was one done in the course of employment. An employer may also be liable directly to a victim if it can be shown that he failed to take care in employing the employee or providing adequate supervision or training, etc.

Company law

Business associations

Summary

- There are four main types of association for running a business: a sole trader, an ordinary partnership, a limited liability partnership and an incorporated company.
- A sole trader is an individual who runs a business on a self-employed basis. That person is responsible for the affairs of the business and any losses or debts incurred.

Partnerships

- An ordinary partnership, as recognised by the Partnership Act (PA) 1890, consists of two or more persons running a business in common with a view to making a profit. Non-profit bodies therefore, such as charities and clubs and societies are not capable of acting as a partnership.
- Forming a partnership does not create a separate legal entity. The partners are liable joint and severally for debts and contractual wrongs done in the ordinary course of business. Such liability extends to other wrongs such as negligence and breach of trust.
- Partners are likely to have a written agreement, but the absence of such an agreement does not preclude the existence of a partnership.
- However, in the event of no agreement or the agreement is silent on a particular matter, the PA 1890 lays down a number of default rules to be applied as affecting the relationship of the partners.
- The most common form of partnership is a partnership at will, which means that a partner can terminate the partnership by giving notice, although it is likely that the partners would have agreed that the partnership will continue with the surviving partners.

Limited liability partnership

- A limited liability partnership formed under the Limited Liability Partnerships Act (LLPA) 2000 is an incorporated body comprising two or more persons called members.

- As with an incorporated company, the members in general incur no personal liability for contractual and tortious wrongs arising from acts done on behalf of the limited liability partnership.
- However, as with the Companies Act (CA) 1985 in respect of incorporated companies, the LLPA 2000 provides a measure of creditor protection. For example, in the event of the insolvency of a limited liability partnership, members can be held liable for fraudulent or wrongful trading and can contribute an agreed sum of money in order to meet creditors' claims.

Incorporated company

- An incorporated company is an artificial legal person with a separate legal entity distinct from its members, officers and employees.
- A company can be formed by registration under the Companies Act 1985 (a registered company), by an Act of Parliament (a statutory company) or on the grant of a Royal Charter (a chartered company).
- Registered companies can be formed as either a public company or a private company.
- The most common form of private company is a one limited by shares, where the members are known as shareholders.
- Another type of private company is one limited by guarantee, such as a number of universities and other non-profit-making organisations. With such a company, the members are known as guarantors. Their liability is limited to a nominal amount stated in the company's memorandum of association.
- In order to incorporate a company, a memorandum of association and articles of association is required to be submitted to the registrar of companies at Companies House, together with other prescribed particulars and a registration fee.
- A company comes into existence on the registrar of companies issuing a certificate of incorporation.

Liability

- A company's liability for its debts are unlimited, except to the extent that it has available assets, but members' liability in the case of a company limited by shares is limited to the amount of the value of their shares.
- Any business, whether a sole trader, a partnership (including limited liability partnerships) or a company, is bound by the provisions of the Business Names Act 1985, which controls the use of certain words by a business as part of its business or trading name.

Key terms

Articles of association — regulations for the management of registered companies (such as Table A), which, with the provisions of the *memorandum of association*, form a company's constitution.

Company name — the title of a registered company as stated in its *memorandum of association* and in the *register of companies* at Companies House.

Company secretary — an officer of a company whose role will vary according to the nature of the company but will generally be concerned with the administrative duties imposed on the company by the CA 1985.

Goodwill — the advantage a business gains from its reputation from the trade and its customers.

Holding company — a company that controls a subsidiary company by holding all or substantially all the shares in that company.

Incorporation — the formation of an association that has corporate personality, i.e. a personality distinct from those of its members.

Limited company — a type of company incorporated by registration under the CA 1985 whose members have limited liability towards the company.

Limited liability partnership — a legally recognised entity defined under the LLPA 2000, which is capable of entering into contracts in its own right and is liable for any debts under those contracts.

Member — a person who holds shares in a company or, in the case of a company that does not issue shares (such as a company limited by guarantee), any of those who have signed the *memorandum of association* or have been admitted to membership by the directors.

Memorandum of association — a constitutional document of a *registered company* that must be drawn up by the person(s) wishing to set it up.

Partnership — an association of two or more people formed for the purpose of carrying on a business with a view to profit.

Private company — a type of *registered company* defined under the CA 1985 as any company that is not a public company.

Registered company — a company incorporated by registration under the CA 1985.

Registered office — the official office of a *registered company*.

Registrar of companies — an official responsible for compiling and maintaining a register of companies.

Statutory company — a company incorporated by the promotion of a private Act of Parliament.

Subsidiary company — a company controlled by a *holding company*.

Unlimited company — a type of *registered company* whose members have an unlimited liability.

Quick Quiz

1 To what extent can a partner be held liable under s5 Partnership Act 1890?

2 What are the particulars that must be sent to the registrar of companies in order to either set up a registered company or a limited liability partnership?

3 Outline the main differences between a public company and a private company.

4 Is a member liable for the debts of a limited liability partnership?

5 On graduating from university with an accounting degree, Bill and Ben are considering setting up a company to run their own business. What advice would you give them as to the advantages and disadvantages of incorporation?

Quick quiz answers

1 Under s5 Partnership Act 1890, partners are agents of their firms and of their fellow partners for acts done as a partner in the ordinary course of partnership business, unless a third party knows that the partner has no authority to do the act or does not know or believe that person to be a partner.

2 Under the CA 1985, the particulars required for the setting up of a registered company are (i) a memorandum of association, (ii) articles of association, (iii) a statement giving the names and particulars of the first directors and of the company secretary, (iv) a statement of the company's registered office address and (v) a statement that all the statutory requirements of registration have been complied with. For a limited liability partnership, the LLPA 2000 requires two or more persons to subscribe to a registration document and a statement that the requirements in respect of the incorporation document have been complied with.

3 Public companies can advertise their shares for sale (e.g. as listed on the London Stock Exchange), whereas shares in private companies are transferable privately. Public companies must have at least £50,000 authorised share capital, of which one-quarter of the nominal value of the shares must be paid up. Public companies need a minimum of two members and two directors and a company secretary. A private company can be formed by one member, having one director and a company secretary. The company secretary of a public company must be professionally qualified. Public companies must have 'public limited company' or 'plc' at the end of the company's registered name. For private companies, the end of the name must be 'limited' or 'ltd' (unless an unlimited company). Private companies can pass written resolutions and can elect to dispense with the requirement for the holding of an annual general meeting.

4 In general, members of a limited liability partnership are not liable for the debts of a limited liability partnership.

5 Given that Bill and Ben are likely to be forming a private company and not a public company, the advantages of incorporation are limited liability of members, vesting of business assets in the company and suing and being sued in the company's name. A disadvantage of incorporation, however, is that it is generally regarded as providing for a greater degree of formality, publicity and expense, although the Company Law Reform Bill 2005, when passed, will ease the administrative burden for private companies.

Incorporation

Summary

- A company is a legal person, separate from its members, directors, employees or those that promoted it.

- A company may own property and it can enter into contracts with others (*Salomon v A Salomon & Co Ltd (1897); Lee v Lee's Air Farming Ltd (1960); Willams v Natural Life Health Foods Ltd (1998)*).

- Members of a limited company are not liable to pay the company's debts. Their liability is limited to the value of their shareholding.

Veil of incorporation

- The veil of incorporation that exists between a company and the members can be lifted in a variety of circumstances, including where a company was formed as a sham or façade (*Gilford Motor Co Ltd v Horne (1933); Trustor AB v Smallbone (No 2) (2001)*), where a company can be characterised as an enemy in time of war (*Daimler Co Ltd v Continental Tyre & Rubber Co Ltd (1916)*), where a company can be treated as an agent of another company (*Firestone Tyre & Rubber Co Ltd v Lewellin (1957)*) or where statutory provisions such as fraudulent and wrongful trading apply.

Criminal liability

- A company can be criminally liable, either in respect of strict liability offences or those which require mens rea where the knowledge of a director (*Tesco Supermarkets Ltd v Nattrass (1972); R v ICR Haualge Ltd (1944)*) or an employee (*Meridian Global Funds Management Asia Ltd v Securities Commission (1995)*) can be attributed to the company.

Promoters

- A promoter is a person who takes the necessary steps to form a company (*Twycross v Grant (1877)*).

- Promoters owe fiduciary duties to the company not to make a secret profit out of the promotion.

- They can avoid liability by disclosure to either an independent board of directors or the shareholders through listing particulars or a prospectus.

- Under s36C CA 1985 a person, such as a promoter, who enters into a contract on behalf of an unformed company is liable on the contract unless there is an agreement to the contrary (*Phonogram v Lane (1982)*).

- Similarly, a promoter can enforce a pre-incorporation contract (*Braymist Ltd v Wise Finance Ltd (2002)*).

- Depending on the construction of the contract, rights can be conferred on a non-existent company by virtue of the Contracts (Rights of Third Parties) Act 1999.

The constitution of a company

- A company's constitution is based on two documents – the memorandum of association (dealing with external matters) and the articles of association (dealing with the internal regulation of the company). Where there is a conflict between the two documents, the memorandum prevails.

- Section 2 CA 1985 provides that the memorandum must state the name of the company, whether the company's registered office is to be situated in England and Wales or Scotland, the company's objects, that the liability of its members is limited and the amount and division of share capital with which the company proposes to be registered.

- The significance of the objects clause in determining a company's capacity to enter into transactions is less now than in the past following the virtual abolition of the doctrine of ultra vires by the CA 1989 (s35(1) CA 1985).

- However, although not affecting the validity of any act done in contravention of the memorandum, directors are under a duty to observe the powers contained in the memorandum, although the company in general meeting (its members) can ratify a breach of duty by the passing of a special resolution (s35(3)).

- A shareholder can seek an injunction preventing a company entering into a proposed ultra vires act (s35(3)) but the company in general meeting can ratify an ultra vires act by the passing of a special resolution (s35(4)).

- Section 14 CA 1985 provides that a company's memorandum and articles of association form a contract between the company and every member so that each member is bound to observe the provisions of both documents. This has been interpreted as applying to company and member (*Hickman v Kent or Romney Marsh Sheepbreeders Association (1915)*) and member and member (*Rayfield v Hands (1958)*), but only to the extent that the member is acting in his capacity as member (*Eley v Positive Security Life Assurance Co Ltd (1876); Pender v Lushington (1877)*). Outsider rights are therefore generally unenforceable.

- Under s9 CA 1985, a company can alter its articles of association by the passing of a special resolution. Any such alteration must be in good faith for the benefit of the company as a whole.

- Challenges to alteration of articles are rare as the courts consider that such business of the company is a matter for the majority shareholders (*Sidebottom v Kershaw, Leese & Co (1920)*).

- However, alterations of articles have been declared invalid where the alteration unfairly discriminates between the majority and minority shareholders (*Dafen Tinpalte Co Ltd v Llanelly Steel Co (1907) Ltd (1920)*).

Key terms

Articles of association — regulations for the management of registered companies (such as Table A), which, with the provisions of the *memorandum of association*, form a company's constitution.

Class rights — rights that attach to a clearly defined class of share (e.g. preference shares) or are conferred on a person for so long as he is a holder of any shares.

Companies House — the office of the *registrar of companies*. Companies with a *registered office* in England or Wales are served by the registry at Cardiff; those in Scotland by the registry in Edinburgh.

Company — an association formed to conduct business or other activities in the name of the association.

Company member — a person who holds shares in a company or, in the case of a company that does not issue shares (such as a company limited by guarantee), any of those who have signed the *memorandum of association* or have been admitted to membership by the directors.

Company name — the title of a registered company, as stated in its *memorandum of association* and in the companies register.

Company secretary — an officer of a company whose role will vary according to the nature of the company but will generally be concerned with the administrative duties imposed on the company by the CA 1985.

Director — an officer of a company appointed by or under the provisions of the *articles of association*.

Fraudulent trading — carrying on business with the intention of defrauding creditors or for any other fraudulent purpose, e.g. accepting advance payment for goods with no intention of either supplying them or returning the money.

General meeting — a meeting of *company members* whose decisions can bind the company.

Incorporation — the formation of an association that has corporate personality, i.e. a personality distinct from those of its members.

Lifting the veil — the act of disregarding the veil of *incorporation* that separates the personality of a corporation from the personalities of its members and directors.

Limited company — a type of company incorporated by registration under the Companies Act 1985 whose members have a limited liability towards their company.

Memorandum of association — a constitutional document of a registered company that must be submitted by the person(s) wishing to form a company.

Partnership — an association of two or more people formed for the purpose of carrying on a business with a view to profit.

Private company — a type of registered company defined under the CA 1985 as any company that is not a public company.

Promoter — a person engaged in the formation of a company.

Registered company — a company incorporated by registration under the CA 1985.

Registered office — the official office of a *registered company*.

Registrar of companies — an official responsible for compiling and maintaining a register of companies.

Share — a unit that measures the holder's interest in and liability to a company.

Special resolution — a decision reached by a majority of not less that 75% of company members voting in person or by proxy at a general meeting.

Subsidiary company — a company controlled by another company, its holding (or parent) company.

Ultra vires — describing an act by a public authority, company or other body that goes beyond the limits of the powers conferred on it.

Unlimited company — a type of *registered company* whose members have an unlimited liability.

Wrongful trading — carrying on business knowing that the company has no reasonable prospect of avoiding an insolvent winding up.

Quick quiz

1 In what circumstances are the courts prepared to lift the veil of incorporation?

2 What are the five compulsory clauses that a company's memorandum of association must contain?

3 What is the purpose of a company's articles of association and in particular Table A of the Company (Tables A–F) Regulations 1985?

4 Advise Corp plc as to the validity of the following transactions entered into by Corp's directors, on the company's behalf and the action, if any, the company can take: (a) an agreement with a third party that is beyond Corp's objects and that has caused a loss to be suffered by Corp; (b) the purchasing of a fleet of vehicles without the directors obtaining general meeting approval as required by Corp's articles of association.

5 Can a promoter be held liable on a pre-incorporation contract?

Quick quiz answers

1 The courts are prepared to lift the veil of incorporation in a variety of circumstances, including (i) where a company was formed for a fraudulent purpose, (ii) where a company can be characterised as an enemy in time of war, (iii) where a company can be treated as an agent of another company and (iv) in applying statutory provisions such as fraudulent and wrongful trading under the IA 1986.

2 A company's memorandum of association must contain (i) the name of the company, (ii) the residence of the company's registered office, (iii) the objects of the company, (iv) that the liability of the members of the company is limited (if at all) and (v) the amount of the company's share capital and how it is divided into shares.

3 The articles of association of a company set out the internal rules of the company, such as the powers of the directors, the proceedings of meetings and rights of members. Table A is a model form of articles for a limited company that can be adopted as a company's articles of association either in full or in part. Where a company does not have articles of association, Table A applies as the company's articles (s8 CA 1985).

4 (i) As the doctrine of ultra vires has been virtually abolished by s35(1) CA 1985, the validity of the transaction between Corp and the third party cannot be challenged on the ground that it is beyond the company's objects. The transaction is valid and binding. However, directors of a company are under a duty to observe the memorandum and failing to do so could lead to action being taken against them for breach of duty (s35(3)). (ii) As the transaction is one that appears to be beyond the directors' powers, the transaction is valid and enforceable by virtue of s35A(1) CA 1985, which provides that a third party acting in good faith can assume that there is no limitation on the powers of the directors. Under s35A(5) CA 1985, directors owe a duty to observe their powers. The transaction, although binding on Corp, could lead to action against the directors for acting in breach of the company's articles of association.

5 A promoter is liable on any contract entered into on a company's behalf before the company was formed (s36C CA 1985).

Capital

Summary

- Capital of a company comprises share capital, i.e. money raised from investors, and loan capital, i.e. money raised from lenders.

- A person becomes a member of a company (i) by subscribing to the memorandum of association of a company or by agreeing to become a member and (ii) being entered in the register of members.

Shares

- A share is a thing in action, conferring certain rights on the holder of the share.

- A company's articles may allow the company to have different classes of shares with different rights attaching to the different classes, e.g. preference shares and ordinary shares.

- A person usually acquires shares in a company by acquiring them from the company or from an existing member or by transmission by operation of law.

Maintenance of capital

- A public company will not be able to begin trading or to borrow money until it has been issued with a certificate under s117 CA 1985. The certificate will be issued where the company has at least a nominal capital of £50,000 of which at least one-quarter of the nominal value of each share is paid up.

- It is a principle of company law that the share capital of a company must be maintained so that creditors have a right to see that a company's capital is not dissipated unlawfully.

- To that extent, as a general rule, a company may not purchase its own shares (*Trevor v Whitworth (1888)*), provide financial assistance for the purchase of its own shares (s151 CA 1985) or pay dividends other than out of distributable profits (s263).

Fixed and floating charges

- A fixed charge is a mortgage over specific assets belonging to the company, which a company cannot realise without obtaining the consent of the charge holder. Examples of assets subject to a fixed charge are land and premises.

- A floating charge is a security over a class of assets that are changing in nature, such as stock in trade, finished articles and book debts, although it is possible for a company to grant a fixed charge over its book debts.

- Assets that are the subject matter of a floating charge can be realised by the company in the company's course of business without the company requiring the consent of the charge holder.

- Once a floating charge crystallises, it becomes a fixed charge on the specific assets of the class of asset charged.

Reservation of title clause

- A reservation of title, or retention of ownership, clause is a device used by sellers of goods in contracts of sale, where the seller reserves title (or ownership) in the goods until he has received payment from the buyer in full.
- Where the goods can be identified and are on the buyer's premises, they can be reclaimed by the seller (*Industries Vaassen BV v Romalpa Aluminium Ltd (1976); Hendy Lennox (Industrial Engines) Ltd v Grahame Puttick Ltd (1984); Armour v Thyssen AG (1990)*).
- A reservation of title clause is unlikely to protect a seller where his goods have been 'lost or destroyed' (*Borden (UK) Ltd v Scottish Timber Products Ltd (1981); Re Peachdart Ltd (1984)*) or where the goods have been sold and he is claiming the proceeds of sale of those goods (*Re Andrabell Ltd (1984)*).

Registration of charges

- Relevant charges (s396 CA 1985) must be registered at Companies House (s399 CA 1985) and a register of charges must be kept by the company (s401 CA 1985).
- A failure to register a charge within 21 days of its creation renders the charge void, although any money secured by the void charge becomes immediately payable (s395 CA 1985).
- The court has the power to permit late registration on such terms it considers 'just and expedient' (s404 CA 1985).

Winding up

- In the event of a winding up of a company, the company's creditors are ranked in the following order:
  1 fixed charge holders
  2 preferential creditors
  3 floating charge holders
  4 unsecured creditors
  5 deferred creditors.
- Any surplus of assets is returned to the members in accordance with their class rights, if any.
- In respect of any insolvency after 15 September 2003, a portion of the assets representing the value of a floating charge can be used to pay unsecured creditors and the Crown loses its status as a preferential creditor.
- Certain transactions that are entered into by a company where insolvency is imminent are void (e.g. s245 IA 1985 in respect of the creation of certain floating charges within 12 months of the onset of insolvency).

Key terms

Articles of association — regulations for the management of registered companies (such as Table A), which, with the provisions of the *memorandum of association*, form a company's constitution.

Authorised capital — the total value of the shares that a registered company is authorised to issue in order to raise capital.

Bonus issue — a method of increasing a company's issued capital by issuing further shares to existing company members.

Call — a demand by a company under the terms of the *articles of association* or an ordinary resolution requiring company members to pay up fully or in part the nominal value of their shares.

Crystallisation — an event or a condition that is complied with, causing a floating charge to become fixed over a company's fluctuating assets (e.g. stock in trade).

Debenture — a document that acknowledges and contains the terms of a loan. A debenture may be unsecured, but more usually it will be subject to a charge and will contain the terms of the charge (e.g. the right to appoint a receiver or an administrative receiver).

Director — an officer of a company appointed by or under the provisions of the *articles of association*.

Dividend — a payment declared either by the directors of a company (an interim dividend) or at the annual general meeting (a final dividend) as being payable to shareholders from profits available for distribution.

Financial assistance — a loan, guarantee, security, indemnity, or gift by a registered company or any of its subsidiaries made for the purpose of assisting someone to acquire its shares.

Memorandum of association — a constitutional document of a registered company that must be drawn up by the person(s) wishing to set it up.

Pre-emption right — a right given to shareholders to purchase the shares of a member wishing to sell their shares or a right of certain shareholders to subscribe to further shares on a new issue.

Preferential debts — certain unsecured debts that are given preferential status on the winding up of a company.

Rights issue — a method of raising share capital for a company from existing members rather than from the public at large.

Share — a unit in the share capital of a company.

Share capital — a fund representing the contributions given to the company by shareholders in return for their shares.

Quick quiz

1 What is the purpose of the rules on maintenance of capital?

2 Can a company pay a dividend out of capital?

3 What is the difference between a fixed and floating charge?

4 In August 2003 ABC Ltd went into liquidation with the following claims of creditors outstanding: in 2000, T Bank plc was granted a floating charge over the company's entire undertaking; 9 months prior to ABC's liquidation, ABC received additional finance from U Bank Ltd with the loan secured against the company's book debts; in 2001, ABC granted a charge over its warehouse in favour of V Bank Ltd; W Ltd is owed £100,000 for unpaid goods – it does not have the benefit of a reservation of title clause in the contract with ABC; ABC's employees are owed £10,000 and HM Revenue and Customs is owed £50,000. Rank the creditors. All charges were registered at Companies House.

Quick quiz answers

1 The purpose of the capital maintenance rules is for the protection of creditors.

2 As an example of the rules on the maintenance of capital, a company may not reduce its capital by paying a dividend. A dividend must be paid out of realisable profits.

3 A fixed charge is a mortgage over specific assets belonging to the company, such as land, the terms of which prevent the company from realising the assets without obtaining the consent of the charge holder. A floating charge provides a lender with security over assets that are changing in nature such as stock in trade. Such assets can be realised in the company's course of business without the company requiring the consent of the charge holder.

4 V Bank's claim would rank first as it is a fixed charge on ABC Ltd's warehouse. Next in line, ranking equally, would be the company's employees and HM Revenue and Customs assuming that they have a preferential debt in accordance with s175 IA 1986. After the preferential creditors, would come U Bank and T Bank as floating charge holders. As floating chargees rank on creation, T Bank will take priority. Although U Bank's charge was created within 12 months of liquidation it appears that the charge is not a void charge under s245 IA 1986 as it appears to represent 'new' moneys. W Ltd has no form of security against the company's assets and ranks as an unsecured creditor.

Company management

Summary

- The division of powers between the general meeting (e.g. the shareholders) and the board of directors is determined by the company's constitution, in particular, the articles of association, which governs the internal regulation of a company.

- As with Art 70, Table A, in practice, the articles give a wide power of management to the directors with little management power retained by the shareholders (e.g. *Automatic Self Cleansing Syndicate v Cuninghame (1906)*).

Shareholder powers

- Where a company's articles are based on Table A, the shareholders can direct the directors on how to act, other than acts already undertaken by the passing of a special resolution.

- Shareholders can also act on the company's behalf where the directors are unable to act (e.g. *Barron v Potter (1914)*, where the board was in deadlock).

- Another option for the shareholders is to remove the directors by the passing of an ordinary resolution under s303 CA 1985.

- However, there are a number of pitfalls standing in the way of shareholders in removing a director in this manner, particularly in relation to a private company, where there is a possibility of a director–shareholder petitioning for relief under s459 CA 1985 or relying on a weighted voting right (*Bushell v Faith (1970)*).

Remedies for wrongdoing

- The power to sue is seen as an example of the power to manage and where the articles are based on Table A, the power to instigate legal proceedings on behalf of the company for a wrong done to the company will be regarded as a matter of management.

- Where, however the directors have caused a wrong to be done to the company, the general meeting can exercise the power to sue in default.

Directors

- The appointment, remuneration and dismissal of directors is dealt with by the company's articles of association, as is whether there is any requirement for a director to hold shares in the company.

- In practice, the directors of a private company hold usually a majority of the shares in a company.

- Executive directors manage the company making business decisions on behalf of the company.

- Non-executive directors, where appointed, do not usually make executive decisions but, given their experience and background, can advise the executive directors on important matters of company mangement.

- A managing director has day-to-day responsibility for the board of directors while the chairman is responsible for the conduct of proceedings of the board and, where permitted by the articles, has an extra vote in the event of deadlock on the board.

- The appointment of non-executive directors is an important feature of the Combined Code as appended to the Stock Exchange Listing Rules.

- To prevent abuse of the corporate form, directors can be disqualified from holding office under the CDDA 1986. A common reason for a court imposing a disqualification order is on the basis that a director's conduct makes him unfit to be concerned with the management of a company (e.g. *Re Barings Bank plc (No 5)(2000)*, which was concerned with directors of a company that collapsed due to the unauthorised activities of one of its employees, Nick Leeson. The maximum period of disqualification is 15 years, which is reserved for the most serious of cases (*Re Sevenoaks Stationers (Retail) Ltd (1991)*). In order to reduce the length and cost of court proceedings a director can make an undertaking to the secretary of state on the same terms as if he were subject to a disqualification order.

Company secretary

- The administrative affairs of a company are left in the hands of the company secretary.

- All companies must have a company secretary, who, in the case of a public company must be professionally qualified.
- The company secretary has usual authority to enter into contracts on behalf of the company that are of an administrative mature (*Panorama v Fidelis Furnishings (1971)*).

Auditors

- Unless a dormant company, every company must appoint a person to act as its auditor.
- The role of an auditor is to examine the records and systems that have been used to prepare the accounts of a company, in order to establish whether those accounts give a true and fair view of the company's affairs.

Meetings

- The holding of meetings is an important part of a company's business.
- Meetings enable the company to pass resolutions in accordance with company legislation and its constitution and to act as a forum for shareholders.
- The procedure relating to notice periods, the calling and the conduct of meetings is provided by the CA 1985 and, where relevant, the company's articles of association.
- A resolution is a decision reached by a majority of the members at a company meeting. There are different types of resolution, as follows. For all companies:
  - *extraordinary resolution*: a decision reached by a majority of not less than 75% of company members voting in person or by proxy at a general meeting
  - *ordinary resolution*: a decision reached by a simple majority (i.e. of more than 50%) of company members voting in person or by proxy
  - *special resolution*: a decision reached by a majority of not less that 75% of company members voting in person or by proxy at a general meeting.
  For private companies:
  - *elective resolution*: a decision by all the members of a private company (at a meeting called on at least 21 days' notice) to dispense with complying with specified provisions of the CA 1985
  - *written resolution*: a resolution signed by all company members and treated as effective even though it is not passed at a properly convened company meeting.
- A number of changes to the law relating to meetings are contained in the Company Law Reform Bill 2005.
- The bill also proposes that a private company will no longer be required to appoint a company secretary.

Key terms

Annual general meeting — a meeting of company members required by the Companies Act 1985 to be held each calendar year.

Articles of association — regulations for the management of registered companies (such as Table A), which, with the provisions of the *memorandum of association*, form a company's constitution.

Auditor — a person appointed to examine the books of account and the accounts of a registered company and to report on them to company members.

Authority — power delegated to a person or body in order to act in a particular way.

Company secretary — an officer of a company whose role will vary according to the nature of the company but will generally be concerned with the administrative duties imposed on the company by the CA 1985.

Elective resolution — a decision by all the members of a private company (at a meeting called on at least 21 days' notice) to dispense with complying with specified provisions of the Companies Act 1985.

Executive director — a director who is either a full time member of the board of directors or under an obligation to devote a substantial amount of time to the management of the company.

Extraordinary general meeting — any meeting of company members other than the *annual general meeting*.

Extraordinary resolution — a decision reached by a majority of not less than 75% of company members *voting* in person or by *proxy* at a general *meeting*.

General meeting — a meeting of company members whose decisions can bind the company.

Memorandum of association — a constitutional document of a registered company that must be drawn up by the person(s) wishing to set it up.

Minutes — records of company business transacted at *general meetings*, board meetings and meetings of managers.

Non-executive director — a director who is usually not under an obligation to devote the whole of their time to the affairs of the company, but who is usually appointed to oversee the decision making of the executive directors by, for example, providing an external perspective.

Ordinary resolution — a decision reached by a simple majority (i.e. of more than 50%) of company members *voting* in person or by *proxy*.

Proxy — a person appointed by a member to attend and vote instead of him at a company meeting.

Quorum — the minimum number of people who must be present at a meeting in order for business to be transacted.

Resolution — a decision reached by a majority of the members at a company meeting.

Special notice — the 28 days' notice that is required to be given to a registered company of an intention to propose certain *resolutions* at a *general meeting* of the company.

Special resolution — a decision reached by a majority of not less that 75% of company members *voting* in person or by *proxy* at a *general meeting*.

Unfair prejudice — unfair conduct on the part of those entrusted to run and control a company as affecting, usually, the interests of minority members.

Voting — the process of casting a vote on a motion proposed at a company meeting.

Written resolution — a *resolution* signed by all company members and treated as effective even though it is not passed at a properly convened company meeting.

Quick quiz

1 What powers do directors have to manage a company?

2 What authority does a company secretary have to enter into contracts on a company's behalf?

3 The articles of association of Alpha Ltd are based on Table A. Last year, one of the company's employees was convicted of stealing property belonging to the company. A general meeting instructed the directors to bring civil proceedings to recover the value of the property stolen, but the directors of Alpha refused to do so. Advise the general meeting.

4 What is the role of a company auditor?

5 What are elective and written resolutions?

Quick quiz answers

1 Directors obtain their powers from a company's articles of association. The company's articles usually provide for a wide power of management to be vested in the board of directors (e.g. Art 70, Table A) and for a power to delegate those powers (e.g. Art 72, Table A).

2 A company secretary may have actual authority to enter into company contracts depending on whether the company has conferred such authority. A company secretary may also possess apparent or usual authority to enter into contracts that relate to company administration.

3 Where a company's articles of association are based on Table A, Art 70 provides for a wide power of management to be vested with the directors who may decide, as a matter of management, whether or not to sue the employee. However, Art 70 enables the general meeting by a passing of a special resolution to instruct the directors on any particular matter, such as instructing the directors to sue the employee, although Art 70 states that no such resolution can invalidate a prior decision of the board. Assuming that the majority shareholders instructed the directors in the form of a special resolution and the directors had not already decided the matter, it would appear that the wishes of the majority shareholders can prevail.

4 An auditor is appointed to audit a company's accounts and to report to the members that the accounts give a true and fair reflection of the company's financial position and have been prepared properly.

5 A private company alone can pass written and elective resolutions. A written resolution is where all the members of a company sign the resolution without the need to hold a meeting to pass it. An elective resolution is one passed by all the members in favour of the resolution, enabling the company to dispense with the holding of annual general meetings or the appointment of auditors, or to give directors the power to allot shares for more than a 5-year period. Elective resolutions need to be registered at Companies House.

Directors' duties

Summary

Directors' duties

- Directors owe duties to the companies they serve.

- A justification for such duties is that, as the directors in practice manage the company, the company relies on the directors to safeguard its assets and interests.

- As the company is a separate legal entity, the duties are owed to the company (*Percival v Wright (1902); Peskin v Anderson (2001)*) and not to individual shareholders, employees or creditors of the company.

- The duties owed by directors are case law based, either in equity or at common law.

- Equity imposes fiduciary duties on directors on the basis of trust and loyalty and good faith.

- The common law insists that directors exercise reasonable care and skill in the discharge of their duties.

- There are three principal fiduciary duties: (i) the non-conflict rule, (ii) the proper purpose rule and (iii) the duty to act in good faith in the interests of the company.

No-conflict rule

- The no-conflict rule requires a director to avoid a conflict between his duty to the company and a personal interest. Examples are where a director has an interest in a company contract, such as receiving an undisclosed commission, or has misused corporate property (*Cook v Deeks (1916); Regal (Hastings) Ltd v Gulliver (1942)); Ball v Eden Project Ltd (2002)*).

- Depending on the nature of the breach of the no-conflict rule, the remedies for breach of the rule are rescission of the contract (*Aberdeen Railway v Riche (1854)*), account of profit (*Boston Deep Sea Fishing Co v Ansell (1888) Cook v Deeks (1916); Regal (Hastings) Ltd v Gulliver (1942)*) or compensation (*Mahesan v Malaysian Government Officers' Co-operative Housing Society (1979)*).

- A director can avoid liability where the company in general meeting, in the absence of fraud or oppression, ratifies (i.e. approves) the actions of the director (*North West Transportation Ltd v Beatty (1887)*).

- A company's articles of association, such as Art 85, Table A, may provide for relief from liability.

- Where Art 85 applies, a director must disclose the nature of any interest in a company contract to the board of directors.

Good faith

- The duty to act in good faith requires directors to act honestly in the interests of the company (*Cook v Deeks (1916)*).

- Where directors have acted honestly, they are required to exercise their powers for a proper and not an improper purpose (*Hogg v Cramphorn (1967)*).

Liability

- Third parties that have participated in a director's breach of duty can be held liable where their participation amounts to 'knowing assistance' or 'knowing 'receipt'.

- Apart from the 'fair dealing' provisions, the CA 1985 provides that a disclaimer excluding a director from liability for breach of duty is void (s310 CA 1985) and a court may excuse a director from liability for breach of duty where it considers that the director has acted honestly and fairly and ought reasonably to be excused (s727 CA 1985).

Reform

- The Company Law Reform Bill 2005 contains a codification of the common law and equitable duties that directors owe the companies they serve.

Key terms

Articles of association — regulations for the management of registered companies (such as Table A), which, with the provisions of the *memorandum of association*, form a company's constitution.

Director — an officer of a company appointed by or under the provisions of the *articles of association*.

Executive director — a director who is either a full-time member of the board of directors or under an obligation to devote a substantial amount of their time to the management of the company.

Fiduciary — a person such as a trustee or director of a company who holds a position of trust or confidence with respect to someone else and who is obliged to act for that person's benefit.

General meeting — a meeting of company members whose decisions can bind the company.

Managing director — a director to whom management powers have been delegated, either absolutely or subject to supervision, by the other directors of the company under the terms of the *articles of association*.

Memorandum of association — a constitutional document of a registered company that must be drawn up by the person(s) wishing to set it up.

Non-executive director — a director who is usually not under an obligation to devote the whole of his time to the affairs of the company, but who is usually appointed to oversee the decision making of the executive directors and to provide an external perspective

Ratification — confirmation of an act by a *resolution* of a *general meeting* adopting an unauthorised act or sanctioning an irregularity in the running of the company, although some acts or irregularities cannot be condoned by a resolution of a general meeting.

Resolution — a decision reached by a majority of the members at a company meeting.

Shadow director — a person who is not a director of a company but who gives instructions, rather than professional advice, on which the directors are accustomed to act.

Voting — the process of casting a vote on a motion proposed at a company meeting.

Quick quiz

1   What are the duties directors owe a company?

2   What are the remedies available to a company where a director breaches the no-conflict rule?

3   Abdul is the managing director of Factorate Ltd. Last month, Abdul purchased goods on Factorate's behalf from Lame Academy plc, which, unknown to Factorate's board of directors, gave Abdul a 'thank you' present of £10,000. The goods were later sold to an unsuspecting purchaser. Advise Factorate as to what action, if any, is available to the company against Abdul. The company does not want to dismiss him as a director.

4   Outline the methods by which a director can be absolved from liability for a breach of duty.

Quick quiz answers

1   There are three main duties directors owe the company they serve. These are the no-conflict rule, the proper purpose rule and the duty to act in good faith in the interests of the company.

2   The no-conflict rule can be divided into two parts – the *requirement* for a director to avoid having an interest in a company contract and an *obligation* on a director not to misuse corporate property. The remedies for breach of either aspect of the no-conflict rule vary. Where appropriate, breach of the first part of the rule entitles the company to rescind the relevant contract, to compel the director to account for any secret profit or to claim compensation for any loss the company suffered.

3   By receiving a gift of £10,000 from a third party, Abdul breached the no-conflict rule as he has an interest in a contract involving Factorate. A consequence of breaching the no-conflict rule is that the company can elect to rescind (avoid) the contract but rescission is not an option as the goods purchased by Factorate are in the hands of an unsuspecting purchaser. In these circumstances, the best remedy for Factorate is to compel Abdul to account for any secret profit he made from the contract, which in this case is the £10,000 he received from Lame Academy. It does not appear that Abdul can rely on the articles for protection as there is a presumption that he did not disclose his interest in the contract to the board of directors.

4   The principal method by which a director can be absolved from liability is for the company to ratify (i.e. approve) a director's breach of duty by the passing of a resolution of the members, although ratification will be ineffective where it is tainted by fraud or oppression. It is also possible for a director to avoid liability by disclosing his interest in a company contract to the board of directors if the articles of association so permit. Another possibility is for a court to relieve a director from liability under s727 CA 1985 where he has acted honestly and fairly and ought reasonably to be excused.

Shareholder protection

Summary

- It is not easy for a minority shareholder to bring legal proceedings against alleged wrongdoers either personally or on behalf of the company.
- Where a wrong is done to a company, the company, as a legal entity, is the proper claimant to bring a claim against the wrongdoers.
- Similarly, the company is the proper entity to condone an internal irregularity. The company's power to litigate will be taken by either the board of directors or the general meeting depending on which organ of the company has the power to sue (e.g. Art 70, Table A).
- Where the wrong caused to the company is committed by those controlling the company, a minority shareholder can bring a derivative claim against the wrongdoers for a fraud on the minority. Both fraud and wrongdoer control need to be established.
- Examples of fraud include expropriation of corporate assets (*Menier v Hooper's Telegraph Works Ltd (1874)*), self-serving negligence (*Daniels v Daniels (1975)*) and a misuse of voting power (*Clemens v Clemens (1976)*).
- Examples of conduct not amounting to fraud include ordinary negligence (*Pavlides v Jensen (1956)*) and acting honestly but for an improper purpose (*Hogg v Cramphorn (1967)*).
- An independent, majority of the minority shareholders can block the bringing of a derivative claim where they object to such action (*Smith v Croft (No 2) (1987)*).

Individual shareholders

- Individual shareholders can bring a personal or representative claim in other circumstances, namely, an infringement of a personal right (*Pender v Lushington (1877)*, *Wood v Odessa Water Works (1889)*), where the business of the company at a general meeting requires a special majority and only a simple majority has been obtained (*Edwards v Halliwell (1950)*) and seeking an injunction preventing the company from entering into a proposed ultra vires act (s35(2) CA 1985).

Minority shareholders

- Minority shareholders aggrieved at the way in which the company is being run by those in control may be able to rely on statutory forms of protection.
- Where their interests have been unfairly prejudiced, they can petition the court for relief under s459 CA 1985.
- Unfair prejudicial conduct means a breach of a legitimate expectation that a minority shareholder has in the way the company's affairs are conducted by those in control of the company (*O'Neill v Phillips (1999)*).
- Common examples of such conduct in relation to private companies are exclusion from management (*Re London School of Electronics (1986)*) and expropriation of corporate assets (*Re Cumana (1986)*).
- It is harder to establish unfair prejudicial conduct within a public company.

- The usual form of relief granted by a court is a buy-out order under s461 CA 1985, i.e. the court orders the majority shareholder or the company to buy the shares of the minority shareholder at a fair value (*Profinance Trust SA v Gladstone (2001)*). A court may refuse relief on the basis of the petitioner's own conduct.

Winding-up orders

- A more drastic remedy for an aggrieved shareholder is to petition the court under s122(1)g IA 1986 for a winding-up order on the just and equitable ground.
- In quasi-partnership companies, examples have included exclusion from management (*Ebrahimi v Westbourne Galleries Ltd (1972)*), loss of confidence (*Loch v John Blackwood Ltd (1924)*) and deadlock (*Re Yenidje Tobacco Co Ltd (1916)*).

Sunstantial corporate loss

- In cases involving substantial corporate losses, the secretary of state may use his powers in the CA 1985 to order an investigation of the company's affairs.

Reform

The Company Law Reform Bill (2005) contains a proposal to place derivative claims on a statutory footing.

Key terms

Articles of association — regulations for the management of registered companies (such as Table A), which, with the provisions of the memorandum of association, form a company's constitution

Derivative action — civil proceedings brought by a minority of company members in their own names seeking a remedy for the company in respect of a wrong done to it.

Director — an officer of a company appointed by or under the provisions of the *articles of association*.

Fraud on the minority — an improper exercise of *voting* power by the majority of members of a company.

General meeting — a meeting of company members whose decisions can bind the company.

Just and equitable gound — a compulsory *winding up* on grounds of fairness under s122(1)g IA 1986.

Majority rule — the principle by which the majority of company members has the power to control the company through *voting* at a company meeting, usually by the passing of an *ordinary resolution*.

Ordinary resolution — a decision reached by a simple majority (i.e. more than 50%) of company members *voting* in person or by proxy.

Personal claim — a claim where some personal individual right has been infringed.

Quasi-partnership — a small private company run like a partnership.

Ratification — confirmation of an act by a *resolution* of a *general meeting* adopting an unauthorised act or sanctioning an irregularity in the running of the company, although some acts or irregularities cannot be condoned by a resolution of a general meeting.

Representative claim — an action brought by or against one or more persons as representative(s) of a larger group.

Resolution — a decision reached by a majority of the members at a company meeting.

Special resolution — a decision reached by a majority of not less that 75% of company members *voting* in person or by proxy at a general meeting.

Ultra vires — an act by a company (or a public authority or other body) that goes beyond the limits of the powers conferred on it.

Unfair prejudice — unfair conduct on the part of those entrusted to run and control a company as affecting the interests, usually, of the minority shareholders.

Voting — the process of casting a vote on a motion proposed at a company meeting.

Winding up — a procedure by which a company can be dissolved. It may be instigated by members or creditors of the company (a voluntary winding up) or by an order of the court (compulsory winding up).

Quick quiz

1 What do you understand by the terms fraud and wrongdoer control?

2 What is the rule in *Smith v Croft (No 2) (1987)*?

3 What are the differences between bringing a derivative claim at common law and a petition under s459 CA 1985?

4 X Ltd, a minority shareholder of Y Ltd, wishes for action to be taken in relation to the disposal by the board of directors of a company asset to Z Ltd at 25% less than its market value. The directors have a majority of the shares in the company. Advise X Ltd as to its legal position.

Quick quiz answers

1 Fraud means abuse or misuse of power. Examples are expropriation of corporate property (*Menier v Hooper's Telegraph Works Ltd (1874)*; *Cook v Deeks (1916)*), self-serving negligence (*Daniels v Daniels (1975)*), acting in bad faith and a misuse of voting power (*Clemens v Clemens (1976)*). Wrongdoer control means the wrongdoers controlling the company, usually by having a majority of the voting power at the general meeting.

2 Where a minority shareholder has established a fraud on the minority by showing fraud and wrongdoer control, his derivative claim may prove unsuccessful if a larger minority shareholder wishes for such proceedings not to be brought. In *Smith v Croft (No 2)*, the court favoured the wishes of the larger of the two minority shareholders where the shareholder with the larger of the shareholdings was independent of the majority shareholder who was alleged to have committed the fraud.

3 A derivative claim enables a shareholder to bring a claim against alleged wrongdoers where the act complained of amounts to a fraud on a minority, such as a misappropriation of corporate assets by directors who are the majority shareholders and control the company. Although a petition under s459 CA 1985 could be used to cover acts that are typically the subject matter of a derivative claim (e.g. *Re Cumana (1986)*), a s459 petition is more likely to be used where the majority and minority shareholders cannot get on with each other to such an extent that their relationship has deteriorated to the point of an irretrievable breakdown of relationship. The most

common example is where a minority shareholder of a quasi-partnership company (i.e. a small, private company built on trust and understanding) had an expectation to continue as a director of the company but was removed by the majority shareholder (as in *Re London School of Electronics (1985)*). The most common remedy is for the court to grant a buy-out order under s461 CA 1985, where the majority shareholder is ordered to buy the shares of the minority at a fair valuation. This enables the warring parties to go their separate ways leaving the company intact.

4   For X Ltd to bring proceedings against the directors, it would have to show that the directors had committed a fraud on the minority. This would mean showing fraud and wrongdoer control. It appears that the directors control the board of directors and the general meeting, but the act complained of may not amount to fraud, i.e. a misuse or abuse of power. The allegation is one based on negligence by the directors and negligence does not amount to fraud (*Pavlides v Jensen (1956)*). However, where the directors benefit from their negligence, as, in this case, where three of the directors have a controlling stake in Z Ltd, that may amount to fraud, as such self-serving negligence is seen as an expropriation of company property (*Daniels v Daniels) (1978)*.

Corporate insolvency

Summary

Dissolution

- Dissolution represents the termination of a company's existence.
- There are four ways in which a company can be dissolved:
  - the striking off from the register of a defunct company
  - following a scheme of arrangement by a court order
  - where the company's objects are illegal on an application by the Attorney-General
  - following a winding up of a company.
- The most common form of dissolution is that following a winding up.
- There are two types of winding up:
  - a voluntary winding up by the members or creditors of the company
  - compulsory winding up by the court.
- The task of the appointed liquidator is to realise the company's assets in order to meet the claims of the company's creditors.
- After meeting the claims of the creditors and the costs of liquidation, any surplus is returned to the members of the company.
- At the end of the winding up, the company is dissolved.
- The most common reason why a company is wound up is due to insolvency, i.e. where the company is unable to meet its day-to-day liabilities.

Administration

- An alternative to winding up on the ground of insolvency is administration. Administration is a process that, on the appointment of a qualified insolvency practitioner to act as administrator, enables the company to avoid creditors bringing claims during the course of the administration.

- The primary purpose of administration is for the administrator to rescue the company as a going concern.
- With effect from 15 September 2003, amendments to the IA 1986 by the Enterprise Act 2002 enable more companies in a state of insolvency to opt for administration.
- This was achieved by allowing for the appointment of an administrator without the need for a court order, placing a moratorium on creditors' claims following an application or petition for administration and preventing charge holders appointing administrative receivers in respect of charges created after 15 September 2003.

Delinquent directors

- Directors responsible for the state of a company's insolvency can have action taken against them for either fraudulent trading (s213 IA 1986) or wrongful trading (s214 IA 1986).
- Delinquent directors can be disqualified from holding the office of director under the CDDA 1986.

Key terms

Administration — a process under the Insolvency Act 1986, directing that, during the period for which it is in force, the affairs, business, and property of a company shall be managed by a person appointed to act as an administrator.

Administrative receiver — a receiver who, under the terms of a debenture secured by floating charge, takes control of all, or substantially all, of a company's assets.

Compulsory winding up — a procedure for *winding up* a company by the court based on a petition made under circumstances listed in the Insolvency Act 1986. The main grounds for this type of petition are that the company is unable to pay its debts or that the court is of the opinion that it is in the interests of the company that a just and equitable winding up should be made.

Director — an officer of a company appointed by or under the provisions of the articles of association.

Dissolution — the dissolving of a registered company.

Fraudulent trading — carrying on business with the intention of defrauding creditors or for any other fraudulent purpose, e.g. accepting advance payment for goods with no intention of either supplying them or returning the money.

Just and equitable ground — a compulsory *winding up* on the ground of fairness under s122(1)g IA 1986.

Liquidator — a person who conducts the *winding up* of a company. Unless he is the Official Receiver, he must be a qualified insolvency practitioner.

Merger — an amalgamation between companies of similar size in which either the members of the merging companies exchange their shares for shares in a new company or the members of some of the merging companies exchange their shares for shares in another merging company.

Scheme of arrangement — an agreement between a debtor and his creditors to arrange the debtor's affairs to satisfy the creditors.

Takeover — the acquisition of control by one company over another, usually smaller, company.

Voluntary winding up — a procedure initiated by a special or extraordinary resolution of the company to dissolve the company.

Winding up — a procedure by which a company can be dissolved. It may be instigated by members or creditors of the company (a voluntary *winding up*) or by order of the court (a compulsory winding up).

Wrongful trading — carrying on business knowing that the company has no reasonable prospect of avoiding an insolvent *winding up*.

Quick quiz

1 Define the different forms of corporate insolvency.

2 What is the rationale behind the changes brought about by the Enterprise Act 2002 and what is the likely effect of these changes on corporate insolvency?

3 Can an action be brought against directors whose conduct may have contributed to or caused the insolvency of a company?

Quick quiz answers

1 Apart from entering into a voluntary agreement with creditors, the likely consequences for an insolvent company is for the company to be placed in receivership, administration or liquidation. Receivership is where an insolvency practitioner is appointed by a secured creditor in order to realise the company assets that are the subject matter of the creditor's security. Liquidation is a formal process by which a company's affairs are wound up by a liquidator (who must be a qualified insolvency practitioner) in order to meet the claims of creditors and to distribute any surplus assets to the members. Administration is designed to enable a company to avoid receivership and liquidation by providing for the appointment of a qualified insolvency practitioner to manage the company's affairs with a view to salvaging the company as a going concern while enabling the company to stave off creditor claims.

2 The changes brought about by the Enterprise Act 2002 were designed to promote a 'rescue culture' for insolvent companies so as to promote administration as a preferred route for such companies. The main change was to enable a company or its directors to appoint an out-of-court administrator as opposed to the costlier and lengthier alternative of seeking a court-appointed administrator. Another change was to prevent floating charge holders from appointing an administrative receiver to realise company property that was subject to the charge.

3 Directors who have contributed to or caused a company to become insolvent can be held liable for fraudulent or wrongful trading under the Insolvency Act 1986. Under the Company Directors Disqualification Act 1986, a director guilty of fraudulent trading is disqualified from holding the office of director for a period between 2 and 15 years. In other cases, a director can be disqualified from holding the office of director where their conduct is judged as such that they are unfit to be concerned with the management of a company.

Consumer, employment and agency law

Consumer protection

Summary

Overview

- Consumer protection legislation is generally intended to protect individuals acting in a private (non-business) capacity against sharp practices by businesses.

- There are various different approaches to consumer protection, including:
    - making certain types of conduct a criminal offence
    - requiring businesses to obtain licences in order to carry out certain activities
    - imposing additional liability on businesses so that it is easier for consumers to sue them for unacceptable performance
    - preventing businesses from relying on unfair contract terms
    - allowing regulators and/or consumer representative bodies to take action against businesses on behalf of consumers
    - encouraging businesses to sign up to voluntary schemes designed to protect consumers.

Criminal conduct

- It is a criminal offence to engage in certain practices that are viewed as harmful to consumers. The sanction against businesses is usually a fine but adverse publicity may also result. Prosecutions are usually brought by local trading standards departments. Examples of offences include:
    - section 20, Consumer Protection Act 1987: giving misleading price indications to consumers in the course of a business (strict liability i.e. no need to show that the business either intended to mislead or did not care whether the indication was misleading)
    - section 1, Trade Descriptions Act 1968: applying a false description to goods or supplying goods carrying a false description (strict liability)
    - section 14, Trade Descriptions Act 1968: making a false statement regarding the provision of services (*not* strict liability; prosecution must show the defendant either knew the statement was false or did not care whether it was true or false)

– regulation 20 of the General Product Safety Regulations 2005: placing a product on the market in the course of a business that is intended for consumers or likely to be used by consumers and that is not safe.

- Note that, in relation to the Trade Descriptions Act offences, the false description or statement does not have to be made to a consumer.

Licensing

- Businesses wishing to provide consumer credit must obtain a licence under the Consumer Credit Act 1974 (CCA) from the Office of Fair Trading (OFT); failure to do so is a criminal offence.

- In order to obtain a licence, a business must show that it is a 'fit and proper person' to provide consumer credit. A licence may be withdrawn if the business does not comply with its terms or the provisions of the CCA. Fines may also be imposed.

- The CCA applies to businesses offering:
  – regulated consumer credit agreements, e.g. personal loans, credit cards, bank overdrafts, 'buy now pay later' deals and hire purchase (but not loans secured against property e.g. mortgages)
  – regulated consumer hire agreements: agreements lasting for at least 3 months under which goods are hired or rented.

- The recipient of the credit must be an individual or a partnership of up to three partners. Limited companies do not qualify for protection. Protection for qualifying partnerships or individuals who are sole traders (rather than consumers) is limited to agreements involving amounts of up to £25,000. There is no financial threshold for credit agreements with individual consumers.

- Regulated agreements must be in writing and follow a special format set out in the CCA. If the credit provider fails to comply with these requirements, the agreement will be unenforceable and the lender may not be able to reclaim the money that has been lent: *Wilson v First County Trust (2003)*.

- Any agreement concluded away from business premises is subject to a 'cooling-off period' of 5 days; if the consumer has second thoughts about the agreement during this period, he is free to cancel it.

- If the interest rate of the loan is very high, consumers can apply to court to have the interest rate reduced to a more reasonable level.

- Lenders must comply with strict rules on advertising to ensure that their publicity is not misleading, e.g. interest rates must be calculated in a particular way set out in legislation.

Imposing additional liability

- Part 1 of the Consumer Protection Act 1987 (CPA) applies to personal injuries or damage to property caused by defective products.

- The injured party must prove that the product was defective and he was injured by it. The defendant will be liable unless it can show that it is covered by a limited range of defences, which include the following:
  – the product was not supplied in the course of a business
  – the defect came into existence after the product had been put into circulation (i.e. it was not a defect inherent in the product but had arisen because of, for example, normal wear and tear)

– the state of scientific and technical knowledge at the time the product was supplied was not such that a producer of products of the same description could have been expected to discover the defect (the 'development risks' or 'state of the art' defence).

- Because the CPA makes it easier for the injured party to establish liability, it may allow a claim to be made where an action based on contract or negligence would fail: *Abouzaid v Mothercare (UK) Ltd (2000)*.

- Amendments made to the Sale of Goods Act 1979 (SGA) and other similar legislation by the Sale and Supply of Goods to Consumers Regulations 2002 also give consumers protection by imposing additional liability on businesses as follows:
  – *guarantees*: manufacturers who choose to offer a guarantee can now be sued by consumers as if there had been a direct contractual relationship between the parties
  – *burden of proof*: goods that prove defective within 6 months of the date of delivery are presumed to have been defective at the time of delivery (unless the supplier can show otherwise).

Contract terms

- See Chapters 6 and 7 for a summary of the protection offered by the Sale of Goods Act 1979, the Supply of Goods and Services Act 1982 and the Unfair Contract Terms Act 1977 (UCTA).

- The Unfair Terms in Consumer Contracts Regulations 1999 (UTCCR) apply to any term in a consumer contract that has not been individually negotiated. Any such term must be:
  – fair (unless the term is a 'core term', i.e. one that sets out the price of the goods or services or is concerned with describing 'the main subject matter of the contract')
  – written in plain, intelligible language (even if it is a 'core term').

- Terms that do not comply with these requirements are not binding on consumers.

- A 'consumer' under the UTCCR is 'any natural person who ... is acting for purposes outside his trade or profession'. This means that businesses are excluded from protection.

- Note that the definition of 'consumer' under UCTA is different and may in certain circumstances apply to businesses: *R&B Customs Brokers v United Dominions Trust Ltd (1988)*.

- The test of fairness in the UTCCR is met if:
  – the term has been presented in a clear and straightforward manner (the requirement of 'good faith')
  – the term did not give rise to a significant imbalance in favour of the supplier: *Director General of Fair Trading v First National Bank (2001)*.

- The requirement of plain, intelligible language normally means that the clause must be written in terms that a non-lawyer would easily understand.

Regulators and consumer bodies

- Individual consumers often do not have the resources to enforce consumer protection legislation. In recognition of this, the Enterprise Act 2002 allows regulators, such as the Office of Fair Trading (OFT), and 'designated consumer representative bodies', such as Which? (formerly the Consumers' Association), to apply for injunctions known as Stop Now Orders to prevent breaches of consumer protection legislation.

- The Enterprise Act 2002 also allows consumer representative bodies to submit 'super-complaints' to the OFT, drawing its attention to practices that may harm consumers. The OFT must respond to such complaints within 90 days.

Voluntary schemes

- In some sectors, voluntary schemes play an important role. For example, consumer protection in relation to misleading advertising claims (other than broadcast advertising) is achieved largely by the British Code of Advertising, Sales Promotion and Direct Marketing (known as the CAP Code), which is administered by the Advertising Standards Authority (ASA) and paid for by the advertising industry.

- Should an advertiser refuse to comply with an ASA ruling, sanctions may be imposed. As a last resort, the ASA may refer the matter to the Office of Fair Trading for investigation under the Control of Misleading Advertisements Regulations 1988.

Conclusion

Different approaches to consumer protection: advantages and disadvantages

Type of approach	Main advantages	Main disadvantages
Criminal conduct, e.g. Trade Descriptions Act 1968	Powerful deterrent effect	Needs to be used sparingly or deterrent effect will be undermined. Does not compensate victims for loss
Licensing, e.g. Consumer Credit Act 1974	Important preventive effect (i.e. can prevent unsuitable businesses being allowed to provide goods or services to consumers)	Costly to enforce (requires careful monitoring by regulators). Costly for businesses to comply with special legal requirements
Liability, e.g. Part 1, Consumer Protection Act 1987	Makes it easier for injured parties to obtain redress	Injured party must still be prepared to take legal action, which may be unattractive due to e.g. cost of lawyers, complex court procedures etc.
Contract terms, e.g. Unfair Terms in Consumer Contracts Regulations 1999	Discourages use of unfair terms (because they cannot be enforced)	Often depends on consumers being aware that the term in question may be unenforceable
Regulators and consumer representative bodies, e.g. Enterprise Act 2002	Allows larger organisations to take action on behalf of consumers to prevent harmful practices	Tends to be more effective at stopping activities of e.g. rogue traders; will not necessarily help an individual consumer who has lost money as a result of a rogue trader
Voluntary schemes, e.g. CAP Code on advertising	More flexible than legislation and less costly to enforce, as paid for by business. Can be more effective than legislation because business is not being forced to comply	Normally requires threat of action under legislation as a 'last resort'. Risk that consumers benefit from a lower level of protection than would be the case if a mainly legislative solution were imposed

Key terms

Caveat emptor — Latin for 'let the buyer beware'. Normally used in the context of the general rule of English law that parties to contracts are expected to look out for themselves and the law will not protect them if they have made a bad bargain.

Core term — a concept under the Unfair Terms in Consumer Contracts Regulations 1999 (UTCCR) referring to a term that sets out the price of the goods or services or is concerned with describing 'the main subject matter of the contract'. Such terms are not required to be fair under the UTCCR although they are required to be in plain, intelligible language.

Designated consumer representative bodies — bodies that represent consumers such as Which? (formerly the Consumers' Association) and that have been designated by the Secretary of State for Trade and Industry under the Enterprise Act 2002 to apply for *Stop Now Orders* or make *super-complaints* to the *Office of Fair Trading*.

Development risks defence — See *'state of the art defence'*.

Good faith — a concept under the Unfair Terms in Consumer Contracts Regulations 1999 (UTCCR) referring to one element of the requirement that terms should be fair, namely that the term must be presented in a clear, straightforward manner.

Mens rea — refers to the state of mind of the defendant in relation to criminal offences that are not *strict liability* offences.

Regulated consumer credit agreements — an agreement regulated by the Consumer Credit Act 1974 for the provision of credit facilities, including personal loans, credit cards, bank overdrafts, 'buy now pay later' deals and hire purchase (i.e. where the customer rents the goods but with an option to purchase them later). Does not include loans secured against land, such as mortgages.

Regulated consumer hire agreement — an agreement regulated by the Consumer Credit Act 1974 under which goods are hired or rented and that lasts for at least 3 months.

Office of Fair Trading — the main consumer protection and competition law regulator, with responsibility for overseeing the licensing system under the Consumer Credit Act 1974 and enforcing competition and consumer protection law generally.

State of the art defence — refers to a defence to liability under the product liability provisions of Part 1 of the Consumer Protection Act 1987. Also called 'development risks defence'. Applies where the state of scientific and technical knowledge at the time the product was supplied was not such that a producer of products of the same description could have been expected to discover the defect.

Stop Now Order — a special type of injunction that can be obtained by the *Office of Fair Trading*, other consumer regulators and *designated consumer representative bodies* under the Enterprise Act 2002. Stop Now Orders are designed to prevent businesses carrying out any further breaches of consumer protection legislation.

Strict liability — means that there is no need to prove anything relating to the state of mind of the defendant.

Super-complaint — a complaint made by a *designated consumer representative body* to the *Office of Fair Trading* (OFT) under the Enterprise Act about an issue affecting consumers. The OFT must respond within 90 days.

Quick quiz

1 You order a computer from a website operated by Too Good to Be True Ltd (TGTBT). The computer is described as costing £800 inclusive of all charges. However, you then find that your credit card has been charged a total of £880 + VAT. You are told that the additional £80 is the delivery charge. You also agreed to pay £10 a month to subscribe to a helpline service that was described as '24 hour' – but it turns out to be office hours only. What offences may have been committed here and what must the prosecution prove?

2 Two weeks ago, following a home visit from a sales representative, you agreed to take out a loan of £1000 from Loans R Us with an interest rate of 130% per year (it seemed like a good idea at the time). It suddenly occurs to you that the loan may not be such a good deal after all. What assistance might the Consumer Credit Act 1974 offer you in this situation?

3 While out jogging, your foot is badly injured by a sharp metal fitting that attaches the sole of your trainers to the uppers. You have to take weeks off work because you cannot walk easily and have had to cancel a holiday at the last minute (losing a substantial deposit). The shop where you bought the trainers has ceased trading. What action can you take to obtain compensation for your injury?

4 In the scenario in the previous question, could you have challenged the holiday company's right to retain your deposit?

5 Fred has bought a van for use in his business. After 13 months, the van develops serious engine problems. The van dealer relies on a term in its standard terms that states that it has no liability for problems arising more than 12 months after the sale. Can Fred challenge this clause using consumer protection legislation?

6 What powers do consumer regulators and 'designated consumer representative bodies' have under the Enterprise Act 2002 to take action against businesses that infringe consumer protection legislation?

7 True or false: if an advertiser refuses to comply with a ruling of the Advertising Standards Authority, the matter is automatically referred to the Office of Fair Trading.

Quick quiz answers

1 In relation to the price, an offence may have been committed under section 20 of the Consumer Protection Act 1987. This is a strict liability offence, so the prosecution only needs to prove that a misleading price indication was given to a consumer, i.e. you. In relation to the helpline service, an offence may have been committed under section 14 of the Trade Descriptions Act 1968. This is not a strict liability offence, so the prosecution must prove not only that TGTBT provided a misleading description but that it either intended to do so or did not care whether the description was true.

2 When a consumer credit agreement is made away from business premises, you have 5 days in which to cancel it. In this case, the 5 days has clearly expired, so on the face of it, the agreement is binding. However, you may

be able to argue that the agreement is unenforceable because the paperwork does not comply with the requirements of the CCA. If that fails, you may be able to apply to court to have the interest rate reduced to a more reasonable level.

3   Ordinarily you could sue the shop where you bought the trainers for breach of contract (the trainers were clearly not of satisfactory quality). However, since the shop has ceased trading, you cannot sue in contract. You could sue the following businesses in tort, either for negligence or breach of statutory duty under Part 1 of the Consumer Protection Act 1987 (CPA): the manufacturer of the trainers and any businesses involved in their importation and distribution in the EU. It will be easier to sue under the CPA because you only need to prove that there was a defect in the trainers and the defect caused the damage.

4   In theory, yes – by arguing that the term allowing the holiday firm to retain the deposit is unfair (and therefore unenforceable) under the Unfair Terms in Consumer Contracts Regulations 1999. However, in order to be unfair, the term must give rise to a significant imbalance in favour of the supplier. In this case, given that you cancelled at the last minute, the holiday firm is unlikely to be able to resell your place on the holiday to someone else. It may well have paid for your seat on the flight and your room at the hotel; it is therefore likely to face costs as a result of your cancellation. Provided that the deposit bears some relation to the loss incurred by the holiday firm, it is unlikely that the term allowing it to retain the deposit is unfair.

5   Fred can challenge this clause, but he will not be able to rely on the Unfair Terms in Consumer Contracts Regulations 1999. This is because he did not buy the van outside the course of his trade or profession; he clearly bought it for business purposes. He might be able to claim protection as a consumer under the Unfair Contract Terms Act 1977 (UCTA) if he can show that the purchase of the van was not integral to his business and such purchases were only made on occasional basis. If that fails (which it might well do if he uses the van regularly in his business), he should still be able to challenge the clause as a business (rather than a consumer). He could argue that it is an unreasonable exclusion under (i) section 3 UCTA (which protects businesses against unreasonable exclusions of liability generally where these are contained in standard terms) and/or (ii) section 6 UCTA (which protects businesses against unreasonable exclusions of the statutory implied terms, e.g. that goods should be of satisfactory quality).

6   Under the Enterprise Act 2002, regulators and 'designated consumer representative bodies' can apply to court for a special form of injunction known as a Stop Now Order, which can be used to prevent businesses from continuing to breach consumer protection legislation.

7   False. The ASA may pursue various other options in order to secure compliance, including asking the advertiser to submit future advertisements for pre-vetting and asking for trade privileges (e.g discounts) to be withdrawn. Matters are generally only referred to the OFT as a last resort.

Aspects of employment law

Summary

The employment relationship

- The nature of an employment relationship is based on the law of contract. However, legislation and EU law have added considerably to employment law in order to provide for the protection of employee interests.

- Employment disputes are heard mainly by an employment tribunal, although cases involving general contractual or tortious claims can be heard in a first instance court, e.g. claims involving wrongful dismissal or personal injuries. An appeal from an employment tribunal lies to the Employment Appeal Tribunal and from there to the Court of Appeal and the House of Lords.

- Employees are employed under a contract of service. Independent contractors work under a contract for services. Whether a person is an employee or an independent contractor is a question of fact for the courts to consider in all the circumstances.

- Employees must be given a written statement of particulars of the employment not later than 2 months after the commencement of the employment.

- Employees are under a duty to pay the employee (and at not less than the minimum rate stipulated by the National Minimum Wage Act 1998), to act faithfully (*Isle of Wight Tourist Board v Coombes (1976)*) and to provide a safe system of work. Employees are under a duty to act in good faith and to use reasonable care and skill in the performance of their job. Acting in bad faith would include obtaining a secret profit or disclosing confidential information (*LC Services Ltd v Brown (2003); Hivac Ltd v Park Royal Scientific Instruments Ltd (1946)*).

Equal pay

- Under the Equal Pay Act (EPA) 1970 an employee is entitled to equal pay for equal work so that no discrimination occurs on the ground of pay as between women and men doing the same job (*Shields v E Coomes (Holdings) Ltd (1978)*).

- So that, for example, where a woman does like work, or work rated as equivalent to that of a male comparator, her contract of employment should be deemed to include an equality clause.

- The employer has a defence where the variation in treatment is due to a genuine material factor that was not the difference in sex.

Health and safety at work

- In contract law, the employer's duty of care to employees particularly involves providing safe plant and equipment, a safe system of work and reasonably competent fellow employees (*Hudson v Ridge Manufacturing Co. Ltd (1957); Pagono v HGS (1976)*). The duty applies to stress-related injury as well as physical injury (*Walker v Northumberland County Council (1995); Johnstone v Bloomsbury Health Authority (1991); Hatton v Sutherland (2002)*).

- An employee will be able to sue his employer in negligence where the employer breached a duty of care owed to that employee and the breach caused a foreseeable type of loss.
- The Health and Safety at Work Act 1974 imposes criminal sanctions on employers who do not look after the health and safety of their employees. The Act is enforced by the Health and Safety Executive.

Dismissal

- An employer or an employee can terminate a contract of employment by giving notice but no such notice cannot be less that the statutory minimum. A failure to give notice in accordance with the contract of employment entitles the employee to bring a claim for wrongful dismissal.
- An employee is dismissed summarily where he is dismissed without notice. This can only be justified in exceptional circumstances such as the employee repudiating the contract through an act of gross misconduct.
- Employees with at least 1 year's continuous service have the right not to be dismissed unfairly.
- Dismissal on a ground not contained in ERA 1996 is unfair. Where the dismissal was on the ground of one of the five specified circumstances, the dismissal may be unfair unless the employer acted reasonably in treating the reason for dismissal as a sufficient reason for dismissing the employee or the employer failed to comply with the statutory dismissal, grievance and disciplinary procedures (*Iceland Frozen Foods Ltd v Jones (1983); Post Office Ltd v Foley (2000)*). There are a number of grounds where dismissal is deemed automatically unfair.
- Remedies for unfair dismissal include re-engagement, reinstatement and compensation. The basic award of compensation is calculated according to a statutory formula. The compensatory award is designed to compensate the employee for losses suffered as a result of having been dismissed unfairly. The compensatory award may not exceed £56,800.

Redundancy

- An employee will have been dismissed by reason of redundancy where the reason for dismissal was wholly or mainly attributable to the employer ceasing to carry on the business, moving the place of business or reducing surplus labour.
- Where an employer fails to follow correct procedures relating to redundancy, the dismissal of the employee is likely to be considered to be unfair.
- Redundancy payments can only be claimed by employees with at least 2 years' continuous service.
- A redundancy payment is the same as the basic award for unfair dismissal.

Sex discrimination

- The Sex Discrimination Act 1975 outlaws discrimination on the ground of a person's sex.
- The SDA 1975 outlaws direct discrimination, indirect discrimination, victimisation and harassment.

- Similar protection is provided by the Employment Equality (Sexual Orientation) Regulations 2003 in respect of discrimination on the ground of a person's sexual orientation.

- Direct discrimination occurs when an employer treats a woman less favourably on the grounds of her sex (*Porcelli v Strathclyde Regional Council (1986)*).

- Indirect discrimination occurs when the employer imposes a requirement that can be complied with by a considerably smaller proportion of women to whom the employer applies it than the proportion of men to whom the employer applies it (*Price v Civil Service Commission (1977)*).

- Victimisation occurs where a woman is treated less favourably on account of having taken other action in respect of the SDA 1986.

- An employer can be vicariously liable for acts of discrimination committed by employees in the course of their employment. However, the employer has a defence if he shows that he took reasonable steps to prevent the act of discrimination or to prevent acts of that description.

- It is permissible for an employer to discriminate where being a man or woman is a 'genuine occupational qualification' of the job.

- A tribunal has the power to award unlimited damages and to order the employer to end the discrimination.

- The Equal Opportunities Commission (EOC) can carry out investigations, require people to give evidence, issue non-discrimination notices and bring individual cases before an employment tribunal.

Race discrimination

- The Race Relations Act (RRA) 1976 outlaws discrimination on the ground of colour, race, nationality or ethnic or national origins.

- Such discrimination can consist of direct discrimination (*Owen & Briggs v James (1981)*), indirect discrimination (*Bayoomi v British Railways Board (1981)*, but compare *Panesar v Nestlé Co Ltd (1980)*), victimisation (*Chief Constable of West Yorkshire v Khan (2000)*) or harassment.

- Being of a particular racial group can be a genuine occupational qualification for a job, such as for reasons of authenticity in works of drama or art.

- Employers can be vicariously liable for discriminatory acts committed by their employees.

- A tribunal has the power to award unlimited damages and to order the employer to end the discrimination.

- The Commission for Racial Equality (CRE) carries out a similar function to that of the EOC.

Other discrimination

- Legislation outlaws discrimination on the grounds of sexual orientation, disability, religion or religious belief and employees on fixed-term contracts.

- When in force, legislation will prohibit discrimination against employees in respect of age.

The Equality Commission

- New legislation will create an Equality Commission, replacing the EOC, the CRE and the DRC.

Key terms

Commission for Racial Equality — a body appointed under the Race Relations Act 1976 with the aim of working towards eliminating discrimination or harassment on the ground of race, to promote equality of opportunity and to keep under review the effectiveness of *race discrimination* legislation.

Continuous employment — the period for which a person's employment for the same employer has subsisted. Certain statutory protection for employees depends on the employee serving a minimum period of continuous employment.

Contract of employment — a contract by which a person, an employee, agrees to undertake certain duties under the direction and control of an employer in return for a wage or salary.

Equal Opportunities Commission — a body established by the Sex Discrimination Act 1975 to eliminate discrimination in accordance with *equal pay* and *sex discrimination* legislation and to keep under review such legislation and its effectiveness in the workplace.

Equal pay — the requirement of the Equal Pay Act 1970 that men and women in the same employment are to be paid at the same rate for like work or work rated as equivalent or of equal value.

Maternity (or paternity) rights — the rights, such as maternity pay and maternity leave, that a woman has against her employer where she is absent from work due to pregnancy or confinement. Similar rights apply to a man whose partner is expecting a baby.

Race discrimination — discrimination or harassment, either direct or indirect, on the ground of race, colour, nationality or ethnic origins.

Sex discrimination — discrimination or harassment, either direct or indirect, on the ground of sex as prohibited by the Equal Pay Act 1970 and the Sex Discrimination Act 1975.

Unfair dismissal — the dismissal of an employee that an employment tribunal finds is unfair according to the Employment Rights Act 1996.

Written particulars of employment — a statement in writing that an employer must provide to certain employees not later than 2 months after the beginning of employment in accordance with the Employment Rights Act 1996, laying down basic terms of the employee's employment (such as date employment began, scale or rate of remuneration, hours of work, holiday entitlement, sickness procedure).

Wrongful dismissal — the termination of an employee's contract of employment in breach of contract, e.g. unless circumstances justify summary dismissal, dismissal of an employee without the employer giving notice in accordance with the contract.

Quick quiz

1 Jim, an employee with a metal works company, slips on the wet floor of the factory that has just been cleaned. The area had been cordoned off and there was a warning notice. Would the company have any contractual liability to Jim?

2 Ahmed has been employed as a bus driver for 3 years. On one of his routes, he was involved in a road accident and he is to be prosecuted for dangerous driving. On hearing the news, Ahmed's manager informs him that he will be dismissed and a week later he received a written notice of his dismissal.

3 What is meant by 'direct and 'indirect discrimination' under the SDA 1975?

4 What are employers' key responsibilities under the provisions of the Health and Safety at Work Act 1974?

Quick quiz answers

1 The company is under a duty to take reasonable care towards its employees. On the face of it, it seems Jim would have difficulty proving breach of the duty. The floor has to be cleaned and reasonable safety measures appear to have been taken.

2 The decision by his employer appears to be hasty and taken before the outcome of any criminal proceedings. It seems questionable as to whether this reason alone would be adequate to justify dismissal and it also appears that the employer failed to follow a disciplinary and dismissal procedure before arriving at the decision to dismiss.

3 The SDA 1975 seeks to protect persons from discrimination on the grounds of their sex or marital status. Direct discrimination occurs when a person is treated less favourably than another because of their sex or marital status. Indirect discrimination is the application of a condition or requirement that the proportion of one sex or married persons that can comply with the condition or requirement is considerably smaller than other sex or single persons that cannot be justified with reference to the demands of the job and, therefore, is detrimental in its effect on one sex or married persons.

4 Under the Health and Safety at Work Act 1974 employers:
   - must ensure the health, safety and welfare of employees; and they must provide and maintain safe plant and systems of work
   - make arrangements for safe use, handling, storage and transport of articles and substances
   - provide health and safety information, instruction, training and supervision
   - provide and maintain a safe working environment and adequate welfare facilities
   - must prepare a written safety policy where there are more than five employees
   - consult safety representatives appointed by recognised trade unions and, where requested by two or more safety representatives, must set up a safety committee.

Agency

Summary

- An agent is a person employed by another, a principal, to make contracts on the principal's behalf with third parties.
- Some agents are employees and some are self-employed.
- Some dealers who sell in their own right call themselves agents but are not so in the legal sense.
- An agent may be appointed orally, in writing or under seal by the principal. The agent is allowed in law to do anything that is reasonably incidental to the powers expressly given by the principal.
- An agency may also come into existence by implication where someone allows a third party the impression that another is acting as agent on his behalf.
- An agency can arise when an unauthorised contract is ratified by the person for whom it is made (*Bolton Partners v Lambert (1889)*). The law may also bind a principal to an unauthorised contract where the agent acted out of necessity (*Great Northern Railway Co v Swaffield (1874)*).

Duties

- Whatever the duties set out in the agency agreement, the law implies duties on both sides.
- The agent's duty of loyalty means that duties must be performed in person, that he must obey lawful instructions (*Bertram Armstrong & Co v Godfray (1830)*), he must exercise reasonable skill and care (*Keppel v Wheeler (1927)*; *Chaudhry v Prabhakar (1988)*) and must not allow his own interest to conflict with that of his principal, e.g. by taking secret profits or bribes (*Boardman v Phipps (1967)*; *Mahesan v Malaysian Cooperative Govt Officers Housing Society Ltd (1979)*).
- In return, the principal must pay the agent his salary and/or commission (*Rolfe & Co v George (1969)*) and indemnify him for any expenses lawfully incurred.

Liability

- An agent, with few exceptions, is not liable on the contract that he brings about on the principal's behalf because the contract is between the principal and the third party.
- However, where the agent does not disclose that he is acting on behalf of the principal, the agent or the principal can be sued on the contract by the third party.

Authority

- An agent acting within his authority binds his principal to the contract.
- Such authority may be express (*SMC Electronics Ltd v Akhter Computers Ltd (2001)*), implied (*Hely-Hutchinson v Brayhead Ltd (1968)*), usual (*Watteau v Fenwick (1893)*) or apparent (*Freeman & Lockyer v Buckhurst Park Properties*

(Mangal) Ltd (1964), Racing UK Ltd v Doncaster Racecourse Ltd (2005)).

- Where an agent has no authority, ratification or necessity may bind the principal.
- However, in the absence of this, an agent who exceeds his authority may be sued by the third party for breach of an implied warranty of authority.

Termination of agency

- An agency agreement may be terminated by the parties in different ways: it may end when the agent's appointed task is completed, on the expiry of a fixed period, or by notice on either side.
- Alternatively, the agreement may be ended by frustration (e.g. on death or insanity) or by bankruptcy.

Key terms

Agent — a person appointed by another (a *principal*) to act on that person's behalf in connection with dealings with third parties.

Authority — power delegated to a person or body in order to act in a particular way. Such authority may be actual (express or implied), usual or apparent.

Commercial agent — an *agent* who solicits business from customers on behalf of a *principal* and for which EU law provides contractual protection relating to such matters as compensation or indemnity on termination of agreement and implied terms relating to payment of commission and notice periods for termination of agreement.

Duty of care — a legal obligation to take reasonable care to avoid causing damage or harm.

Principal — a person on whose behalf another person (an *agent*) acts.

Ratification — confirmation of an act, e.g. where a *principal* adopts the unauthorised act of an *agent* with a third party.

Undisclosed principal — a *principal* whose existence is not disclosed by an *agent* to a third party.

Quick quiz

1 What are the requirements for apparent authority?

2 How can a principal ratify a contract entered into by an agent who exceeded their authority?

3 What is the cause of action against the agent by the third party when the agent exceeds this authority?

4 Jackie owns a hotel and employs Keith as manager to run it. With Jackie's permission, Keith is often visited at work by his fiancé, Lisa, who sometimes helps him out when he is busy. A week ago, Lisa ordered 20 sets of bath towels for the hotel from a local supplier. On delivery, Jackie refused to pay for the towels. Is Jackie liable on the contract?